£10

NORTH WALES,

DELINEATED FROM

TWO EXCURSIONS

THROUGH ALL THE

INTERESTING PARTS OF THAT HIGHLY BEAUTIFUL
AND ROMANTIC COUNTRY,

AND

INTENDED AS A GUIDE TO FUTURE TOURISTS.

NORTH WALES

Delineated from two excursions through all the interesting parts of that highly beautiful and romantic country, and intended as a guide to future tourists

By

Rev. W. Bingley

Cyngor Sir Ddinbych / Denbighshire County Council
Gwasanaeth Llyfrgell a Gwybodaeth / Library and Information Service
This book is number

142

of a limited edition of 450 copies

First published 1814

This edition specially produced by
Cedric Chivers Limited, Bristol
for the publisher
Cyngor Sir **Ddinbych / Denbighshire** County Council
Gwasanaeth Llyfrgell a Gwybodaeth
Library & Information Service
Rhuthun LL15 1HP

ISBN 1 900941 13 9

Printed in Great Britain by J.W. Arrowsmith Limited, Bristol
Bound by Cedric Chivers Limited, Bristol

Dayes delin.

Storer sculp.

_ *Pistyll Rhaiadr.*)

Published, for Longman & Rees, May 14.ᵗʰ 1804.

NORTH WALES,

DELINEATED FROM

TWO EXCURSIONS

THROUGH ALL THE

INTERESTING PARTS OF THAT HIGHLY BEAUTIFUL
AND ROMANTIC COUNTRY,

AND

INTENDED AS A GUIDE TO FUTURE TOURISTS.

By the REV. W. BINGLEY, A.M.

FELLOW OF THE LINNEAN SOCIETY,

AND LATE OF PETER-HOUSE, CAMBRIDGE.

Illustrated with Plates, and a whole Sheet Map coloured.

SECOND EDITION.

London;

PRINTED FOR LONGMAN, HURST, REES, ORME, AND BROWN,
PATERNOSTER-ROW.

1814.

TO

JAMES EDWARD SMITH, M.D. F.R.S.

PRESIDENT OF THE LINNEAN SOCIETY,

THIS VOLUME,

DESCRIPTIVE OF

A HIGHLY ROMANTIC AND INTERESTING

PART OF THE

BRITISH EMPIRE,

IS INSCRIBED,

AS A TESTIMONY OF THE SINCERE ESTEEM,

OF HIS VERY AFFECTIONATE,

AND OBEDIENT SERVANT,

WILLIAM BINGLEY.

PREFACE.

In the summer of the year 1798, I was first induced, from the various accounts that had reached, me respecting the grandeur of the mountain scenery of North Wales, to appropriate three months to a ramble through all its most interesting parts. I accordingly set out from Cambridge, (where I was then resident,) soon after the commencement of the long vacation, and proceeded, in the cross-country coaches, immediately to Chester. From Chester I leisurely skirted the north coast of Wales, along the great Irish road*, through St. Asaph and Conwy, to Bangor. At Caernarvon I remained for a considerable time, making excursions in all directions among the mountains, and through the principal parts of the island of Anglesea. When I had examined all the places that I could learn were worth notice, I continued my route, entirely *round* the country, visiting, in my course, Harlech, Barmouth, Dolgelle, Machynlleth, Llanydloes, Newtown, Montgomery, Welsh Pool, Oswestry, Wrexham, and Mold. From Mold I crossed over (towards the interior) to Ruthin, and proceeded

* Except only in going from the village of Northop to Flint, and thence to Holywell, in the whole not more than eight miles.

through Llangollen, Corwen, and Bala, to Shrewsbury, whence, in the month of September, I returned to Cambridge.

Not satisfied with this single journey, I returned into North Wales, in the year 1801, and resided there four months more; during June, July, August, and September. In this latter excursion my time was chiefly. occupied in examining the counties of Caernarvon and Merioneth, and the island of Anglesea, visiting again, in these counties, all the places that I had before seen, ascending most of the principal mountains, and searching around for other, new and interesting, objects.

Previously to my first journey, I had made several tours through nearly all the romantic parts of the North of England. I can, however, with truth declare, that, taken in the whole, I have not found these by any means so interesting as four of the six counties of North Wales, namely, Denbighshire, Caernarvonshire, Merionethshire, and Anglesea. The traveller of taste (in search of grand and stupendous scenery,) the naturalist, and the antiquary, have all, in this romantic country, full scope for their respective pursuits.

My mode of travelling was principally as a pedestrian, but sometimes I took horses, and at other times proceeded in carriages, as I found it convenient. A traveller on foot, if he have health and spirits, has, in my opinion, many advantages over all others : of these the most essential is that complete independance of every thing but his own exertions, which will enable him, without difficulty to visit and examine various places that are altogether inaccessible to persons either in carriages or horseback.

From my first entrance into the country I had formed a determination, if I found my observations sufficiently interesting, to lay the result of them before the public. This I did in my *Tour round North Wales*, published about ten years ago. Till that journey was nearly completed, no tour of any importance, later than that of Mr. Pennant, (originally published in 1778,) had come to my knowledge. I had not then heard of those either of Mr. Aikin, Mr. Warner, or Mr. Skrine, and therefore, not without reason, considered myself as filling an unoccupied place in British topography. The work, notwithstanding there were no fewer than half a dozen others of a nearly similar nature, published about the same time, was so well received by the public, as to afford reasonable hopes of success to fresh exertions.

To the present work is attached a *Map of North Wales*, compiled from the most authentic sources, to which I could have access, and corrected by my own observations I fear that, in many instances, it may be found inaccurate, but as Mr. Evans's " Map of North Wales," which contains by far the fewest errors of any that has been yet published, now sells at the enormous price of a guinea, I was, from this circumstance, induced to attempt the compilation of a new one to illustrate my own journey. If it only tend to reduce the price of Evans's map, I shall consider the labour and expence that have been bestowed upon it as sufficiently repaid.

The *Itinerary*, inserted at the conclusion of the

volume, will be found of considerable use to the traveller, as it contains a notice of almost every object worth visiting throughout the whole of North Wales. It contains also an account of the distances, and a character (as I found them) of most of the inns.

CONTENTS.

CHAP. I.

CHESTER.

CHAP. II.

CHESTER TO FLINT.

CHAP. III.

FLINT TO HOLYWELL.

b

CHAP. VIII.

EXCURSION FROM CONWY ROUND THE CREIDDIN.

CHAP. IX.

EXCURSION FROM CONWY TO CAER RHUN.

CHAP. X.

CONWY TO BANGOR.

CHAP. XI.

EXCURSION FROM BANGOR FERRY THROUGH
NANT FRANGON.

CHAP. XII.

BANGOR TO CAERNARVON.

CHAP. XIII.

EXCURSION FROM CAERNARVON TO LLAN-
BERIS.

CHAP. XIV.

EXCURSION FROM CAERNARVON TO THE SUMMIT OF SNOWDON.

CHAP. XV.

EXCURSION FROM LLANBERIS TO THE SUMMIT OF SNOWDON.

ASCENT OF SNOWDON FROM LLYN CWELLYN.

CHAP. XVI.

EXCURSION FROM CAERNARVON TO THE SUMMITS OF THE MOUNTAINS GLYDER AND TRIVAEN.

CHAP. XVII.

EXCURSION FROM CAERNARVON INTO ANGLESEA.

CHAP. XVIII.

VOYAGE FROM CAERNARVON TO PRIEST-HOLME.

CHAP. XIX.

EXCURSION FROM CAERNARVON TO BEDDGE-LERT; AND THENCE TO PONT ABERGLAS-LLYN, INTO NANT HWYNAN, AND TO THE SUMMIT OF SNOWDON.

CHAP. XX.

CHAP. XXI.

CHAP. XXII.

VOYAGE FROM CAERNARVON TO THE ISLE OF BARDSEY, AND THENCE TO PWLLHELI.

CHAP. XXIII.

EXCURSION FROM CAERNARVON, BY CAPEL CURIG, TO LLANRWST; AND FROM THENCE, BY THE VALE OF FFESTINIOG, AND TAN-Y-BWLCH AGAIN TO CAERNARVON.

CHAP. XXIV.

CAERNARVON THROUGH BEDDGELERT TO HARLECH.

EXCURSION FROM HARLECH TO CWM BYCHAN.

CHAP. XXV.

HARLECH TO BARMOUTH.

CHAP. XXVI.

BARMOUTH TO DOLGELLE.

EXCURSION FROM DOLGELLE TO KEMMER ABBEY AND THE WATERFALLS.

CHAP. XXVII.

DOLGELLE TO MACHYNLLETH.

CHAP. XXXIII.

OSWESTRY TO RUABON.

EXCURSION FROM RUABON TO BANGOR ISCOED.

CHAP. XXXIV.

RUABON TO WREXHAM.

EXCURSION FROM WREXHAM TO HOLT.

CHAP. XXXV.

WREXHAM TO MOLD.

CHAP. XXXVI.

MOLD TO RUTHIN.

CHAP. XXXVII.

RUTHIN TO LLANGOLLEN.

CHAP. XXXVIII.

LLANGOLLEN TO CORWEN.

CHAP. XXXIX.

CORWEN TO BALA.

CHAP. XL.

BALA TO SHREWSBURY.

CHAP. XLI.

SHREWSBURY.

CHAP. XLII.

THE MANNERS AND CUSTOMS OF THE WELSH.

NORTH WALES.

CHAP. I.

CHESTER.

Rows. — Walls.—Roodee.—Singular Tradition. — Cathedral. — Churches. — Castle.—Glover's Stone. — Bull-Baiting.— Public Buildings. — Singular Events. — Anecdote of Dr. Cole. — Anecdote of King James I. — Manufactures and Trade.

THERE are few towns in Great Britain, which, for antiquity and singularity, are more remarkable than Chester. The houses are, for the most part, a motly collection of buildings modern and antique, which afford a character in many situations not a little grotesque. The streets, which are tolerably broad, are excavated to a considerable depth. On a level with these are warehouses and kitchens; whilst above, and on a level with the shops and court-yards, are galleries, or, as they are called,

ROWS,

which run, on each side, along the fronts of the houses, and afford a sheltered walk for foot-

B

passengers. These are tolerably wide, but low
and close, and often very dirty. As they are
eight or ten feet, at least, above the street, persons are under the necessity of descending and
ascending the steps wherever a lane crosses
them. Their width, in many places admitting
of stalls betwixt the passage and the street, give
to a stranger the idea of a public road through
the midst of shops. Over them, and supported
in front by wooden posts, are the higher stories
of the houses. These Rows, are what tend principally to give its air of singularity to this town :
and to see the chief business of the place trans-
acting in these covered ways, which one might
almost fancy had once been a middle story cut
out of all the houses, appears to a stranger truly
singular.

THE WALLS

round this city, which, except those of Carlisle,
are the only entire specimen of ancient fortification now existing in Britain, are built of a soft
red stone, found on the spot, that gives them at
a distance the appearance of brick. Their circuit is nearly two miles, and they are sufficiently
broad at the top to admit conveniently of two
persons walking abreast. They are at present
kept in repair for the purposes merely of pleasure and recreation. This is done principally
by the murage duty of two-pence on every hundred yards of Irish linen that enters the port of
Chester. In different parts they command extensive and varied prospects. On the east, the
Broxton hills and the castle-crowned rock of

Beeston are seen at a distance; whilst finely cultivated grounds fill the intervening space. Towards the west, the mountains of Flintshire, that bound the beautiful vale of Clwyd, are very visible: and almost immediately beneath are the river and canal which present to the observer, in contrast, a scene of bustle and commerce.

Betwixt the river and the walls is a piece of pasture-land about a mile in circumference, called

THE ROODEE.

This is used as a race-ground; and few places in the kingdom, of its size (for it is only about a mile in circuit), are better calculated for the purpose, as it is nearly surrounded by eminences that command a view directly upon it.

Tradition says that in the year 946, an image of the Virgin mother and a large cross were interred here. The story is curious:—This image belonged to the church of Hawarden, and, during the invocations of the inhabitants for relief from a season of drought, by which they were greatly suffering, being either not securely fixed in its place, or not possessing that share of infallibility which has frequently been ascribed to the image of the Virgin, it somewhat unexpectedly, fell upon the head of Lady Trawst, the governor's wife; the effect of which was fatal. In consequence of this catastrophe, the inhabitants of the place held a consultation as to the most proper mode of disposing of the image; and after due deliberation, its sentence was;—" To be banished from that place by being laid on the sands of the

river, from whence the tide might convey it to
whatever other quarter the virgin whom it represented should think proper." As it was low
water when the image was taken to the sands,
the tide of flood, carried it of course, up the river;
and on the day following it was found near the
Roodee, where it was immediately interred by
the inhabitants of Chester with all due pomp
and solemnity, and a large stone was placed over
the grave with this inscription:

> The Jewes theire God dide crucifie,
>   The Hardeners theires dide drowne,
> 'Cause with theire wantes she'd not complye;
>   And lyes under thys colde stone.

THE CATHEDRAL.

Near the walls, at the north-east side of the
city, stands this, one of the most heavy, irregular, and ragged piles of building I ever beheld.
It is constructed of the same red stone as the
walls; from the softness of which, its exterior
seems fast mouldering to decay.

There is, however, much neatness and beauty
in the choir, and the Gothic work around its
sides has a very pleasing effect. About the walls
are dispersed the monuments of several bishops
and clergymen, but none of them of any magnificence.

The bishop's throne stands on what is generally, though improperly, denominated the shrine
of St. Werburgh; a large stone richly ornamented with Gothic carving. Round the top of
this there is a range of thirty small images, at
present neatly *gilded,* supposed to have been in-

tended for the kings and saints of the Mercian kingdom. The shrine, in which the sacred relics were deposited, was somewhat more portable than this mass of stone, (a vessel no doubt either of silver or gold,) for in the year 1180, Mr. Pennant informs us, " it was brought out to stop the raging of a fire in the city, which, for a long time, had been invincible by every other means: but the approach of the holy remains *instantly proved their sanctity by putting an end to its furious desolation.*"*

The altar-piece, which is of very fine tapestry, is executed after one of the cartoons of Raphael, and represents the history of Elymas the sorcerer. Wright, in his travels through France and Italy, expresses his opinion, that this is much superior to any of the tapestry which he saw in the Vatican.

Behind the altar is the chapel of St. Mary, where prayers are read every morning at six o'clock.---The south transept forms the parish church of St. Oswald.

On the south side of the altar there is an ancient tomb, which is shewn to strangers as that of Henry IV. emperor of Germany. Camden says, that in order to escape from the troubles which his own unguarded conduct had brought upon his empire, this prince fled in disguise to England, and resided at Chester, unknown as to his real character for nearly ten years: but, death approaching, he discovered himself, and was afterwards interred in the Abbey church. The story seems altogether

* Pennant's Tour in North Wales, vol. i.

doubtful, and the latter part of it is certainly untrue, for he is well known both to have died and been buried at Liege.

The chapter-house stands on the east side of the cloister court: but neither in this place, nor in the vestibule, did I observe any thing which was in the least interesting.—In 1724, on repairing the building the remains of the celebrated Hugh Lupus, the first earl of Chester, after lying undisturbed upwards of six hundred years, were discovered here, wrapped in leather, and deposited in a stone coffin. Part of his shroud is still in preservation.

Near the cathedral is the Abbey-court, on the south side of which is situated the bishop's palace, a handsome modern stone building. The other houses of the court are occupied principally by the prebendaries, minor canons, and vicars choral.

The cathedral was erected on the site of a nunnery founded about the year 660, by Wulpherus king of Mercia, for his daughter Werburgh, afterwards sainted, to whom it is dedicated. The chief part of the present fabric was erected during the reigns of the three last Henries.

CHURCHES.

There are at Chester eight parish churches within the walls:

St. Oswald's	St. Michael's,
St. Peter's,	St. Mary's,
Trinity,	St. Olave's, and
St. Bridget's,	St. Martin's*.

* In the parish of St. Martin there were formerly two religious houses; one appropriated to the Carmelites, or Grey

St. John's church stands just beyond the walls, and not far from the river, in the south-east part of the town. This, which was once a collegiate church, has been a large and magnificent pile.of Saxon architecture; and even yet exhibits some curious specimens of the massive strength of the Saxon columns and arches. It was founded, by Ethelred king of Mercia, about the year 689; in consequence, says tradition, of a visionary admonition to found a place of religious worship on the first piece of ground where he should afterwards see a white hind. This legend is supposed to be represented by a sculpture, now almost defaced, on the west side of the tower.

On the south side of the church-yard there was a small anchorite's cell, to which the wounded Harold retired after his defeat at the battle of Hastings; and where, in meditation and solitude, he is said to have closed his life.

THE CASTLE.

In the south angle of the town walls is situated the castle, founded by Hugh Lupus in the reign of William the Conqueror; but of the ancient building there is not, at present, much left: what remains, however, is of the same red stone as the cathedral and walls. Some years ago a design was entered into, to take down such of the ancient parts as were necessary to the purpose, and erect in their stead, a new gaol, shire-hall, &c. upon an improved and extensive plan.

Friars; and the other a convent of Benedictine nuns, dedi- cated to St. Mary. Of these, the present remains are very few.

The present shire-hall is a truly elegant stone fabric, with a portico in front. The court-room is semicircular, and lighted from above. Few rooms in the kingdom exceed this either in purity of design, or in the taste exhibited in its execution.

The new county-gaol is a very considerable structure; it contains five different yards for the prisoners, upwards of forty cells for criminals, and fourteen solitary cells for the condemned.

Among other remarkable objects that were pointed out to me in Chester, was

GLOVER'S STONE.

Which stands at the head of Castle-street and is the boundary, in this direction, of the jurisdiction of the city. Here the criminals are delivered to the city sheriffs for execution. Opinions are divided as to the origin of this singular custom. There is a tradition, that when Chester was made a separate county by Henry VII., the citizens, tenacious of *privilege*, took upon themselves this unpleasant task, rather than suffer the county officers to exercise any authority within their jurisdiction.—Others say that this duty was imposed upon them as a punishment for having once rescued a felon from the hands of the officers, as he was on the way to execution.

BULL-BAITING.

In few places has the barbarous and unmanly sport of bull-baiting been more assiduously attended to, or sanctioned by the presence of persons in more respectable stations of life, than in this. It is not many years since the mayor and corporation, habited in their robes, regularly attended, in their *official capacity*, as participators in this brutal amusement! On the accustomed day, as soon as their presence announced that the entertainment might commence, the town crier opened the business by proclaiming aloud to the gaping audience :—" Oyez! Oyez! Oyez! if any man stands within twenty yards of the bull-ring, let him take—*what comes :*" and after some other customary ceremonies, the scene of cruelty and slaughter began.

PUBLIC BUILDINGS.

The principal public buildings in Chester, besides those I have already mentioned, are

The Exchange; an elegant fabric, supported on columns, and containing a large and commodious common-hall, in which the quarter-sessions are held, and all the city-officers are elected. Here are also held the city-courts of crown-mote, and port-mote.—The exchange likewise contains a mansion house, where the corporation entertainments are given, and the citizens have their assemblies during the winter; and the subscription library.

The House of Industry stands near the river on the west side of the town. In this the poor, not only of the parishes of Chester, but even of distant parishes, on agreement with the governor, are supported and employed. The number of persons it generally contains is betwixt two and three hundred.

The Infirmary is also on the west side of the town, but within the walls. It was opened in the year 1761, and is very amply supported by voluntary contributions.

The Blue-Coat School, near the north gate, was founded by Bishop Stratford in the year 1706. By this institution thirty-five boys are maintained and educated for four years, at the end of which term they are put out apprentices to business. Here is also a similar institution for ten girls, who, at the end of four years receive each forty shillings, and are placed out to service.

The North-Gate Gaol is the city-prison for felons and debtors.

The Bridewell, or House of Correction, where small crimes are punished by hard labour and confinement, is near the north-gate, on the opposite side of the canal*.

* *Sketch of the History of Chester.*—From the very form of the place, we are led to conjecture, that Chester was indebted to the Romans for its foundation: for the four principal streets, Bridge-street, Northgate-street, Watergate-street, and Eastgate-street, crossing each other at right angles, still retain the original appearance of a Roman camp. Of this, however, we have no direct historical evidence, though Chester is well known to have been one of the principal military stations that the Romans had in this island.

At different times there have been various remains of Roman antiquity discovered here, such as altars, statues, coins, and two hypocausts; one in a field near the Watergate, and another near the Feathers Inn in Watergate-street. The latter is yet left unfilled up, and may be inspected by the curious. It is entered through a blacksmith's shop and pantry, and, from the lowness and darkness of the place, few but antiquaries will be induced to visit it. Its form is rectangular, and it had formerly thirty two low pillars that supported square tiles perforated for the passage of the

In a chronological list of remarkable events at Chester, I find the following singular occurrences:

1489. This year St. Peter's steeple was pointed, when a goose was eaten by the parson and others on the top thereof, and part cast into the four streets.

warm vapour into the sudatorium, or sweating-room above, which is now destroyed.

After the Romans departed from Britain in the fifth century, Chester fell under the government of the British princes. In their hands it remained till the year 603, when it was wrested from them by Ethelfrid, king of Northumbria.

Chester now seems to have been alternately possessed by the Britons, the Saxons, and the Danes; by the latter, however, it was held but a very short time, being restored to the Saxons by the valiant daughter of Alfred the Great, Elfleda, the wife of Ethelred duke of Mercia.

After the Norman conquest, William created his nephew, Hugh Lupus, earl of Chester, and delegated the same sovereign jurisdiction to him in this county, which he himself possessed in the rest of the island. By virtue of this grant, the earls held parliaments at Chester, consisting of the barons and tenants, which were not bound by the acts of the English parliament. The earls were petty princes, and all the landholders in the county were mediately or immediately their vassals, and under the same allegiance to them as to the kings of England.

Hugh Lupus, immediately after receiving the earldom, in order to secure himself from any incroachments either of Welsh or English, repaired the town walls, and erected the castle.

In several of the reigns subsequent to the Norman conquest, Chester was made a place of rendezvous for the English troops in all expeditions against the Welsh. In consequence of this it frequently suffered very considerably. Camden informs us that the " skirmishes here betwixt the Welsh and English, in the beginning of the Norman times, were so numerous, the inroads and incursions, and the firing of the suburbs of Hanbrid beyond the bridge so frequent,

1517. The plague raged so shockingly, that the streets were deserted, and grass grew a foot high at the cross.

1552. The magistrates of Chester were restrained, by act of parliament, from licensing more than four persons to sell wine within the town.

that the Welshmen called it *Treboeth*, that is, Burnt Town. They tell us also that there was a long wall made there of *Welshmen's Skulls.*"

From the time of Hugh Lupus, for near two centuries, Chester continued entirely under the jurisdiction of its earls; but on the death of John Scott, without issue male, in 1237. Henry III. took the earldom, and all the powers annexed to it, into his own hands; and in return, granted to the city its first royal charter.

Henry bestowed it on his son Edward, afterwards king Edward I., from whom it successively devolved upon Simon de Montfort, earl of Leicester, Edward of Caernarvon, Edward of Windsor, Edward the Black Prince, Richard of Bourdeaux, Henry V., Henry VI., Edward V., Arthur the son of Henry VII., and afterwards to Henry VIII. The next person on whom the earldom was conferred, was Henry Frederick Stuart, son of James I. He was succeeded by his brother, afterwards Charles I., and from him it went to Charles II. After a period of more than eighty years, George, the son of George I. succeeded, afterwards Frederic his elder brother, then his present Majesty, and in 1762 it was transferred to the Prince of Wales, in whom it still continues.

In the civil wars, during the reign of Charles I., Chester adhered with great fidelity to the royal cause, and was consequently besieged by the parliament's army: but it was not till every hope had been cut off by the important victory which the latter had gained at Rowton Heath, of which, from the leads of the Phœnix Tower, the king himself was an anxious spectator, that it was surrendered on the 3d of February 1645-6, on the most honourable terms, after a gallant resistance for near five months, during part of which time the garrison were so much distressed for provisions, as to eat even their horses, dogs, and cats.

1569. This year the two sheriffs, Peter Licherband, and William Massey, Gent. fought a battle, for which they were fined ten pounds towards the repair of the walls.

1617. King James visited Chester, and was presented by the body corporate with a *gilt* cup, and a hundred Jacobins of gold, as a rich token of the attachment of the city to his crown and person.

To a singular stratagem of Elizabeth Edmunds, a female of this place, was owing the entire safety of the protestants of Ireland, in the reign of queen Mary. Dr. Cole, a commissioner from the queen, on his way to that country, stopped one night at Chester. The mayor, in his official capacity, waited on him: he unguardedly spoke of the business in which he was engaged, and took out his commission in the presence of the hostess, who had a brother, a protestant, in Dublin. When the mayor left him, Dr. Cole politely attended him down stairs, and Mrs. Edmunds in the mean time took the commission from the box, and substituted for it a pack of cards, with the knave of clubs placed uppermost. The doctor, on his return, put up the box, and on his arrival in Dublin, presented it in form at the castle to the lord deputy and privy council. His lordship opened it, and the whole assembly, as well as the commissioner himself, were in the utmost astonishment at its contents. He assured them that it *had* contained a commission, but why it was not there then, and how the cards came into its place, he was as ignorant as they. Disappointed and chagrined, he returned to the English court for a

fresh commission, which he obtained, but before
he could again arrive in Ireland, the queen died.
Her successor, queen Elizabeth, rewarded the
woman for this meritorious act with a pension
of forty pounds a year for her life.

A whimsical story is told by Mr. Yorke respecting an expedition of James I. into Wales.
When he was on the road near Chester, he was
met by such numbers of the Welsh, who came out
of curiosity to see him, the weather was so dry,
and the roads so dusty, that he was nearly suffocated. He was completely at a loss in what
manner to rid himself of them civilly: at last
one of his attendants putting his head out of the
coach, said: " It is his Majesty's pleasure that
those who are the best gentlemen shall ride for-
wards." Away scampered the Welsh; and but
one solitary man was left behind. " And so,
Sir," says the king to him, " you are not a gentleman then?" " Oh yes, and please hur majesty,
hur is as good a shentleman as the rest; but hur
ceffyl, God help her, is not so good." *

MANUFACTURES AND TRADE.

The only manufacture of any consequence in
Chester, is that of gloves, which is carried on
to some extent. There are also snuff mills; a
small manufactory for tobacco pipes; an iron
foundry; patent shot manufactory; ship builders'
yards, and other concerns, which afford some
but not much employment for the poor.

* Royal tribes of North Wales. *Ceffyl* is the Welsh word
for horse.

The maritime business is of no great extent.
It consists chiefly of the coasting and Irish
trades; and a small portion of commerce with
foreign countries. Great quantities of cheese,
coals, and lead, are exported. The imports
are principally linen cloth from Ireland; and
hides, tallow, feathers, &c. from other quarters.
The number of ships belonging to the port is
but small. The business of ship-building is,
however, carried on to a considerable extent,
many vessels of from one hundred to five hundred tons burthen being annually built here.

Till the new channel was made for the river
Dee, which was finished about the middle of
the last century, vessels of twenty tons could
scarcely reach the town, and ships of burthen
were obliged to lie ten miles lower down, by
Park-Gate. But now, at the spring tides, vessels of near four hundred tons burthen are able
to come up almost to the bridge.

CHAP. II.

CHESTER TO FLINT.

Hawarden and Castle.—Euloe Castle.—Coed Euloe.—Defeat of the Army of Henry the Second by the Welsh.—Northop. —Flint.—Flint Gaol and Castle.—Richard the Second betrayed to Bolingbroke.—Borough.

IT was early in the morning of the sixth of July that I commenced my route from Chester into Wales, in a direction towards St. Asaph and Conwy. The day had not dawned more than two hours, the dew then sparkled upon the leaves and grass, and the sun shot his red beams through the undispersed fog. The birds on every side were pouring forth their melodious notes, and the cheering coolness of the air corresponding with my own disposition at the time, to enjoy in the full all these beauties of nature, rendered the outset of this journey infinitely more pleasing than that of any of my rambles through the romantic parts of England. The fog soon cleared away, and the now unclouded sky seemed to indicate a continuance of the most delightful weather. I wandered so slowly along, that it was near seven o'clock before I arrived at

HAWARDEN.

This is a small clean-looking town in Flintshire, celebrated only for its *castle*, which has been an extensive building, and was formerly of considerable importance to the interests both of the Welsh and the English. This building, of which at present little more than the fragments of the walls and keep are left, stood on a considerable eminence, near the road, at the east end of the town, within the grounds of Sir Richard Stephen Glynne, Bart. It commands an extensive prospect towards the river Dee and the county of Chester.

The late Sir John Glynne was at the expence of having much of the rubbish removed from the ruins : and in one place there was discovered a long flight of steps, at the bottom of which was a door, and formerly a draw-bridge. This crossed a deep long chasm, to another door leading to two or three small rooms, probably places of confinement, where prisoners, after pulling up the bridge over the chasm, might be lodged in the utmost security.*

The circular keep, which is more elevated and perfect than the other parts of the building, has a room fitted up in it in the modern stile. This addition, however, and the painted statues interspersed in the grounds, but ill accord with the wild and shattered ruins around them.†

---

* Pennant's Tour, i. 104.

† *History of Hawarden Castle.*—The time of the foundation of this fortress is not known. It appears however to have been in existence soon after the Norman conquest ; for it was then possessed by Roger Fitzvalerine, son of one of the noble adventurers who followed the fortunes of William the Conqueror. It was held by the seneschalship to the earls of Chester, and was afterwards the seat of the barons of Mont Alt, who were stewards of the palatinate of Chester.

On the extinction of the ancient earls in 1237, Hawarden

C

I continued my route towards Northop. A
little beyond the ninth mile-stone from Chester,
1 turned, on the right, over some meadows, in
search of a small fortress called

castle and some other fortresses belonging to them were resumed by the crown. But, about thirty years afterwards,
when Henry III. and his son Edward were taken prisoners
by Simon de Montfort at the battle of Lewes, their libe-
ration was purchased by the resignation to him of the earldom of Chester from Edward, who then held it, and by
the absolute cession to the prince Llewelyn, not only of this
place, but of the absolute sovereignty of Wales.

Shortly after this time it must have been destroyed; for
Llewelyn, in 1267, when he restored to Robert de Mont
Alt the lands of Hawarden that he had formerly possessed,
strictly enjoined him not to build any castle there for thirty
years. A fortress seems, however, to have been raised
long before the expiration of that period ; for in the night
of Palm Sunday, 1281, David, the brother of Llewelyn,
ungrateful for the favours which had been so lavishly conferred upon him by Edward I. surprized and took this castle,
cruelly massacring all who resisted.

Hawarden seems to have continued in the barons of
Mont Alt for nearly fifty years from the death of David;
when Robert, the last baron, having no male issue, conveyed it to Isabella, queen of Edward II. but on her disgrace it came once more to the crown.

In 1336 Edward III. granted it, along with the steward-
ship of Chester, to William de Montacute, earl of Salisbury ; in whose family it continued till the year 1400, when
John, his great nephew, was beheaded by the townsmen of
Cirencester, after attempting an insurrection in favour of
his deposed master, Richard II. The earl, however, prior
to this event, had made over his estates in fee to four of
his friends ; but, after his attainder ; by an act of parliament
they became forfeited to the crown.

Thomas, duke of Clarence, the son of Henry IV. who
was afterwards slain at the battle of Baugy in 1420,
had a grant of Hawarden ; and about twenty years after
his death it was given to Sir Thomas Stanley, who held it
till the year 1450, when it was resumed, and granted to
Edward Prince of Wales.

EULOE CASTLE.

It is about a quarter of a mile distant from the road, and from its situation on the edge of a glen, and being surrounded with wood, I had no little difficulty in finding it. It formerly consisted of two parts; the larger of which was an oblong tower, rounded at one end, and about

The surviving feoffee of the Earl of Salisbury now laid claim to his estates, on the plea that the Earl was not possessed of them at the time of his forfeiture. An inquisition was taken, his plea found good, and complete restitution was made to him.

In 1454 Hawarden was again conveyed to Sir Thomas, afterwards Lord Stanley; and on the death of his son Thomas, earl of Derby, it descended to his second wife Margaret, the mother of Henry VII. After her decease it continued in the family till the execution of the gallant James, Earl of Derby, in 1651; and was subsequently purchased of the agents of sequestration by serjeant Glynne, in one of whose descendants it still continues.

In the civil wars Hawarden was betrayed by its governor to the parliament and kept for them till 1643, when part of the English forces, who had been serving against the rebels in Ireland, upon the cessation there, came over to assist the king, and landed at Mostyn, a place about sixteen miles distant. Soon after their arrival they made an attack on this castle, and after a fortnight's siege, it was surrendered to them.

In the hands of the Royalists it continued until after the surrender of Chester in 1645, when it was vigorously besieged by the parliament's forces under general Mytton, and in about a month was taken.

On the twenty-second of December, in the same year, the parliament, alarmed at some disturbances which had taken place amongst their soldiers, ordered this and four other castles to be dismantled. These orders extended only to the rendering of it untenable; its further destruction is said to have been subsequently effected by its owner, Sir William Glynne.

c 2

fourteen yards long, and ten or twelve in width,
guarded on the accessible side by a strong wall.
The other part consists of an oblong court, at
the extremity of which are the remains of a
circular tower.   Leland says that Euloe Castle
was the property of a gentleman in Flintshire,
of the name of Howell, who, by ancient custom,
a privilege he inherited from his ancestors, used
to give the badge of a silver harp to the best
harper in North Wales. In his own time it
was, he informs us, " a ruinous castelet or
pile *."

It was in the wood adjoining to this place,
called

COED EULOE,

that king Henry the Second, in an expedition
against Owen Gwynedd, prince of North Wales,
received a severe and most memorable repulse
from David and Conan, the two sons of that
hero. The army of Owen was encamped, and
seemed ready for engagement, and some slight
skirmishes were commenced. These, however,
were but artifices to draw the English into a
narrow and dangerous pass between the hills,
where a numerous ambuscade was secretly
placed under the command of his sons. Henry,
too confident in the strength of his men, and
not relying sufficiently on the opinion of those
who had a more perfect knowledge of the
country than himself, fell into the snare, and
paid dearly for his rashness; for when he and

* Leland's Itinerary, v. 53.

his vanguard, following the Welsh into the valley, were engaged in fight, another party, with horrible outcries, arose on a sudden from under the cover of the woods, which hung over the steep, and assaulted them with stones, arrows, and other missile weapons. The disadvantageous situation of the English army, and the confusion into which they were thrown, totally disabled them from resisting this unexpected attack; and they were routed with dreadful slaughter.

NORTHOP.

When I arrived at Northop, a small village, containing a handsome and somewhat ancient church, I turned out of the usual road to Holywell, and went towards Flint *. About two miles from this place, and from the slope of a hill, at the bottom of which stands the town, the scenery opened in a most pleasing manner. It was high water ; and the estuary of the Dee, which runs up towards Chester, enlivened by the vessels " lightly floating on its surface," the towns of Park-Gate, and some others on the opposite shore, appeared to peculiar advantage. At the ebb of the tide this wide arm of the sea dwindles into a narrow stream, inclosed on each side by long and dreary banks of sand.

* It is not worth the while of any tourist to follow my route to Flint, as he will find there scarcely any thing worth his notice.

FLINT

is a market town, small, irregularly built, and
by no means pleasant. It has once been surrounded by a ditch and ramparts, but these
are now nearly destroyed. Being situated near
the sea, it is resorted to by a few persons from
the adjacent country, as a bathing-place; but
the marshy coast which extends from the edge
of the water almost to the town, must render
it, in this respect, extremely disagreeable. The
church, or rather chapel, for it is but a chapel
of ease to Northop, is a dirty ill-looking building, with a boarded turret.—From this place
there are packets which sail every tide, when
the wind permits, for Chester and Park-Gate.

Though the great sessions for the county are
held at Mold, the *county gaol* is at Flint, situated in the castle-yard, in a fine healthy situation.
It is a good building, and constructed on a plan
similar to the gaol of Ruthin. Over the front
door of this prison, there is a marble slab,
containing an elegant inscription, the compo-
siton of Mr. Pennant.

The *castle* stands upon a rock in the marsh,
and so near the river, that sometimes at high-
water the walls are washed by the tide.* It has
been a square building, with towers at the
angles, some remains of each of which are yet

---

* The channel of the Dee is at present at some distance,
but the river formerly flowed close under the walls. There
are still in some parts rings left to which ships were moored.
—*Pennant.*

left. That at the south-east corner, which is called the Double-Tower, is much larger than the others. In its outward diameter it measures forty feet. It is formed by two concentric walls, each six feet thick, having a gallery eight feet wide included between them, and leaving a circular area of about twenty feet in diameter, into which there was an entry from the gallery by four doors. This appears to have been the keep. The interior of the castle is a square court, containing about an acre of ground. In the curtain on the west side there are yet left several windows with pointed arches*.

* *History of Flint Castle.*—The founder of this castle has not yet been decidedly ascertained. Camden and Lord Littleton each attribute it to Henry II. after his defeat at Coed Euloe, and concur in the opinion that it was finished by Edward 1.; whilst Fabian, Stowe, and many others, say that it was built by Edward only, about the year 1275, not mentioning a word of its being begun by Henry, though in the same sentence they each tell us that Edward strengthened Rhyddlan Castle; which plainly evinces that they distinguished betwixt building and repairing.

In the year 1332 Edward III. granted this and other castles, with all his lands here, to the Black Prince, to hold to him and his heirs, kings of England: and in 1385 it was bestowed by Richard II. with the chief-justiceship of Chester, upon Robert Vere, Earl of Oxford

It was surrendered fourteen years afterwards to Percy Earl of Northumberland, who betrayed into it the unfortunate Richard II. under the insidious pretence that Bolingbroke, who was waiting for him here, desired only to have his property restored, and that the kingdom should have a parliament. Northumberland met the king at Conwy, where he had gone after his return from Ireland; and they were proceeding together towards this place, when among the recesses of the mountains near Penmaen Rhôs, the latter observed a band of soldiers. Alarmed for his safety, and now fearful of the snare that was laid for him, he attempted to return; but Percy springing forward, caught his

In the year 1283 Flint was made a free
borough, and received its charter, which was
afterwards confirmed in the reign of Philip

horse's bridle, and forcibly directed his course. They dined
at Rhyddlan, and arrived in the same evening at Flint.
The next day, " after dinner, (says Stowe), the Duke of
Lancaster entered the castle all armed, his basenet except·
ed. King Richard came down to meet him; and the duke,
as soon as he saw the king, fell on his knees, and coming
near unto him, he kneeled a second time with his hat in
his hand : and the king then put off his hoode and spoke
first : ' Fair cousin of Lancaster, you are right wellcome.'
The duke, bowing low to the ground, answered, ' My
lord, I am come before you sent for me ; the reason why I
will shewe you. The common fame among your people is
such, that ye have for the space of twenty or two and
twenty years, ruled them very rigorously: but, if it please
our lord, I will helpe you to govern better !' The king
answered, ' Faire cousin of Lancaster, sith it pleaseth you,
it pleaseth me well !' The duke then with a high sharp
voyce, bad bring forth the king's horses, and two little
nagges, not worth fourtie franks, were brought forthe : the
king was set on the one, and the earl of Salisbury on the
other : and thus the duke brought them from Flint to
Chester ;" from whence, after a night's rest, they were
taken to London *.

From this period I have been able to meet with no documents relative to the castle of Flint, until the civil wars of the
reign of Charles I. when it appears to have been garrisoned
for the king, after having been repaired at the expence
of Sir Roger Mostyn, who was appointed governor. In
1643 it was besieged by Sir William Brereton and Sir
Thomas Middleton, and was defended till all the provisions,
even to horses, failing, the governor surrendered it upon
honourable terms. It must afterwards have been retaken
by the royalists ; for in August 1646 it appears to have
been surrendered to major-general Mytton. In December
of the same year it was, with Hawarden, and three other
castles, ordered by the parliament to be so far destroyed as
to render it untenable.

---

* Stowe's Annals, 321. Pennant, i. 50.

and Mary, and again in the twelfth of William
III.

This place, in conjunction with Caerwys,
Rhyddlan, Caergwrle, and Overton, sends a
member to parliament. The election is made
by such of the inhabitants as pay parochial
taxes; and the returning officers are the two
bailiffs appointed by the mayor.

CHAP. III.

FLINT TO HOLYWELL.

*Holywell.—Mode of assembling to Church.—Wenefred's Well.
—Legend of St. Wenefred.— Miracles.— Mosses.—Devotees.—Mills and Manufactories on the Stream.—Well for
weak Eyes. — Basingwerk Abbey. — Basingwerk Castle. —
Tradition respecting it.—Watt's Dyke.*

Nothing very interesting occurred in the road
betwixt Flint and Holywell; and had it not
been for the shortness of the journey, scarcely
six miles, it would have appeared extremely
tedious.—I soon became in a great measure
separated as it were from the country, by a
range of hills on the left of the road, which did
not allow me one pleasing prospect: and on the
opposite side a long and dreary marsh, with an
extent of sand in the bed of the river not less
than two miles in any direction beyond it, presented such a dull uniformity of objects, that I
was glad to be indebted even to a few straggling
gulls, which at intervals came whirling over
my head, uttering their harsh screams, for
sources of reflection and amusement.

HOLYWELL.

I know no town in North Wales which in a
commercial view is of more importance than

Holywell. The numerous manufactures in its vicinity, and its easy access to the sea, have rendered it the great mart of this part of the kingdom. The town is spacious, but irregular; and pleasantly situated on the slope of a mountain which extends nearly to the water. Many of the houses are good, and give to it an air of considerable opulence.

The parish-church is singular only for its situation, being so much below the rest of the town, that the bell is scarcely audible even at a little distance. When the inhabitants are to be called to prayers, they are therefore under the necessity of adopting the following singular remedy for this defect :—a person hired for the purpose, fastens a leathern strap round his neck, to the end of which a bell of tolerable weight is suspended, and over one of his knees he buckles a cushion ; thus accoutred he sets out a certain time before the service commences, and walks through the principal parts of the town, jingling the bell every time his cushioned knee comes forward.

WENEFRED'S WELL,

From which the name of Holywell was given to this place, springs with vast impetuosity from a rock at the foot of a steep hill near the bottom of the town. It is covered by a small Gothic building, said to have been erected by Margaret the mother of Henry the VII., but Mr. Grose was of opinion, that the frieze of the outside cornice, which is ornamented with monkies, and other grotesque figures, indicates it to be of

more ancient date.   Nothing, observes this
accurate writer, can exceed the delicacy and
elegance of the Gothic work on the inside of
this building, which forms a canopy over the
well, having in the centre, and serving as
origin to the gothic arches, a circular shield on
which was once carved a coat of arms.   Above
this was the chapel; at present converted into a
charity-school.   The water passes from the small
well, under an arch, into a larger one, which
was intended for the bath.

THE LEGEND.

The legendary origin of this well is singular.
Wenefred*, who is supposed to have lived in
the early part of the seventh century, is reported
to have been a beautiful and devout virgin, of
noble descent.   She was placed under the protection of her relation Bueno, a descendant
from the kings of Powys, who had founded a
church here.   A young prince, whose name was
Cradoc, struck with the elegance of her person,
resolved to attempt her virtue; and, seizing an
opportunity when all except herself were at
prayers, he declared to her his passion.   She
made some excuse to escape from the room, and
then fled from the house to the church, which
appears to have been situated at the foot of the
hill.   Before she could reach this sanctuary he
overtook her, and with his sword, in an extacy

* The Welsh name of this female was Gwenvrewi; Tudur
Aled, a Welsh bard who flourished about the year 1450, has
celebrated her sanctity and the reputed miracles of her well,
in a poem still extant.

of rage and disappointment, struck off her head. This, like an elastic ball, bounded down the side of the hill, through the door of the church, and up one of the aisles directly to the altar where her friends were assembled at prayer : resting here, a clear and copious fountain immediately gushed out. St. Bueno snatched up the head, and again joining it to the body, it was, to the surprize and admiration of all present, immediately re-united, the place of separation being only marked by a white line encircling the neck. Cradoc dropped down on the spot where he had committed the atrocious act; and the legend informs us that it was not known whether the earth opened to receive his impious corpse, or whether his master, the devil, carried it off, but that it was certainly never seen afterwards. The sides of the well were covered with a sweet-scented moss, and the stones at the bottom became tinctured with her blood!

The liveless tears shee shed into a fountaine turne,
And, that for her alone, the water should not mourne,
The pure vermillion blood that issued from her veines
Unto this very day the pearly gravel staines;
As erst the white and red were mixed in her cheeke,
And that one part of her might be the other like,
Her haire was turned to mosse, whose sweetness doth declare
In liveliness of youth the natural sweets she bare*.

Wenefred survived her decapitation about fifteen years, and having, towards the latter end of that time, received the veil from St. Elerius at Gwytherin, in Denbighshire, died abbess of that monastery.

* Drayton's Polyolbion, p. 160.

The well, after her death, was endowed with many miraculous properties: it healed the diseases of all who plunged into its water, and Drayton says that no animal whatever could be drowned in it.

The following is one of the numerous wonders that have been recorded of its powerful influence: a party of depredators stole a cow from a pasture not far distant, and, that their footsteps might not be traced, dragged her along some neighbouring rocks. But how were the impious wretches deceived: not one step was set without leaving an impression on the stones, as if they had been passing over soft clay; nay, the learned editor of the life of St. Wenefred says that the original describes them as at every step *sinking up to the very knees!* The owner was, by this means enabled to recover his beast; and the terrified wretches, coming in penitence to the altar, confessed their crime, and, no doubt by the intercession of the saint, were forgiven.

The sweet-scented moss, growing plentifully on the sides of this well, is nothing more than *jungermannia asplenoides* of Linnæus; it is found in many other springs in the kingdom, and is also occasionally to be met with in moist places, by road sides, and in woods. The supposed tincture of the blood is likewise a vegetable production, *byssus jolithus.* I have some doubt whether the moss, as it is called, does not entirely derive its smell from that of the byssus, which is very powerful, and which I have known it to retain on a stone in a cabinet for a great length of time, even though itself was almost dried away and become invisible.

The day of the commemoration of St. Wenefred is the 3d of November, and it is yet observed by the Roman catholics of this part of the country.

The devotees of this saint were formerly very numerous, and in the last age the well was so noted, that, according to Mr. Pennant, a crowned head dignified the place with a visit. " The prince who lost three kingdoms for a mass, payed his respects on the 29th of August, 1686, to our saint, and received as a reward a present of the very shift in which his great grandmother, Mary Queen of Scots, lost her head*." Of late years the visitors have much fallen off: however, if I may judge from seven crutches and two hand-barrows stuck among the gothic ornaments of the roof, I should suppose that the well was not yet entirely forsaken. Indeed the sanative properties of this water, in common with those of cold baths in general, are not to be disputed; but to attribute to the intercession of a saint those things which from the common course of nature are to be accounted for, is only worthy the ages of superstition and ignorance.

The quantity of water thrown up here has been found, on an accurate calculation, not less than *eighty-four hogsheads* in a minute. The well has never been known to be frozen, and it scarcely ever varies in quantity, either in droughts, or after the greatest rains. These circumstances render it of inestimable value: for, although the water has only a mile and a hundred and twenty-four yards to run, before it

---

* History of Whitford and Holywell,

arrives at the sea, it turned, a few years ago, the machinery to eleven different

MILLS AND MANUFACTORIES.

1. *A Corn Mill,* a large building that stands near the head of the stream.

2. *The Upper Cotton Mill,* erected in the autumn of the year 1783, and finished in the short space of six weeks from the laying of the foundation. It is six stories high, and forty yards long.

3. *The Old Cotton Mill,* erected in the spring of 1777. This is only three stories high : it is thirty-three yards long, and eight wide.

4. *The Crescent Cotton Mill,* erected in the spring of 1790. It is six stories high ; twenty-six yards long, and ten wide.

5. *The Brass Battery Mills,* built in the year 1765. Goods are here prepared for Africa, America, and other parts of the globe. For Africa, large brass pans, called *Neptunes,* in which the negroes make salt: pans for getting the gold out of the beds of the rivers, that has been washed from the mountains by the violence of the torrents: bright and black *manillas ;* the latter are the current coin of some parts of the African coast, and the first are rings to ornament the arms and the legs of the negroes. Brass vessels are also made here for various other purposes; and brass and copper rods.

6. *A Copper Rolling Mill,* erected in 1787. This is the largest and most commodious building of the kind in the kingdom, being eighty-

six feet long, sixty-nine wide, and near thirty high in the centre.

7. *The Lower Cotton Mill*, was built in the summer of 1785. It is six stories high; thirty-six yards long, and ten wide.

8. *A Copper Wire Mill*, belonging to the Parys Mine Company, situated on the east side of the stream. This is a manufactory for brass wire of every denomination. Square materials are also drawn at this place for making copper nails, in the common way of beating and heading.

9. *A Copper Rolling Mill* of the Parys Mine Company.

10. *Brass Melting Houses*, where plate brass is made for the purpose of being manufactured at their Battery Mills; plate-brass for wire for the pin manufacturers, and ingot brass for the founders, &c.

11. *A Copper Forge*. This is the property of the Parys Mine Company, and stands on the lower part of the stream, next the sea. It was finished in the year 1780. Here is a great forge for heating the cakes of copper previously to their being beat into pans, or rolled into sheathings, &c. From hence our navy is in part supplied with sheathing, bolts, and nails. Some of the bolts are twenty feet long, and so hardened by rolling and battering as, when facilitated, by boring with an auger two-thirds of their length, to be capable of being driven almost to their heads, into places where the beds of timber are extremely thick. Rudder bands and braces are manufactured here; and nails, from a foot long to the size of a sadler's tack. Braziers are furnished from hence with all kinds

of copper vessels.—These, and all the other works on the stream of this description, are furnished with copper from the Anglesea mines.

The Mine Companies employ near forty vessels of from thirty to fifty tons burthen each, to convey the several manufactures, or the materials, to and from Liverpool, and other places where they have connections.

By the road side, near the larger well, there is a *small spring*, that was once famous for the cure of weak eyes. An offering was made to the tutelar saint (for most of the springs in this country are dedicated to some imaginary saint) of a crooked pin, and at the time of laving the eyes, an ejaculation, by way of addition to the charm, was uttered by the patient. In the present age the waters have lost nearly all their efficacy.

BASINGWERK ABBEY*.

In search of Basingwerk Abbey, I proceeded along the road by the side of the stream, for about a mile, till I came to the marsh, and then crossing it to the right, I found myself within sight of this ruin, which stands on an eminence just above. These shattered time-worn remains, with the surrounding sycamores, are from some points of view highly picturesque and beautiful.

> The ivy now in rude luxuriance bends
>   Its tangled foliage through the cloistered space,
> O'er the green window's mould'ring height ascends,
>   And fondly clasps it in a last embrace.

* Maes glâs, or Greenfield monastery.

The little at present left is scarcely sufficient to indicate to us what this Abbey was when in its flourishing state. The church which was situated on the east side, is totally destroyed. The refectory is the most entire part of the building, and has on one side a large recess with a couple of circular arches. Above the refectory was the dormitory where the monks had their cells. The chapel of the Knights Templars, founded here by Henry II, is spacious and elegant. The brick building striped with timber, that joins the Abbey, and certainly adds nothing to its beauty, is conjectured by Mr. Grose to have been the granary. The situation is delightful, commanding an extensive prospect of the river Dee, Chester, Park-gate, and the Lancastrian hills. The architecture is mixed, the round arches and short massy columns exhibiting the Saxon, and the narrow pointed windows the Gothic-style*.

BASINGWERK CASTLE.

Vestiges of this fortress are yet visible in the foundation of a wall on the edge of Watt's

---

* Tanner and Dugdale say that Basingwerk Abbey was founded by Ranulph Earl of Chester, about the year 1131, and that this foundation was afterwards confirmed by Henry II. and Llewelyn prince of North Wales. Many of the old writers ascribe the original foundation to Henry, but Mr. Pennant is of opinion that it ought to be referred to a period considerably anterior to either of these.

At the dissolution of Abbeys in the reign of Henry VIII. its revenues appear to have amounted to somewhat more than a hundred and fifty pounds *per annum*.

Dyke, and by the road side near the turnpike
gate, at a little distance from the Abbey: but
these are very trifling. It is supposed to have
been indebted for its erection to Richard the
son of Hugh Lupus earl of Chester. In the
year 1119, after his return from Normandy,
where he had been educated, he attempted a
pilgrimage to Wenefred's well, but either in
his journey thither, or on his return, he was attacked by a party of Welsh, and compelled to
seek for shelter in Basingwerk Abbey. Thus
situated, he implored protection from Wenefred, who, tradition says, raised certain sands
betwixt Flintshire and the opposite coast, to
permit his constable and men to pass over to
his relief, which, from that circumstance, were
called *Constable's Sands!* If any reliance whatever were to be placed in the origin of this
tradition, it tends to prove that the foundation
of the Abbey was considerably anterior to the
date generally assigned to it.

The castle is well known to have been rebuilt in the the year 1157, by Henry II. after
his escape in the battle near Euloe; he, however, first cleared all the passes and cut down
the woods around it, which at that time were
impenetrable forests, affording shelter, as he
had keenly experienced, to powerful enemies.

The Welsh ever looked upon this fortress as
a disagreeable check upon their proceedings
and liberty, and therefore about eight years afterwards, Owen Gwynedd, after many unsuccessful attempts, took it at last by storm, and
immediately levelled it with the ground. From
this time it does not appear to have been the
cause of any further contentions.

WATT'S DYKE.

This barrier begins at Maesbury near Oswestry, passes by that town, through the grounds at Wynnstay, near Wrexham, Hope, and Northop, and terminates in the Dee at this place. Churchyard is almost the only writer that has not confounded this with Offa's Dyke. He assigns as the object of its formation that the space betwixt the two, for they run to a considerable distance nearly parallel with each other, was to be free ground, where the Britons and Danes might meet for all commercial purposes.

> There is a famous thing,
> Call'd Offa's Dyke that reacheth farre in length,
> All kind of ware the Danes might thither bring,
> It was free ground and call'd the Briton's strength.
> Watt's Dyke, likewise, about the same was set,
> Between which two the Danes and Britons met,
> And traffic still, but passing bounds by sleight,
> The one did take the other pris'ner streight.

CHAP. IV.

HOLYWELL TO ST. ASAPH.

Lead Mines.—Calamine,—Roman Pharos.—Memoranda of Mr. Pennant.—Vale of Clwyd —St. Asaph.—History of the Cathedral.—Miracle performed by St. Asaph.—Vale of Clwyd.

THE road from Holywell to St. Asaph is rugged but pleasant. This country abounds in *lead mines*, and I passed some very considerable ones about a mile beyond Holywell. The veins of ore, as I was informed, run in directions either north and south, or east and west, but of these the latter are by much the richest. They are found in a matrix either of chert or lime-stone, and often extend to unknown depths. The common, or lamellated ore, yields above fifteen hundred of lead to twenty of the ore, and, in general, about fourteen ounces of silver to the ton.

Calamine is also found in great quantities in this neighbourhood, and in veins like the lead, sometimes mixed with ore, but frequently alone. Nearly the whole of Flintshire abounds with it, and so entirely ignorant were the inhabitants of its use, as, within the last sixty years, even to have mended their roads with it. These roads have, however, been since turned up in many places, and their materials converted to more valuable purposes.

I had not passed the lead mines far before I came within sight of an ancient circular building, in form not much unlike a windmill, on the summit of a lofty hill, called Carreg, in the parish of Whitford, and about two miles to the right of the road. This, Mr. Pennant, entreating his friends not to consider him an *antiquarian Quixote* for doing it, conjectures to have been a Roman pharos, constructed to direct the navigators to and from Deva, along the difficult channel of Seteia Portus.

MEMORANDA OF THE LATE MR. PENNANT.

A large mansion called Downing, which stands about half way betwixt the road and the seashore, was, not long ago, the residence of Mr. Pennant.

This indefatigable and useful writer was born at Bychton, in the parish of Whitford, on the 14th of June 1726. He was a lineal descendant from Tudor Trevor, who married Angharad the daughter of Howel Dda, prince of North Wales*.

He became possessed of the estate at Downing by the death of his father David Pennant: and having discovered a rich mine of lead ore on it, he was enabled, by means of the emoluments arising from this, to make considerable improvements. Here he principally resided.

---

* The name is truly Welsh, derived from *pen* the head or end, and *nant*, a narrow valley; the house of Bychton, the ancient family mansion, being seated at the head of a very considerable dingle.

" The house itself," he informs us, " has little to boast of. I fortunately found it incapable of being improved into a magnitude exceeding the revenue of the family. It has a hall, which I prefer to the rural impropriety of a *paltry vestibule:* a *library*; a parlour capable of containing more guests than I ever wish to see in it at a time, *septem convivium ; novem convicium!* and a smoking-room, most anti. quely furnished with ancient carvings, and the horns of all the European beasts of chace. This room is now quite out of use as to its original purpose. Above stairs is a good drawing-room, in times of old called the dining-room, and a tea-room, the sum of all that are really wanted. I have Cowley's wish realized, a small house and a large garden!"

In his history of Whitford and Holywell, Mr. Pennant mentions another house called Downing, on the opposite side of the dingle, about three hundred yards from this mansion, the property of Thomas Thomas, Esq. Fierce feuds, as usual in days of yore, raged according to his relation, between the two families. " These Montagues used to take a cruel revenge on their neighbour Capulet, by the advantage of a stream, which ran through their grounds, in its way to our kitchen, where it was applied to the turning of a spit. How often," says he, " has that important engine being stopped, before it had performed half its evolutions! our poor Capulet swearing, lady crying, cook fuming, and nurse screaming ! But

> To hear the children mutter,
> When they lost their bread and butter,
> It would move a heart of stone."

Till the advancement of Richard Pennant, Esq. in the year 1783, to the title of Penrhyn, the family, according to his own account, was never distinguished by any honours beyond the most useful one, that of a justice of the peace.

The first sheriff of this house was Pyers Pennant, who discharged that trust in 1612. He had the fortune to marry the daughter of a family not famed for placidity, or the milder virtues. *Valdè, valdè, irritabile genus!* " And from them, Tom," an aunt used often to tell him, " we got our passion ;" and frequently added the wise Welsh caution, *Beware of a breed!*

The fruits of this marriage soon appeared, for Thomas, the eldest son, in a *furor brevis* killed his miller. He was indicted for manslaughter, tried, and convicted, but afterwards pardoned.

When Mr. Pennant was about twelve years old, the father of Mrs. Piozzi presented him with a copy of Willughby's Ornithology. This first gave a taste for the study of natural history, which he afterwards pursued with so much avidity, and from which the world has derived so much instruction and benefit.

In the year 1755 he began a correspondence with Linnæus, which ended only when the age and infirmities of that justly celebrated man obliged him to desist. To the talents of Mr. Pennant, Linnæus subscribed in the highest terms ; and two years after the commencement of their acquaintance, Mr. Pennant was, at his instance, elected a member of the Royal Society at Upsal.

In 1761, he published his first work, the folio edition of his British Zoology.

Four years after this he made a short tour to the continent, during which he became personally acquainted with Le Comte de Buffon. While in Paris, he passed much of his time with this naturalist, and afterwards spent some days with him at his seat at Monbard.

At Ferney he visited Voltaire, " who happened," says Mr. P , which is nearly the whole account he gives of him, " to be in good humour, and was very entertaining; and in his attempt to speak English, convinced us that he was a perfect master of our oaths and our curses."

At Bern he commenced an acquaintance with Baron Haller, and at the Hague with Dr. Pallas. His meeting with the latter gave rise to his Synopsis of Quadrupeds; and afterwards, in a second edition, to his History of Quadrupeds.

In 1769, he made his first tour into Scotland, a country at that time almost as little known to its southern brethren as Kamtschatka. He published an account of this journey, which proved that the northern parts of Great Britain might be visited with safety, and even with pleasure; and from this time Scotland has formed one of the fashionable British tours. A candid account of this country was so great a novelty, that the impression was instantly bought up, and the following year another was printed, and as soon sold. In 1772, he performed his longest journey; his second tour in Scotland, and voyage to the Hebrides; and he returned rich in civic honours, receiving the usual compliments of every corporated town. The publication of this tour obtained the applause which it justly merited.

He made, previously to the year 1778, several journies over the six counties of North Wales, in which he collected ample materials even for their history. His work on this country appeared, at different periods, in two volumes in quarto. Of its merits I am able to speak in terms somewhat positive, having myself examined nearly every place, in this division of the principality, that Mr. Pennant had visited. I can pronounce of it, that, for accuracy, it is throughout (when the necessary allowance is made for alterations that have taken place in the lapse of thirty years) almost unexceptionable. What it wants in elegance of style is sufficiently compensated by quantity of matter, and the antiquary, the artist, and the philosopher, may alike derive from it information and instruction.

His Arctic Zoology appears to have been commenced about this period. This work was so well received by the public, as to be translated into German by Professor Zimmerman; that part of it which relates to the north of Europe was translated into Swedish, and the introduction into French.

The following is an enumeration of Mr. Pennant's different publications, with their dates:

British Zoology,	folio edition,	-	-	-	-	1761
——————————	second edition, two vols. 8vo.			-		1768
———————	vol. iii 8vo.	-	-	-	-	1769
——————————	103 additional plates, &c. 8vo.			-		1770
——————————	fourth edition, three vols. 8vo.			-		1776
——————————	vol. iv. containing worms, &c.			-		1777

Synopsis of Quadrupeds, 8vo.   -   -   -   -   1771
History of Quadrupeds, being the second edition of
the Synopsis, two vols. 4to.   -   -   -   -   1781
———————————— third edition, two vols. 4to.   1792
Genera of Birds, 8vo.   -   -   -   -   -   -   1773
Indian Zoology, folio,   -   -   -   1779
————— second edition, 4to.   -   -   1792
Arctic Zoology, two vols. 4to.   -   -   1784
————— Supplement to, 4to.   -   -   1787
————— second edition, two vols. 4to.   -   1792
Tour in Scotland in 1769, 8vo.   -   -   -   1771
———————————— second edition, 8vo.   -   1772
———————————— third edition, 4to.   -   1774
Tour in Scotland in 1772, forming vol. ii. 4to.   -   1774
————————————— vol. iii. 4to.   -   1775
———————————— fifth edition, three vols. 4to.   1790
Tour in Wales, vol. i. 4to.   -   -   -   1778
————— vol. ii. 4to.   -   -   -   1781
————— second edition, two vols. 4to.   -   1784
Journey from Chester to London, 4to.   -   -   1782
Account of London, 4to.   -   -   1790
——————— second and third editions,   -   1791
Literary Life, 4to.   -   -   -   -   1793
History of Whitford and Holywell, 4to.   -   1796
Outlines of the Globe, vols. i. and ii. 4to.   -   1798
Miscellanies, only 30 copies, from a private press.
History of the Patagonians, from the same press.

Posthumous Publications.

Outlines of the Globe, vols. iii. and iv. 4to.   -   1801
Journey from London to Dover, 4to.   -   -   1801
Journey from Dover to the Isle of Wight, 4to.   -   1801

The two last of these form also two of the
volumes of the work denominated by Mr. Pennant, " Outlines of the Globe." This, in manuscript, occupies two-and-twenty folio volumes,
and great expence was bestowed on them in
ornaments and illuminations. No more, however, than six have been yet published.

The writing of his numerous works, their
correction, and the additions to the subsequent

editions, with his various other duties, kept both his mind and his body in active and continual employment.

To his regular and temperate mode of life, and his riding exercise, for he performed all his different tours on horseback, with the perfect ease of mind that he enjoyed on these pleasing excursions, he attributes the almost uninterrupted good health that he enjoyed for near seventy years. His general time of retiring to rest was ten o'clock; and he rose both in summer and winter at seven.

His favourite exercise seems to have been on horseback, and this he continued, as far as he was able, to the latest period of his life, " considering the absolute resignation of the person to the luxury of a carriage, to forbode a very short interval betwixt that and the vehicle which is to carry us to our last stage."

In the year 1792, the sixty-seventh of his age, he says of himself, " though my body may have somewhat abated its wonted vigour, yet my mind still retains its powers, its longing after improvement, its wish to see new lights through the chinks which time has made." And speaking of his great attempt, the Outlines of the Globe : " Happy is the life that could beguile its fleeting hours without injury to any one, and, with addition of years, continue to rise in its pursuits.—But more interesting, and still more exalted subjects, must employ my future span."

Some of these latter observations appear in his " Literary Life," which contains his biography, so far as relates, principally, to his literary concerns, to the commencement of the

year 1793. This although published by himself, he whimsically denominates a posthumous
work, the name in dotted characters,

THOMAS PENNANT.

subscribed to the advertisement, indicating it to
be sent into the world by his departed *literary*
spirit. From this time he declares himself determined to appear in no new works before the
public, yet the activity of his mind would not
suffer him, even in his advanced age, entirely
to resign himself to private labours and domestic
concerns; accordingly he wrote, and in 1796
printed, the "History of Whitford and Holywell," the word

RESURGAM

appropriately occupying the leaf preceding the
title. He afterwards published also the two
first volumes of the "Outlines of the Globe."

The loss of an amiable daughter, in the year
1794, had so great an effect upon his mind,
that he was never able perfectly to recover it.

Towards the latter end of the year 1796 he
began to be affected by the pulmonary complaint, which at length terminated his life.
His mental faculties, however, still continued
in a great measure unimpaired till the month of
October 1798, when his disorder began to wear
a serious aspect. He was from this time confined to his bed, and on the 16th of December
closed his existence without a groan. Conscious
of approaching dissolution, he met the stroke
with the utmost composure and resignation.

In the writings of Mr. Pennant, we are not to look for any of those brilliant effusions of genius that mark the pen of some of the modern naturalists and travellers. But if he did not possess their fire, he had the more valuable requisites of untarnished principle, and a scrupulous adherence to truth. Perseverance, industry, and correctness, are their leading characteristics. His reading was extensive, particularly in the zoological branches of natural history. He possessed a retentive memory, and a considerable rapidity of composition, his works being generally printed, with little or no correction, as they flowed from the pen.

As to his private character ; he was religious without bigotry, and, from principles the most pure and disinterested, firmly attached to the established church. He was a steady friend to our excellent constitution, and when the spirit of democracy with which the mania of a neighbouring country appeared desirous of overwhelming our kingdom, was spreading abroad, he resisted its efforts with all his might. To sum up the general character of Mr. Pennant in few words, he was a man of upright conduct and the most unshaken integrity, uniting to a good head that valuable counterpart so often wanting, an excellent heart.

VALE OF CLWYD.

About two miles from St. Asaph, I entered the celebrated vale of Clwyd, and, favoured by a charmingly serene morning, the whole scene, from the side of the hill, appeared to the greatest

advantage. Towards the south stood Denbigh,
with the shattered remains of its castle crowning
the summit of a rocky steep in the middle of
the vale; and on the north, clad in its sober
hue, I observed the castle of Rhyddlan. The
intervening space was enlivened with meadows,
woods, cottages, herds, and flocks scattered in
every pleasing direction, whilst the whole was
bounded by the sea and the dark retiring
mountains. This, from the extent of picture,
is not a scene fitted for the pencil, though its
numerous beauties must attract the attention of
every lover of nature. When we enter a rugged
scene of rock and mountain, where the shelving
sides scarcely afford soil for vegetation, and
where the whole character is that of savage
grandeur, we are struck with astonishment and
awe ; but, when nature presents us with a scene
like this, which seems to abound in health,
fertility, and happiness, every nerve vibrates to
the heart the pleasure we receive. Here the
pencil fails :

I admire—
None more admires—the painter's magic skill,
Who shews me that which I shall never see,
Conveys a distant country into mine,
And throws Italian light on English walls :
But imitative strokes can do no more
Than please the eye—sweet Nature every sense.
The air salubrious of her lofty hills,
The cheering fragrance of her dewy vales,
And music of her woods,—no works of man
May rival these ; they all bespeak a pow'r
Peculiar, and exclusively her own.

ST. ASAPH.

After enjoying this lovely scene for some time, I descended into the vale, crossed the bridge over the little river Clwyd, and soon afterwards arrived at St. Asaph, or, as it is called by the Welsh, Llan Elwy, *the Church of Elwy*, a name obtained from its situation on the bank of the river Elwy, which runs along the west side of the place. It consists of little more than a single street, the houses pretty uniformly built, up the side of a hill. It has a cathedral and parish church; and, as a city, is, except one or two, the most insignificant in the kingdom. The cathedral, though small, is plain and neat. The episcopal palace is a large and convenient building, under the grounds of which the Elwy flows. The deanery is on the opposite side of the river, and stands due west of the cathedral *.

* *History of the Cathedral.*—Cyndeyrn Garthwys, or Kentigern, the son of Owain ap Urien Reged, was bishop of Glasgow and primate of Scotland, but was driven thence by the persecutions of one of the Scottish princes. He fled into Wales, where he was taken into the protection of Cadwallon, uncle to Maelgwn Gwynedd, prince of North Wales, who assigned to him Llan Elwy as a place of residence. Here, about the year 560, he founded an episcopal seat and monastery, and became himself the first bishop. On the death of his persecutor he was recalled into Scotland, but first nominated his disciple Asa or Asaph, his successor, from whom both the church and place received their names. In the time of Asa, the number of monks were nine hundred and sixty-five; of these three hundred were labourers in the fields, three hundred servants about the monastery, and the rest were religious. Asa died about the year 596, and was interred in the cathedral.

E

During the protectorship of Oliver Cromwell, the post-master of St. Asaph, who had attached himself to the puritanical party, occupied the bishop's palace, in which he kept the post-office. He used the font belonging to the cathedral as a trough for watering his horses, and, by way of venting his spleen on the established clergy, he tied up his calves in the bishop's throne.

The following are mortuaries that were formerly due to the bishop of this diocese on the death of every beneficed clergyman. On the interference of bishop Fleetwood they were set aside by act of parliament, and the living of Northop was annexed to the bishopric in their stead.

His best gelding, horse, or mare.	His waistcoat.
	His hat and cap.
His best gown.	His falchion.
His best cloak.	His best book.
His best coat, jerkin, doublet, and breeches.	His surplice.
	His purse and girdle.
His hose or nether stockings, shoes, and garters.	His knife and gloves.
	His signet, or ring of gold,

Not many years ago a mark on a black stone in the pavement of the street, about the middle

About the year 1247, in the wars betwixt Henry III. and the Welsh, the bishops both of St. Asaph and Bangor were driven from their sees, and became indebted to voluntary contributions for subsistence. In somewhat more than thirty years after this period, the cathedral was consumed by fire, and two years were occupied in rebuilding it. The roof and upper parts, with the bishop's palace and canons' houses, were again destroyed by Owen Glyndwr in 1404; and they continued in ruins for upwards of seventy years, when they were rebuilt by bishop Redman.

of the hill between the two churches, used to be pointed out to strangers as the print of St. Asaph's horse-shoe, when he leaped with him from Onan-hassa, which is about two miles off. This, however, observes Mr. Grose, who relates the story, seems to have been a miracle performed rather by the horse than by the saint, to whom it is ascribed, unless the keeping of his seat at so great a leap may be deemed such. What was the occasion of this extraordinary leap we are not told; whether only to shew the agility of his horse, or to escape the assaults of the foul fiend, who, in those days, took unaccountable liberties even with saints *.

VALE OF CLWYD.

The tower of the cathedral commands a most extensive prospect of the vale of Clwyd, in every direction; and it is almost the only situation that I could find for seeing it to advantage. The river Clwyd, from which the vale takes its name, is a diminutive stream that meanders along its bottom, scarcely three yards over in the widest part. Its banks are low, and after sudden rains it is subject to the most dreadful overflowings, the torrent at these times frequently sweeping along with it even the very soil of the land it passes over. From this circumstance it is that much of the land near its banks is let at very low rents. This vale is perhaps the most extensive of any in the king-

---

* Grose's Antiquities, vol. vii. p. 43.

E 2

dom, being near twenty-four miles in length,
and about seven in width; containing the three
considerable towns of St. Asaph, Denbigh, and
Ruthin; and though it is impossible to exhibit
a more beautiful scene of fertility, yet, from its
great width and its want of water, I believe the
painter will prefer to it many of the deep and
picturesque glens of Caernarvonshire and Merionethshire.

CHAP. V.

EXCURSION FROM ST. ASAPH TO RHYDDLAN.

*View of St. Asaph. — Rhyddlan. — Edward 1. — Morfa
Rhyddlan. — Rhyddlan Castle.—Friary —Port.—Diserth.
—Diserth Castle.—Plants.—Siamber Wen.—Anecdote of
Sir Robert Pounderling.*

F ROM St. Asaph I wandered along the vale
three miles, towards the village of Rhyddlan, or
the *Red Shore*, so called from the colour of its
site. The country all the way was interesting.
At the distance of about a mile I looked back
upon the little city I had left. Its single street
occupied the slope of the hill, at the top of
which stood the cathedral ; and the intermingled
trees and houses, with the turbulent river Elwy
flowing at the bottom, under a majestic bridge
of five arches, altogether formed an extremely
beautiful scene.

RHYDDLAN

Lies in a flat, on the eastern bank of the river
Clwyd, about two miles from its influx into the
sea. This is here a little extended in width, so
as, at high water, to admit of small vessels riding
up, as far as the bridge. Although Rhyddlan
is now a very insignificant village, it was formerly a place of considerable magnitude and

importance; but no traces whatever of these are left except in the ruins of its castle *. Edward I. annexed to it the privileges of a free borough, in order to facilitate an intercourse betwixt the Welsh and English, and for the purpose of allaying the rooted enmity and the unhappy jealousies that had for centuries rent the two countries. In all his proceedings our monarch exhibited strong features of policy. He had been early taught, that when stratagem would supply the place of men and treasure, it was at least wise, if not always just, to adopt it. Hence originated likewise the statute of Rhyddlan, and hence was his infant son proclaimed prince of Wales. This statute, which was passed in a parliament assembled here in the year 1283, contains a set of regulations for the government of Wales; it also recites many curious particulars relative to the Welsh customs previous to Edward's conquest, against which it was in a great measure directed. His imposing upon them his son, who had, not long before, been born at Caernarvon, for a prince, is an instance of craft which we are surprised to observe in so great a monarch as Edward. He assembled the Welsh barons and chief men, and informed them, that in consequence of their long expressed desire to have a prince, a native of their own country, he had at length determined to indulge them, in nominating one whose whole life had been hitherto irreproachable, and who could not even speak a word of English. Little

* "Non procul a mari Rudlana in Tegenia, olim magnus urbs, nunc exiguus vicus situatur." Lhuyd Comment. Brit. 56.

did they think, when expressing their acclamations of joy and unbounded promises of obedience, that the prince he was about to invest, who was so immaculate, had scarcely been born twelve months, and was at least able to speak as much English as Welsh. The scheme in a great measure succeeded; and, aided by the strength he at that time had obtained in the country, and the additional forces that he brought into it from England, he totally subdued this warlike people.

MORFA RHYDDLAN.

Betwixt the village and the sea is a large marsh, called Morfa Rhyddlan, *the Marsh of Rhyddlan*, where, in the year 795, a dreadful battle was fought betwixt the Welsh people under their leader Caradoc, and the Saxon forces headed by Offa king of Mercia. The Welsh were routed, and their commander was slain. The Saxon prince, in the heat of his revenge, cruelly ordered all the men and children of the enemy that fell into his hands to be massacred, the women alone escaping his fury. This tragical event is supposed to have been recorded by a poem, written shortly afterwards, copies of which are now extant. The plaintive air called Morfa Rhyddlan, as we are told by some, had its origin about the same period; but, from its construction, infinitely too artificial for those dark ages, it is easy to discern that it must be attributed to a much more recent date.*

* See this air amongst the specimens of Welsh music.

RHYDDLAN CASTLE.

The castle is of red stone, nearly square, and
has six towers, two at each of two opposite corners, and only one at each of the others. One
of these was called the *King's Tower*, Twr y
Brenin. It had a double ditch on the north,
and a strong wall and foss all round. In this
wall a tower called Twr y Silod is yet standing.
The principal entrance appears to have been
at the north-west angle, betwixt two round
towers: the two opposite to these are much
shattered, but the remainder are tolerably
entire*.

* *History of Rhyddlan Castle.*—There is some difference
of opinion as to the period at which this castle was first
erected. Two celebrated historians, Powel and Camden,
attribute it, and apparently with justice, to Llewelyn ap
Sitsylt, who reigned in Wales at the commencement of the
eleventh century, and who, they inform us, made it the
place of his residence.

In 1063, three years before William the Conqeror came
to the throne, Rhyddlan castle was in the possession of
Griffith ap Llewelyn, prince of North Wales. It was in
that year attacked and burnt by Harold, the son of Godwin
earl of Kent (afterwards king of England), in retaliation
for some depredations committed by the Welsh on the
English borders.

The Welsh soon rebuilt this their barrier fortress, which
appears to have been of no small importance to them, in
the excursions upon their neighbours, affording them a
refuge, whenever they were driven back, or had the misfortune to be worsted in combat. But in 1098 it appears to
have been wrested from them by Robert, surnamed from
the event de Rhyddlan, the nephew and lieutenant of
Hugh, earl of Chester. Considerable additions were now
made to it, and this hero was stationed in it with sufficient force to overawe the Welsh, and repel any attacks
they might make. While situated here, Griffith ap Cynan,

BLACK FRIARY.

Not far from the castle there was formerly a house of Black Friars, founded some time before 1268; for in that year Anian, who is related to have been prior of this house, was created bishop

prince of Wales, earnestly intreated for aid against some foes by whom he had been assailed, and Robert afforded him every assistance in his power; but, on some quarrel that afterwards took place, Griffith attacked him in the castle, burnt part of the buildings, and slew a great number of his men.

It was repaired and fortified by Henry II. who gave it to Hugh de Beauchamp; but in 1169, whilst Henry was engaged in foreign affairs, it was attacked by Owen Gwynedd, and his brother Cadwaladr, assisted by Ryse ap Griffith, and, after two months' blockade, was surrendered to them. The English recovered it, and about 1214, in the reign of King John, it was again attacked and taken by the Welsh, under their prince Llewelyn ap Iorwerth. It is mentioned as being the last fortress which John held in this country, the Welsh having now entirely driven him out.

Towards the latter end of the reign of Richard I., Ranulph Blundeville earl of Chester, being surprised by the Welsh army whilst in this castle, sent express to his constable of Chester, Roger Lacy, to hasten to his relief with the best forces he could collect. It was on Midsummer's day, and there happened to be a fair at Chester. Roger, therefore, immediately got together a mob of fidlers, players, and other idle fellows, and marched with them towards Rhyddlan. The Welsh, with Llewelyn at their head, observing at a distance an immense crowd, concluded it to be the English army; they therefore immediately raised the siege, and fled with precipitation. As a recompence for this service, the earl granted to Lacy and his heirs the government over all the people of the above motley description in the county of Chester. This was afterwards, in part, assigned by the son of Lacy to Hugh Dutton, his steward, and his heirs, by the following deed:

of St. Asaph. It suffered greatly in the wars
betwixt Edward and Llewelyn, but recovered,

" *Sciant præsentes et futuri, quod ego, Johannes constabu-*
" *larius Cestriæ, dedi et concessi, et hâc presenti meâ chartâ*
" *confirmavi Hugoni de Dutton et hæredibus suis, magistra-*
" *tum omnium leccatorum* et meretricum totius Cestershiriæ,*
" *sicut liberius illum magistratum teneo de comite. Salvo*
" *jure meo, mihi et hæredibus meis.*"

This instrument is without a date, but it appears to have
been given some time about the year 1220. By virtue of
this, the heirs of Hugh Dutton claimed, in the reign of
Henry VII., an annual payment of four-pence from every
female of *a certain description* who exercised her profession
within the precincts of the county of Chester. They also
claimed that all the minstrels of the county should appear
before them, or their stewards, yearly, at the feast of St.
John the Baptist, and present to them four flaggons of wine
and a lance; and that every minstrel should also pay four-
pence halfpenny as a licence to exercise his calling. This
anniversary and custom was observed so lately as the year
1758, when it appears to have been first discontinued. On this
festival the minstrels always went in procession to divine
service in St. John's Church in Chester.

The Welsh, after the surrender to them of Rhyddlan
castle, in the reign of King John, appear to have had possession of it many years. The next circumstance which has
been recorded of it is that, on the refusal of Llewelyn ap
Griffith to do homage to Edward the First, this monarch, at
the head of a considerable army, marched into Wales, and,
amongst others, took this castle, fortified it, and placed in
it a strong garrison.

Not long afterwards it was taken by Ryse ap Maelgwn,
and Griffith ap Meredith ap Owen, but they were soon compelled to abandon it, for in 1283, Edward held a parliament
at Rhyddlan, and appears to have himself resided for a while
in the castle.

In 1399 it was seized by the earl of Northumberland, previously to the deposition of Richard II., who dined here, in

* *Leccator* in the old law Latin signified a riotous and debauched
person.

and subsisted until the dissolution, although it does not appear in the valuations either of Dugdale or Speed*. I did not remark when I was here, whether any part of the building was remaining.

From the *port,* (about two miles from the village,) where the river Clwyd discharges itself into the sea, considerable quantities of corn and timber, the produce of the vale and neighbourhood, are annually exported.

DISERTH.

The village of Diserth is about two miles and a half east of Rhyddlan. The church stands in a romantic bottom, and is finely overshadowed with several large yew trees that grow around it. In the churchyard are many very singular tomb-stones; two in particular attracted my attention, they were not, as usual, altar-shaped, but had each a semicircular stone on the top. They were of ancient date, and belonged to a family of the name of Hughes. Here was also a curious and much ornamented old pillar, of whose use I could form no conception.

company with the earl, in his way to Flint, where he was treacherously delivered into the power of his rival Bolingbroke.

In the civil wars Rhyddlan castle was garrisoned for the king, but was surrendered to general Mytton in July 1646, and in the December following was ordered by the parliament to be dismantled. It is at present the property of the crown.

* Tanner.—Brown Willis says it was reported that there was an abbey here, the religious of which were of a military order.

DISERTH CASTLE*,

Stands on the summit of a high lime-stone rock, at the distance of about half a mile from the village. Its present remains consist only of a few shattered walls†. From hence there is a fine prospect of part of the vale of Clwyd.

On the castle-hill I collected some fine specimens of *VeronicaSpicata,* a plant that I had never before met with : its blue spikes appeared very beautiful, mixed with the delicate flowers of *Geranium sanguineum,* and in some places with the brilliant yellow of the *Cistus helianthemum,* which abounds on this dry calcareous soil. *Cistus Marifolius* was nearly in equal plenty with its relative ; and *Thalictrum minus, Conyza squarrosa,* and *Carduus marianus,* with some other plants not so rare, were the principal of my discoveries here.

SIR ROBERT POUNDERLING.

In a field somewhat south of this place, I observed a ruinous building, which, on inquiry,

* The word Diserth seems to be derived from the Welsh *dy,* very, and *serth,* steep, from the elevated situation of its castle.

† This castle, which was formerly a British post, the last of the chain on the Clwydian hills, had, also, the name of Castell y Craig, *The Castle of the Rock.* The time of its foundation is not known. It was fortified by Henry III. about the year 1241 ; and appears to have been the property of the earls of Chester. In the thirty-first of Henry III. on the extinction of this family, it became annexed to the crown ; and about twenty years afterwards was destroyed, along with the castle of Digunwy, near Conwy, by Llewelyn ap Griffith.

I found was called Siamber Wen, *the White Hall.* This was the mansion of Sir Robert Pounderling, a valiant knight, who was many years constable of the castle. This illustrious hero, we are told, was so celebrated for his prowess, that, amongst other challenges, he received one at a tournament in this country from a Welshman, who in the combat beat out one of his eyes. Being afterwards at the English court, he was requested to challenge him in return, but he wisely shewed that he had prudence as well as valour, by declining a second combat, alleging as his excuse, that he had no desire to have the Welshman knock out his other eye.

From this place I retraced my road through Rhyddlan to St. Asaph, from whence the next morning I made an excursion to Denbigh.—I must remark, for the benefit of those who may follow me, that in the latter part of this day's ramble from Rhyddlan to Diserth, I received little amusement, except in my botanical pursuits. Neither the village nor the castle of Diserth afford any thing very deserving of attention.

CHAP. VI.

EXCURSION FROM ST. ASAPH TO DENBIGH.

*Road and Views.—Town of Denbigh.—Denbigh Castle.—Fine
View.—Old Town.—Privileges.—White Friary.—Whit-
church.—Memoranda of Humphrey Lhwyd.—View of
Denbigh from the East.*

O DENBIGH now appeare, thy turne is next,
I need no gloss, nor shade to set thee out:
For if my pen doe follow playnest text,
And passe right way, and goe nothing about,
Thou shalt be knowne, as worthie well thou art,
The noblest soyle that is in any part:
And for thy seate, and castle do compare,
With any one of Wales, what'ere they are.

So says honest Churchyard in a poetical account of " the Worthines of Wales," written
about the middle of the sixteenth century, when
Denbigh was accounted a place of considerable
importance, and when its walls and castle were
entire.

I was much disappointed in the walk from St.
Asaph to Denbigh. From remarking in the
maps that it lay entirely along the vale of
Clwyd, I had expected many elegant and varied
prospects. The road, however, lies so low,
and the vale is so wide, and so much intersected
with lofty hedge-rows, that it was only in two
or three places that I had any interesting prospect whatever. A woody dell, watered by the
river Elwy, and ornamented with a gentleman's

seat or two, pleasingly situated amongst the trees on its rising bank, afforded a picturesque scene on the right of the road, about three miles from St. Asaph.

DENBIGH.

The town of Denbigh was concealed from the sight by low intervening mountains, until I had arrived within about a mile of it. It is situated on a rock, whose summit is crowned by the fine ruins of its castle, nearly in the middle of the vale of Clwyd. All the streets, except one, are very irregular, and the houses are in general ill built. I wandered alone to the castle, but, from the great number of turnings in the narrow streets, experienced some difficulty in reaching it, although I had it in view nearly the whole time.—A late tourist (Mr. Skrine) has remarked, that Denbigh, from its situation has been thought to resemble Edinburgh. But though some slight traces of similiarity may be found, he is of opinion that the boldness of the position of Edinburgh, and the grandeur of its surrounding objects, far surpass every thing here.

DENBIGH CASTLE.

The entrance into the castle is through a large Gothic arch, which was formerly flanked by two octagonal towers, both now in ruins. In an ornamental niche over the arch, there is a figure of its founder Henry de Lacy, and over another gate, that formerly stood on the left of this, there was also a statue of his wife, Margaret, the

daughter of William Longspee, earl of Salisbury.
This castle has once been a most extensive building; and from the strength and thickness of its
walls, it appears to have been impregnable, except by artillery or famine.—The breaches in
the walls (observes Mr. Grose) plainly shew in
what manner they were constructed. Two walls,
occupying the extremities, of the intended thickness, were first built in the ordinary manner, with
a vacuity betwixt them, into which was poured
a mixture of hot mortar and rough stones of all
sizes, which, on cooling, consolidated into a
mass as hard as stone. This kind of building
was called *grouting.*

The parish church of Denbigh is Whitchurch, about a mile distant; but there is a
chapel of ease within the walls of the castle, a
building which was formerly used as the chapel
to the garrison. At a little distance from this
there is also part of the body of a church begun by Robert Dudley, earl of Leicester, in
1579. Elizabeth granted to this nobleman the
castle and lordship of Denbigh. But having
incurred the hatred of the inhabitants by his
tyrannical and oppressive conduct, he chose to
leave it in its present unfinished state.

From the walls of the castle I had a fine
view of all the country for many miles
round. From hence the vale, in all its pastoral beauty, is displayed before the eye. The
banks of the little river are pleasingly decorated; and the bounding mountains finely contrast their naked barren sides with the delightful scene of fertility between them*.

* *History of Denbigh Castle.*—After the death of Llewelyn,
the last prince of Wales, Edward I. granted the lordship

With respect to the town of Denbigh, Leland informs us that there had been many streets within the walls, but that in his time (before the middle of the sixteenth century) these were nearly all demolished, the householders

of Denbigh to Henry de Lacy, earl of Lincoln, who began the castle, and fortified the town with a strong wall. But before the castle was completed, his son was thrown by accident into the well, and killed. This misfortune had such an effect on the earl, that he had not resolution to finish what he had begun ; and Leland states that the interior never was finished‡.

After the death of the earl, the castle and lordship devolved by marriage with his daughter, upon Thomas, earl of Lancaster. On his attainder they were given by Edward II. to Hugh D'Espencer, on whose execution, they again escheated to the crown, and were granted by Edward III. to Roger Mortimer, earl of March, in exchange for lands to the value of a thousand pounds *per annum*. But his attainder and execution enabled the king, not long afterwards, to grant them to Sir William de Montacute, whom he created earl of Salisbury. This earl seems to have been the first owner of Denbigh, since the founder of its castle, who had not been arraigned for high treason ; he was, however, a most zealous and active adherent to the state. He died in 1333 ; and on the subsequent reversal of the attainder of the earl of March, the lordship and castle of Denbigh were restored to that family. By the marriage of Ann, the sister to the last earl of March, with Richard Plantagenet, earl of Cambridge, they came into the house of York, and thence to the crown.

King Edward IV., while duke of York, was besieged in Denbigh castle by the army of Henry VI.; and the king declared it his intention, if Edward was taken, to give him his life, but, on condition only that he should forever banish himself from the realm§. He however escaped.

In 1563 queen Elizabeth bestowed this castle and lord-

‡ Leland's Itiner. v. 56—58.
* Leland's Itin. v. 58. The words are " King Edward IV. was besieged in Denbigh castelle, and ther it was pactid betwene *king Henry's* men and *hym* (self) that he should with life departe the reaulme never to returne. If they had taken king Edward there, debellatum fuisset."

within the walls scarcely then exceeding eighty in number. This decay is supposed to have arisen from the joint inconveniences of the want of water, and the steep situation of the old town. It became gradually abandoned till at length it was wholly deserted, and a new town much more convenient, was formed about the bottom of the rock.—The town walls, like those of the castle, appear to have had great strength. There were only two gates, the Exchequer and the Burgess's Gate. In the former (which was on the west side) the lord's courts were holden; and in the other (which was on

ship on her favourite Robert Dudley, earl of Leicester, who raised the rents from two to nine hundred pounds a year, and arbitrarily inclosed much of the common lands. An insurrection was the consequence, and two of the principal insurgents were hanged at Shrewsbury. The disputes arose to so alarming an height, that it at length became necessary to request the interference of the queen, who by granting them a charter, confirmed to the tenants the quiet possession of their lands. A new cause of disturbance arose, in the reign of William III., from the vast grant that had been made to the earl of Portland: the people were, however, hushed by the same means that had been adopted in the former reign.—The castle and lordship belong at present to the crown.

After the retreat of Charles the first, from Chester in September 1645, he came to Denbigh castle, and the tower in which he had apartments still retains the name of the King's Tower. The castle continued till the following year in the hands of the royalists, colonel William Salisbury being the governor; and, in the month of July it was besieged by a party of the parliament's forces under the command of general Mytton. Three months, however, elapsed before the garrison would surrender.—After the restoration of Charles II., it is said to have blown up with gunpowder, and thus rendered altogether untenable by the forces of an enemy.

the north) the burgesses held their courts. Besides these the walls had only four towers*.

This place was endowed with the privileges of a free borough by Richard the Second. Queen Elizabeth formed here a body corporate, consisting of two aldermen, two bailiffs, two co-roners, and twenty-five capital burgesses, a re-corder, and inferior officers. It returns one member to parliament†.

WHITE FRIARY.

At the east end of the town there was for-merly a house of Carmelite, or white friars, de-dicated to St. Mary. This is said by some historians to have been founded by John de Salisbury, who died in 1289; but, according to others, it was the work of John de Sanis-more, towards the close of the fourteenth cen-tury.

Whitchurch, the parish church to Denbigh, and about a mile distant, is a white-washed structure of no very elegant appearance. It is chiefly celebrated as containing the re-mains of Sir Richard Middleton, governor of Denbigh castle, under Edward VI., Mary, and Elizabeth, who died in 1576; and of

HUMPHREY LLWYD,

The antiquary, to whose memory there is a mural monument, containing a figure of him-self in the attitude of prayer. This person

---

* Leland's Itin. v. 56.   † Pennant, ii. 45.

was a native of Denbigh, and a student of Brason-nose college, Oxford. He adopted the profession of physic, and became family physician in the house of the last Fitzalan, earl of Arundel, the chancellor of the university. He represented his native place in parliament, and died there in the forty-first year of his age. He compiled a map of England for his friend Ortelius, to whom he dedicated his *" Commentariolum Britanniæ,* and his epistle *" De Mona Druidum insulâ, antiquitati suæ restitutâ."* He left in manuscript, among various other tracts, a Welsh Chronicle from king Cadwaladr, and a History of Cambria. He collected many curious books for lord Lumley, (whose sister he married,) which form at this time a valuable part in the library of the British Museum.

The approach to Denbigh from Whitchurch is much more august and grand than from any other side. The castle, from this road, is seen finely situated on the summit of its rock, which being nearly perpendicular, affords one a good idea of the ancient strength of the place. From hence, also, the accompanying scenery appears more open and varied than from any other part of the immediate neighbourhood of the town.

CHAP. VII.

ST. ASAPH TO CONWY.

*Abergeley.—Llandulas.—Penmaen Rhôs.—River Conwy.—
Ferry.—Impositions practised there.—Pearl Fishery.—
Town of Conwy.—Castle.—Church.—Abbey.—Plâs Mawr.
—Ancient Privileges.*

MY next stage was Conwy. The road now
became somewhat more hilly, but it was hard
and good, and the surrounding country, for
the most part very pleasant. After passing
Abergeley, *the conflux of the concealed water,*
a small village about seven miles from St. Asaph,
I had the sea on the right, and a range of low
rocks on the left of the road.—Beyond Llandulas, *The Dark Village,* the road winds round
a huge limestone rock, called Penmaen Rhôs.

It is supposed to have been in some of the
deep glens of this neighbourhood, that king
Richard the second was surprized by a band of
armed ruffians, secreted there by the earl of
Northumberland, for the purpose of betraying
him into the hands of Bolingbroke, who was
waiting the event at Flint.

I had wandered for some time leisurely along
this road, my eyes fixed upon the ground in
search of plants, when suddenly raising my

head, I was astonished with the magnificence of the landscape before me. The fine old town of Conwy, with its gloomy walls and towers, and its majestic, turretted castle, appeared with the wide river in front, and backed by rising, wooded, and meadowy grounds, and beyond these by the vast mountains of Caernarvonshire.

RIVER CONWY AND FERRY.

The river Conwy runs on this, the east side of the town. It is here about half a mile across, and at present passed by means of ferry-boats. Besides the inconveniences naturally attending so wide a stream, in a place subject to all the variations produced by the flowing and ebbing of tides that run sometimes very high, most of the travellers who have crossed here (except the passengers in the mail-coach, who by order of the post-office, have a boat always waiting for them,) know what it is to experience the wilful delays, and the gross and barefaced impositions of the ferry-men. The charges ought to be *a penny* for every person on foot, except with respect to those who come in the public coaches or in post chaises, who are required, though from what principle I cannot learn, to pay *a shilling* each; *two-pence* for a man and horse, and *half-a-crown* a wheel for gentlemen's carriages. Instead of the latter fare, I have myself known them with the most impudent assurance possible, charge half-a-guinea for ferrying over a gig, and after receiving that, importune in addition for liquor. These impositions, however, unpleasant as they may be, are trifling inconveniences to those suffered from their wilful and needless delays. I have more than once experienced both their impositions and delays myself, and am acquainted with several gentlemen who have suffered infinitely more inconveniences from them than I ever did. It was, some years ago, in contemplation to erect a bridge across the stream, which, on account of the narrowness of the channel at low water, was considered to be perfectly practicable, when all these inconveniences would have been obviated; but it is to be feared that this project is now entirely given up.

PEARL FISHERY.

This river was celebrated in former times as a pearl-fishery; and pearls have been found here at different intervals ever since the Romam conquest. The shell in which they are found is called the Pearl Muscle, and is the *Mya margaritifera* of Linnæus*. It is peculiar to stoney and rapid rivers, burying itself with its open end downward in the sand. The pearl is a calculus, or morbid concretion, supposed to be produced by some disease, and is at times found even in the common oyster and muscle. It is sometimes within the body of the animal, and sometimes on the inside of the shell; and

---

* GEN. CHAR. Shell bivalve, gaping at one end. Hinge with a broad thick tooth, not let into the opposite valve.

SPEC. CHAR. Shape oval, bending in on one side. Shell thick, opake, and heavy. Tooth of the hinge smooth and conical. Length 5 or 6 inches; breadth about $2\frac{1}{4}$.

one muscle frequently contains more than a single pearl. The shells that bear the best pearls are not smooth and equal like the rest, but are crooked and wrinkled; and the larger the pearls are, the greater is their deformity. Linnæus informed Mr. Pennant that he had discovered the art of causing the pearls to form: he however refused to communicate it, and it is supposed to have died with him. When there are pearls in the shells, the animals, on being squeezed, will eject them, and they even sometimes spontaneously cast them on the sand of the river. It is reported in the country that sir Richard Wynne of Gwydir presented the queen of Charles II. with a pearl from the river Conwy, which was afterwards placed in the regal crown. About twenty-five years ago the late Sir Robert Vaughan went to court with a button and loop in his hat set with pearls from the Conwy.

CONWY

Though somewhat gloomy from the antiquity of many of its buildings, is, on the whole a most beautiful and picturesque town. Its walls, which are founded for the most part on the solid rock, and in many places above twelve feet in thickness, are nearly entire. The houses are irregular, but by no means bad.

THE CASTLE

Stands upon a rock, two sides of which are washed by the river. Its architecture and situation are truly grand. The heap of rubbish at present remaining in the river nearly opposite to the end of the castle, is the relic of a tower, which terminated a curtain coming from that angle of the town-wall; and at the other end there was a similar one, which has been long destroyed. Besides these, the castle was also defended by eight large circular towers, from each of which formerly issued a slender turret of use as a watch-tower: of the latter only four are remaining. The exterior walls are of the same thickness as those round the town. These, as well as the towers, except one on the south side of the castle, are, in their general external appearance tolerably entire. The lower part of that, however, from the stones having been taken away from the foundation, has fallen down the rock. The upper part remains still suspended at a great height above, and exhibits in the breach, observes Mr. Pennant, " such vast strength of walling, as might have given to the architect the most reasonable hope that his work would have endured to the end of time "

The chief entrance into the castle is at the north-west end, formerly over a deep trench and drawbridge.

The hall is the most remarkable part of the building now left, and has once been a magnificent apartment. It is a hundred and thirty feet long, about thirty broad, and upwards of twenty in height. The ceiling was supported by eight flat gothic arches. It was lighted by six narrow windows towards the river, and three much larger and more ornamented toward the court. It appears to have had cellars under

the south side and at the east end, the roof of
which has long been destroyed. Only four of
the arches above the hall are left, and from
these and the walls the ivy hangs in the greatest
luxuriance.

The two towers at the end of the castle opposite to the great gate, are called, one the
King's, and the other the *Queen's Tower,* from
Edward 1. and his consort Eleanor, who had
their respective apartments in them. Those of
the former are altogether plain; but in the
room on the second story of the latter, there is
an elegant gothic niche of considerable size in
the wall. This is formed by six arches crossing
each other, and in the recesses betwixt the
pillars which support these there have once been
seats. In the three middle recesses, which command a prospect of the river, are the remains
of three small gothic windows. This is supposed to have been what was anciently called
the *Oriel,* and to have contained the queen's
toilet. In the front of the towers is a court,
from whence probably the royal pair, when at
this castle, used to admire together the numerous beauties of the surrounding country*.

---

* *History of Conwy Castle.*—Edward the first, erected
this castle in the year 1283, and at the same time built the
walls of the town, and repaired several of his other castles
in Wales These were principally to guard against the insurrections of the Welsh under Llewelyn, which for some
years before, had been very frequent. The situation fully
evinced the judgment of its founder, having a complete
command of the river, and by its vicinity to the strong pass
of Penmaen Mawr, enabling the king's troops to occupy it
on the least commotion, and thus cut off all communication
from the interior of the mountains.

In one instance Edward found himself very unpleasantly
situated here. He, with a few of his men, had preceded

THE CHURCH,

Said to have been the conventual church belonging to the monastery, is an inelegant structure; bearing however marks of considerable anti-

the body of his army, and crossed the river, soon after which the tide flowed in, and prevented his men from following. The Welsh in the mountains receiving intelligence of this, descended upon the castle in a body, and made a furious attack upon him and his handful of men within. Destitute of every kind of provision, except a little honey and water, they were reduced to great distress: but, by the strength of the walls, and their own activity and bravery, they were enabled to hold out until the water again retired, and the rest of the army came over to their relief.

In the year 1399, Richard the second, on his return from Ireland, having landed in Wales, heard that the duke of Lancaster had prepared against him immense forces : fearing the weakness of his own army, he therefore, in company with a few friends, stole in the night to Conwy castle. Here he hoped to remain secure till something effectual could be resolved upon ; but his hope was vain, for the insinuating treachery of Northumberland drew him into the very snare that he had so much dreaded, and which in the end cost him his crown and life.

In the civil wars this castle was repaired and fortified for Charles the first, by Dr. John Williams, archbishop of York, this was done at the king's express request, who faithfully promised, that, it should remain in the immediate possession of the archbishop, or of any one whom he chose to appoint until the money expended was repaid. When it was finished, several of the neighbouring families deposited in it their writings, plate, and valuables to a great amount: for these, the archbishop gave to each owner a receipt, rendering himself liable to account for their loss. In May 1645, however, Sir John Owen, a colonel, in the king's service, obtained of prince Rupert a commission appointing him governor of the castle. By virtue of this he surprised and took it, dispossessing the archbishop, notwithstanding the solemn engagement of the king to the contrary; and refused to give any security for the valuables within. The

quity. There are within it a few modern monuments to the memory of different branches
of the Wynne family, formerly of this place.
Among other inscriptions, I found one recording an instance of fecundity somewhat uncommon. It was on a plain stone over the body of
Nicholas Hookes, of Conwy, gentleman, who
was interred here in the year 1637, and is
stated to have been the forty-first child of his
father, and himself the father of twenty-seven
children.

prelate applied to the court, for redress but in vain; and
being persuaded by general Mytton, he quitted that party,
and went over to the side of the parliament. He now fortified his own house, which was not far distant, and Mytton
supplied him with forces to garrison it. "The governor,"
says Rushworth, "upon notice of such his revolt, sent out
a party from Conwy to besiege him in his house; but, he
sending to colonel Mytton for assistance, a party was
dispatched thither to interpose for and assist him, the
archbishop became active on that side in person, and was
wounded in the neck. Mytton, having drawn out his forces,
it was resolved to storm the place, which was accordingly
attempted, and with some loss accomplished; and a few
days afterwards, the castle surrendered; the colonel, with
relentless antipathy to the Irish, ordered all who were seized
within the walls to be tied back to back, and flung into
the river.—For his services, the parliament granted to the
archbishop a general pardon, and in addition a release from
all his sequestrations.

After the restoration this fortress was granted by
Charles the second, to Edward earl of Conwy, who, in
1665, ordered all the iron, timber, and lead, to be taken
down and transported to Ireland, under the pretence that
it was to be used there in his majesty's service. Several
principal gentlemen of the country opposed the design,
but their remonstrances were over-ruled, and this noble
pile was reduced nearly to its present condition.—It is at
this time held of the crown at an annual rent of six
shillings and eight pence, and a dish of fish to Lord Hertford as often as he passes through the town.

CONWY ABBEY.

The remains of the Cistertian abbey founded here by prince Llewelyn ap Iorwerth in 1185, are at present very few. In this convent, and that of Stratflur in Cardiganshire, were kept the Welsh historical records, from 1126 till the year 1270.—The founder was buried in the church of the abbey ; but after the dissolution, his coffin was removed to Llanrwst, a town twelve miles distant. In the same church, A. D. 1220, was also interred Cynan ap Owen Gwynedd : his body was inclosed in the habiliments of a monk, holy garments, which in those superstitious days were deemed proof against every power of Satan ; and thus, as Moret said of Albertus, " he turned monk after he was dead."

PLAS MAWR.

In the principal street there is a large uncouth pile of building called Plâs Mawr, *The Great Mansion.* This appears to have been erected somewhat more than two centuries ago by Robert Wynne, Esq. of Gwydir. In front of the house are the letters J. H. S. X. P. S. signifying, *Jesus hominum salvator, Christiani populi salus ;* and over the gateway a Greek inscription, Ανεχυ, απεχυ, *bear, forbear.* The apartments, which are very numerous, are ornamented in a rude style with arms and uncouth figures in stucco work.

Edward made Conwy a free borough; and the mayor for the time being was the constable of the castle. Amongst other privileges, it possessed one, in common with all other English garrisons on the west side of the Clwyd, that when any person committed a crime within that district, he could not be convicted but by a jury empannelled within it.

CHAP. VIII.

EXCURSION FROM CONWY ROUND THE CREIDDIN.

*Creiddin.—Diganwy.—Teganwy.—Taliesin, the British Bard.
—Watch Tower.—Great Orme's Head, or Llandudno Rocks.
—Adventures there.—Llandudno.—Tradition of Tudno and
Cybi.—Hwylfar Ceirw.—Copper Mine.—Gloddaeth.*

CREIDDIN is a commot, or hundred of Caernarvonshire, situated on the side of the river opposite to Conwy, and forming a considerable promontory into the Irish sea. It is terminated by an extensive rock, on many sides very precipitous, of about two miles in length, called the Great Orme's Head. This is connected to the main land, by a neck of ground, altogether so flat, that Leland says, " the way to it is over a made causey, through a marsh often overflown*." This is never the case at present : it is, on the contrary, supposed to be amongst the finest corn and meadow land in this part of Wales.

After having examined the town of Conwy, I again crossed the river, in company with an intimate friend, to make the tour of this celebrated cape. We strolled along the shore, botanizing

* Leland, Itin. vol. v. p. 49.

in our progress, for about a mile and a half, till
we came to the ruins of the ancient

DIGANWY,

Or Dinas Gonwy, *The Fort on the Conwy*, at
present called by the common people, though
for what reason I cannot learn, *Y Fardre* *.
The remains are just sufficient to enable us to
form some judgement as to the original extent
of this castle. The exterior wall inclosed the
summits of two high and almost conical rocks,
except on one part, where this defence was
rendered unnecessary from the depth of the precipice. On the two summits appear to have
been the principal buildings ; but although it
has been well guarded from its elevated situation, and has been successively the habitation
of several of the Welsh princes, it is impossible
that this castle should have ever been a place of
any magnitude. The ruins are now almost
covered with earth and shrubs, and in different
parts of them the young botanist may meet with
much amusement. These rocks are high, and
form conspicuous objects from the walls of
Conwy. From the summit of the one which is
most elevated, we had a good view of the principal parts of the promontory : we saw Gloddaeth
in its woods at the foot of a considerable rocky
eminence, and in a different direction, about
two miles east of us, the woods of Bodscallon,

* It is frequently called *Gannoc* by the old monkish
writers.

and again, somewhat south of these, the woods round Marl *.

Near the foot of these rocks, and close upon the shore, is a house belonging to Mrs. Williams, built some years ago, probably in a great measure out of the ruins. To this structure the name of Teganwy, or Deganwy, was given to perpetuate that of the place.

TALIESIN, THE BRITISH BARD.

During part of the sixth century, Maelgwn Gwynedd, prince of North Wales, kept his court at Diganwy; and his brother Gwyddno Garan-

---

* Diganwy is supposed by some to have been a Roman station, the *Dictum*, where the Nervii Dictenses, under the late emperors, had their reserve guard. In the sixth century it was occupied as a place of residence by Maelgwn Gwynedd, and for two centuries afterwards formed one of the royal mansions, till the year 808, when it was destroyed by lightning. It was soon rebuilt, and being thought a post of great strength and consequence, suffered much in the struggles of this country. In the year 1246, Henry III. attempted to rebuild this castle, then in a ruinous state; and the English army appears for a considerable length of time to have suffered great distress. A letter, preserved by Matthew Paris, from a soldier of fashion, describes this in very spirited terms. " We lie here," says he, " watching, praying, fasting, and freezing : we watch in defence against the Welsh, who beat up our quarters every night; we pray for a safe passage home ; we fast because we have scarcely any food left, and we freeze from the want of warm clothing, and having only linen tents to keep out the cold." The army was at length so harassed, that Henry was compelled to retreat, heartily weary of his fruitless attempt. In 1263, the place was completely destroyed by Llewelyn; and, Conwy castle being erected not long afterwards, it was thought a needless task to commence a new building here.

hîr, *Gwyddno with the High Crown*, the lord of
Cantref Gwaelod, a hundred in Merionethshire,
since overflowed by the sea, resided also for
some time in the neighbourhood. The latter had,
near his residence, a weir called Gored Wyddno,
Gwyddno's Weir, which is even yet known by the
same name, and belongs to Sir Thomas Mostyn,
as owner of the house of Bodscallon. Elphin, the
son of Gwyddno, was an extravagant youth, and
at one time he had so greatly exhausted his
finances, that he was compelled, as a temporary
relief, to ask of his father the benefit of the weir
for a single night. The request was complied
with, but not a single fish was caught. A
leathern basket was however taken up, which,
on examination, was found to contain a child.
This was an unfortunate circumstance to one so
much in want of even a successful tide. Elphin
had, however, the humanity to direct that the
child should be taken care of, and that no expence should be spared in his education. The
youth, who was named Taliesin, was introduced
by Elphin at his father's court; and his first
step towards fame was in reciting there a poem
containing the history of his life, called *Hanes
Taliesin*. Maelgwn Gwynedd, was greatly surprized at his talents, and himself became afterwards his patron. Some time after this a dispute took place at Diganwy, betwixt Elphin
and his father, of so serious a nature as to cause
the former to be thrown into prison. His attentions to Taliesin now proved of the utmost
importance to him : the bard addressed to the
prince a poem on his patron which excited his
commiseration, and caused him to issue an immediate order for Elphin's release.—Taliesin

throughout the whole of his life continued to receive the attentions, the admirations, and the applause which his talents justly merited ; and after his death he was honoured with the appellation of *The Prince of the British Bards.* His works are very numerous, and many spurious pieces have been imposed on the world among his productions, some of them forged by the monks, to answer the purposes of the church of Rome, and others by the Welsh bards, in the times of their last princes, to spirit up their countrymen to resist the English yoke. Those that are known to be his own bear marks of the highest excellence. His " Beddau Milwyr Ynys Prydain," *The Tombs of the Warriors of Britain,* is a noble piece of antiquity, and will last while the country and the language exist. All his productions are extremely difficult to be understood, so much so that even the best Welsh scholars of the present day will confess that they cannot entirely comprehend them. If his writings were not so obscure, there appear to be in them many particulars which would throw much light on the history, the opinions, and the manners of the ancient Britons, and particularly on those of the Druids, much of whose learning he had himself imbibed.

On a rock towards the north of Diganwy we observed a circular watch-tower, of some antiquity.

We now crossed the flat, and under the south-west side of Llandudno rock, passed the shell of a large mansion that, some centuries ago, was a palace belonging to the bishops of Bangor.

ORME'S HEAD, OR LLANDUDNO ROCKS.

From thence we were led by steep tracks along the steep and slippery sides of the elevated down of Llandudno, for about two miles, to the end of the promontory. Here the rocks were for the most part perfectly perpendicular, of amazing height, and extended to a great depth into the sea. It was awful to hear the roaring of the water among the hollows below us, while at the same time we could not see the breakers till we were upon the very edge of the steep. The stench of putrid fish, the remains of those with which the sea-fowl on these rocks supply their young, was almost insupportable. Not contented to go away without seeing every thing curious within the bounds of prudence that the place afforded, we each pulled off our boots, and crept with caution to the very verge of the precipice. A slight trip of the foot might have sent either of us headlong into a corvorant's nest, or amongst the fishermen who were employed with their boats below. The view had enough of sublimity in it;

> The crows and choughs that wing'd the midway air,
> Shewed scarce so gross as beetles.

The sea dashing in foam against the breakers, the deep hollows, and rude prominences of the rocks several hundred feet below us, were exceedingly tremendous. Our unexpected appearance near their nesting places disturbed the birds, and the flights of so many hundreds, at different depths, with their various harsh and dissonant notes, produced altogether a grand effect. This was considerably heightened by the contrast of the white plumage of many of them against the gloomy sides of the steep. The fishermen, who were almost immediately under us, appeared in their little skiffs, diminished to children, and it was not without using our glasses that we could well discover their operations. When the sea-fowl had become somewhat familiarized with us, they again quietly settled upon their places on the various ledges below. The corvorants were extremely numerous, and we observed unfledged young ones in several of the nests. In order to rouse them we pelted the old birds with stones, but as if confident of our inability to injure them with these feeble weapons, they seemed to ridicule our utmost efforts. Though almost close upon them, they always avoided our blows by a short flight, after which they again returned, apparently unconcerned, to their nests. These we could observe to be ranged on most of the ledges at distances of not more than a yard or two from each other. The rock in places was rendered perfectly white with the dung of the birds. The sea reflected a beautiful green colour, and its surface was enlivened by numerous flocks of birds scudding along it in search of prey, and by their whiteness but just visible to us as spots from above.—My companion, I shuddered with horror while he was doing it, descended by means of his hands and knees to a green patch on one of the steep precipices some yards below. To me he seemed scarcely to have footing enough to stand in safety, without clinging to the rock, and to furnish me with a more perfect idea of his situation, he dropped a stone from his hand immediately into the sea.   He fixed himself with his left hand firmly to the rock, and with all the force he dared exert, darted a stone at a corvorant that was near him.   The effort was rash, and he might have paid dearly for it. With some persuasion, and not without some difficulty, he returned in safety to the top.—On these rocks, which extend entirely along the end of the cape, the samphire, *Crithmum mari-timum,* is found in considerable quantity.   It is collected by the inhabitants of the adjacent parishes both for home-use and for sale.   The process, where it is out of immediate reach, is too well known to need a description here.

LLANDUDNO.

Having spent upwards of two hours upon these rocks, we directed our course towards the little church of Llandudno, which is on the north-east side of the promontory.   It stands alone on an elevated and extensive plain, just above the sea, in the very seat of desolation and barrenness ; exposed to every wind that blows, destitute even of a single tree to shelter or pro-tect it.   I could not distinguish a hut or cottage of any description in its neighbourhood.—It is dedicated to St. Tudno, who, tradition says, was a Romish recluse of extreme purity of manners and sanctity, that lived and died here. On the very spot where so holy a man had yielded his last breath, it was thought a suitable token of respect to found a place of worship to his memory. This, therefore, or some former one similar to it, appeared.—Tudno and Cybi, the founder of the church at Holyhead, it is said were intimate friends, and were accustomed to meet once every week near Priestholme, for the purpose of joining in prayer. The former was called the *White Tudno*, from his always going westward, from the sun, and the other the *Tawny Cybi*, because his route led him always to meet it.

Not far from the church are two rows of upright stones called Hwylfar Ceirw, *The High Road of the Deer*. Tradition says of these, that it was a path by which the deer, which once abounded in the mountains of Caernarvonshire. used to descend to a meadow below, long since covered by the sea. This explanation is extremely absurd, and, till some better is found, we must rest in ignorance both as to their origin and use.

Near the road betwixt Llandudno and Eglwys Rhôs, *The Chapel in Rhôs*, there is a copper mine, which, though formerly not productive, is now worked to some extent. The miners here descend by shafts, and do not, as in most of the Welsh mines, enter through levels.—By an unaccountable neglect I have mislaid all the particulars that I had obtained respecting it.

GLODDAETH.

Not far from the mine is Gloddaeth, the well-known seat of Sir Thomas Mostyn, Bart. built by his ancestor Sir Roger Mostyn in the reign of Queen Elizabeth. It is situated on an extensive slope, covered with modern plantations, and commanding many delightful prospects. The library, which abounds in valuable manuscripts, principally of Welsh literature, has rendered it very celebrated among the lovers of ancient learning. About the grounds are to be found, in a native state, many plants that are extremely rare in other parts of Great Britain.

From Gloddaeth, without visiting, on account of the lateness of the evening, either Bodscallon, another house belonging to Sir Thomas Mostyn, or Marl, we immediately proceeded to the ferry, where, after waiting a considerable time (sufficiently wearied with our excursion), we at length stepped into the ferry-boat, and in about twenty minutes afterwards were again landed under the walls of old Conwy.

CHAP. IX.

EXCURSION FROM CONWY TO CAER RHUN.

Vale of Conwy.—Caer Rhûn.—The Conovium of the Romans. —Account of some late Discoveries there.—Description of a Cataract in the Mountains beyond Caer Rhûn.

From Conwy I wandered along the road lead-ing towards Llanrwst, for about five miles, to the village of Caer Rhûn, *The fort of Rhûn,* (ap Maelgwn, prince of North Wales,) and the site of the ancient Conovium; and about three miles farther to a remarkably grand cataract in the mountains on the right of the road.

Having passed the village of Kyffin, I looked back upon the town of Conwy, and saw its black walls and towers, with the river flowing beneath them. They closed the vale, and had the appearance of great strength and grandeur.

THE VALE OF CONWY

Affords many very interesting prospects. It is adorned with all the variety that can arise from a well wooded and highly cultivated country, bounded by lofty mountains. It is more elegant, from its being more varied, and coming more completely under the eye than the vale of

Clwyd. The river forms, for a few miles, a broad and expansive water.

CAER RHUN*

Is a charming little village on the western bank of the river, and surrounded with wood. —From various discoveries of antiquities in the place and neighbourhood, and from other circumstances, there is good reason for supposing that this was the site of the Roman *Conovium*. During the summer of 1801, considerable pains were taken to investigate this station by the owner of the ground, the Rev. H. D. Griffith, the worthy rector of Llanbeder, who is since dead, and in whom not only his immediate friends, but society and literature, have experienced an irretrievable loss.

In the platform, which was on a low mount, and formed a parallelogram, measuring a hundred and fifty yards in length, and about a hundred in breath, many apartments were cleared, some of which appeared, as Mr. Griffith informed me, to have been a Roman pottery. He shewed me some of his few discoveries, of which I made no memorandum, as he promised me a full account of the place, at the conclusion of his last summer's research; but this, unfortunately, he did not live to complete. I recollect only that there were two small earthen lamps, one of which was very neatly constructed. A

---

* This place is called by Camden and some other writers Caer hên, *The Old City*. This, however, appears to be done erroneously, for all the ancient MSS. now extant, that mention the place, have it *Caer Rhûn*.

few years previously to this, several broken
vases, dishes, and other culinary utensils of
earthen ware, though none of them entire, were
taken up here; some of them stamped with
devices of men in armour, others with dogs in
chace of the stag ; some of them were of a fine
sky blue colour, others red, and one in particular, the most perfect of them all, was a sort
of hollow dish, with its surface beautifully
glazed, and of a lively red colour, bearing the
letters PATRICI very visibly stamped in its
centre. Its diameter was about six inches.
The most curious piece of antiquity found at
this time was a brazen shield of circular form,
curiously embossed circle within circle, with
small brass studs, from the circumference nearly
to the centre, where a sharp piece of wrought
iron, about four inches and a half in length,
was fixed. This shield, which was somewhat
more than a foot in diameter, had on its under
side, when discovered, a covering of leather
stuffed with hair.—Mr. Griffith thought there
were good grounds to contradict the generally
received opinion, of a bath and hypocaust having been discovered here.

CATARACT.

From the road, near the bridge called *Pont
Porthlwyd*, not quite seven miles from Conwy,
I observed, high up the mountain, at some
distance from the road, a waterfall of very con-
siderable height, called by the country people
Rhaiadr Mawr, *The Great Waterfall.* I

ascended along a winding path, which, after about a quarter of an hour's walk, conducted me to the bed of the river, near the station from whence it was to be seen to the greatest advantage. The water, from the late dry weather, was very inconsiderable, still, however, the scene was highly picturesque. From the upper part two streams descended at some distance from each other. The range of rock down which the water was thrown was very wide and extremely rude, being formed, in horizontal ledges, into deep clefts and enormous chasms. On the various lodgments of the rocks, were numerous pendant shrubs. The dark shades of the clefts, and the irregular brilliancy of the prominent features of the scene, from the reflected rays of the sun, contrasted, again, with the foaming of the water, were truly grand. The colours of the rock, which were every where also very dark, were rich and highly varied. The streams united a little above the middle of the fall: they rushed from thence in foam over the rocks, and from the deep shelvings, in many places the water was entirely hidden from me below. In addition to this, nearly every different stratum of rock threw it into a fresh direction. In the whole scene there was the utmost irregularity. On the right of the cataract the inclosing rocks were nearly perpendicular, very lofty, and crowned with pendant foliage. Those on the left were very high and towering, adorned on the lodgements with grass and ferns.—I should have made a drawing of this cataract, had it been possible to have expressed it, with any justice, on an octavo plate: this, however, was altogether impossible. The above description is expressed in terms infinitely too feeble to give any correct idea of the scene:—this waterfall appeared to me by much the most grand and picturesque of any that I have seen in North Wales.

In descending to the road I had an extensive view along the whole vale of Conwy. It appeared from this eminence to be much varied, and on the whole very beautiful.

CHAP. X.

CONWY TO BANGOR.

In my route from Conwy to Bangor, I began
to find myself in a country that was truly
mountainous and romantic : the hills of Flintshire and Denbighshire, which I had just
passed, bear no comparison in picturesque
beauty with the stupendous scenery of Caernarvonshire. The mountains here, instead of being,
as those were, gentle in ascent, and frequently
covered with grass and verdure to their summits, began to wear the savage and majestic
face of nature,—they were precipitous, rugged,
and gloomy.

SYCHNANT,

The dry hollow, which commences about two
miles from Conwy, is the first scene of moun-

tain horror that the traveller in this direction is presented with. The road descends along a steep betwixt the rocks. Immediately below it on one side is this deep and narrow vale : from the bottom arises Penmaen bach, *the lesser Penmaen,* whose head is raised several hundred feet above, and whose broad and sombre front constitutes all the boundary on the right. The ledges of many of the rocks were covered with the flowers of the different species of heaths, which gave a purple tint to the scene. The opening of the rocks towards the bottom, and the gradual unfolding of a distant view of the bay of Beaumaris, the island of Anglesea, and the verdure of the intervening country, was extremely beautiful. The contrast heightened the elegance, and added to it a singularity of character that does not often occur even in mountain-scenery.

PENMAEN MAWR.

Near the fifth mile-stone from Conwy is the celebrated mountain called Penmaen Mawr, *The Great Penmaen,* a huge rock that rises nearly 1550 feet in perpendicular height above the sea. Along a shelf of this tremendous precipice is formed part of the great Irish road. This is well guarded towards the sea by a strong wall, and supported in many parts by arches turned beneath it, a method, in point of expence, found far preferable to that of hewing it out of the solid rock. Before the wall was built, accidents were continually happening by people falling down the precipices ; but, since that time, I believe it has been accounted perfectly safe. Of these accidents the following have been recorded:

An exciseman fell from the highest part, and escaped unhurt.

A clergyman who lived in Anglesea, about forty years ago, fell over with his horse and a midwife behind him. The female and the horse both perished; but the clergyman escaped.

Somewhat more than a century back, Sion Humphries of Llanfair vechan, paid his addresses to a female who lived in some part of Creiddin, beyond Conwy. They agreed to meet at a fair at that town. He was thrown down Penmaen Mawr: she was overset in the Conwy ferry-boat, and was the only person that escaped out of more than fourscore. This story seems romantic, but it is well authenticated. They were afterwards united, and lived many years together in the parish of Llanfair. The female died in 1744, at the great age of one hundred and sixteen; and he survived her five years. Their graves are close together in the churchyard, and are yet familiarly shewn by the inhabitants.

On the evening of the 31st of July 1801, during a tremendous storm of thunder, a mass of stone, supposed to weigh several thousand tons, was loosened from its bed, and precipitated with a dreadful crash to the sea; it swept down part of the wall, and left about a hundred and fifty tons lodged upon the road. A woman and horse narrowly escaped destruction, having but just passed the place before the accident happened. This body of rock appears to have been unfixed by the torrent of water that was pouring down on all sides. I was not many miles distant from the place at the time. All the carriages, among which was the mail, were stopped for several hours, until a body of the country people, who were immediately set to work upon it, were able to clear away so much of the rubbish as to allow them a passage.

Before this pass was formed, which is now near forty years ago, the usual mode of going betwixt Conwy and Bangor was either in boats, or, waiting the departure of the tides, to proceed along the sands, at low water. The latter mode was frequently attended with danger, owing to the soft places left by the fresh water streams, and the hollows formed by the tide, of the depth of which, when filled with water, the guides could not always be certain.

There was a horse-path along the side of the mountain, but it is said to have been excessively dangerous and bad; in some parts it lay above, and in others below, the present road.

ASCENT TO THE SUMMIT OF PENMAEN MAWR.

From the sixth mile-stone I began an ascent to the summit of Penmaen Mawr. I chose this place in order that I might have a guide not to the summit merely, but to the spot where I could find a shrub of which I had heard many nonsensical accounts, called by the Welsh Pren Lemwn, or *Lemon-tree*. This I had been told grew in a situation almost inaccessible, and bore a fruit resembling a small lemon: that many persons had planted cuttings, and even roots of it, in their gardens, but that these had

II

invariably dwindled and died. I questioned
my guide, as we proceeded, respecting the figure
and colour of its leaves and flowers, and I immediately conjectured it to be, what I soon afterwards found it, nothing more than *Cratægus aria*
of Linnæus, which does not often occur among
the Welsh mountains. It grows on the perpendicular rocks just above the road; and of
the three small trees that were pointed out to
me, one had been cut on all sides, for the purpose of planting into gardens.

From hence I scrambled up a steep ascent,
covered entirely with loose stones, which often
gave way the moment I trusted my weight
upon them, to the summit; and, as I walked
pretty quick, it was not before I had experienced several severe tumbles, that I reached
it. I had frequent occasion, from heat and
exertion, to turn round and catch the cool and
refreshing breezes from the sea; and in each of
these restings, as I gradually rose above the
intervening obstacles, I found new objects to
admire. From the summit the view was extensive, and, towards the isle of Anglesea, and
from thence round to the Cheshire and Lancashire hills, was very beautiful. The whole of
the bay of Beaumaris seemed to lie directly
underneath, as well as all the coast from the
abrupt termination of Ormes Head to the little
island of Priestholme. I could just discern the
isle of Man. The prospect over the Conwy
into Denbighshire was also extremely pleasing;
but the mountains towards the south not being
in themselves sufficiently varied, were destitute
of character, and almost entirely of interest.

On the summit, and extending in an oval

form, from north to south, are some evident remains of antiquity. Many ruins of ancient massy walls, formed apparently without cement, are yet visible; and on the east the fragments of several small circular buildings that seem to have been originally formed for soldiers' huts. On the highest part there are the remains of what appeared to me to have been watchtowers; and near one of these I observed a small square well, in which, although then in the midst of a dry season, I found a considerable quantity of water.

This ruin is called Braich y Ddinas, *The Arm of the City*, and is supposed to have been an ancient British fortification. A correspondent of bishop Gibson says of it: "This castle seems to have been impregnable, there being no way to offer any assault to it, from the hill being so high, steep, and rocky, and the walls of such vast strength. The way or entrance into it ascends with many twinings, so that a hundred men might here defend themselves against a whole legion; and yet it should seem there were lodgings within these walls for twenty thousand men. By the tradition of our ancestors, this was the strongest and safest refuge, or place of defence, that the ancient Britons had in all Snowdon, to secure them from the incursions of their enemies."—Governor Pownall, contrary to the commonly received opinion, conjectures it to have been one of the Druids consecrated high places of worship, and that it was never intended for a place of defence*.

* Gibson's Camden, 805. Archæologia of the Antiq. Soc. vol. iii. p. 303.

Penmaen Mawr is not so interesting a mountain, except to the antiquary, as I afterwards found Snowdon, Glyder, and many others in the interior of the country ; the prospects from the summit being neither so grand nor so varied as from these.

The easiest points to ascend from are either along a wall that extends from the road far up the side of the mountain on the extremity nearest to Conwy, or at the other extremity a little beyond the sixth mile-stone. If the traveller be a pedestrian he can ascend one way and descend by the other : this will save him at least a mile or two of journey. The loose stones that lie scattered apparently on every part of the mountain render an expedition to its summit very unpleasant : but the distance is so short, that a person who walks pretty quick may overcome it in little more than an hour.

ABER.

About nine miles from Conwy stands the pleasing little village of Aber, or, as it is called bp way of distinction, Aber gwyngregin, *The Conflux of the White Shells.* Here I found a comfortable little inn. This is a very convenient station for such persons as wish to examine Penmain Mawr, and the adjacent country, either as naturalists or artists.

On a small artificial mount on the west side of the river, just above the bridge, called the *Mwd,* stood formerly a castle belonging to Llewelyn ap Griffith, prince of Wales; and it was here that he received his summons from our Edward to deliver up the principality to the crown of England. The mount is nearly circular at the top, and not more than twenty yards in diameter.

From this place, persons frequently cross immediately into Anglesea, in a direction towards Beaumaris. The distance is about four miles, and at low water they may walk to the bank of the channel, within a mile of Beaumaris, where the ferry-boat plies. In fogs, the passage over these sands has been found very dangerous, and many lives have been lost in attempting to cross them at such times. As some precaution, however, the bell of the church is now generally rung during foggy weather, which prevents persons from wandering very widely from the line they ought to keep.

A deep glen runs from the village amongst the mountains, at whose extremity I had been informed there was a waterfall. I therefore wandered along the bank of the stream, which passes under the bridge, as the most sure mode of reaching it. The distance I found near two miles. The mountains that inclosed the hollow were some of them clad with wood, which, with the prominences of the rocks, and the verdure of the lower grounds, give a pleasing character to many of the scenes. About half-way is a bridge, over which the road leads to Caer Rhun and the vale of Conwy. A little beyond this I turned round to take a view down the vale; and when I descended to the bed of the stream,

I had before me a most charming landscape. The stones of the stream, over which the water broke in a very pleasing manner, with a high bank on the left, formed a rude foreground, that in some measure hid from the sight the regular outline of a green mountain on that side. About the middle was the single arch of the bridge, with a few scattered cottages near it. The road was seen to pass over the mountain-hollow above; and the trees were thinly scattered over one hill, but at the bottom of the rock behind the bridge were collected into a tolerably thick and large copse. The background was occupied by this round and lofty, but well varied rock, in which stony prominences and verdant, but abrupt slopes, were the principal features. This is a scene to which the pencil alone can do justice, description is much too feeble.

RHAIADR MAWR.

Following still the course of the stream, I soon came within sight of the waterfall, called **Rhaiadr Mawr,** *The Great Cataract.* At a distance this appears to have no one character of picturesque beauty. I fancied it merely a narrow stream, falling down the flat and uninteresting face of a lofty rock, and its appearance continued much the same, until I had arrived very nearly to the foot of the cataract, the lower part of which is upwards of sixty feet in height. Its character is extremely simple : at some distance two or three divisions of the upper rock are seen, but immediately at the foot little more than the lower fall is visible. In the bed of the river, as in those of most mountain torrents, are scattered numerous fragments of rock. On each side of the cataract, the mountain had the same flat appearance; this, with the nearly regular outline of the whole scene, at the top forming a segment of a large circle, and some other characteristics, gives to it that kind of simple grandeur, though on a much smaller scale, which is conspicuous in Pistyll Rhaiadr, the celebrated waterfall of Montgomeryshire.

> Smooth to the shelving brink a copious flood
> Rolls fair and placid; where collected,
> In one impetuous torrent, down the steep,
> It thundering shoots, and shakes the country round.
> At first an azure sheet it rushes broad;
> Then whitening by degrees as prone it falls,
> And from the loud resounding rocks below
> Dash'd in a cloud of foam, it sends aloft
> A hoary mist, and forms a ceaseless shower.

LLANDYGAI.

At Llandygai, *The Church of Tygai*, a village beautifully situated on the banks of the Ogwen, is a church, one of the neatest in the principality, built in the form of a cross, having the tower in the centre. Its style is gothic, and it is supposed to have been erected about the reign of Edward III.; but its being washed with ochre to render it in some measure correspondent with the neighbouring mansion of Penrhyn castle, gives it unfortunately a modern cast.

I obtained the key in order to examine the tomb of archbishop Williams, lord keeper of

the great seal, in the reign of James the First,
who was interred here. This is placed in the
wall on the south-side of the chancel, and is
protected from the dust by a long green curtain,
which has a singular appearance. The tomb
has lately been ornamented afresh, at the expence of Lady Penrhyn, a descendant of the
archbishop's family. He is represented in his
episcopal dress at an altar, and (save in the
glare of the gilded ornaments) there is a considerable air of elegance about it.* On a table
monument in the south-east corner, just beyond
this, are two antique figures, supposed to represent some of the Penrhyn family that were
interred here.

Near the river Ogwen, and a little above the
bridge, are two mills belonging to Messrs.
Worthington and Co. of Liverpool. One of
these is for the purpose of grinding materials
for an earthenware manufactory at Liverpool.
The other is an oil and paint mill : oil colours
are here prepared, from the mineral, entirely
to their finished state, and are shipped for
Liverpool at Port Penrhyn. The walks that
have been formed near these buildings are somewhat interesting; and the planting of the adjacent grounds with trees and shrubs, will, in the
course of a few years, render this neighbourhood much more pleasing than it is at present.

---

* This prelate, who acted so conspicuous a part during
the reigns of James the First and Charles, was a native of
Conwy, and born on the 25th of March, 1582. He died at
Gloddaeth, in 1650, aged sixty-eight.

PENRHYN CASTLE.

On the right of the road, not far from Bangor, is Penrhyn castle, the seat of Lord Penrhyn. The grounds are entered through one of the most elegant gates I ever beheld. The house is a fine but by no means a superb building, faced with the yellow Devonshire bricks, which give to it the appearance of being washed with ochre. It has nothing of state magnificence or parade about it, but it can boast considerable elegance. The architecture is the military gothic of the reign of Henry VI., with embattled turrets, which rise to some height above the roof. The grounds are well wooded.

The *stables* are excellent, and are supposed to be among the first in the kingdom in point of accommodation and utility. They are fronted with the purple slate obtained from lord Penrhyn's quarries : which indeed seems to be applied to every possible use on the whole of the property here. The grounds are fenced with it : narrow upright slabs, to imitate palisadoes, are fixed each by two small holdfasts to the railing. The effect is exceedingly neat, but as slate is generally liable to snap, sometimes with a slight blow, and the edges are sharp, I should think them dangerous to sheep in their attempts to escape through the spaces which accident may thus create.

The *chapel* is at a little distance from the house, in front of one part of the plantation. It is a small gothic building, apparently of some antiquity. It formerly stood much nearer the house, but was taken down, and rebuilt of the same materials, put together in the same manner, on its present site. The interior is elegant, and has a brilliantly painted gothic window, the performance of Mr. Eggington of Birmingham. The modern porch by no means accords with the other parts.

From the chapel I was led through the grounds to the baths, which are upon the beach, about half a mile distant. In the way I passed the cottage of the under-steward Mr. Lloyd, designed, like all the improvements about this place, by Mr. Benjamin Wyatt. This station commands a view, though too extensive to be accounted picturesque, yet, in many respects, enchantingly lovely. Nature seems to have crowded here every beauty of mountain, water, wood, and meadow. In front is an expanse of sea, terminated on the right by the Llandudno, or Orme's Head rock, to appearance perfectly insulated, the flat that connects it to the main land not being visible at high water. Penmaen Mawr, along whose side, though near six miles distant, I could plainly distinguish the white line of the road, and the neighbouring mountains, appear to rise abruptly from the water's edge; from hence a long range is seen to stretch into the interior of the country, in which Carnedd Llewelyn and Carnedd Ddafydd are peculiarly conspicuous. On the other side is the island of Anglesea from Beaumaris northward to Penmon, and Priestholme, with the woods of Baron-Hill.

The *Bath* is a plain but elegant building, entered through a portico, fronted by four columns, which admits carriages to pass underneath. There are three rooms for dressing, &c. The baths are, a circular one open at the top, of size sufficient to allow a person to swim without inconvenience, being apparently about thirty feet in diameter; and a small one that will allow of the water being heated. The latter is within the building, and is lined with white and cream-coloured earthen-ware, from a manufactory near Liverpool: under the window is a large and beautiful oval of the same, with a wreath of oak-leaves within the rim, and a coronet and Lady Penrhyn's initials in the centre.

Not far from the bath, there is, upon the sands, an extensive weir, occupying several acres of ground, and forming the segment of a large circle, its ends bending towards the land. It is made by means of stakes driven deep into the beach, secured by stones, and interwoven with the pliant branches of trees. This is a fishery which produces to those who rent it of his lordship, a comfortable subsistence. The fish are taken at the ebb of the tide; and during the herring season the fishermen have their principal harvest. Immense numbers of these are sometimes caught. In one instance so many were taken at a single tide, as, when sold at two shillings, and the worst at eighteen-pence a hundred, produced nearly eighty pounds; besides the quantities that were obliged to be left on the return of the tide, from want of hands sufficient to carry them away, and those that were taken by people who flocked from all parts of the neighbourhood to obtain the refuse fish.

BANGOR.

Passing Port Penrhyn, (a description of which will with greater propriety occupy a place in my next than in the present chapter,) I arrived at Bangor, *The Chief Choir*. This, although at present only a very small place, had formerly so much importance, as to be denominated from its size Bangor Vawr, *The Great Bangor*, to distinguish it probably from Bangor is-coed in Flintshire. It is seated in a vale, from the back of which arise the vast mountains of Caernarvonshire. The streets are narrow, and the houses bad and irregular: a spirit of improvement would, however, render it one of the most beautiful places in Great Britain. From the entrance either way it is seen to advantage, the square tower of its cathedral, and some of the best houses which are near it, presenting themselves from among the trees. The cathedral is small, but every thing around it is kept exceedingly neat *. From near the churchyard there

---

* *History of the Cathedral.*—Deiniol ap Dunawd or Dinothus, abbot of Bangor is-coed in Flintshire, founded here some time about the year 525, a college for the instruction of youth and support of clergy, intending it probably as a cell or appurtenant to that celebrated monastery. It had scarcely been founded thirty years, when Maelgwn Gwynedd raised it into a bishopric, dedicated the new church to Deiniol, and created him the first bishop.

In the tenth century, Edgar coming into North Wales, confirmed all the privileges which had been granted by the founder: he also gave to the college a considerable quantity of land, and founded a new chapel on the south side of the cathedral, which he dedicated to the blessed Virgin. This was afterwards converted into a chantry of singing priests, and is at present supposed to form part of the vicar's house.

is a fine prospect of part of Anglesea, and the town and bay of Beaumaris.

History has recorded, though with what truth it is impossible now to say, that Condagius, a king of Britain, who reigned about eight hundred years prior to the coming of Christ, erected here a *temple*, which he dedicated to Minerva.

On an eminence at a little distance from Bangor there was formerly a *castle*, built by Hugh, earl of Chester, some time during the

The cathedral has been several times destroyed during the troubles in which this country has been involved; in the reigns of William the Conqueror, king John, Henry III. and Henry IV. After the latter demolition, which was by the army of Owen Glyndwr, it continued in ruins near ninety years, when the choir was rebuilt by the bishop, Henry Dean or Denys, formerly prior of Lanthony. He recovered many parcels of land belonging to the see, and was also himself a great benefactor. The tower and the nave, as well as the palace, were built in the year 1532 by bishop Sheffington: the bishop, however, died, and the tower was left at little more than half the intended height. He gave three bells to the church, and directed in his will that his executors should provide a fourth, but they refused in every respect to complete what he had begun. On the tower was this inscription, which is now become illegible:

" Thomas Sheffington episcopus Bangorensis hoc campanile et hanc ecclesiam fieri fecit, anno partus virginis 1532."

Owen Gwynedd, prince of Wales, who died in 1169, is supposed to have been buried in the south transept, beneath an arch with a flowery cross cut on a flat stone. When Baldwyn, archbishop of Canterbury, visited Wales, to preach the crusades and invite soldiers to the holy wars, he saw the tomb of this prince, and directed the bishop to remove the body out of the church: this was on account of his having been excommunicated by Becket for marrying a first cousin, and continuing to cohabit with her till his death. The bishop, in obedience to the charge, made, not long afterwards, a passage from the vault through the south wall of the building, through which he caused the body to be shoved secretly into the churchyard.

reign of **William Rufus.** It has been so long demolished, that even the period of its destruction cannot be ascertained.

Not far from the town there was also formerly a *house of friars preachers.* This was founded about the year 1299 by Tudor ap Gronw, lord of Penmynydd and Trecastle. Some time during the reign of Edward VI. this building was converted into a free school.

St. Mary's de Garthlaman, the ancient parish church, which stood about four hundred yards from the cathedral, appears to have been erected prior to the commencement of the fourteenth century.

BANGOR FERRY,

Called by the Welsh Porthaethwy, *The Ferry of the confined Waters,* is about a mile beyond the town. Here the passengers from England to Ireland cross the strait of Menai into Anglesea. The ferry-house is situated on the eastern bank of this elegant river, expansive as some of the American torrents, and is certainly one of the most charmingly retired spots in the kingdom. Here is an inn to which most travellers resort, from the unaccountable want of comfortable accommodation in the town. The views from the house and garden are principally confined to the opposite shore and the intervening stream; but the numerous trading vessels that pass, the rocky banks, and altogether varied scene, are too pleasing to be overlooked even by the most tasteless traveller.

It was at this inn that I was, for the first time since my arrival in Wales, entertained with the music of the harp, the indigenous instrument of this country.

In the thirteenth century a *battle* was fought near Bangor Ferry, which none of the historians have mentioned. It is, however, described by a bard who lived about the time, Llywarch Brydydd y Moch, in a poem on the death of Llewelyn ap Iorwerth. His language is animated and expressive, and may be taken as a specimen of the Welsh bardic style of that period. " Dark ran the purple gore over the breasts of the warriors : loud was the shout ; havoc and carnage stalked around. The blood-stained waves flowed over the broken spear, and mournful silence hung on the brows of the warriors. The briny wave, rolling into the channel, mingled with waves of blood. Furiously raged the spear, and the tide of blood rushed with force. Our attack was sudden and fierce. Death was displayed in all its horrors. Noble troops, in the fatal hour, trampled on the dead, like prancing steeds. Before Rodri was subdued, the churchyards became like fallow ground."

CHAP. XI.

EXCURSION FROM BANGOR FERRY THROUGH NANT FRANGON.

Port Penrhyn.—Fine Situation.—Writing-Slate Manufactory.—Iron Rail-Road —Lord Penrhyn's Slate Quarries.—Cottages of the Workmen.—Ogwen Bank.—Carnedd Llewelyn—Nant Frangon.—Rude Landscape.—Falling of a Rock.—Waterfalls of Ben Glog.— Y Trivaen.—Anecdotes respecting two upright Stones on the Summit of Trivaen.— Llyn Ogwen.—New Road.

On the following morning I rose early in order that I might have sufficient time to examine the romantic vale of Nant Frangon, *The Beaver's Hollow*, and the different commercial undertakings of Lord Penrhyn and others in its neighbourhood. The boundary of my excursion I had fixed at Llyn Ogwen, about twelve miles distant, and the principal objects were to be Port Penrhyn, Lord Penrhyn's slate quarries, and the waterfalls of Ben Glog.

I therefore repassed the town of Bangor, and took an early breakfast at the *Penrhyn Arms*, a comfortable and most delightfully situated inn that overlooks

PORT PENRHYN.

This was built by his lordship from a design of Mr. Benjamin Wyatt; and had it been large enough for general accommodation, would be a most eligible place for every traveller on pleasure. One end of the house, that commands a view over Beaumaris bay towards the sea, is occupied by a subscription news-room for the inhabitants of Bangor and its neighbourhood, and few places of this nature possess so much either of internal or external elegance. Mr. Wyatt's taste is here very conspicuous, not only in the neat design of the room, but in the choice of a situation commanding an uncommonly beautiful prospect of land and water. This is the same in general character as that I have described from Mr. Lloyd's cottage in Lord Penrhyn's grounds *: but, in addition to all the elegance of that scene, the towers of Penrhyn castle from hence appear in front, rising above the dark surrounding woods. Immediately below the bowling-green, into which the room opens, the observer has the busy scene of the port. Here the appearance of the numerous vessels with which this is at all times crowded, and the bustle and noise that necessarily attend the shipping of goods, form a singular contrast with the other mild and beautiful features.

From the inn I descended to the *quay*. On one side of this there is a long yellow building, in which is carried on one of the most extensive manufactures of *writing-slates* in Great Britain. This belongs to Messrs. Worthington and Co. of Liverpool: and Mr. Worthington (to whose civility and attentions in himself conducting me through all his concerns in this neighbourhood,

* See p. 106.

I

I acknowledge myself greatly indebted) informed
me that as many as between three and four
hundred dozen were, on an average, manufactured here every week. A few inkstands, and
some other fancy articles, are also made, but
these are found not to answer to any extent.
The slates used are of the finest quality that the
quarries afford. The process of smoothing and
framing them is extremely simple, and unnecessary here to be described.

Port Penhryn is principally used by vessels
coming from different parts of the kingdom for
the slates obtained from lord Penrhyn's quarries,
between five and six miles distant. About six
hundred tons are shipped per week. These,
for many years, were conveyed to the port at
an enormous expence, by means of carts and
horses, but there is now an iron rail-road which
extends all the way from the quarries to the
quay. In consequence of this, two horses are
able, in fifteen waggons chained to each other,
to draw upwards of twelve ton weight of slates.
Pursuing this rail-road, I arrived, after a walk
of about two hours, at

LORD PENRHYN'S SLATE QUARRIES,

Which are at Braich y Cafn, in the mountains
on the south-west side of Nant Frangon. Here
I found several immense openings, with sides
and bottoms as rude as imagination can paint,
that had been formed in the getting of the slate.
On first surveying them, a degree of surprize
is excited how such yawning chasms could have

been formed by any but the immediate operations of nature.

As a place to engage the attention of the tourist, few will be found more worthy than these quarries, which, even in singularity of appearance, great depth, and the rude forms of the remaining rocks, will scarcely be found inferior to the copper mines in Anglesea. The bustle of the workmen on the various ledges, the breaking up of the strata, and the noises of splitting and shaping, with at intervals the loud explosion from the blasting of the rocks, and the subsequent crash of the pieces thrown in every direction, will be novel to most of the travellers through this country.

Nearly opposite to the quarries there is a small *public house*, where the traveller may obtain such poor, yet acceptable refreshment, as the neighbourhood affords, viz. bacon, eggs, and ale : and he will find the inhabitants, at least equally cleanly, with any among the mountains.—In different parts around are scattered the white-washed cottages of the workmen, built from the designs of Mr. Wyatt, and on the exterior, affording at a little distance, an air of considerable neatness and comfort ; but from the broken windows, and the ragged and filthy appearance of the children of two or three into which I ventured to put my head, nothing but the extreme of wretchedness and poverty could be supposed to reign within.

By the road-side, not far distant, there is a large mill for the purpose of sawing the slate into slabs, for grave stones, cottage hearths, mantle pieces, fences, &c.

I 2

Descending from the quarry, I crossed the road to visit Lady Penrhyn's grounds at

OGWEN BANK,

Of which a Welsh writer has said, though perhaps somewhat affectedly, that " 'tis an acre of *Tempe* among the rocks of *Norway !*" In these grounds there is a small ornamented building containing a dining-room and such other accommodations as are necessary for the family or their friends in their visits to the quarry. In front of this the stream of the river Ogwen breaks in a small cascade among the rocks. The grounds are laid out in too *gay* a stile to accord with the bleakness of the surrounding mountain scenery ; yet prejudice itself must allow that it is on the whole a most delightful spot.

I do not remember from what exact point it was that the summit of the celebrated mountain

CARNEDD LLEWELYN

Was pointed out to me : it, however, appeared in a direction exactly west, and in a straight line, was scarcely more than three miles distant. Except Snowdon, which exceeds it not more than fifteen or twenty yards, this is the highest of the Welsh mountains. Its rocks are said to afford to the botanist numerous alpine plants, but one in particular, *Ajuga alpina,* that has not hitherto been elsewhere found in Wales. — The neighbouring inhabitants have a tradition, that formerly a giant called Rhitta had his residence on this mountain, and, as in all other stories of giants, that he was the terror of the whole country. They even assert that he wore a garment woven from the beards of several of the princes and most redoubted warriors whom he had slain in combat.—Taking leave of our giant and his residence at the same time, I shall descend into the rude mountain vale of

NANT FRANGON,

The Beaver's Hollow. This tremendous glen is destitute of wood, and almost even of cultivation, except in a narrow slip of meadow, that lies along its bottom. The sides, however, which are truly,

> Huge hills that heap'd in crowded order stand,

sufficiently repay their want of verdure, by the pleasing and fantastic appearance of the rocks that compose them. These rise abruptly from their base, and stretch their barren points into the clouds, unvaried with trees or shrubs, and uncheered even by the cottager's hut.

In the year 1685, part of a rock of one of the impending cliffs at the upper end of this vale, became so undermined by storms and rain, that, losing its hold, it fell down in several immense masses, and in its passage along one of the steep and shaggy cliffs, dislodged some hundreds of other pieces. Many of these were intercepted in their progress into the vale, but so much forced its way to the bottom as entirely destroyed a small piece of meadow ground, and several of the fragments were thrown at least two hundred yards asunder. In this accident one great stone, the largest remaining piece of the upper rock, made in its descent, a trench as large as those in which the mountain streams usually run : this is yet pointed out by the inhabitants of the vale. When it arrived at the plain, it continued its passage through a small meadow, and across the river Ogwen, and lodged itself on the opposite bank.

The mountains at the upper end of this vale form a scene singularly grand : on each side the hollow appears guarded by a huge conical rock, Trivaen on the right, and Braich Dû on the left. These, with Glyder Bach and Glyder Vawr, *The Lesser and Greater Glyder*, and some others, fill up the distance, and so close the vale, that no access could possibly be supposed to be had from beyond them*.

WATERFALLS OF BEN GLOG.

At the end of the vale the road winds up a steep rock, betwixt Trivaen and Braich Dû, called Ben Glog. And from the bottom, at the distance of about half a mile on the left, may be seen the three falls of the Ogwen. These are called Rhaiadr Benglog, *The Cataracts of Benglog,* and they are so fine that the traveller in search of romantic scenery will be highly

---

* Near this place, by a little gothic cottage, there is a small *hone quarry*. The stones obtained here are said to equal the Turkey hones in quality. These are taken to a mill at Llandygai to be sawn and ground into shape. When I was here, the quarry was worked by only a single man.

gratified by visiting them. I descended from
the road into the bottom of the vale, and went
along the bank of the river until I arrived at
the foot of the lower cataract. Here the stream
roared with vast fury, and in one sheet of
foam, down an unbroken and almost perpendicular rock. The sun shone directly upon it,
and a prismatic bow was beautifully formed by
the spray. The tremendous roar of the water,
and the broken and uncouth disposition of the
immediately surrounding rocks, added greatly
to the interest of the scene.—After awhile I
climbed a rocky steep to the second or middle
fall. Here the river is precipitated, in a fine
stream, through a chasm between two perpendicular rocks that each rise several yards above.
From the station I took, the immense mountain
Trivaen was seen to fill up the wide space at
the top, and to form a rude and sublime
distance, heightened greatly in effect by a dark
aërial tint arising from the extreme heat of the
day, and the lowering clouds that were floating
around. The masses of black rocks, surrounded
by foam, near the top of the fall, 1 could have
fancied were floating along the torrent, and
rushing to the bottom. The stream widens as
it descends, and below passes over a slanting
rock, which gives it a somewhat different direction. In the foreground was the rugged bed
of the stream, and the water was seen to dash
in various directions among the broken masses
of rock.—The third cataract, to which I now
clambered, I found very grand and majestic,
yet by no means equal to either of the former.
—These waterfalls are scarcely known in the
adjacent country, and have been unaccountably

omitted even in Mr. Pennant's Tour, although this gentleman accurately describes most of the scenery around them.

Leaving the falls, the trouble of visiting which had been amply repaid by the pleasure I had derived from them, I regained the road.— On crossing the upper end of the vale, I was delighted with a very beautiful and unexpected view for nearly its whole length, where the mountains down each side appeared, to a great distance, falling off in beautiful perspective.

Y TRIVAEN,

The Three Summits, so called from its appearing on one side to have three separate heads, forms, as I have before said, the right boundary of this extremity of the hollow. It is singular from having on its highest point two tall upright stones, which from below have the appearance of two men standing together. These are each about fourteen feet high, and they are not more than a yard and half asunder. So exact is their resemblance to human figures, (for the eye does not take cognizance of their distance, and consequently their real size is not discovered,) that I am by no means surprized at the circumstance of many travellers having been deceived in fancying them a Welsh tourist and his guide. I was credibly informed that one gentleman who was on horseback, stopped by the edge of Llyn Ogwen, (for this is the place from whence alone they can be seen,) nearly half an hour to watch their motions; but being somewhat sooner satisfied with gazing at them than he thought they were at the surrounding country, he rode on to Capel Curig, where he related the circumstance, adding an expression of surprize at their remaining so long on one spot. The people at the public-house laughed heartily at the joke, and immediately undeceived him. A gentleman of my acquaintance, also, who some years was in the country, related to me some particulars of his journey, and among other things told me, that having passed through Nant Frangon a little way, he observed on the top of one of the mountains two men that seemed very earnestly engaged in admiring the country. He said, that although he went on very slowly, and was constantly looking back at them, till an intervening rock shut them from his sight, yet they still remained in the same position. This story was told so seriously, that it was not without difficulty I could keep my countenance to hear it to the end; and even when I had, I was scarcely able to persuade him that what he had imagined to be men were nothing but blocks of stone*.

LLYN OGWEN,

The source of the little river Ogwen, is a tolerably large pool, for it does not deserve the appellation of lake, well stocked with trout, and some other kinds of fish common to mountain pools.—Near this place the scenery changes its rough aspect, and assumes a more placid, but

---

* This mountain will be more particularly described in an ensuing chapter.

still rude character, which it retains for some miles.

NEW ROAD.

An act of parliament has lately been obtained for forming a road from near Llanrwst to Bangor Ferry, on which the mail-coach from London to Holyhead now runs. Till within these few years, the road along these vales was a mere horse-path, and that one of the worst in the country. The principal advantages of this new road consist in having upwards of ten miles saved (in thirty-eight) betwixt Capel Voelas and Bangor Ferry; and in its passing almost entirely along vallies in the most mountainous and romantic parts of North Wales, and thus avoiding the immense steeps of Penmaen Mawr and Sychnant. There is only one material declivity, that of Ben Glog, (betwixt Llyn Ogwen and Nant Frangon,) the whole way. The principal objection to the road seems to arise from the circumstance of immense drifts of snow in winter rolling down from the mountains into the vallies, and at times entirely blocking up the passage, against which, unhappily, there car be no remedy.

CHAP. XII.

BANGOR TO CAERNARVON.

Fine Scenery.— Caernarvon.—Extensive Prospect.—Llan-bublic Church.—Harbour.—Caernarvon Castle.—Birth of Edward, first Prince of Wales.—History of Caernarvon Castle.—Roman city of Segontium.—Jumpers.

LONG before I had conceived the thought of making a tour through Wales, I had heard much said in praise of the ride from Bangor to Caernarvon. It had invariably been represented to me as affording more exquisite scenery than almost any other part of the country.—For four miles I sauntered along from the inn, expecting every moment to be delighted with a prospect of these boasted scenes, and was indulging some reflections, not altogether favourable to the taste and judgment of my informers, when, on a sudden turn of the road, the straits of Menai, the well wooded island of Anglesea, and beyond these the far distant Rival mountains on one side, opened into a placid scene, whilst the black precipices and shagged sides of the rocks of Caernarvonshire on the other, formed a most delightful contrast. This transition was so momentary, that it seemed almost the effect of enchantment. Proceeding onward, the town and castle of Caernarvon after a while entered the scene, and completed a landscape one of the most charming I ever beheld.

At Caernarvon I went to the hotel, an inn built some years ago by the earl of Uxbridge on a very extensive scale. It is an elegant stone building situated on the left of the entrance into the town, a little above the Menai, of which it commands an extended prospect.

CAERNARVON

Is, on the whole, the most beautiful town in North Wales. It is situated on the eastern bank of the Menai, the strait that divides the isle of Anglesea from the other parts of Wales, and is a place extremely well adapted to afford during summer a few months retreat for a thinking mind from the busy scenes of the world.— Its situation between the mountains and the island renders it a convenient place of residence for travellers who wish to visit both.

The walls round the town are even yet nearly entire, and, as well as the castle, seem to bear much the same external appearance which they did in the time of their founder Edward the First. They have a number of round towers, and two principal gates, entrances to the town. Over one of these is a spacious room, which is used as the town-hall, and in which the dancing assemblies are frequently held.— The houses are, for the most part, tolerably regular, but the streets, as in all other ancient towns, are very narrow and confined.—On the outside of the walls there is a broad and pleasant terrace walk along the side of the Menai, extending from the quay to the north end of the town walls, which is the fashionable promenade,

in fine evenings, for all descriptions of people.
—The court-house, in which the great sessions
for the county are held, and where all the county
business is done, stands nearly opposite to the
castle gates.—The custom-house, a small and
mean building, is on the outside of the walls, not
far from the quay.

From the top of Tuthill, the rock behind the
hotel, I had an excellent bird's-eye view of the
town. From hence the castle, and the whole of
the town walls, are seen to the greatest advantage; and, on a fine day, the isle of Anglesea,
bounded on two sides by the Holyhead, and
Paris mountains, appears spread out like a map
beneath the eye. Sometimes, even the far distant mountains of Wicklow may be seen towering beyond the channel. On the opposite side
to these is the fine and varied range of British
Alps, where Snowdon, whose

> Hoary head,
> Conspicuous many a league, the mariner,
> Bound homeward, and in hope already there,
> Greets, with three cheers, exulting,

is seen to far overtop the rest.

Caernarvon is in the parish of Llanbublic, and
the *church* is situated about half a mile from
the town. In this, which contains nothing
curious except a marble monument, with two
recumbent figures of sir William and lady
Griffith, of Penrhyn, who died in the year 1587,
the service is always performed in the Welsh
language. There is an English service every
Sunday morning and afternoon, in the chapel
of ease to this church, situated in the north-
west corner of the town walls, and originally

built for the use of the garrison. The former of these is generally very well attended.

At Caernarvon there is a small, but tolerably good harbour. This is used principally by the vessels that trade here for slates, of which many thousand tons are exported every year to different parts of the kingdom.

CAERNARVON CASTLE.

The entrance into this stupendous monument of ancient grandeur is through a lofty gateway, over which is yet left a mutilated figure, supposed by most writers to be that of Edward the the First. In this gate there are the grooves of no fewer than four port-cullises, evidences of the former strength of the fortress. The building is large but irregular, and much more shattered within, than, from viewing it on the outside, one would be led to imagine. The towers are chiefly octagonal, but three or four of them have each ten sides: among the latter is the *Eagle Tower*, the largest and by far the most elegant in the whole building. This tower, which received its name from the figure of an eagle yet left (though somewhat mutilated) at the top of it, stands at one end of the oblong court of the castle, and has three handsome turrets issuing from it.

It was in the Eagle Tower that Edward, the first prince of Wales, afterwards Edward II. was born on St. Mark's day, the 25th of April 1284*. Pennant says, that the prince was

---

* Matt. West. 372.

brought forth " in a little dark room not twelve feet long, nor eight in breadth." This assertion he alleges to be founded on tradition, but I cannot conceive how that gentleman should retain the opinion after he had once examined the place. This room has indeed had a window and a fire place in it, but it very evidently was nothing more than a passage-room to some of the other apartments, which, though nearly the most magnificent in the castle, must, during the queen's confinement, have been shut up as useless. If the prince was born in the Eagle Tower, it must have been in one of the rooms, occupying in width the whole interior, in an apartment suitable to the majesty of the heir apparent to the English throne, and not as honest Coleforks, who has the care of the castle, and who pointed out to me the place, said, " in such a dog-hole as this."—From the top of the Eagle Tower I was highly gratified by a very extensive view of the isle of Anglesea, the Menai, and the country for many miles round.

At the other end of the court, and opposite to this tower, is a gate called the Queen's Gate. This is said to be that through which the faithful Eleanor, queen of Edward I., first entered the castle. It appears to have been guarded by two portcullises, and it anciently had a communication with the outside of the castle by means of a draw-bridge over a deep moat. At present it is considerably above the level of the ground, owing probably to the moat having been filled up with earth from this part.

The state apartments are larger, and appear to have been much more commodious, than any of the others. The windows were wide, and not inelegant for the times. On the outside, the building containing these apartments is square, but I was surprized, on entering them, to find all the rooms perfectly polygonal, the sides being formed out of the vast thickness of the walls.

A narrow gallery, or covered way, formerly extended round this fortress, by which, during a siege, a communication could be had with the other parts without danger. On one side this gallery remains yet undemolished. It was next to the outer wall, and was lighted by narrow slits that served as stations, from whence arrows, and other missile weapons, could be discharged with advantage upon an enemy.

The castle occupies the whole west end of the town; and was a place of such strength, as, before the introduction of artillery, to have been capable of withstanding the most furious attacks of an enemy The exterior walls are in general about nine feet in thickness.

From a heap of rubbish near the end of the court opposite to the Eagle Tower, an echo may be heard which repeats several syllables very distinctly. There is, however, only a single reverberation.

Caernarvon castle, it has very justly been observed, from whatever point, or at whatever distance it is viewed, has a romantic singularity, and an air of dignity that commands an awe, at the same time that it pleases the beholder. Its ivy-clad walls are in some parts going fast to decay, while in others they even yet retain their ancient external form and appearance*.

* *History of Caernarvon Castle.*—After Edward the First had subdued the Welsh people, he began to think of secur-

PRIVILEGES AND GOVERNMENT OF CAER-
NARVON.

This town is governed by a mayor, one alderman, two bailiffs, a town clerk, and two ser-
geants at mace.—The representative in parlia-

ing his conquests by erecting several strong holds in different
parts of their country. And, as it appeared to him that
Caernarvonshire, on account of its mountains and morasses,
was a country likely to encourage insurrections, he determined to guard as much as possible against such, by
erecting the castles of Conwy and Caernarvon, two of the
strongest in the whole principality.

We are informed by Mr. Pennant, from the authority of
the Sebright manuscripts, that Edward began this castle in
the early part of 1283, and completed it within that year*.
A record, however, formerly belonging to the exchequer
of Caernarvon, states decisively that it occupied twelve
years in building. The revenues of the archbishopric of
York, which about that time was vacant, were applied
towards defraying the expences†.

The reason of the queen of Edward I. being brought here
I have already mentioned in the account of the village of
Rhyddlan.

Very few events relative to Caernarvon or its castle have
been given to posterity. In an insurrection of the Welsh,
during a fair, in the year 1294, the town was suddenly
attacked: after the surrender it was set on fire, and all the
English found within the walls were murdered in cold
blood.—This place, in 1404, was blockaded by Owen
Glyndwr's adherents, but was bravely defended for the
king by Jevan ap Meredydd and Meredydd ap Hwlkin
Llwyd of Glyn Llivon in Evionedd. During the siege Jevan
died in the castle, and his body was conveyed out privately
by sea to be buried in his parish-church of Llanvihangel.
Owen's men, at length finding all their efforts to take the
castle fruitless, thought proper to raise the siege, and retire
for the purpose of harassing the English in some other
quarter.

Caernarvon was seized in the year 1644, for the parliament, by captain Swanly, who took at the same time four

* Pennant, ii. 215.   † Grose, vii. 8.

K

ment is elected by the burgesses, in conjunction with those of Pwllheli, Nefyn, and Criccieth. The right of voting is in every one resident or non-resident, who has been admitted to his freedom.

About half a mile south of Caernarvon there are yet to be seen a few walls, the small remains of

SEGONTIUM*,

The ancient Roman city, mentioned in the Itinerary of Antoninus. This appears to have

hundred prisoners, and a great quantity of arms and ammunition. It must have been soon afterwards retaken; for, in the following year, I find it amongst the castles that were fortified for the king. Lord Byron was appointed governor, but, on its being attacked in 1646 by general Mytton and general Langhorn, he surrendered it on honourable terms.

General Mytton and colonel Mason were besieged here in 1648 by sir John Owen with a small force consisting of only a hundred and fifty horse, and a hundred and twenty foot soldiers; and it is by no means improbable that the bravery of this handful of men would have been crowned with success, had not notice been brought to sir John that a considerable detachment from the parliament's army were on their march to join general Mytton. He immediately drew off his troops from the castle, and determinately marched to attack them. The two forces met on the sands betwixt Conwy and Bangor, and, after a furious encounter, his party was routed, thirty of his men were killed, and himself, and about a hundred others, were taken prisoners. After this contest, the whole of North Wales became subject to the parliament.

The property of Caernarvon castle is at present in the crown. It was formerly held by the Wynnes of Glynllivon and Gwydir, the Bulkeleys of Baron Hill, and the Mostyns of Gloddaeth.

* This place is called by the Welsh *Caer Custeint*, the Fort of Constantine, and *Caer Segont*, the Fort of the river Seiont.

been the principal station which the Romans had in North Wales, all the rest being subordinate to it. It received its name from the river Seiont, which rises in the lower lake of Llanberis, passes under the walls, and discharges itself into the Menai near Caernarvon castle. Its form was oblong; and it appears originally to have occupied about six acres of ground. The road which leads from Caernarvon to Beddgelert now divides it into two parts.

Not far from hence was the fort which belonged to it: this was also of an oblong figure, and stood upon about an acre of ground. The walls are at present about eleven feet high, and six in thickness, and at each corner there has formerly been a tower.

Along these walls there are three parallel rows of circular holes, each nearly three inches in diameter, which pass through the whole thickness: and at the ends are others of a similar kind. Much learned conjecture has been employed as to the original design of these holes. Some antiquaries have supposed them to have been used for discharging arrows through at an enemy, but their great length and narrowness render it impossible that this should ever have been the case. Others have fancied they might have been left in the walls to admit air for the purpose of hardening the liquid cement that was poured in; but this cannot have been so, since there are such at Salisbury that appear to have been closed with stone at the ends, and others have been found even below the natural surface of the ground at Manchester. Mr. Whitaker, in his history of that place, says, that he

K 2

by chance met with a hole that was accidentally laid open from end to end : this, he thought, disclosed the design of all the rest, and he supposes, that as the Romans carried their ramparts upwards, they took off from the pressure on the parts below, and gave a greater strength to the whole, by turning little arches in their work, and fixing the rest of the wall upon them. At Segontium, however, this cannot have been the case, for the holes are not only too small, but are at by far too great a distance from each other to have been of any material use in lightening the work. It appears to me, that these were formed for no other purpose than merely to bear the horizontal poles for resting the scaffolding upon, necessary in the building of the fabric: they may have been left unfilled up in order to admit air into the interior of the work, or for some other purpose with which we are not now acquainted. I am the more strongly inclined to this conjecture from their being exactly parellel, and the rows at a proper height above each other to admit the masons to work.

It was the opinion of Mr. Camden that this was the *Setantiorum Portus* of Ptolemy, but that place has been referred with greater propriety to the Neb of the Nese, a high promontory in the river Ribble, about eight miles west of Preston in Lancashire.

JUMPERS.

Whilst I was at Caernarvon, I was induced, more than once, to attend the chapel of a singular branch of calvinistical methodists, who, from certain enthusiastical extravagancies which they exhibit in their religious meetings, are denominated *Jumpers*. Their service here is in the Welsh language, and, as among other methodists, commences and concludes with a prayer. It is not until the last hymn is sung that any uncommon symptoms are exhibited. The tune consists only of a single strain, and the hymn having but one verse, this verse is, in consequence, repeated over and over, sometimes for half an hour, and sometimes, if their spirit of enthusiasm is much excited, for upwards of an hour. With this begin their motions. It is sung once or twice over without any apparent effect. The first motion to be observed is that of the upper parts of their body from right to left. They then raise their hands, and often strike one hand violently against the other. Such is the effect produced even on strangers, that I confess whenever I have been among them at these times, my intellects became greatly confused : the noise of their groaning and singing, or oftentimes rather bellowing, the clapping of their hands, the beating of their feet against the ground, the excessive heat of the place, and the various motions on all sides of me, almost stupified my senses. The less enthusiastic move off soon after the hymn is begun : among these, every time I attended them, I observed the preacher to make one ; he always threw a silk handkerchief over his head, and, descending from the pulpit, left his congregation to jump by themselves. At intervals the word " *gogoniant*" (praise or glory !) is frequently to be heard. The conclu-

sion of this extravagance, has been described
by one of their own countrymen with more
justice than I am able to give to it. " The
phrenzy (he says) so far spreads, that to any
observation made to them, they seem altogether
insensible. Men and women indiscriminately,
cry and laugh, jump and sing, with the wildest
extravagance imaginable. That their dress becomes deranged, or the hair dishevelled, is no
longer an object of attention. And their rap-
tures continue, till, spent with fatigue of mind
and body, the women are frequently carried
out in a state of apparent insensibility. In
these scenes, indeed, the youthful part of the
congregation are principally concerned, the
more elderly generally contenting themselves
in admiring, with devout gratitude, what they
deem the operations of the spirit." Their
exertions on these occasions are so violent, that
were they often repeated in the week, the
health of the people must be materially affected.
When they leave the place, they often seem so
much exhausted, as scarcely to be able to support the weight of their bodies; and the hardest
labour they could be employed in would not
so much waste the animal spirits, or weary
their limbs, as an hour spent in this religious
frenzy.

Besides these common meetings, they have
their general assemblies, which are held twice
or thrice in the year at Caernarvon, Pwllheli,
and Bala, in rotation. At the latter meetings
they sometimes assemble so many as five or six
thousand people, who come from all parts of
the adjacent country to hear the popular
preachers. The general meeting at Caernarvon

is holden in the open air, upon the green near the castle. Here, not contented with their enthusiastic extravagancies on the spot, many of the country people have been known to continue them for three or four miles of their road home.

After so far describing this singular sect of enthusiasts, I may be allowed a few observations on the general increase of methodism, and on what appear to me the modes of conduct to be adopted in order to check the torrent that seems bearing forward to overwhelm us in its vortex, and that appears to strike deeply at the root of government, both in church and state.—In too many instances the established clergy must blame themselves for the influx of methodism into their respective parishes. Buoyed up with the idea that the church is under the immediate protection of the state, they look on as idle spectators, and carelessly watch the trap into which, some time or other, even they may themselves fall. No one will contend that the clergy have not the power of keeping the great body of the people united to them. Talent is certainly not wanting, as is evident from the success obtained by a set of men, many of whom are among the most ignorant and illiterate of the community. It is in too many instances the want of inclination and industry, on which the clergy split. The non-residence of the beneficed clergy, and the paltry stipends of the curates, equally aid the cause of methodism. Where a clergyman, to obtain a livelihood, is under the necessity of serving several churches, the duty, from the indivisibility of the person, is often hurried over

with a carelessness that ill becomes the ambas-
sador of God. I could mention an instance of
a clergyman in one of the midland counties,
serving four cures, and teaching a school ; and
all this for little more than a hundred pounds
a year. This person has to support a wife and
children.—Religion, in too many cases, is made,
as an old writer has justly observed, " a stalk-
ing-horse for interest and ambition ;" the shadow only is present, whilst the substance is far
removed. Hence the innumerable instances of
men who have enlisted under the banner of the
shepherd, and yet starve that flock which it is
their duty to feed. —Another cause is the neglect
of public worship among the higher classes of
the community. Examples are of essential
consequence in influencing the actions of men ;
and, where the common people observe that
their superiors in knowledge and station are
inattentive to their duty, at least they have
from this circumstance some colour for their
own neglect.—If it be asserted that the methodists increase their numbers by the enthusiastic rant which flows from their pulpits, and
that it would ill become the members of the
establishment to adopt such a mode of preach-
ing, it is easy to reply, that the clergy are too
often contented with *reading* dry and tedious
essays on morality. The grand subject of
human redemption, and the important doctrines
of revelation, seem kept entirely in the back
ground. Even Cicero would have preached as
much to the purpose as many of the Christian
pastors of the present day. The irreverent
mode in which the prayers are often read is
also an evil that should be corrected. The

liturgy of our church, allowedly one of the finest compositions that ever flowed from the pen of man, is frequently hurried over in such a manner, that the only merit seems to consist in the expedition. The earnestness of dissenters in their extemporary prayers, often affords a striking contrast to this, which alone might induce some converts.—If the clergy are sensible of the danger to which the church may be exposed by the continued increase of sectaries, they should exert all their abilities and all their influence to bring their stray sheep again to the fold. They should, in the place of moral essays, preach the gospel of peace; and they should prove that they are at least as earnest for the welfare of their flock, as those who endeavour to lead them astray.—It has always appeared to me of essential importance, where the size of the parish would admit of its being done, that the clergyman should make himself personally acquainted with all his parishioners. This would unite them to him, and prevent any attempts at what is called their conversion. There is no doubt, whatever, but the clergy might have the utmost influence in their respective parishes, if they only adopted the proper methods of obtaining it.—In pointing out these defects in the church, I have done it in the most anxious desire for its safety and protection. To have errors exposed, is assuredly the best mode of teaching how to avoid them; and the benefits arising to society from a religious establishment, are, in the present state of Christianity, of the utmost importance. This was too fully proved during the unhappy contests that took place a century and a half ago.

If, therefore, I say, the clergy would only exert their talents and influence, the wild zeal, and furious bigotry that lays such hold on the passions of the illiterate part of the community, (which, it should ever be recollected, forms the great mass of the people), would soon defeat the purposes for which they are adopted.   Unaffected piety, and the steady principles of true religion, would flourish in the face of all the efforts of methodism.   Let the clergy but be united, and deserve the character which they have pledged themselves to maintain, and every struggle of our adversaries to overturn the established church will but tend to unite its parts, and fix it still more firmly upon its foundation.

CHAP. XIII.

EXCURSION FROM CAERNARVON TO LLAN-BERIS.

HE walk from Caernarvon to Llanberis, *The Church of Peris,* a village about ten miles distant, I found, for the most part, rugged and unpleasant. The road, for nearly half way, lies over a flat barren country; and, beyond that, as far as Cwm y Clo, near the first or lower lake, over mountains, which, affording no varied prospects, are still, dull, and uninteresting. But when I had passed these, and was arrived in

THE VALE OF LLANBERIS,

A scene presented itself so truly grand, that I do not recollect one equal to it, even in the most romantic parts of Westmoreland or Cumberland. It reminded me most of the scenery about Ulswater; but this view, though much less extensive, is still more picturesque than any thing I saw there. The bold and prominent rocks, which ascend almost immediately from the edges of the lakes, and tower into the sky, cast a pleasing gloom upon the whole landscape. The more distant mountains of the vale, embosoming the moss-grown village, with the meadowy flat around it, are seen retiring in lines crossing behind in the most picturesque manner possible, whilst the intermediate space, betwixt the village and the observer, is occupied by a small lake, whose waters, reflecting the mountains which bound it, contract their sombre hue, and render the scene still more interesting.

There is no carriage road from Caernarvon nearer to Llanberis than Cwm Clo, which is not quite half way; the road from thence being only a horse-path, and that one of the worst I ever saw. The best mode for those persons who are not able to walk so far, is to go on horseback, or in carriages, as far as the bottom of the lower lake, from whence they may see the waterfall, the old castle of Dolbadarn, or the village.—I have found every part about this romantic spot so extremely interesting, that I cannot too earnestly recommend to all persons who visit Caernarvon to prolong their route by coming here. There are no difficulties to be encountered but what the scenery will amply repay.

In one of my subsequent journies I went up the lakes in a boat.—The vale at the foot of the lower lake is called

CWM Y CLO.

The Vale of the Eminence, from the insulated
rock that forms one side of it, on which the
Britons had a strong hold called Caer Cwm y
Clo. I ascended this rock, and found on its
summit the remains of walls, of such a nature
as plainly to indicate their pristine use. The
fortification seems, however, to have been of no
great importance.

From the top of a low rock on the left of
this, I had an extensive and a very varied prospect. Towards Llanberis, the vale and the
lakes were seen bounded on each side by their
lofty and precipitous rocks: on the right was
Snowdon, the monarch of the British Alps; he
here presented himself the broadest and most
tremendous of the group: on the opposite side
of the vale were Llidei Vawr and Glyder Vawr.
Behind all these, in the far distant landscape, I
observed the point of Crib Coch, *The Red
Ridge:* it was well contrasted by its distance
with the sombre mountains that intervened.
The narrow isthmus that separates the lakes,
and the insulated rock on its right bank, with
the remains of Dolbadarn tower, formed distinct
features in this interesting scene. The intervening space between the lake and my station
was occupied by a dreary extent of moor. On
the north-east, over a vast length of wastes,
were seen the bay of Beaumaris, the island of
Priestholme, and the sea: the isle of Anglesea
was visible in its whole range from Abermenai
to Penmôn.

We had just seated ourselves in a boat that was to carry us up the lake, when my intelligent friend, the Rev. Peter Williams, the rector of Llanrûg and Llanberis, who was my companion in most of my rambles amongst the mountains, pointed out to me the cottage that once was inhabited by

MARGARET UCH EVAN.

This is on the left side of the bottom of the lake, near a stable lately built by Thomas Asheton Smith, Esq. Few females in this country have attained so great celebrity as Margaret. Being passionately fond of the sports of the chace, she kept a great number of all the various kinds of dogs used in this pursuit. She is said to have destroyed more foxes in one year than all the confederate hunts did in ten. She rowed well; and could play both on the harp and the fiddle. Margaret was also an excellent joiner; and, at the age of seventy, was the best wrestler in the country. She was likewise a good blacksmith, shoe-maker, and boat-builder. She shod her own horses, made her own shoes, and, while she was under contract to convey the ore from the Llanberis copper mine, down the lakes, she built her own boats. This wonderful female died about eighteen years ago at a very advanced age.

VALE OF LLANBERIS.

The entrance into the vale of Llanberis from the bottom of the lower lake is exceedingly grand and romantic. Seated as we were in the boat, nearly on a level with the surface of the water, the lake, on looking along its whole extent, had the appearance of being large and expansive. The mountains arrange in the most beautiful manner imaginable. Among some rocks on the right bank of the lake, about half a mile from the bottom, there is a scene remarkably picturesque. Snowdon, with its deep and perpendicular precipice, and two summits, forms an immense mass of mountain, which constitutes the principal feature. The lake, the round tower of Dolbadarn, the distant vale and mountains, and on the other side the huge rock of Glyder Vawr, lend each its character to heighten the effect of the whole.

The vale of Llanberis is nearly straight, and of no great width throughout. It contains two small lakes, or rather pools; for their size will scarcely admit of the former appellation. The upper pool is about a mile in length, and somewhat less than half a mile across; and the other, though longer, is so very narrow, as to bear more the appearance of a wide river than a lake. These are separated by a small neck of land, but have a communication by a stream which runs from one into the other.

In both the pools the fish called *Char* used formerly to be caught, but, owing to the copper works carried on here, these have all been long since destroyed.

DOLBADARN CASTLE.

On a rocky eminence between the two pools stands the old tower of Dolbadarn castle. This is about nine yards in its inner diameter, and, with a few shattered remains of walls and offices, occupies the entire summit of the steep. Its name of Castell Dolbadarn, *The Castle of Padarn's Meadow*, is supposed to have originated in its having been erected on the verge of a piece of ground called Padarn's Meadow, to which a holy recluse of that name retired from the world, to enjoy religious meditation and solitude.

Dolbadarn castle very evidently appears, from its construction, to have been of British origin. It was built, no doubt, to defend the narrow pass through the vale into the interior of the mountains; and, from its situation, it seems to have been capable of affording perfect security to two or three hundred persons in cases of emergency.—In this castle it was that Owen Goch, *Owen the Red*, was confined by his brother Llewelyn ap Iorwerth, prince of Wales, upwards of twenty years, for having attempted to excite an insurrection among the people, injurious to his rights and dignity.—It has been long in ruins, for Leland mentions it in his time as only " a piece of a tower. * "

* Leland's Itin. v. 44. It is highly probable that this was anciently called *Bere Castle* †, which some of the his-

† A corruption probably of *Peris* or *Beris castle.*

SLATE QUARRY.

In the mountain, on the opposite side of the lake, called Allt Dû, *The Black Cliff*, there is a large slate quarry belonging to Thomas Asheton Smith, Esq. As this is high up among the rocks, the men, in conveying the slates down to the lake, are under the necessity, as well as one horse before the cart, to have one yoked behind. This prevents these aukward vehicles from being dashed to the bottom of some of the dangerous steeps, in which the mountains abound, and which must inevitably be the case without some such contrivance. It however appears to me, that sledges similar to those adopted in many parts of Westmoreland and Cumberland for the same purpose, would not only be less expensive, but would also be found more safe and commodious.

CATARACT.

About half a mile south of the castle, at the end of a long and deep glen, there is a tremendous cataract called Caunant Mawr, *The Waterfall of the Great Chasm*. It is upwards of sixty feet in height, and is formed by the

torians relate to have been in Caernarvonshire, seated in the midst of a morass, inaccessible but by a single causeway, and not to be approached except through the narrow and rugged defiles of the mountains. About the thirteenth century it was esteemed the strongest castle that the Welsh possessed in this part of the country.

L

mountain torrent from **Cwm Brwynog**. This rushes through a cleft in the rock above, and, after proceeding for a few yards in a direct line, suddenly takes a turn with a broad stratum of the rock, and thus descends aslaunt, with a thundering noise, into the deep black pool below.

ANECDOTES OF FOULKE JONES.

Not quite a mile and a half from **Dalbadarn** castle, and on the road leading to Caernarvon, is an old farm-house called **Ty Dû**, *The Black House*, formerly the property of **Dr. Goodman**, who was bishop of Gloucester in the reign of Charles I. It was not many years ago the residence of **Foulke Jones**, a man celebrated throughout the principality for his extreme muscular powers.—It was at a very early age that these were first brought into action. When about three years old, as he was sitting before the door at Ty Dû, he was attacked by a gander whose female and brood he had been pursuing: he seized the bird by the neck, and leisurely tore him into a thousand pieces.—His strength increased with his years, till at last it was far beyond that of any man in the principality. Three men were engaged in building a wall near his house, and they found one stone which their utmost united efforts could not remove to its proper place. Jones advised them to leave it for a while, and go into the house to dinner. During their absence Jones lifted it up by himself. On their return they went to the place where the stone had lain, in order to make, if possible, a more effectual attempt: they found it gone, and were in the utmost astonishment when they saw that one man had been able to effect what their united efforts had been exerted on in vain.—The disposition of Jones inclined him at all times to live on the most amicable and peaceful terms with his neighbours, seldom exerting his uncommon powers but in acts of utility, or for their amusement. Two men were fighting in a public house at Caernarvon, and on his entering he was requested to separate them. He did this effectually by seizing one in each hand, beating their stupid heads together, and then pushing them asunder.—He was one day standing on a bridge near Caernarvon, when an impertinent fellow, half drunk, grossly insulted him, in order to induce him to fight, and at length went so far as to strike him in the face. This was not to be borne. Jones took the fellow in one hand, and lifting him over the wall of the bridge, held him for some seconds suspended over the water. The man loudly intreated that he would not throw him in, and expressed so much contrition for his conduct, that Jones returned him in safety, but dismissed him with an ignominious kick.—A Welshman, a native of the county of Denbigh, who believed himself superior to every one in the principality in all the feats of activity, walked over to Llanberis for the express purpose of contending with Jones. Our hero was at work in a field, by the road-side, near his house, when the stranger requested to be informed where he should find the residence of Foulke Jones, as he was come to prove that there was one in the principality more strong

and more active than he. " My master (says
Jones) lives at that house (pointing towards
Ty Dû), but it may be prudent in you first
to try the strength of the servant, before you
venture to contend with one that is even very
greatly his superior." The man looking on
him with ineffable contempt, stepped over the
wall; and, after some little altercation, and
much boasted prowess on his side, they closed,
when Jones, almost in a moment, flung him
violently back again into the road. The man
had met with too serious a rebuff from the person
whom he conceived to be the servant, to
inquire any further respecting the master, but
made the best of his way home again.—Jones
died about eighteen years ago at the advanced
age of seventy-five.

LLANBERIS COPPER MINE.

Pursuing the path leading from the castle to the
village, I came to a copper mine near the edge
of the lake, belonging to a company of gentlemen who reside at Macclesfield. The ore here
is in general very rich, being worth on an
average from twenty to twenty-five pounds per
ton, whilst that of the Paris mine is not often
worth more than fifteen. The work was commenced in the year 1791; and the number of
hands now employed is about a hundred. The
ore is brought in small waggons to the mouth of
the mine : here it is broken into small pieces
with hammers. It is then sorted, and the best
and smallest pieces are taken out, and con-

veyed in boats down the lakes, whence it is carted to the Menai, where a vessel is ready to carry it into Glamorganshire, to be melted and wrought into copper. The larger fragments are conveyed to a stamping-mill on the opposite side of the lake, where they are crushed into powder by six stampers. The proprietors have a few pits for the corrosion of iron, as in the Paris mines; and they have also lately begun to roast their ore here, which a short time ago were not even thought of.

Whilst I, and three gentlemen, who happened to be with me the day I visited the mine, were watching the women break the ore, a loaded waggon was brought out of the level. This gave us an opportunity of returning in an empty one for the purpose of examining the interior of the work. One miner was employed to drag, and two others to push the waggon along the narrow cavern. This was about two hundred yards in length, and, in the whole distance, it was seldom more than six feet wide, and seven or eight high. In some places the rugged arch of the roof was so low, that we were under the necessity of stooping down in order to pass it. The day was one of those excessively hot ones that we frequently have about the middle of August; and the chilling damp which immediately struck us on entering, added not a little to the terrors of the place. The level lying in a direct line, we took no lights along with us. I sat with my back towards the entrance, and the perfect darkness of the place, the confused noise (from the arched and low roof) of the talking of our guides, and the rumbling of the wheels, re-

echoed in deep and imperfect sounds along the
cavern, added to the frequent jolting of our
vehicle, from the badness of the wooden rail-
road, inspired me with some ideas not perhaps
altogether agreeable.   The length of the journey
seemed more than double what it really was.
When almost at the end of the riding part of
the expedition, one of our infernia left us in
order to bring a light from the interior of the
mine.   He was absent about five minutes, during which time we remained in perfect darkness.   When I first saw him at some distance,
his candle appeared reflected in the water
which was lodged in the middle of the level,
and the confused appearance of two lights, the
one above and the other below, added to the
man's grotesque and dingy countenance, for
the other parts of his body were obscured by the
gloom, produced an effect that I can scarcely
describe, and which I shall not very soon forget.
—When we came to the end of the level we got
out of the waggon, and each lighting his candle, followed our guides into a cavern so high,
that all our lights did not render the roof visible.
The sides were rude as the exterior of the rock,
and the black chasms along them, nearly all
impenetrable by our lights, rendered it to one
of our friends, more timorous than the rest, a
scene of horror.   A skilful artist might have
found us a good subject for his pencil : the glare
of light on *our* countenances expressive of
inquiry, and not perhaps entirely free from
those lines which ideas of terror will create ;
the blackened visages of our guides ; our different dresses ; and the rude scenery around,
aided by a little picturesque grouping, and that

allowable exaggeration which both painters
and poets lay claim to in their descriptions,
might have produced an admirable picture.   In
the cavern where we were standing, a shaft
about sixty feet deep, was driven to a vein of ore
below.   On looking down this we could just
discover in the darkness of the gloom, the reflection of a light from the workmen there.
Soon afterwards a light was seen to cross the
bottom; and, on calling aloud for it to stop,
the man returned, and stood with it immediately below.   It was a mere speck, and its
rays were just discernible striking on the thick
vapour immediately around it.   Near the bottom
of this shaft, our guides informed us, there was
another about fifty feet in depth.   We left the
cavern, and after visiting another, nearly similar
to it, from which all the ore had been got, we
ended our adventure by returning along our
former road into the light of day.

LLANBERIS.

The village of Llanberis is romantic in the
extreme.   It is situated in a narrow grassy dell,
surrounded by immense rocks, whose summits
cloudcapped, are seldom visible to the inhabitants from below.   " Nature has here (says
Camden, speaking of these parts of Caernarvonshire) reared huge groups of mountains, as
if she meant to bind the island fast to the bowels
of the earth, and make a safe retreat for the
Britons in time of war.   For here are so many
crags and rocks, so many wooded vallies ren-

dered impassable by so many lakes, that the lightest troops, much less an army, could never find their way among them. These mountains may be truly called the British Alps; for besides that they are the highest in the whole island, they are like the Alps, bespread with broken crags on every side, all surrounding one, which, towering in the centre, far above the rest, lifts its head so loftily, as if it meant not only to threaten, but to thrust it into the sky."

All the parts immediately surrounding the village were formerly covered with wood; but, except some saplings from the old roots, there are at present very few trees left. In the memory of persons now living there were great woods of oak in several different parts about these mountains. In the tenth century the whole country must have been nearly covered with wood, for one of the laws of **Howel Dda**, *Howel the Good*, directs that " whoever cleared away timber from any land, even without the consent of the owner, he should, for five years, have a right to the land so cleared; and after that time it should revert to the owner."

Except two tolerable houses in the vale, the one occupied by Mr. Jones the agent to the copper mine, and the other, which is on the side of the lake opposite to Dolbadarn castle, occupied by the agent to the slate quarries, the whole village consists but of a few scattered cottages, and these apparently the most miserable. They are in general constructed of the shaly stone with which the country abounds, and have but just so much cement as to keep out the keenest of the mountain blasts. The windows are invariably small, and many of them that have been broken, are so blocked up with boards, that the light down the chimney is greater than that from the window.

There are two cottages in this village where the wearied traveller, may take such poor refreshments as the place affords. One of these belonged, when I first was at this place, to John Close, a grey-headed old man, who was born and brought up in the north of Yorkshire. He had occasion to come into Wales with some cattle in his younger days, and preferring this to his Yorkshire home, resided here the rest of his life.—Neither of these places affords a bed, nor any thing eatable better than bread and butter, or cheese, and, perhaps, eggs and bacon.

The first time that I came to Llanberis, being somewhat fatigued with traversing the adjacent mountains, I went to the former of these houses to rest myself and obtain some refreshment. It was just at the dinner hour, and a scene was exhibited altogether novel to me. At one table were seated the family of the house, consisting of the old host, his wife, and their son and daughter, eating their bread and milk, the common food of the labouring people here: a large overgrown old sow was devouring her dinner, with considerable dissatisfaction on account of the short allowance, from a pail placed for her by the daughter in one corner; whilst I was eating my bread and butter, with an appetite steeled against niceties by the keenness of the mountain air, at a table covered with a dirty napkin, in the other corner. This scene, however, induced me always afterwards to bring with me refreshments from

Caernarvon, and enjoy my dinner, in quiet, in the open air.

The *church* of Llanberis* was some years ago, without exception, the most ill-looking place of worship I ever beheld. The first time I came to the village, I absolutely mistook it for a large antique cottage, for even the bell-turret was so over-grown with ivy, as to bear much the appearance of a weather-beaten chimney; and the grass in the church-yard was so long as completely to hide the few grave-stones therein from the view. Since this time it has, however, undergone some repairs, but it is still sufficiently rude to accord excellently well with the surrounding mountains.

THE CURATE

I saw, and was introduced to: he resided in a mean-looking cottage not far from the church, which seemed to consist of but few other rooms than a kitchen and bed-room, the latter of which served also for his study. When I entered the room he was en-gaged over an old folio volume of sermons. His dress was somewhat singular; he had on a blue coat that long had been worn threadbare, and in various places exhibited marks of the industry of his wife, a pair of antique corderoy

---

* This is dedicated to Peris, a cardinal missioned from Rome as a legate to this island. He is said to have settled and died here.

breeches, and a black waistcoat, and round his head was tied a blue handkerchief. His library might have been the very same that Hurdis has described in the *Village Curate.*

Yon half a dozen shelves support, vast weight,
The curate's library. There marshalled stand,
Sages and heroes, modern and antique :
He, their commander, like the vanquished fiend,
Out-cast of heaven, oft through their armed files,
Darts an experienced eye, and feels his heart
Distend with pride, to be their only chief:
Yet needs he not the tedious muster-roll,
The title page of each well-known, its name,
And character.

From the exterior of the cottage, it seemed but the habitation of misery; but the smi es of the good man were such as would render even misery cheerful. His salary was about forty pounds, on which, with his little farm, he contrived to support himself and his family, and with this slender pittance he seemed perfectly contented and comfortable. His wife was absent, but from a wheel which I observed in the room I conjectured, and was afterwards informed, that her time was principally employed in spinning wool. The account I had from the parishioners of the character of this man was, that he was respected and beloved by all, and that his whole time and attention were occupied in doing such good to his fellow creatures as his very slender circumstances would allow.

I venerate the man whose heart is warm,
Whose hands are pure, whose doctrine, and whose life

Coincident, *exhibit lucid proof*
That he is honest in the sacred cause.
To such I render more than mere respect,
Whose actions shew that they respect themselves.

This person, after sustaining a severe illness with the utmost resignation and fortitude, died in the beginning of the year 1801, leaving a widow and one daughter to survive him.

WELSH FUNERAL.

During my residence in Caernarvonshire I one day rode with the worthy rec*or of Llanberis, to attend the funeral of a girl, a child about seven years old, whose parents resided in the parish of Llanddiniolen, somewhat more than five miles distant. The coffin was tied on the bier, and covered with a sheet, tied also at the corners. It was borne on the shoulders of four men. The number of attendants at the outset was near an hundred, but this increased by the continued addition of men, women, and children, some on foot and some on horseback, till, by the time we arrived at the church, we had more than double that number. At the head of this cavalcade my friend and myself ascended the stee paths of the rocks, passed over mountains, and wound our way along some of the most rugged defiles of this dreary country. To any stranger who could have observed, at a little distance, our solemn procession, in this unfrequented tract of mountains, in one place some hundred feet above the lake of Llanberis, to the edge of which we had to descend, it would have borne much the air of romantic times. When we came to the church, we found that place nearly full of people awaiting our arrival. The service was read in Welsh in a most impressive manner; and the coffin was let down into the grave by four of the female mourners. A more solemn office I had never witnessed, and the circumstance of the body being committed to the bosom of the earth by the hands of relatives or friends was altogether new to me.—The ceremony being over, the grave was filled up and planted with slips of box and some other evergreens.—The offerings in the church amounted to near two pounds, of which more than thirty shillings were in silver*.

At no great distance from the church there is a *well* dedicated to St. Peris, and inclosed within a square wall. In the holes of this a person of the adjoining cottage generally has a small fish, from the appearance or non-appearance of which, when a bit of bread is thrown into the water, the common Welsh people pretend to foretel good or ill fortune. The general reward of a piece of silver from such strangers as visit the place, affords a temptation for them still to keep on foot at least the appearance of this superstition.

I was one day strolling with my friend Williams along the vale, when he pointed out

---

* For an account of the nature of these offerings, see the chapter on the Welsh Customs.

to me a female well known in this village, and who, from the masculine tone of her voice, her manners, and appearance, might have been a descendant of the celebrated Margaret Uch Evan, called

CADDY OF CWM GLAS.

This athletic female does not often visit the town of Caernarvon; but, whenever she does, the boys run after, and call her, "the woman with a beard." Caddy resides in Cwm Glâs, a romantic vale, about two miles from Llanberis. She is accustomed to masculine employments of every description, and such is her muscular power, that no man of the village would dare to try a fall with her. Mr. Jones of the copper-mine had often rallied her on the subject of her great strength, and told her that he did not believe half the stories that he had heard related: she, one day, in perfect good humour, came behind him, as he was standing on the bank of the pier, near the stamping mill, and lifting him from the ground, held him in her arm, though by no means a small man, with great apparent ease, over the water. " Now, Sir, (says she) I suppose you will believe that I am tolerably strong: you must confess it, or I shall throw you in." He immediately acknowledged her powers, and was relieved from his predicament.—A man some years ago entered her cottage, during her absence, and had collected together some eatables and clothes, with which he was escaping, just as she returned. Though this cottage is in a very solitary situation, and she was entirely alone, she resolutely went up and insisted on his returning every thing he had taken. He opened his wallet, and gave up the eatables. Supposing these to be all, she returned with them to the cottage. But soon after discovering that a silk handkerchief, which she had left on the table, was gone, she immediately seiz d one of the bars of a small gate in her hand, and went in pursuit of the thief. She overtook him in the most solitary part of the vale, and, brandishing her cudgel over his head, with the utmost courage, demanded restitution of the remainder of her property. An answer she did not wait for, but seizing the bag, shook the whole contents upon the ground. When she had selected her own property, she threw the bag in the fellow's face; and, after bestowing a hearty thwack with her cudgel on each of his shoulders, left her opponent to comfort himself with the idea of having escaped a more sound drubbing, which, as she afterwards declared, she would have inflicted, had she thought it necessary.

CWM GLAS.

A bad horse-path led me from the village of Llanberis into Cwn Glâs, *The Blue Vale**. For

---

* Whence the epithet of glâs, *blue,* could be attached to this vale, I can form no conception.

four miles I was hemmed in on each side by
high rocks that almost approach each other.
The sun cast a sloping shade on those of the
right, which fully marked all their deepened
hollows. Various in themselves, and varied in
their tints and colourings, I was at every step
interested by their terrific grandeur. They had
no characters of softened beauty, there were
here none of the delicate features of a cultivated
vale, not even a single tree, but rocks towered
over rocks, till their summits reached the clouds,
whose partial gloominess added still greater
sublimity to the scene. Sometimes I beheld
above me a gentle hollow, then a few steps farther, the deepened precipice and towering ba-
saltic like columns of an adjoining range of rocks.
In some places there appeared three or four
ranges, one above another, with the most fantastic outlines imaginable, and receding in
distance as in height. The tints on the prominences were of darkened purple, in the hollows
sombre, and olive-brown on the nearer ranges.
The fore-ground was overspread with masses
of rock, and a rapid mountain stream forced
its way along the middle of the narrow vale.
Such is this tremendous hollow, whose grandeur
continues undiminished for almost four miles.
The rocks on each side are nearly perpendicular
throughout.

About three miles from Llanberis there is an
immense stone, that has once been precipitated
from above called

THE CROMLECH.

This stone is of some thousand tons weight, and many times larger than the celebrated mass of rock in Borrowdale, called *Bowdar Stone*. It lies in a place called Ynys Hettws, *Hetty's Island;* and two of its sides meeting at an angle with the ground, it was once used as the habitation of an old woman, who, in summer, resided in the vale to tend and milk her cows. The inclosures are yet nearly entire, and are at present used as a sheepfold.

Not far from this stone, on the opposite side of the stream, is the cottage of Caddy of Cwm Glâs, the female whom I mentioned a few pages back. There is, at a little distance from the cottage, another immense mass of rock insulated like the former.

GORPHWYSFA,

The resting Place, is an eminence, four miles from Llanberis, that overlooks a considerable part of this vale. It also commands a view into the mountain vale, that joins Nan Hwynan, and the vale Capel Curig.

From hence I returned to Caernarvon.

The tourist, if he chooses it, may, from this place, proceed onwards nearly in a direct

M

line, through the village of Capel Curig, to
Llanrwst; or adopting another route, may
keep the right-hand path, which will lead him
through the vale, called Nan Hwynan, to Beddgelert. From Beddgelert, he may either return to Caernarvon or continue his journey, in
a direction towards Dolgelle, or Bala.

CHAP. XIV.

EXCURSION FROM CAERNARVON TO THE SUMMIT OF SNOWDON.

Instructions to the Tourist.—Clogwyn du'r Arddu.—Dangerous Adventure.—Height of Snowdon.—Prospect from the Summit.—Name.—Royal Forest.—Clogwyn y Garnedd. —List of Snowdon Plants.—Well near the Summit.—Snowdon Copper Mine.—Uncommon Snow Drift.—Accidents that have happened to the Workmen.—Further Intructions to the Tourist.

THE distance of the summit of Snowdon from Caernarvon is somewhat more than ten miles; and from Dolbadarn castle, in the vale of Llanberis, the ascent is so gradual, that a person, mounted on a little Welsh poney, may ride up very nearly to the top.

From Dolbadarn castle the traveller must go, by the waterfall, Caunant Mawr, to Cwm Brwynog, *The rushy Hollow.* He must proceed up this vale, and then along the ridge immediately over the vale of Llanberis, till he comes within sight of a black, and almost perpendicular rock, with a small lake at its foot, called Clogwyn du'r Arddu, *The Black Precipice.* This he is to leave about a quarter of a mile on his right, and then ascending a

M 2

steep called Llechwedd y Rè, *The rapid Descent,*
must direct his course south-west to the well, (a
place sufficiently known to the guides,) from
whence he will find it about a mile to the highest
peak of the mountain.

In my first journey I went from the castle to
Cwm Brwynog, but, instead of following the
above route, I wandered to *Clogwyn du'r Arddu,*
to search that rock for some plants which
Lhwyd and Ray have described as growing
there. The Reverend Mr. Williams accompanied me, and he started the wild idea of attempting to climb the precipice. I was too
eager in my pursuit to object to the adventure,
and we began our laborious task without once
reflecting on the dangers that might attend it.
For a little while we got on without much difficulty, but we were soon obliged to have recourse both to our hands and knees, in clambering from one crag to another. Every step
now required the utmost caution, and it was necessary to try that every stone was firm in its
place before the weight of the body was trusted
upon it. I had once lain hold of a piece of
the rock, and was in the act of raising myself
upon it, when it loosened from its bed, and I
should have been precipitated headlong, had I
not in a moment snatched hold of a tuft of
rushes, and saved myself. When we had ascended somewhat more than half-way, there
seemed no chance of our being able to proceed much farther, on account of the increasing
size of the masses of rock above us. We rested a moment from our labour to consider what
was to be done. The danger of descending
was much too great for us to think of attempt-

ing it, unless we found it absolutely impossible to proceed. On looking down, the precipice, for at least three hundred feet, seemed almost perpendicular. We were eager in our botanical pursuit, and extremely desirous to be at the top, but I believe it was the prospect downwards that determined us to brave every difficulty. It happened fortunately that the steep immediately above us was the only one that presented any material danger. Mr. Williams having on a pair of strong shoes with nails in them, which would hold their footing better than mine, requested to make the first attempt, and after some difficulty he succeeded. We had along with us a small basket to contain our provisions, and hold the roots of such plants as we wished to transfer to his garden; this he carried behind him by means of a leathern belt fastened round his waist. When, therefore, he had fixed himself securely to a part of the rock, he took off his belt, and holding firmly by one end, gave the other to me: I laid hold, and, with a little aid from the stones, fairly pulled myself up by it. After this we got on pretty well, and in about an hour and a quarter from the commencement of our labour, found ourselves on the brow of this dreadful precipice, and in possession of all the plants we expected to find.

It would be difficult to describe my sensations when my companion pointed out to me the summit of Snowdon at the distance of only about a mile and a half from us, and, from its great elevation, appearing scarcely more than half a mile. The sight was so unexpectedly agreeable, that I proceeded from hence to the summit with considerably greater alacrity than I should have done had we encountered no dangers, or experienced no interruptions. Thus situated, the well known story of the Pedlar immediately recurred to me, and if he had found relief from the wearisome burthen of his pack by throwing from it the additional weight of a large stone that he had attached to it for the purpose, so I, after the labour of clambering the steep of Clogwyn du'r Arddu, found ascending to the summit of Snowdon perfectly easy.   Had I gone along the regular track, I have not a doubt but I should have *fancied* myself much more wearied than I now really felt.

The perpendicular height of this mountain, according to late admeasurements, is 1190 yards (somewhat less than three quarters of a mile) from the level of the sea.   It rises to a mere point, its summit not being more than three or four yards in diameter.

The view from the summit I found beyond my expectation extensive.   From this point the eye is able to trace, on a clear day, part of the coast, with the hills of Scotland; the high mountains of Ingleborough and Penygent in Yorkshire; beyond these the mountains of Westmoreland and Cumberland; and, on this side, some of the hills of Lancashire.   When the atmosphere is very transparent, even part of the county of Wicklow, and the whole of the isle of Man, become visible.   The immediately surrounding mountains of Caernavonshire and Merionethshire all seem directly under the eye, and the highest of the whole appear from this station, much lower than Snowdon.

Many of the vales were exposed to the view, which, by their verdure, relieved the eye from the dreary scene of barren rocks. The numerous pools visible from hence, betwixt thirty and forty, lend also a varied character to the prospect.—The mountain itself, from the summit, seems as it were propped by five immense rocks as buttresses. These are *Crib y Ddistil,* and *Crib Coch,* between Llanberis and Capel Curig; *Lliewedd* towards Nan Hwynan; *Clawdd Coch* towards Beddgelert; and *Llechog,* the mountain which forms the south side of the vale of Llanberis, towards Dolbadarn*.

The summit of Snowdon is so frequently enveloped in clouds and mist, that, except when the weather is perfectly fine and settled, the traveller through this country will find it somewhat difficult to have a day sufficiently clear to permit him to ascend the mountain with any degree of pleasure. When the wind blows from the west it is almost always completely covered ; and at other times, even when the state of the weather seems favourable, it will often become suddenly enveloped, and will remain in that state for hours. Most persons, however, agree that the prospects are the more interesting, as they are more varied, when the clouds just cover the summit. The following description of the scenery from Snowdon when the mountain is in this state, is perfectly accurate.

> Now high and swift flits the thin rack along
> Skirted with rainbow dies, now deep below

* See a further description of Snowdon in the ensuing chapter, and in chap. xix.

(While the fierce sun strikes the illumin'd top)
Slow sails the gloomy storm, and all beneath
By vaporous exhalation hid, lies lost
In darkness ; save at once where drifted mists
Cut by strong gusts of eddying winds, expose
The transitory scenes.
Now swift on either side the gather'd clouds
As by a sudden touch of magic, wide
Recede, and the fair face of heaven and earth
Appears. Amid the vast horizon's stretch,
In restless gaze the eye of wonder darts
O'er the expanse ; mountains on mountains piled,
And winding bays, and promontories huge,
Lakes and meandering rivers, from their source
Traced to the distant ocean.

The name of Snowdon was first given to this
mountain by the Saxons, its signification is *A
Hill covered with Snow*. The Welsh call all
this cluster of mountains that lie in the county
of Caernarvon, Creigiau yr Eryri, the *Snowy
Cliffs*. The highest point of Snowdon is called
Yr Wyddfa, *The Conspicuous*.—Most of the
old writers who have mentioned this mountain,
assert that it is covered with snow through the
whole year. Such, however, is by no means
the case, for this, as well as all the other Welsh
mountains, has in general no snow whatever
upon it betwixt the months of June and November.

Snowdon was formerly a *royal forest* that
abounded with deer; but the last of these were
destroyed early in the seventeenth century.

The parts of this mountain on which the uncommon alpine plants are chiefly to be found,
are the east and north-east sides. These form a
range of rocks called *Clogwyn y Garnedd*, which
abound in the most dangerous steeps. There
is at all times some difficulty in searching them,

but when the rocks are rendered slippery from heavy mists or rain, this becomes, from the insecurity of the footing, greatly increased.—A list of the plants that I have found here may not be unacceptable, at least to a young botanist.

Poa alpina.
—— glauca.
Festuca cambrica.
Rumex digynus.
Chrysosplenium oppositifolium.
Saxifraga stellaris.
————nivalis.
———oppositifolia.
———hypnoides.
Lycopodium alpinum.
——— ———selaginoides.
Pteris crispa.
Asplenium viride.

Arenaria verna.
——— var 1. laricifolia.
——— var. 2. juniperina.
Cerastium alpinum.
——— latifolium.
Geum rivale.
Serratula alpina.
Salix herbacea.
Rhodiola rosea.
Lycopodium selago.
Polypodium lonchitis.
——— ilvense.
———— arvonicum.
Cyathea fragile.

It is a singular fact that nearly at the top of Snowdon there is a fine *spring of water*, which, I am informed, is seldom increased or diminished in quantity either in winter or summer. From its very elevated situation, this water is the coldest I ever recollect to have tasted.

SNOWDON COPPER MINE.

A considerable vein of copper ore was discovered a few years ago in Cwn Glâs Llyn, *The Hollow of the Blue Pool*, near the foot of Clogwyn y Garnedd. Some of the gentlemen of the county entered into an association for the purpose of getting this ore, and the work now

goes on with considerable spirit. It is, however, by no means so rich or valuable as that from
the Llanberis mine, and this circumstance, together with the expence of conveying it nearly
over the summit of the monntain to Caernarvon,
may possibly prevent its ever being worked to
any extent. The proprietors have made a tolerably good sledge-path from the Beddgelert
road, near Lln Cwellyn, to Bwlch Glâs, a
hollow just below the highest point of Snowdon,
and from thence a winding footpath down to
the mine. To Bwlch Glâs the men carry the
ore in bags on their shoulders: here it is loaded
on small one-horse sledges, in which it is dragged
to the road.—A house has lately been erected
near the mine for the accommodation of the
workmen during bad weather: some of them
live here altogether.

Much difficulty and many hardships are to
be overcome by the workmen in the variable
climate of these alpine vales. In winter,
heavy snows, which frequently drift many
yards in thickness; in spring and autumn,
the most violent hurricanes; and, in the height
of summer, thunder-storms uncommonly tremendous, are to be withstood by the labourers
in this copper mine.—In the winter of 1801
the snow drifted so deep before the mouth of
the mine, that the men were under the
necessity of cutting a level through it, and of
thus going to their work under a long arch
of snow. Sometimes the mouth of the new
level they were forming in the rock was so
closed round with snow, that they were not
able to tell exactly where it was; and when

with difficulty they had found it, it cost some labour to clear an entrance. This snow-drift was in many places near twenty yards deep, and some of it was to be seen in the recesses of the rocks till even the middle of May.

I was informed that the wind had often been so furious among the rocks that the workmen had found the utmost difficulty in preventing themselves from being blown over the edge of the precipices. Sometimes when they heard its approach by the roaring along the vales, they were compelled to fall down on their hands and knees, and, laying fast hold on each other, to wait in this position till the violence of the gust was passed; or when it was likely to continue, they had to creep along till, under shelter of the side of the mountain, they could proceed in safety. A party of the men were one morning going to the mine, when the wind was heard to roar loudly along one of the hollows. They all, except one man, laid down till the gust had passed by : he ridiculed their cowardice, and holding out his jacket on each side, observed, that " as a fine breeze was springing up, he should spread his sails, and make the best of his way by scudding before the gale, to his work." The wind in a moment bore him from the ground to the distance of ten or twelve yards, where he was thrown down with the utmost violence. He repented his folly, and though he was not much hurt, the accident had a good effect in teaching the men in future to act with becoming prudence.

Two Denbighshire gentlemen, who are also partners in this concern, have caused a tolerably good horse-path to be made from Gorphwysfa, beyond Llanberis, to the copper mine. This will now render the ascent to the summit of Snowdon from Capel Curig and the village of Llanberis perfectly easy.

Welsh tourists have been much in the habit of over-rating the difficulties that are to be encountered in the journey to the summit of this mountain. To provide against these, one of them recommends a strong stick with a spike in the end, as a thing absolutely necessary; another advises that the soles of the shoes be set round with large nails; and a third inveighs against attempting so arduous and so difficult an undertaking in boots. I can only say, that to have nails in the shoes, and to take a stick in one's hand, may both be useful in their way, but if a person is in good health and spirits, he will find that he can do very well without either. I should recommend to the traveller to allow himself sufficient time: to be upon the journey by five or six o'clock in the morning, when the sun has not yet attained much power, and when the air is cool and refreshing. The chief thing required is a little labour, and this, by going gently along, will be rendered very easy. There is also another advantage in having sufficient time by stopping frequently to rest himself, he will be enabled to enjoy the different distant prospects as he rises above the mountains, and to observe how the objects around him gradually change their appearance as he ascends.—It will always be necessary to take a guide, for otherwise a sudden change in the weather might render the attempt extremely perilous to a stranger. But these changes are of no consequence to men who are in the habits of frequently ascending the mountain, as they have marks by which they would know the path in the most cloudy weather.—A sufficient supply of eatables is also absolutely necessary: the traveller will find the utility of these long before he returns.

CHAP. XV.

EXCURSION FROM LLANBERIS TO THE SUM-MIT OF SNOWDON.

Small Pool called Ffynnon Frech.—Llyn Llwydaw.- Llyn y Cwm Glás.—Romantic Scenery.—Descent to the Village of Llanberis.

ASCENT OF SNOWDON FROM LLYN CWELLYN.

Bwlch cwm Brwynog.—Llyn Ffynnon y Gwás.—Account of a Mountain Storm.

In the present excursion I proceeded about a mile beyond the village of Llanberis, and, crossing the brook that runs into the pool, commenced my ascent up the steep mountains on the right.—After some fatigue, for the sun shone bright, and the reflection from the rocks was very powerful, I gained the top of the first range of rocks which overlook the vale I had left.—In a hollow among these mountains I found the little pool called Ffynnon Frech, *The Spotted Well.* In its bottom were growing in great abundance those rare plants, almost wholly confined to alpine pools, *Subularia aquatica, Isoetes lacustris,* and *Lobelia dortmanna.*

From hence I continued my journey up another steep, and from its top observed two other pools in a vale at a great depth below me, called Llyn Llwydaw, *The Dusky Pool,* and Llyn y Cwm Glâs, *The Blue Pool in the Hollow.* A small island in the former is, in spring, the haunt of the Black-backed Gulls *, which here lay their eggs, and nurture their young. I did not descend, as I could observe nothing about them likely to repay me for the trouble, but proceeded onward, for about a mile, along the sloping sides of the mountains, till I came to the hollow called Bwlch Glâs. After leaving this place I was not long in attaining the summit of the monarch of the British Alps.

From the top of the first mountains, after I left Llanberis, till I came within sight of Llyn Llwydaw, the scenery was awfully rude. It was one continued series of rocks, infinitely varied in their figure and disposition. The nimble-footed sheep that brouzed on their dark sides, and skipped along their tremendous precipices, looked down upon us with the utmost composure, fearless of any danger from their seemingly precarious situation. In some places the rocks, overhanging the path, seemed ready to start from their bases, threatening destruction to the travellers who had dared to approach their gloomy shade.

The latter part of the excursion, along the sloping sides of the mountains, was somewhat unpleasant. The stones I had to traverse for above a mile were so small and loose, as at

* *Larus marinus* of Linnæus.

every step to give way : this not only rendered
the walk fatiguing, but sometimes, indeed, dangerous.   The scenery was wild, but little interesting.   The hollow beneath me, hemmed in
by the gloomy mountains around, had, from a
few points of view, a considerable degree of
grandeur, but, in this respect, it was far inferior
to what I had passed.   Wandering along this
dreary scene, I once or twice heard, sweetly
mellowed by the distance,

> The wildly winding brook
> Fall hoarse from steep to steep.

The light clouds swept briskly over the mountains, sometimes entirely obscuring them, and
then again shewing their serrated tops visible
through the thinness of the mist.

    I descended from Snowdon this time along
what may with propriety be denominated a
mountain stair-case, down the rocks immediately
opposite to the village of Llanberis.   This road
was so very steep and unpleasant, that I would
at any time rather go three or four miles round
than venture down it again.

ASCENT OF SNOWDON FROM LLYN CWELLYN.

    On the following day I once again ascended
to the summit of Snowdon, and this time I
chose, as the place of my outset, the cottage of
the ' mountain guide, who lives near Llyn
Cwellyn, a pool about six miles from Caernarvon, on the side of the road leading from

thence to Beddgelert.—We first went along
some meadows, which extend up the sides of
the mountains for about half a mile. Leaving
these, we, after some time, came to Bwlch Cwm
Brwynog, *The Hollow of the Vale of Brwynog,*
a kind of gap betwixt the mountains, which
overlook that vale. This place is reckoned about
half way to the top, and persons who visit the
mountain on horseback usually ride thus far,
leaving their horses here till they return.—We
passed by Llyn Ffynnon y Gwâs, *The Servant's
Pool,* so called, it is said, from the shepherd of
a farmer in the neighbourhood having some time
ago been drowned there as he was washing
his sheep. The road then lies along a steep
ridge, one of those denominated the buttresses
of Snowdon.

The path I found all the way exceedingly
tiresome. A little above the pool, I had to pass,
for nearly a quarter of a mile, over immense
masses of rocks, lying over each other in almost
every different direction, and entirely destitute
of vegetation.—The sledge-way to the copper-
mine (mentioned in the last chapter) will, however, now have done away all these inconveniences.

During the whole former part of this excursion the sky was clear, and the sun shone excessively hot: not a single cloud was to be seen
on the whole concave of the heavens. Notwithstanding this very favourable appearance, the
guide, while we were on the top of Snowdon,
suddenly advised that we should hasten our
descent, as a storm would otherwise soon be
upon us. I ridiculed the idea, without once

N

considering that the knowledge of the mountaineers in the symptoms of the weather, must
be much more correct than that of an entire
stranger, and I had occasion to repent of it. The
wind had not long before veered round from east
to south-west, and a narrow skirt of cloud
seemed rising from the ocean. We packed up
our napkin and eating-vessels in the basket, and
footed our way with all possible expedition,
springing over the ledges, and among the
broken fragments of the rocks, like mountain
goats. The cloud increased rapidly, and every
time I could take my attention for a moment
from my feet, 1 discovered that it had become
more condensed and black than before. Its
misty extremity now eclipsed the sun, and from
the streaks with which it was marked, it was
too plain what we had soon to expect. I advised that we should seek for shelter under two
fragments of rock a few hundred yards in front
of us, till the fury of the storm abated. The
velocity with which the lower clouds were
moved, dashed them among the hollows of the
mountains, and whirled them round with great
violence. In a few seconds we found ourselves
enveloped in a mist so dense that we could
scarcely find the stones we had before seen, and
under which we intended to seek for shelter.
No sooner had we reached them than the torrent
descended in mingled hail and rain. The hail-
stones by rebounding came into my retreat, and
the rain so filled the floor, that, in a short time,
1 found the water flowing over my shoes. I
was, however, under the necessity of quietly
submitting to this evil, in order to avoid being
wet in other parts. Every moment I expected

to be assailed by a tremendous flash of lightning, and deafened by its consequent thunder.
Happily, however, these did not occur. The
clouds blocked up the mouth of my retreat, and
left me looking apparently into an expanse of
air : from the abrupt appearance of the rocks
before me, I seemed to be sheltered on the
verge of a precipice. In about half an hour
the fury of the storm abated, and soon afterwards the heavens again became serene. The
brilliancy of the drops of rain on the grass, and
the moisture on all sides, rendered the surrounding objects very beautiful. The channels were
now filled, and torrents of water were seen
pouring down all the mountains into their pools
and hollows. Some of the larger streams overflowed their banks into the meadows. Our
walking was rendered very uncomfortable from
the grass and rocks being so slippery, as several
times to throw us on our backs with considerable
violence. At length, however, we arrived in
safety at the bottom.—After resting myself here
about a quarter of an hour, I again returned to
Caernarvon.

CHAP. XVI.

EXCURSION FROM CAERNARVON TO THE
SUMMITS OF THE MOUNTAINS GLYDER
AND TRIVAEN.

*View of Llanberis from the Sides of the Mountains.—Llyn
y Cwn.—Llyn Idwel.—Cwm Idwel.—Tremendous Precipice
and Cataract of Tull Dû.—Cwm Bochlwyd.—Trivaen.—
Difficult Ascent.—Description of the Summit of Trivaen.—
Daring Leap.—Glyder Bach.—Strange Masses of Stone.
—Glyder Vawr.—Extensive Prospect.—Evening Scene in
Llanberis.—Plants found near Tull Dû.*

Mr. Jones of Llanberis having obligingly
offered me accommodations at his house for a
few days, in order that I might, with greater
ease and convenience, examine every thing remarkable in the neighbourhood of the village,
I rose early one morning to undertake, in company with my friend Mr. Williams, by far the
most laborious walk that I ever ventured upon
in the course of one day. This was no less
than to ascend the summits of three mountains,
Trivaen, Glyder Bach, and Glyder Vawr, none
of them very much inferior to Snowdon.

About seven o'clock we set out from the
village, and directed our route up the mountains
on the north-east side of the vale of Llanberis.

When we had attained the brow of the first
eminence, immediately above the village, we
agreed to rest about five minutes, in order to
observe the appearance of the vale and mountains. The church, with its half a dozen houses,
and a few trees and meadows, were seen almost
as on a map. Beyond these, and exactly
opposite to us, extended a long range of serrated rocks, marked with innumerable intersecting streaks of red, the effect of the mountain
storms. The sun shone with great brilliancy
on these rocks, whilst Snowdon, and all the
other mountains behind them, were entirely
veiled in clouds. The lakes of Llanberis were
in part visible.—Having ascended to the eminence next above us, we found that the whole
extent of the lakes was now brought into the
view. The scene became altogether more extended, for we had now a view over the intervening mountains to the other parts of Caernarvonshire. Part of the island of Anglesea,
and the strait of Menai, were seen filling
up the openings of the mountains. We observed a few light and semitransparent clouds
float down the vale of Llanberis, and over the
dark pools, frequently whirled by the wind in
eddies. We at length arrived at a very small
pool known to all Welsh botanists, and called

LLYN Y CWN,

The Pool of the Dogs. This alpine lake was
first made generally known from the assertion
of Giraldus Cambrensis, that it contained a

singular kind of trout, perch, and eels, which all wanted the left eye. Few people seem to have given credit to this account. Mr. Edward Lhwyd, however, says that a Caernarvonshire fisherman informed him that he had several times caught monocular trout in Llyn y Cwn, and that these had all a distortion in the spine. The honourable Daines Barrington also declares, that on accurate inquiry he had heard of monocular trout being taken here within the memory of persons then living. There are no fish of any description in the pool at present *.

From Llyn y Cwn we proceeded, about three quarters of a mile, along a flat swampy piece of ground, till we came to an immense precipice above a hundred yards in perpendicular height, which forms one side of the hollow that incloses the black waters of

LLYN IDWEL.

This hollow, surrounded on all sides by dark and prominent rocks, is called *Cwm Idwel*. It is said to have been the place where Idwal, the son of Owen Gwynedd, prince of North Wales, was murdered by a person to whose care and protection his father had entrusted him. The shepherds believe the place to be the haunt of demons, and that, fatal as that of Avernus, no bird dare fly over its water.

* Phil. Trans. vol. xxvii. p. 464. and the volume for the year 1767.

We descended along the broken rocks on one side of this precipice to a great depth into the hollow; and turning among the larger masses that lay in rude heaps, somewhat more than half way down, where the descent became more gradual, we soon found ourselves at the foot of a tremendous rent, or chasm in the mountain, called

TULL DU,

The Black Cleft. A more grand, or more sublime scene, the pencil even of Salvator Rosa could not have traced. The stream that runs from Llyn y Cwn is seen to roll down the deep cleft at a vast height above, and is broken in its descent by numerous interrupting rocks. There had been much rain the day before we were here, and the accumulated volume of water rushing from the astonishing height of *a hundred and fifty yards,*

> In one impetuous torrent down the steep,
> Now thundering shot, and shook the country round.

Amongst the rocks at the bottom I observed a great number of circular holes of different sizes, from a few inches in diameter to two feet and upwards, which had been formed by the eddy of the torrent from above. These hollows are frequently called by the Welsh people *Devil's Pots,* and, from this circumstance, the place itself is sometimes denominated the Devil's Kitchen.

We descended from Tull Dû, and crossing the foot of the range of rocks on the east side of Cwm Idwell, came at length so close to Nant Frangon, as to have a view nearly of its whole extent. Still proceeding, after a while we attained the highest part of the rocks immediately surrounding Cwm Idwel. Here we found ourselves on the verge of another mountain hollow, smaller indeed than the last, but equally cheerless and dreary, called *Cwm Boch-lwyd*, containing a small black pool, *Llyn Bochlwyd*. From this situation we had the whole conical summit of

TRIVAEN

In view before us. Its sides appeared not greatly inclining from a perpendicular; and the huge masses of rock that covered them seemed destitute of vegetation, except where the clefts gave lodgement to a few mosses, bilberries, and a few species of saxifrage. To ascend its summit appeared, as in truth we found it, a most arduous undertaking: no part of Snowdon, frequented by travellers, can be in any degree compared to it.—We were determined not to be alarmed by appearances, however unfavourable they might be, and though I believe we each felt a secret persuasion that all our attempts would be to no purpose, we crossed Cwm Bochlwyd, and approached the foot of this upper part of the mountain. Here we mustered all our resolution, and commenced the laborious task; and, after a continued climbing of about three quarters of an hour, for we could scarcely take half a dozen steps together in any place, without at the same time using our hands, we found ourselves on the summit. Here, from the massy crag, we contemplated all the scene around us, which was rude as mountain horror could render it. We stood on a mere point, and on one side of us was a precipice more deep than any I had before seen. We united our strength, and rolled down it several huge pieces of rock : these continued their thundering noise for several seconds, and by their friction and dashing into hundreds of pieces, emitted a strong sulphureous smell, which ascended even to our station. The summit of Trivaen, as I have remarked at the end of my observations on Nant Frangon, in a former chapter *, is crowned by two upright stones, twelve or fourteen feet in height, about a yard and a half asunder, and each somewhat more than a yard across at the top. To stand upright on one of these, and look down the side of the mountain, would inspire even a tolerably stout heart with terror : to fall from hence would be inevitable destruction. But my companion stepped from the top of one to that of the other. I am not easily alarmed by passing among precipices, and my head is, I believe, as steady as that of most persons, but I must confess I felt my blood chill with horror at an act which seemed to me so rash. The force necessary for the leap, without great management in its counteraction, would have sent him a step farther than he had intended to have gone, would have sent

* See page 117.

him headlong down the precipice. He informed me that a female of an adjacent parish was
celebrated for having often performed this daring leap, and when he was standing on one of
the stones, dangerous as it was, he was determined to attempt the same.

We descended from the summit, and, crossing
a mountain vale, ascended the side of

GLYDER BACH,

The Lesser Glyder. This mountain, though
considerably higher than Trivaen, is neither so
steep, nor, on its exterior, so rocky. On its
summit there are several groups of columnar
stones, some standing upright, others laid across,
and, in short, in all directions. On measuring
them, we found many of them to be from sixteen to twenty feet long, and twelve or fourteen
broad. In one place there is a particularly
large one, laid over some others, and projecting
far beyond them. My companion walked to
the end, and evidently moved it by jumping
on it. " Many of the stones (says Mr. Pennant
in his account of this mountain) had shells
bedded in them; and in the neighbourhood I
found several pieces of lava. I therefore consider this mountain to have been a sort of a
wreck of nature, formed and flung up by some
mighty internal convulsion, which has given
these vast groups of stones fortuitously such a
strange disposition, for had they been the settled
strata bared of their earth by a long series of
rains, they would have retained the same regular

appearance that we observe in all other beds of similar matter *."

From hence we passed to the summit of

GLYDER VAWR,

The Greater Glyder, and observed in our way several of the same kind of insulated masses of rock scattered in different directions around us. —From this situation we had a grand and unbounded prospect. On one side, the immense mountains of Caernarvonshire and Merionethshire appeared with their towering precipices in such rude order, that they seemed " the fragments of a shattered world :" these were intersected by green meadowy vales and deep glens. On the other side, towards the town of Caernarvon, we had the whole of the isle of Anglesea in sight, and at a great distance northward we saw the Isle of Man, resembling a faintly formed cloud. All the intervening space in that direction betwixt us and the sea was filled up by the varied scenery of mountains and vales, interspersed with their lakes and streams.—Glyder Vawr is the most lofty of all the Caernarvonshire mountains, except Snowdon and Carnedd Llewelyn ; and in all the scenery of the vale of Llanberis it forms a prominent feature.

Having admired this delightful prospect for some time, we descended, and shortly afterwards arrived at the bank of Llyn y Cwn.

* Pennant's Tour, ii. 160.

About eight o'clock, after a fourteen hours' ramble, among crags and precipices, we found ourselves once again in the vale of Llanberis, and not a little fatigued with our day's excursion.

As it was not probable that I should remain another night here, after resting myself about a quarter of an hour, I determined to make the best of my time, tired as I was, and watch the close of an

EVENING SCENE IN LLANBERIS.

I left my hospitable friends, and strolled to the end of the lake. Scarcely a breath of air was to be felt. A white fog was extended, in long dense streaks, low down in the vale. The evening clouds appeared across the end of the lakes, tinged with various hues of red and orange, from the refracted rays of the departing sun. These were reflected in full splendour along the water. The rocks reflected various shades of purple, as the prominences were presented to the eye, or as the heath or verdure most prevailed. These colours after a while became one mass of dark greenish blue. The clouds lost their splendour; and the pool began to darken from the shades of the mountains. Scattered clouds now settled on various parts of the rocks, their light colours singularly contrasting with the sombre mountain tints. On turning round and looking from the pool towards the village, I was just able to distinguish it in the gloom, its place being marked by the smoke of the peat fires, rising a few yards perpendicularly from the chimnies, and then spreading into a cloud, and hovering directly over it. The rocks and precipices softened by degrees into an uniform mass of shade. The general features now became entirely lost, and only the upper outline was distinguishable in the obscurity. The evening fogs soon after came on, and in a short time so enveloped the whole scene, that not a single former trace was visible.

I shall conclude this chapter with a catalogue of the *plants* that have been found near Tull Dû, and about the pool of Llyn y Cwn; and I much doubt whether any other part of the kingdom, in so small a space of ground, will afford so many uncommon plants as are to be met with here.

Melica cœrulea.
Festuca rubra.
———— Cambrica.
Plantago maritima.
Galium boreale.
Lobelia dortmanna.
Parnassia palustris.
Saxifraga stellaris.
———— nivalis.
———— oppositifolia.
———— hypnoides.
———— palmata.
———— cœspitosa.
Silene acaulis.
Arenaria verna.
———— var. 1. laricifolia.
———— var. 2. juniperina.
Sedum rupestre.
Rubus saxatalis.

Rubus chamæmorus.
Thalictrum alpinum.
———— minus.
Subularia aquatica.
Draba incana.
Cochlearia officinalis.
———— grœnlandica.
Hieracium alpinum.
———— taraxaci.
———— sylvaticum.
Statice armeria.
Anthericum serotinum.
Juncus triglumis.
Rumex digynus.
Vaccinium myrtillus.
Chrysosplenium oppositifolium.
Gnaphalium dioicum.
Carex dioica.

Carex flava.
—— atrata.
—— pilulifera.
Empetrum nigrum.
Rhodiola rosea.
Juniperus communis, *var.*
Lycopodium selaginoides.
——————— selago.

Lycopodium alpinum.
Isoetes lacustris.
Pteris crispa.
Asplenium viride.
Polypodium phegopteris.
——————— rhæticum.
Cyathea fragile.

CHAP. XVII.

EXCURSION FROM CAERNARVON INTO ANGLESEA.

The Menai.—Ferries.—Loss of Ferry-Boats.—Particulars of the Loss of the Abermenai Boat in 1785.—Tal y Moel Fre. —Anglesea —Llanddwyn Abbey.—Beautiful Prospect — Llanedwen.—Tradition respecting a Woman Sixteen Feet high.—Invasion by the Romans.—Battle at Moel y Don.— Plâs Newydd.—Cromlech.—List of Cromlechs in Anglesea. —Ancient Place of Interment.—Gwyndy.—Wine Houses. —Holyhead.—Amlwch.—Anglesea Copper Mines.—Vitriol and Alum Work.—Smelting Houses and Port.—Llanelian. —Elian's Closet and Chest.—Wakes and Superstitions.— Memoranda of Goronwy Owen.—Pentraeth.—Plâs Gwynn. — Tradition of an extraordinary Leap. — Beaumaris.— Beaumaris Castle.—History of the Castle.—Ridiculous De- fence of the Anglesea Royalists.—Beaumaris Bay.—Baron Hill.—Observations on the general Deformity of what are called ornamental Buildings. — Llanvaes. — Penmon. — Marine Productions of Anglesea.

I CROSSED from Caernarvon into Anglesea by the ferry-boat, which every day, when the weather will admit, takes passengers over the Menai, *The Narrow Water*, to and from the island. This is a distance of somewhat more than a mile. The boat always goes at high water, and, when ready to set out, one of the men blows a horn, in the town, for the purpose of collecting toge- ther the passengers.

FERRIES.

There are six ferries from Caernarvonshire into Anglesea; *Abermenai*, about three miles south-west of Caernarvon; *Tal y Voel*, from Caernarvon; *Moel y Don*, about half way betwixt Caernarvon and Bangor Ferry; Porthaethwy, or *Bangor Ferry;* that from the promontory of *Garth*, near the town of Bangor; and from *Aber*, across the Lavan Sands to Beaumaris.—Several accidents have at different times happened at these ferries.

1664. The Abermenai ferry-boat (which is sometimes brought to take passengers from Caernarvon to the Abermenai house, in Anglesea), had arrived at the Anglesea shore from Caernarvon, the oars were laid aside, and the passengers were about to land, when a misunderstanding occurred concerning a penny more than the people were willing to pay. During the dispute the boat was carried into a deep place, where it upset, and although it was at that time within a few yards of the shore, *seventy-nine* of the passengers perished, one only escaping.—The country people believed that this was a visitation of heaven, because the boat was built of timber that had been stolen from Llanddwyn abbey.

1723. The Tal y Voel boat was upset on the thirteenth of April, and *thirty* persons perished. A man and a boy only escaped, the former by floating on the keel of the boat, and the other by laying hold of the tail of one of the horses, was dragged to the shore.

1726. The Bangor ferry-boat was so overloaded with people in their return from Bangor fair, that it sunk, and all the passengers (the number not known) were drowned, except one man and a woman. The latter floated on her clothes till she was taken up by another boat.—She was alive in the year 1798.

1785. In the month of December, the Abermenai boat in going from Caernarvon was swamped in the opposite sandbank, and all the passengers perished except one, Mr. Hugh Williams, a respectable farmer now living at Tyn Llwydan, near Aberffraw, in Anglesea.

LOSS OF THE ABERMENAI FERRY-BOAT.

The unaffected narrative of the latter melancholy event I received from Mr. Williams himself, and his story is too interesting and too simple to be related in any other than nearly his own words :

" The Abermenai ferry-boat usually leaves Caernarvon on the return of the tide, but the 5th of December being the fair-day, and there being much difficulty, on that account, in collecting the passengers, the boat did not leave Caernarvon that evening till near four o'clock, though it was low water at five, and the wind, which blew strong from south-east, was right upon our larboard bow. It was necessary that the boat should be kept in pretty close to the Caernarvonshire side, not only that we might have the benefit of the channel, which runs near the shore, but also that we might be sheltered from this wind, which blew directly towards two sand-banks, at that time divided by a channel, called Traethau Gwylltion, *The shifting Sands.* These lay somewhat more than half way betwixt the Caernarvonshire and the Anglesea coasts.—It was not long before I perceived that the boat was not kept sufficiently in the channel, and I immediately communicated to a friend, who was along with me*, my apprehensions that we were approaching too near the bank. He agreed in my opinion, and we accordingly requested the ferry-men to use their

* Thomas Coledock, gardener to O. P. Meyrick, Esq. of Bodorgan.

best efforts to keep her off. Every possible
exertion was made to this purpose, with the oars,
for we had no sail, but without effect, for we
soon after grounded upon the bank; and the
wind blew at this time so fresh as at intervals to
throw the spray entirely over us.

" Alarmed at our situation, as it was nearly
low water, and as there was every prospect,
without the utmost exertion, of being left on the
bank, some of the tallest and strongest of the
passengers leapt into the water, and, with their
joint force, endeavoured to thrust the boat off.
This, however, was to no purpose, for every
time they moved her fr m the spot, she was
with violence driven back.—In this distressing
situation the boat half filled with water, and a
heavy sea breaking over us, we thought it best
to quit her, and remain on the bank in hopes,
before the rising again of the tide, that we
should receive some assistance from Caernarvon.
We accordingly did so, and almost the moment
after we had quitted her, she filled with water,
and swamped.—Before I left her I had however
the precaution to secure the mast, on which, in
case of necessity, I was resolved to attempt my
escape : this I carried to a part of the bank
nearest to the Anglesea shore, where I observed
my friend with one of the oars, which he had also
secured for a similar purpose.

" We were at this time, including men,
women, and children, *fifty-five* in number, in a
situation that can much better be conceived than
described. Exposed, on a quick-sand, in a dark
cold night, to all the horrors of a premature
death, which, without assistance from Caernarvon, we knew must be certain on the return

of the tide, our only remaining hope was that we could make our distress known there. We accordingly united our voices in repeated cries for assistance, and we were heard. The alarm bell was rung, and, tempestuous as the night was, several boats, amongst which was that be‧longing to the custom-house, put off to our assistance. We now entertained hopes that we should shortly be rescued from the impending danger;—but how were we sunk in despair when we found that not one of them, on dis-covering our situation, dared to approach us, lest a similar fate should also involve them. A sloop from Barmouth, lying at Port'‧ Leidiog, had likewise slipt her cable to drop down to our assistance, the only effectual relief we could have received;—but before she floated the scene was closed.

" Finding that our danger was now every mo-ment increasing, and that no hopes of help what-ever could be entertained, I determined to con-tinue no longer on the bank, but to trust myself to the mercy of the sea. Being a tolerably good swimmer, I had full confidence that, with the mast, I should be able to gain the Anglesea shore. I accordingly went to the spot where I had deposited it, and found my friend there, with the oar in his hand. I proposed to him that we should tie the mast and oar together with two straw ropes, which he also had along with him, and endeavoured to persuade him to trust our-selves upon them. I fastened them together as securely as possible, and finding, after repeated endeavours to prevail on him to accompany me, that he had not fortitude enough to do it, I was determined to make the effort alone. I pulled off my boots and great coat, as likely to impede me in swimming : he committed his watch to my care, and we took a last farewell. I pushed the raft a little off the bank, and placed myself upon it, but at that moment it turned round, and threw me underneath.—In this position, with one of my arms slung through the rope, and exerting all my endeavours to keep my head above water, overwhelmed at intervals with the spray which was blown over me with great violence, I was carried entirely off the bank. When I had been in the water, as near as I could recollect, about an hour, I perceived, at a considerable distance, a light. This I believed to be (as it afterwards proved), in Tal y Voel ferry-house: my drooping spirits were revived, and I made every exertion to gain the shore, by pushing the raft towards it, at the same time calling out loudly for help. But judge of my disappointment when, in spite of every effort, I was carried past the light, and found myself driving on rapidly before the wind and tide, deprived now of every hope of relief. Dreadful as my situation was, I had, however, still strength enough to persevere in my endeavours to gain the shore. These, after being for some time beaten about by the surge, which several times carried me back into the water, were at length effectual. After having been upwards of two hours tossed about by the sea, in a cold and tempestuous night, supported only by clinging hold of the mast and oar of a small boat, I was thus providentially retrieved from otherwise inevitable death. — I now felt the dreadful effect of the cold I had endured, for, on endeavouring to rise, that I might seek assistance, my limbs refused their office. Exerting myself to the utmost, I endeavoured to crawl towards the place where I had seen the light, distant at least a mile from me, but at last was obliged to desist, and lie down under a hedge, till my strength was somewhat recovered. The wind and rain soon roused me, and after repeated struggles, and the most painful efforts, I at length reached the Tal y Voel ferry-house. I was first seen by a female of the family, who immediately ran screaming away, under the idea that she had encountered a ghost. The family, however, by this means were roused, and I was taken into the house. They put me into a warm bed, gave me some brandy, and applied heated bricks to my extremities : this treatment had so good an effect, that on the following morning no other unpleasant sensation was left than that of extreme debility.—Having been married but a very short time, I determined to be the welcome messenger to my wife of my own deliverance. I therefore hastened home as early as possible, and had the good fortune to find that the news of the melancholy event had not before reached my dwelling.

" This morning presented a spectacle along the shore which I cannot attempt to describe. Several of the bodies had been cast up during the night. The friends of the sufferers crowded the banks, and the agitated inquiries of the relatives after those whose fate was doubtful or unknown, and the affliction of the friends of those already discovered, to this day fill me with horror in the recollection :—I, alas, was the only surviving witness of the melancholy event.—Besides those bodies thrown upon the

shore by the tide, so many were found in various
positions, sunk in the sand-bank, that it was
not till after several tides that they could all be
dug out.—My boots and great coat were found
under the sand, nearly in the place where I
had left them. The boat was never seen afterwards, and it is supposed to be even yet lodged
in the bank."

Tal y Moel Fre, or, Tal y Voel Fre, *The End
of the Hill*, where I landed in Anglesea, is so
called, from the coast being somewhat more
steep there than any where else in its immediate
neighbourhood.

ANGLESEA,

Prior to the invasion of the Romans, had the
name of *Môn*, which signified merely an insula-
tion from the continent of Wales; this name
they latinized into Mona. It received its first
appellation of *Anglesea* on its reduction to the
Saxon yoke.

The princes of North Wales had here their
residence, except when driven out for two centuries by the Irish and Picts, until the close of
the reign of their last prince. The palace was
at Aberffraw; and I have been informed that
some few fragments of the walls are yet standing, forming now part of the walls of a barn.

LLANDDWYN ABBEY.

In describing the places which I have visited in the island of Anglesea, I shall begin with the Llanddwyn rocks and abbey, at the extreme south point, and distant from Caernarvon in a direct line about six miles.

The ruins of this abbey are situated about the middle of a sandy flat surrounded by rocks, and also, except on one side, by the sea. Some of the walls are yet standing, but they possess nothing whatever either of interest or elegance. If I may judge from the present traces of its site, the erection altogether has never been of any considerable magnitude.

This place, I have been informed, is a noted resort of smugglers, and their traces are indeed sufficiently evident in several large and deep holes dug in the sand for concealing their cargoes. I have seen few places more inviting to this species of illicit commerce. Several narrow entrances between the rocks, with a fine sandy bottom, seem particularly calculated to hide their little vessels from the careless eye of the revenue officers of this district. Here they can run in, and (being four or five miles from any inhabited place, and surrounded by eminences,) unload and deliver their cargoes to their emissaries without danger.

From the Anglesea coast, near the Tal y Voel ferry-house, the town of Caernarvon, with the straits of Menai in front, and the high grand mountains in the back ground, were strikingly beautiful. Snowdon, the day I was here, was

perfectly unclouded, and his red sides, brightened by the beams of the sun, were seen gradually
sloping till they ended in a point far above the
tops of all the adjoining mountains; each of
which had its beauty in the disposition of its
lights and shades, and of its prominences and
hollows.

It was my original intention to have proceeded entirely round the island, by Newborough, Aberffraw, and Holyhead. But on inquiry into the practicability of this scheme, I
found that I should meet with considerable difficulty, from the circumstance of a bank having
been burst by the sea, near Aberffraw, and
several hundred acres of land being constantly
flooded at high water. My route was therefore
necessarily changed, and instead of making
the circuit I had intended, I botanized along
the Anglesea coast as far as Moel y Don ferry,
from whence I took the direct road to Holyhead.

About three miles from the place where I
landed, I passed *Llanedwen*, a village now celebrated principally from its having been the
place of interment of Henry Rowlands, the
learned author of " Mona Antiqua Restaurata,"
who died in the year 1723. A black slab, near
the south end of the church, contains a Latin
inscription to his memory: this was his own
composition, but it is now nearly obliterated.—
The Welsh people have a strange tradition, that
the body of a woman *sixteen feet* long, lies
buried across the path leading to the south door
of the church. The present gardener at Plâs
Newydd, to satisfy some inquirers, was induced

to dig up the place a few years ago, but no bones, nor any other evidence occurred that could support so ridiculous a story.

The place where the Roman general Suetonius Paulinus first landed, when he invaded this island, is not far from Llanedwen. About two hundred yards from the Menai there is a field yet called Maes Mawr Gâd, *The Field of the Great Army*, and at a little distance eastward, just on the shore, a place still retains thé name of Rheidd, or *The Chief Men's Post*.

MOEL Y DON.

The Hill of the Wave, is celebrated as being the place where, in the year 1282, part of the English army experienced from the Welsh a severe defeat, attended with great slaughter. Edward I. had led out his men to contend with the Welsh soldiers in the open plains, but, on their retiring to the mountains, he did not dare an attack in their fastnesses. He therefore sent over a party of them into Anglesea, and ordered them to encamp on the bank of the Menai, near Moel y Don; at the same time giving directions for a bridge of boats, of width sufficient for sixty men to march abreast, to be built across the straits. He retired to Conwy castle with the remainder of his army; and the workmen proceeded in their operations. The bridge was so far finished, that part of it only wanted boarding over, when, at the ebb of the tide, several of the English nobility, and about three hundred soldiers, rashly crossed it, and remained on the opposite side till the tide had

cut off their access to the bridge. The Welsh
soon received information of this circumstance,
and, descending like a torrent from the mountains, rushed with such fury upon the affrighted
Englishmen, that every one of them, except Sir
William Latimer, who escaped from the excellence of his horse, was either put to the sword,
or perished in the water. The historians inform
us that, besides the common soldiers, the Welsh
slew, in this encounter, thirteen knights, and
seventeen young gentlemen, probably officers
commanding in the English army.

PLAS NEWYDD.

I deviated from the Holyhead road about a
mile at Moel y Don, for the purpose of examining the house and grounds of lord Uxbridge at
Plâs Newydd, *The New Mansion.* The house
is a very elegant building. It stands upon the
bank of the Menai, is almost surrounded by
woods, and commands from the front windows
a beautifully picturesque and extensive prospect
of those British Alps, the mountains of Caernarvonshire.

At a little distance are some druidical remains, a large and a small *cromlech,* which stand
close together. The former of these is about
thirteen feet long, and twelve broad. The
upper stone, which, in some parts, is about
four feet in thickness, formerly rested on five
upright supporters; but, some years ago, after
some heavy rain, the one at the back suddenly

split, since which time it has been necessary to prop it with supporters of wood.

The original design of the cromlech, notwithstanding the contrary opinion of various antiquaries, seems only to have been as a sepulchral monument; for, under several cromlechs in Cornwall and other parts of England, bones have been found deposited. It appears to have been the original of our present altar tombs, which are but a more diminutive and elegantly formed cromlech.

The following is a list of twenty-eight cromlechs, which, I believe, are yet to be found in the island of Anglesea:

Two at Plâs Newydd, in the parish of	Llan Edwen.
One at Bodowyr,	Llanidan.
One at Trevor,	Llansadwrn.
Two at Rhôs Fawr,	Llanfair yn Mathafarn.
One at Marian Pant y Saer,	Ibid.
One at Llugwy,	Penrhôs Llugwy.
One at Parkiau,	Ibid.
Three on Bodafon mountain,	Llanvihangel Tre'r-beirdd.
Three at Boddeiniol,	Llanbaleo.
One at Cromlech,	Llanfechell.
One at Henblas,	Llan Gristiolis.
One at Tynewyddland,	Llanfaelog.
One, partly demolished, on Mynydd y Cnwe,	Ibid.
Three small ones near Cryghyll river,	Ibid.
One near Towyn Trewen,	Llanfihangel Yneibwl.
One near Llanallgo,	Llanallgo.
One at Cremlyn,	Llandone.
One at Myfyrian, in the parish of Llanidan.	
One at Bodlew, and	
One at Rhôs y Ceryg.	

In returning from the house at Plâs Newydd, to the Holyhead road, I observed, at a little distance from the path, a *tumulus,* of considerable size. There is upon it a large flat stone, beneath which I found a low entrance into a subterraneous recess, apparently ten or twelve feet long, and four feet wide and high. The sides are formed by flat upright stones, one of which, opposite to the entrance, is said to close the passage into a vault considerably larger than this. This place was first exposed in the time of sir Nicholas Bailey, about seventy years ago; and, when the workmen had opened the entrance into the larger recess, he ordered them to discontinue their operations, as it seemed to contain nothing but bones. A servant of the earl of Uxbridge, at the request of some gentleman who visited the place, dug to the depth of about twelve feet in the bottom of the smaller vault, and discovered a few human bones, and a very old clasp knife, which might probably have been lost by the men who before dug in the same place, for the man could give me no satisfactory description of it.

Having finished my examination of this ancient place of interment, I pursued my journey towards Holyhead; and, evening coming on, I took up my abode for the night at

GWYNDY,

The Wine House, an inn standing nearly equidistant from Bangor and Holyhead.—About the reign of Edward the Fourth, and for some years subsequent to that period, the gentlemen of Wales frequently invited their friends, in large parties, to exercise in wrestling, tournaments, and other feats of activity : but, as these meetings, in consequence of the numbers invited, were usually attended with great expence, they were always held in the house of some neighbouring tenant, who was supplied with wine from his lord's cellar, and this was sold to the visitors, and his master received the profits. These houses were denominated *Gwyndu,* or wine houses and from this circumstance the present place had its name.

HOLYHEAD.

In the morning I proceeded towards this place, distant about thirteen miles. Holyhead is situated on an island, at the extreme west point of Anglesea, but, except at high water, the dividing channel is passable without boats. The island is seven or eight miles long, and, in most parts towards the sea, so rocky, as to be inhabited only by the various species of sea-fowl, which breed among the cliffs.—From being the nearest point of this kingdom that lies towards Dublin, it has always been much resorted to by company passing to and from Ireland. In itself, however, it possesses but few attractions for the tourist on pleasure.—The distance from Holyhead to Dublin is about twenty leagues, which the packets generally make in about twelve hours.

The church-yard is on a rock directly above the sea : it forms a quadrangle of about ninety yards, by forty. Three sides are inclosed by strong walls, and the fourth is nearly open to the sea, having only a parapet defended by steep rocks.

The church is a handsome embattled edifice, built in the form of a cross. It is supposed to have been once a college of prebendaries, founded by Hwfa ap Cyndelw, lord of Llys Lliven in Anglesea, and one of the fifteen tribes of North Wales, who lived in the twelfth century. In the reign of Edward the Third, the whole of the church, except the chancel, was rebuilt; and the latter was repaired in the beginning of the last century.

A number of cross roads, sufficiently disagreeable, led me, over a most uninteresting country, to

AMLWCH,

Near the Lake*, a small market town about a mile from the *Paris mountain*, that inexhaustible mine of copper, a mine of wealth to all its proprietors. Almwch seems entirely dependent, for its prosperity, on the copper mines, for most of its inhabitants have some concern in them, either as miners or agents.—The church, dedicated to Elaeth, a saint of the British calendar, is a neat modern structure. Of the town itself, I observed nothing remarkable except that it was in general a most black, and dismal place, owing to the scoria of the metal, of which all the roads are formed. On the exterior of the

---

* This loch, or lake, from which the town has its name, was situated betwixt the church and the port. It has long been drained, and is now in a state of cultivation.

town the country is a scene of barrenness and desolation. The sulphureous fumes from the mine have entirely destroyed the vegetation for a considerable space around, and little else than earth and rock are to be seen even within a short distance of Amlwch. On the Paris mountain, there is not even a single moss or lichen to be found.

ANGLESEA COPPER MINES.

On the morning after my arrival, at Amlwch, I walked to the Paris mountain. Having ascended to the top, I found myself standing on the verge of a vast and tremendous chasm. I stepped on one of the stages suspended over the edge of the steep, and the prospect was dreadful. The number of caverns at different heights along the sides; the broken and irregular masses of rock which every where presented themselves; the multitudes of men at work in different parts, and apparently in the most perilous situations; the motions of the whimsies, and the raising and lowering of the buckets, to draw out the ore and the rubbish; the noise of picking the ore from the rock, and of hammering the wadding, when it was about to be blasted; with, at intervals, the roar of the blasts in distant parts of the mine, altogether excited the most sublime ideas, intermixed, however, with sensations of terror. I left this situation, and followed the road that leads into the mine; and the moment I entered, my astonishment was again excited. The shagged arches, and overhanging rocks, which seemed to threaten anni-

hilation to any one daring enough to approach
them, fixed me almost motionless to the spot.
The roofs of the work, having in many places
fallen in, have left some of the rudest scenes
that imagination can paint: these, with the sulphureous fumes, from the kilns in which the ore
is roasted, rendered it to me a perfect counterpart to Virgil's entrance into Tartarus*.

> Hac iter Elysium nobis; at læva malorum
> Exercet pœnas, et ad impia Tartarus mittit.

> 'Tis here in different paths the way divides,
> The right to Pluto's golden palace guides;
> The left to that unhappy region tends,
> Which to the depth of Tartarus descends;
> The seat of night profound, and punish'd fiends.

To look up from hence, and observe the people on the stages, a hundred and fifty feet above
one's head; to see the immense number of ropes
and buckets, most of them in motion; and to
reflect, that a single stone casually thrown from
above, or falling from a bucket, might in a
moment destroy a fellow creature, a man must
have a strong mind, not to feel impressed with
many unpleasant sensations. A few days before
I was last here, a bucket caught against the
point of a rock, emptied its contents on the head
of one of the miners, and killed him on the spot.
The sides of this dreadful hollow are mostly
perpendicular. Along the edges, and in general slung by ropes over the precipices, are the
stages with windlasses, or *whimsies*, as they are

---

* I am informed that the appearance of this part of the
mine has lately been much changed, from some of the insulated rocks, &c. having been cleared away.

here termed, from which the buckets are lowered; and from which those men descend, who work upon the sides. Here, suspended in mid air, they pick, with their iron instrument, a small place for a footing, cut out the ore in vast masses, and tumble it with a thundering crash to the bottom. In these seemingly precarious situations they make caverns, in which they work for a certain time, until the rope is again lowered to take them up.

Much of the ore is blasted by gunpowder, eight tons of which, we are told, was some time ago annually used for this purpose.—The manner of preparing for the blasting was entirely new to me, and may be so to some of my readers. A hole is bored in the rock of about the diameter of a wide gun barrel, and of depth in proportion to the quantity of matter to be thrown up. At the bottom is lodged the gunpowder, and the man then taking a thin iron rod, tapering to a point, and about two feet in length, he places it perpendicularly in the middle of the hole, and fills it up on all sides with stones, clay, &c. ramming these hard down by means of an iron projecting at the bottom, with a nick in it, that it may pass freely round the rod. When this is prepared the rod is taken out, and a straw filled with gunpowder is substituted. A match is then put to it, that will burn so long, before it communicates the fire to the powder, as to allow all the workmen within reach, to escape into different retreats from the danger attendant on the explosion. Several blasts are generally ready at the same time, and notice is given to the workmen to run into shelter, by a cry in Welsh of *fire*. Whilst I was in the mine, the

P

cry was several times given, and I, with the rest, crept into shelter. In one instance, six or seven blasts went off in different parts successively, one of which was within thirty yards of my station, and the splinters of the rock dashed furiously past me. The process of blasting is frequently attended with danger, from the carelessness with which the men retire to their hiding-places : and it sometimes happens that, in ramming down the wadding, the iron strikes against the stone, and fires the gunpowder. This generally proves fatal to the man employed. During the short time I remained here, I observed upwards of forty men in different places, occupied in this work ; and I felt somewhat uncomfortable under the idea that in such a number, some one might be careless enough to have his gunpowder take fire before he was aware of it.

There are in the Paris mountain two mines : of these, the one on the east side is the *Mona mine*, the entire property of the earl of Uxbridge. The *Paris mine* is the joint property of the earl of Uxbridge and the rev. Edward Hughes of Kinmael, near St. Asaph. Thomas Williams, esq. of Llanidan, the member for Marlow, when I was last there, had a lease of half the earl's share in these mines, and they worked conjointly ; Mr. Hughes worked his share of the Paris mine alone.

It is generally believed that the Romans got copper ore from this mountain ; for vestiges are yet left of what have been taken for their operations ; and some very ancient stone utensils have, at different times, been found here. From the time of the Romans, till the year 1764, these mines seem to have been entirely neglected. Copper had, about two years before this period, been found here, and Messrs. Roe and Co. of Macclesfield, had, with a mine in Caernarvonshire, a lease of part of the Paris mountain from sir Nicholas Bailey, the father of the earl of Uxbridge, which expired about nine years ago. They spent considerable sums of money in making levels to drain off the water, without any great success, and were about to give up any further attempts, when their agent requested that a final experiment might be tried in another part of the mountain. This succeeded, for in less than two days, ore of almost pure copper was discovered not two yards from the surface, which proved to be that vast bed which has since been worked to such advantage. The day of this discovery was the second of March, 1768, and it has ever since been observed as a festival by the miners.—The rev. Edward Hughes, who was the owner of the remainder of the mountain, was roused by this success to attempt a similar adventure, which has also succeeded beyond the most sanguine expectations of the time.

The bed of ore is in some places more than sixty feet in thickness; and the proprietors are said to ship annually about 20,000 tons. The number of hands employed is upwards of a thousand. The ore has lately been supposed to be fast decreasing, but the discovery of a new vein in the Mona mine, will keep that property still in a flourishing state for many years.

The ore, as I have already remarked, is obtained partly by picking and partly by blasting.

P 2

It is then broken with hammers, into small pieces, by women and children, armed with iron gloves. After this operation it is piled in kilns of great length, and about six feet high, where it is set on fire in different places, to undergo the process of roasting; for as the ore in its natural state contains a great quantity of sulphur, it is necessary that this should be separated (which can only be done by means of fire) before it is fluxed into copper. The sulphur passes off in the form of vapour, and is conveyed by a flue, connected with the kiln, to the sulphur chamber, a place built to receive it, where it sublimes, and becomes the flower of sulphur of the shops. It is afterwards taken from hence, melted in large copper pans, and cast in moulds for sale.

After the ore has been thus roasted, which is rather a tedious operation, occupying from three to ten months, according to the quantity in the furnaces, (which is generally from three hundred to a thousand tons,) it is taken to the slacking pits, places constructed of stone, about six yards long, five wide, and two deep, to be washed, and made merchantable. The poorest of this, that is, such as contains from one and a half to two *per cent.* of metal, is then conveyed to the smelting houses at Amlwch port; the rest is sent to the company's furnaces at Swansea and Ravenhead. By the processes of roasting and washing, though the ore is much reduced in quantity, it is considerably improved in quality: and the water is so richly impregnated with copper, which is dissolved by the acid quality of the sulphur, that, by means of old iron immersed in it, according to the German method, it produces such quantities of fine copper, that the proprietors have obtained in one year, upwards of a hundred tons of the copper precipitated from the water. Their average export of precipitate is sixty tons *per annum*.

The proprietors also turn the water drawn from the beds of copper, which is highly impregnated, through rectangular pits similar to those used in the above process. These are each about thirty feet long, twelve broad, and two deep. Any kind of iron, either old or new, is used, but in general, for the sake of convenience, they procure small plates of cast iron. The iron becomes dissolved by the acid, and is suspended in the water, whilst the copper is precipitated. Care is taken to turn the iron every day, in order to shake off the incrustation of copper formed upon it, and this is continued till the iron is perfectly dissolved. The workmen then drain off the water, and rake together the ore in the form of mud, which, when it is become, by drying, of the consistency of a softish paste, they bake in ovens constructed for the purpose. After this process it is exported with the other ore, to Ravenhead or Swansea. One ton of iron thus immersed, produces nearly two tons of copper mud, each of which, when melted, will yield sixteen hundred weight of copper; and this sells at a considerably higher price than the copper which is fluxed from the ore.

Several of the shafts which have been formed in these mines for taking off the water, are driven very deep. One that I saw was upwards of a hundred and sixty feet in depth, below the open bottom of the mine. One of the miners, whilst I was looking at it, brought a lighted candle, and fixed it on the rim of one of the buckets in which they draw up the water. It was curious to watch it in its dark and confined descent, till it became a mere speck of light, when, suddenly immersing in the water, it was lost.

These mines have increased the value of lands in the parish of Amlwch, from about fourteen hundred to five thousand pounds *per annum,* and upwards; the number of houses from two hundred to upwards of a thousand; and the population from nine hundred to about five thousand persons.

VITRIOL AND ALUM WORK.

At a little distance from the mine is a building appropriated to the making of vitriol and alum. The proprietor is Dr. Joshua Parr, who resides in Carmarthenshire. The argillaceous earth from which the alum is extracted, is found on the spot, in a stratum about six feet beneath the surface of the ground. About one ton a week was the average quantity manufactured here. A small quantity of white vitriol continues to be made; but the attempts to prepare green and blue vitriol have been attended with no success. Indeed the whole concern has answered so ill, that, when I was here, I was informed, it would probably be altogether given up in the course of a very short time.

SMELTING HOUSES AND PORT.

These are about a mile from Amlwch. The former contain thirty furnaces: each capable of holding half a ton weight of roasted ore, which produce not quite one hundred weight of metal. As it is the refuse ore only that is smelted here, it is necessary when it arrives at Swansea, to have it smelted again four or five times before the metal is sufficiently pure.

The port is very small, but excellently adapted to the business of exportation. It is a chasm between two rocks, running far into the land, and has in a great measure been formed by art: its width is not more than to allow two vessels to ride abreast; it is however sufficiently long and deep to receive thirty vessels of two hundred tons burthen each. This port was first made at the expence of the copper companies, for the convenience of their shipping, and is not therefore frequented by any others than vessels concerned with them.

About two miles east of Amlwch, and at a little distance from the coast, is the village of

LLANELIAN.

The church is by no means an inelegant structure; and adjoining to it is a small chapel of very ancient foundation, that measures in its interior, twelve feet by fifteen, called Myfyr, *the confessional.*—A curious closet of wood, of an hexagonal form, called *St. Elian's closet*, is yet left in the east wall, and is supposed to have

served both the office of a communion table, and
as a chest to contain the vestments and other
utensils belonging to the chapel. There is a
hole in the wall of the chapel, through which
the priests are supposed to have received con-
fessions : the people believe this hole to have
been used in returning oracular answers, to per·
sons who made inquiries of the saint respecting
future events.—Near the door is placed Cyff
Elian, *Elian's chest*, or poor box. People out
of health, even to this day, send their offering
to the saint, which they put, through a hole,
into the box. A silver groat, though not a very
common coin, is said to be a present peculiarly
acceptable, and has been known to procure his
intercession, when all other kinds of coin have
failed! The sum, thus deposited, which in the
course of a year frequently amounts to several
pounds, the churchwardens annually divide
among the poor of the parish.

The wakes of Llanelian were formerly held
on the three first Friday evenings in August;
but they are now confined to only one of those
days. Young persons from all parts of the adjacent country, and even from distant counties,
assemble here, most of whom have along with
them some offering for the saint, to ensure their
future prosperity, palliate their offences, and
secure blessings on their families, their cattle,
and corn.

The misguided devotees assemble about the
chapel, and having deposited their offerings,
many of them proceed to search into their future
destiny, in a very singular manner, by means
of the wooden closet. Persons of both sexes,
of all ages and sizes, enter the small door way,

and if they can succeed in turning themselves round within the narrow limits of the place, (which measures only betwixt three and four feet in height, about four feet across the back, and eighteen inches in width,) they believe that they shall be fortunate till at least the ensuing wake. But if they do not succeed, in this difficult undertaking, they esteem it an omen of ill fortune, or of their death within the year.—I have been told, that it is curious enough to see a stout lusty fellow, weighing perhaps sixteen or eighteen stone, striving to creep into these narrow confines, with as much confidence of success as a stripling a yard high; and when he fails in the attempt, to see him fuming and fretting because his body, which contains in solid bulk more than the place could hold, were it crammed into all corners, cannot be got in. But when we consider, that superstition and enthusiasm have generally little to do with reason, we must not wonder at this addition to the heap of incongruities that all ages have afforded us.

Llanelian was formerly a sanctuary, or place of refuge for criminals.—In digging a grave in the church-yard, about sixteen years ago, a deep trench was discovered, which extended about twenty yards in a transverse direction across. It was found to contain a great quantity of human bones; and is supposed to have been the place of interment of a number of sailors who perished in a storm that drove them upon this coast.

The distance betwixt Amlwch and Beaumaris, by Dulas and Red-wharf bays, is about sixteen miles, and the country, the whole way, was sufficiently pleasant to render the walk very agreeable ; but it so greatly resembles the country in many parts of England, that the traveller will not observe its character to be either new or particularly interesting.—I passed, at the distance of about a mile on the right, the village of Llanfair, celebrated as the birth-place of

GORONWY OWEN,

A man inferior in talent and genius to none which Wales has produced. He was born in the year 1722; and his father having only a small farm to support his family upon, the principal of Goronwy's schooling was acquired in the neighbouring village of Llanallgo. During his early years, he exhibited such marks of application and abilities, that at the age of fifteen he was taken as an assistant in the grammar-school at Pwllheli. Here he found employment for some time. In 1741 he went to Oxford; but, from the poverty of his parents, he was supported in that university by the munificence of Mr. Lewis Morris. Four years afterwards he received holy orders at Bangor, and became curate to the bishop, at Llanfair. The bishop soon removing him, to make way for one of his own friends, he accepted the curacy of Oswestry, and in the same year received priest's orders at St. Asaph. In the year following he married, and in 1748 removed to Donnington, near Shrewsbury, where he served a church, and taught a school, for about twenty-six pounds a year. He changed his residence in 1753, (with his wife and two children,) to serve the curacy

of Walton, near Liverpool, for which, and the
are of a school, he was allowed forty pounds
and a house.— On this slender, and hard-earned
pittance, his family was almost starving, when,
two years afterwards, he was induced to remove
to the curacy of North-holt in Middlesex. Here
he was once more on the point of starving, when
the rectory of St. Andrews, in the county of
Brunswic, in Virginia, worth about two hundred
pounds *per annum*, was obtained for him; and,
in the month of November 1757, he sailed from
this country to take possession of it.   Here his
situation seems to have been still distressing.
He had to live among men whose whole character and conduct he had every reason to detest.
In only two letters that were received by
his friends in this country, of the great number
that he wrote, he complains, that all his letters
from hence had been opened before they came to
his hands.   With one of these letters he himself
travelled seventy miles, and with the other
nearly as far, to secure them a passage, by de-
livering them himself to captains of vessels.   In
one of them, dated July 1767, he states the loss
of all his family, except one boy.

Thus had he, though a man of the highest
talents, to struggle with affliction through every
part of his life; and the close attention that,
in England, he had paid to the duties of his station as a schoolmaster, and his application to
the study of languages and general literature,
during what ought to have been hours dedicated
to rest, with the necessary anxieties for his
family, tended greatly to undermine his health.
His character throughout appears to have been
free from stain. He was not ambitious; a com-

fortable subsistence seems to have been the utmost limit of his wishes, yet his country did not
give it ; and with every qualification that could
render him useful to society, he was banished
from his native home, to seek an asylum, for a
mere existence, in a voluntary transportation
from every thing he held dear and valuable.

The acquirements of Goronwy Owen were
very extensive. To a perfect acquaintance with
the Latin and Greek languages, he added a
knowledge of Hebrew, Chaldee, Arabic, and
Syriac. His Latin odes have been universally
admired for the purity of their language, and
for the elegance of their expression.—As a Welsh
poet he ranks superior to all since the days of
Dafydd ap Gwilym. Those parts of his works
that have been printed, are considered as perfect models of Welsh poetry.—His poetry consists chiefly of odes, moral, serious, and religious;
but his most celebrated performance is a poem
on the Day of Judgment, " Cywydd y Farn
fawr." The ideas in this are so grand, and it
is throughout so crowded with poetic images, as
deservedly to raise it superior to the works of
any but a few of the most eminent bards.—He
had also a general knowledge of antiquities,
which, from his various letters that are extant,
he seems to have pursued with considerable
ardour.—Goronwy Owen died in Virginia, but
the time of his death I have not been able to
ascertain.

About a mile from Red-Wharf bay, I passed
the village of Pentraeth, *The End of the Sands.*
It is pleasantly situated, and its little church is
so picturesque, that from this circumstance only,

Mr. Grose was induced to insert a print of it in his Antiquities. The ash and sycamore trees around seem to shelter it from the observation of the world.—It is the place of interment of the Panton family, whose seat, Plâs Gwynn, *The White Mansion,* is about half a mile distant.

In a field near the porter's lodge of Plâs Gwynn, there are two stones, at a considerable distance from each other, which were pointed out to me as the place where tradition says Einion ap Gwalchmai, some centuries ago, obtained his wife by an uncommon exhibition of activity, in leaping *fifty feet!* There were two competitors, and the female decided their claims by taking the man who could leap farthest. Einion, it is said, some time afterwards, went to a distant part of the country, where he had occasion to reside several years, and he found, on his return, that his wife had, on that very morning, been married to another person. He took his harp, and, sitting down at the door, explained in Welsh metre who he was, and where he had been resident. His wife narrowly scrutinized his person, unwilling to give up her new spouse, when he exclaimed:

> Look not, Angharad, on my silver hair,
>   Which once shone bright of golden lively hue:
> Man doth not last like gold,—he that was fair
>   Will soon decay, though gold continue new.
>
> If I have lost Angharad, lovely fair!
>   The gift of brave Ednyfed, and my spouse,
> All I've not lost, (all must from hence repair,)
>   Nor bed, nor harp, nor yet my ancient house.

I once have leap'd to shew my active power,
A leap which none could equal or exceed,
The leap in Aber Nowydd, which thou, fair flower!
Did once so much admire, thyself the meed.

Full fifty feet, as still the truth is known,
And many witnesses can still attest,
How there the prize I won, thyself must own,
This action stamp'd my worth within thy breast.

BEAUMARIS.

From Plâs Gwynn I had a walk of about five
miles to Beaumaris. The entrance into the
town was pretty : the bay and castle, with Penmaen Mawr, and the Ormes Head at a distance,
are seen in a direct line in front; and the road,
which lies down a steep hill, is shaded on each
side with trees. The town itself is finely situated on the western bank of the Menai, just
where it opens into an extensive bay. The
houses are in general neat, and well built, and
one of the streets is very good.—On examining
the church and church-yard, I found nothing
worth notice, except a whimsical inscription on
Meredith Davies,

Who has been our parish clark
Full one and thirty years, I say ;
But here, alas ! lies in the dark,
Bemoan'd for ever and aye.

BEAUMARIS CASTLE

Is situated close to the town, within the grounds
of Baron Hill, the seat of Lord Bulkeley. It

covers a considerable space of ground, but its walls are at present so low, that it does not excite much attention. When it was in a perfect state, it consisted of an outer ballium, or envelope, surrounded by a broad ditch flanked by several round towers ; and it had on the east side an advanced work, called the gunner's walk. Within these was the body of the castle,* which was nearly square, having a round tower at each angle, and another in the centre of each face. The area is a square, with the corners cut off, and measures about sixty yards on each side. In the middle of the north side is the hall, which is twenty yards long, and twelve broad, and has

---

* *History of the Castle.*—After Edward I. had secured his conquests in Caernarvonshire by the erection of the castles of Caernarvon and Conwy, he found it was also necessary to have a fortress of some strength in the island of Anglesea, to prevent the Welsh from taking refuge there, and becoming sufficiently collected and powerful to harass his forces in other parts. Beaumaris castle was therefore founded for this purpose about the year 1295 : it was built on private property, but Edward made full satisfaction to the proprietors of the ground, by bestowing on them other lands free from rent and service. The name of the town, which before had been Bonover, was now changed to Beaumaris, indicative, says Holinshed, of its pleasant situation in a low ground.

From the time of the foundation of the castle, to the reign of Charles I., I have been able to find no incident recorded of any importance. It is said to have been extremely burthensome to the country, on account of the frequent quarrels which took place betwixt the garrison and the people of the neighbourhood.

In the civil wars of the reign of Charles I., Beaumaris castle was garrisoned for the king by Thomas lord Bulkeley; and, in the year 1648, the people of the whole island rose, in imitation of those in several counties of England, to set the king at liberty, and restore monarchy to the oppressed kingdom. Multitudes of royalists, from different parts of North Wales, resorted here, and a general muster was made, under

had five elegant windows in front.*—There has been a communication round the buildings of the inner court by means of a gallery somewhat more than a yard wide, which is yet in a great measure entire. In recesses in the sides of this gallery are several square openings, which seem to have been furnished with trap doors, entrances to dungeons beneath. The use of these I have not been able to learn: they must have been descended by ladders, for there are no remains of steps to be discovered in any of them. The two eastern towers of this building served the purpose of dungeons for the confinement of prisoners.—On the east side of the area are the remains of a very small chapel, arched and ribbed with pointed and intersecting arches. Between each of the gothic pilasters is a narrow window,

the direction of lord Bulkeley, in the middle of the island. The parliament, determining to bring them to submission, sent against them a division of their army, under the command of general Mytton. Some of the loyalist officers conducted themselves with bravery and spirit, but the islanders in general proved cowards. An Anglesea captain was directed to keep the church of Beaumaris: he posted his men in it, locked them safely up, and then ran away, with the key in his pocket. In consequence of this he was ever afterwards stigmatized with the title of captain Church.— When the enemy were seen marching over the heights of Penmaen Mawr, at least four miles distant, the Anglesea people began to bustle about, drums were beat, trumpets sounded, and vollies of both small and great shot were discharged The parliament's army, somewhat more accustomed to fighting than to be alarmed at an enemy who could fire small shot at them when four miles off, approached the place, and with little difficulty put the whole to flight. The garrison surrendered on honourable terms, and Mytton was immediately made governor.—The castle is now the property of the crown.

* Grose.

and, behind some of them, there have been small closets, gained out of the thickness of the wall.

When Edward the First built the castle, he surrounded the town with walls. He also incorporated it, and endowed it with great privileges, and lands to a considerable value.—It sends one member to parliament.

THE BAY OF BEAUMARIS

Forms a fine opening before the town; and it is so sheltered, that vessels of considerable burthen can lie secure in it, even during stormy weather. The depth of the water near the town is six or seven fathoms, even when the tide is out; but this deep channel scarcely extends more than a quarter of a mile in width. All the rest of the bay, for several miles, is left dry at low water, and has the name of the *Lavan Sands*. These are supposed by the Welsh people to have once formed a habitable hundred of Caernarvonshire, that was first overflowed during the sixth century. It seems by no means improbable that this was the case, for there is decided proof of the sea having incroached very greatly on some parts of this coast. In the church-yard of Abergeley, a village on the coast of Caernarvonshire, about eighteen miles distant, there is the following inscription:

> Yma mae'n gorwedd
> Ym monwent Mihangel;
> Gwr oedd a'i annedd,
> Dair milltir yn y gogledd.

Q

Under this stone lieth,
In this church yard of St. Michael,
A man whose dwelling was
Three miles to the northward.

Another evidence arises from the bodies of oak
trees, tolerably entire, having been discovered,
at low water, in a long tract of hard loam, far
from the present banks of the sea.

BARON HILL.

On an eminence behind the town of Beaumaris stands this charming residence of lord
Bulkeley, commanding a most delightful prospect of all the northern mountains of Caernarvonshire, of the bay of Beaumaris, and a
great expanse of sea. The house stands in
front of the woods, and is esteemed by many
tourists an ornament to this corner of Anglesea.
It was built originally in the reign of James I.,
for the reception of Henry, the eldest son of
that monarch, when on his way to Ireland.
But his untimely death so much affected sir
Richard Bulkeley, the owner, that he gave up
his original and magnificent plan, and used the
part only that was then completed, for his
family seat. The house has been enlarged, and
greatly improved, by its present worthy possessor.* I was sorry (in the year 1802) to observe the effect of the elegant view of the Welsh
mountains from the house totally destroyed, by
the small square building in front, called a
fort. I cannot conceive how gentlemen should

* Beaumaris Bay, p. 11.

suffer themselves to be so much misled, as to permit their agents to construct these, singularly called, *ornamental buildings.* The present is a white, church-like castle, an apparent excrescence evidently useless, and glaringly unnatural. Lord Uxbridge has one of these white *ornamental* structures on the side of the Menai, opposite to Plâs Newydd: but superior to all that I have ever seen of this description, is that of Mr. Thomas of Coed Halen, which provokingly obtrudes itself into almost every good view of the fine old walls and castle of Caernarvon. If the formation of any of these buildings is to be defended, as I know that of some of them is, on the score of their being land-marks to the mariner, my objection must cease; utility must ever be considered to supersede elegance. But this is not often the case; lord Uxbridge's building is far distant from the sea, and other eminences near Caernarvon might have been adopted besides the present, standing, as it does, almost close to the castle. A friend of mine remarked, to some observations I had made on this subject, that, in a tour through South Wales, he had almost invariably observed, that the only rage for spoiling the scenes by these monstrosities, was where the surrounding country was more than usually beautiful. Near old castles, or monastic remains, he had generally been provoked with a deformed castellated pleasure-house, or a lately erected ruin, and invariably in the very place from whence of all others it should have been kept away. The ideas of these gentlemen must be nearly on a par with those of Mr. Pocklington, which stimulated him to

Q 2

improve one of his views by white-washing an oak tree.

About a mile from Beaumaris, near the seat of sir Robert Williams, bart. and not far from the shore, are yet to be seen, in the walls of a barn, the poor remains of the house of Franciscan friars, founded in the thirteenth century, by Llewelyn ap Iorwerth, prince of Wales, called

LLANVAES,

Or *The Friars*. It is at present principally known as having been the place of interment of Joan, the wife of Llewelyn, and natural daughter of King John. The stone coffin of this princess, though now removed, served, not long ago, as a watering trough for horses. In this church there were also interred, at different times, a son of one of the kings of Denmark, lord Clifford, and many barons and knights who were slain in the Welsh wars.

The church, and some other parts of the buildings, were destroyed soon after the death of Llewelyn, in an insurrection of the Welsh against the English forces; and Henry IV. again nearly destroyed it, on account of the friars having espoused the cause of Owen Glyndwr. His son, Henry V., re-established it, and added a provision for eight friars, of which, however, only two were to be Welshmen. At the dissolution the convent and its possessions were sold: they are at present the property of lord Bulkeley.

PENMON.

Two miles north of Friars is the priory of
Penmon, at present consisting of little more than
the ruinous refectory, and part of the church.
This was a house of Benedictine monks, dedicated to St. Mary, and endowed, if not founded,
by Llewelyn ap Iorwerth, before the year 1221.
In the twenty-sixth of Henry VIII., the revenues were valued at about forty-eight pounds
per annum.

The island of Anglesea is celebrated for some
of its rare marine productions, and particularly
for the variety of its shells and crabs. The
places from whence the latter are principally to
be obtained are the rocky coasts about Llanddwyn, Roscolin, Holyhead, and Penmon; and
the best times for discovering them are at low
water, during the spring tides, which sometimes
rise and fall near twenty feet. The mode is to
turn up the stones, near low-water mark, under
which they will be found to lurk, hidden among
the sea-weed. The shells are principally taken
in the dredges of the oyster-catchers betwixt
Beaumaris and the island of Priestholme, and
in Red Wharf bay.

CHAP. XVIII.

VOYAGE FROM CAERNARVON TO PRIEST-HOLME.

The Straits of Menai.—Charming Sail.—Swelly Rocks.—Llandysilio Church, on a small Island in the Menai —Fine View.—Priestholme.—Tradition respecting this Island — Extraordinary Flight of Sea-Fowl.—Puffins.—Account of the Manners and Economy of these Birds.

ONE day, during my residence at Caernarvon, I took the cutter belonging to the hotel, a beautiful little decked vessel, with accommodations for ten or twelve persons, and sailed to the island of Priestholme, off the Anglesea coast, about five miles beyond Beaumaris.

THE MENAI,

As a river, is a remarkably fine piece of water, seldom less than half a mile, and in several places near two miles in width; and, to those persons who are fond of excursions on the water, the sail from Caernarvon to Beaumaris on a fine day, with a brisk wind, will be found extremely pleasant. At different times of the day the scenery will be found very different; and a cloudy and dense, or a transparent and rare atmosphere, render a material change to the appearance of the various scenes that occur in sailing along this charming water; so that how often soever excursions are made, some new appearance will always occur. The shores, in a few places, are bold and steep; in others, the ascent is gentle and unvaried: sometimes they are barren and rocky, and sometimes adorned with woods and cultivated grounds. The dark wooded banks of the island of Anglesea, sloping gently to the water's edge, afford, in many points of view, an elegant contrast (with the translucent waves between,) to the more rude shores of Caernarvonshire. In a brisk side gale, tacking across the stream affords many beautiful views which are lost when sailing before the wind; and when many vessels are on the water at the same time, it is a pleasing sight to observe them passing along in different directions, and crossing each other in the different tacks.

We had proceeded about five miles, when we passed the front of Plâs Newydd, the seat of the earl of Uxbridge; soon after which the channel straightened very considerably, and the distance was terminated on one side by an almost perpendicular coast, and on the other by a sloping and wooded ascent. Not far from hence are the well known rocks, called, from the numerous currents that set in different directions around them,

THE SWELLY ROCKS.

At low water many of these are to be seen, which, at other times, are hidden by the flood;

and the channel betwixt those that are always
exposed is very narrow and dangerous. When
the lower rocks are covered with water, from
the tide running with great rapidity among
them, many circling eddies are formed, the
vortexes of which the mariners sometimes find
it difficult to avoid.

LLANDYSILIO CHURCH.

At a little distance beyond the Swellies we
passed two low rocks, with a flat between them,
forming at high water an island called *Bên
Glas.* This island, though it affords only a few
acres of ground for the grazing of sheep, has upon
it the small church of Llandysilio. On the
Anglesea side there is a causeway to the island,
but passable only at low water. What should
induce the foundation of a church in so singular
and precarious a situation, where the service can
only be performed when the tide serves, I am
not able even to conjecture.

A little beyond Bangor Ferry a fine expansive view opened upon us. Penmaen Mawr
here forms, in the distance, a bold extremity to
the ridge of mountains which extends into the
interior of Caernarvonshire. Beyond this are
seen Penmaen Bach, the little Ormes Head, and
the great Ormes Head, all presenting their steep
sides towards the sea. The town of Beaumaris,
appearing just above the level of the sea, on a
promontory that forms from hence an extreme
point of Anglesea, is observed on the other side
of the water. Under the mountains of Caernarvonshire, and sheltered by them nearly on

all sides, we observed the town of Bangor; and, a little beyond it, Port Penrhyn, with its numerous vessels. A gale of wind soon drove us past the town of Beaumaris, whose castle appeared, from the water, a large and strong building: these received additional beauty from the high woods of Baron Hill rising behind them.

A tolerably fair wind soon brought us under the rocks of the south side of

PRIESTHOLME.

This island is nearly three quarters of a mile distant from the Anglesea shore; and is about a mile in length, and half a mile across. On all sides, except that towards Anglesea, it presents steep and inaccessible rocks, inhabited only by various species of sea-fowl. Its interior affords feed for a few sheep. Near the middle of the island there is an old square tower, supposed to have once been an appurtenant to the monastery of Penmon. There is a considerable quantity of rubbish and stones around it, the remains of other buildings. The island is at present uninhabited by man. I was much surprized, in wandering about it, to find an upright stone, with the following inscription :—

> Bar⁵. Stout
> belonging to the
> Sally died in
> the small pox
> Novr. yᵉ 3d. 1767.
> N. B. The ship was cast
> away here.

It is called by the Welsh Ynys Seiriol, *Seiriol's*

island*. This people have a tradition respecting Priestholme, that when what are now the Lavan sands formed a habitable part of Caernarvonshire, their ancestors had a communication from hence across the channel, by means of a bridge; and they yet pretend to shew the remains of an ancient causeway, which they say was made from this place to the foot of Penman bach near Conwy, for the convenience of the devotees who made pilgrimages to the island.— It is at present the property of lord Bulkeley, and is rented of him as a rabbit and puffin warren.

When we had arrived under the rock, and had cast anchor, we fired a swivel gun, to try the effect of the report round the island, when such a scream of puffins, gulls, and other sea birds, was heard, as beyond all conception astonished me. The immense multitudes that in a moment rose into the air, were unparalleled by any thing I had before seen. They flew in a thousand different directions, uttering as many harsh and discordant screams: some darted into the water, some scudded about on its surface, others were seen dipping into the deep, others rising out, and others again came flapping almost close to our heads: in short, the air, the sea, and the rocks seemed alive with their numbers.—We landed, and I clambered up the rocks, and walked alone to the other side

---

* Seiriol was the son of Owen Danwyn, the son of Eineon Urdd, who chose this as a place of retreat from the world. He is believed to have built a chapel here, about the year 630, and some have supposed the present tower to be the remains of that foundation : This, however, cannot have been the case, as it is comparatively a modern erection.

of the island, when I had a sight that even surpassed the former. Upwards of fifty acres of land were literally covered with *Puffins**. I speak much within compass, when I declare that the number here must have been upwards of 50,000. I walked gently towards them, and found them either so tame or so stupid, as to suffer me to approach near enough to have knocked one or two of them down with a stick. In their habits and manners, these birds remind one very much of the Penguins of the tropical climates. Their legs are placed so far back, that they walk with their heads nearly upright. —Puffins are birds of passage; they arrive in the beginning of April, and remain until about the eleventh of August. On their arrival they immediately take possession of the burrows in the crevices of the rocks, or on the sloping ground of the island; and those that come last, if they find all the holes occupied, form for themselves new ones. They have nearly expelled the rabbits by seizing on their burrows. They put together usually a few sticks and grass, and on this the female lays a single white egg, which is generally hatched in the beginning of July. The males and females are said to sit alternately, relieving each other at intervals for the purpose of procuring food. Both during incubation and while attending on their young, they may without much difficulty be seized in their holes; but it is necessary to be somewhat careful in trusting the naked hand near their beaks, for they have the power of inflicting a most severe bite. With a glove on I amused myself by taking out several of them, in order to observe the truth of Mr.

* *Alca arctica* of Linnæus.

Pennant's assertion, that from their extreme affection for their young, when " laid hold of " by the wings, they will give themselves the " most cruel bites on any part of their body " that they can reach, as if actuated by des- " pair; and when released, instead of flying " away, they will often hurry again into their " burrows." They bit *me* with great violence, but none of them seized any parts of their own body: a few of them, on being released, ran into the burrows, but not always into those from whence I had taken them. If it was more easy for them to escape into a hole, than to raise themselves into the air, they did so; but if not, they ran down the slope and flew away. The noise they make, when along with their young, is a singular kind of humming, much resembling that produced by the large wheels used for spinning worsted. When I first went amongst their burrows, I heard this noise on every side of me, and could not conceive from whence it proceeded, till the sound of my footsteps frightened many of the birds out of their holes, and it was immediately explained. On being seized, they emitted the noise with greater violence, and from its being interrupted, by their struggling to escape, it sounded not much unlike the efforts of a dumb man to speak.— The young ones are entirely covered with a long blackish down, and in shape are altogether so different from the parent birds, that no one could, at first sight, suppose them the same species. Puffins do not breed, till they are three years old; and they are said to change their bills annually.—Their usual food is sprats and sea-weeds, which render the flesh of the old birdse xcessively rank. The young ones, however, are pickled for sale by the renters of the island, and form an article of traffic peculiar to this neighbourhood. The oil is extracted from them by a peculiar process, and the bones are taken out, after which the skin is closed round the flesh, and they are immersed in vinegar impregnated with spices.

CHAP. XIX.

THE distance from Caernarvon to Beddgelert,
the grave of Gélert, is about twelve miles, and
the road is in general very excellent; being the

great road from Caernarvonshire into South
Wales.

GLANGWNA,

About two miles from Caernarvon, I passed,
on the left, Glangwna, one of the most charming retreats in the principality. The house is
small, but surrounded with wood, and so completely sequestered, as scarcely to be seen from
the road. The grounds are not extensive, but
they have an elegant wildness; and the walks
through the woods and along the banks of the
river Seiont, whose stream dashes in foam
among the rocks of its bed, are scarcely exceeded by any on a small scale, that I have yet
seen. This beautiful place is the property of
Thomas Lloyd, Esq. of Shrewsbury.

From an eminence in the road, about four
miles from Caernarvon, I was presented in front
with a view extremely fine, along Nant Gwyrfai,
the Vale of Freshwater. A range of sloping
rocks formed the middle distance. The dark
and towering rock of Mynyd Mawr, was seen
to rise from behind, on the right of the vale;
and, on the opposite side, this was well contrasted by the smooth and verdant mountain
Moel Aelir. The vale appeared closed at some
distance, by part of the side of the lofty Arran.
Just at this station, there are several rude, but
extremely picturesque cottages, some of which
were half obscured by trees. The road is at
first hidden, but it is seen at a little distance in
front, sloping down into the vale: the latter

was intersected by moss-grown walls, and rude hedge-rows.

I left the road for the purpose of ascending the summit of the hemispherical mountain, called

MOEL AELIR,

The frosty hill. This I did without much difficulty, and found the prospect from the top to far surpass my expectations. The Rival mountains appeared quite near, and beyond them the whole remaining extent of the promontory of Llyn, as far as Aberdaron, was visible. Part of Cwellyn Pool (by the road leading to Beddgelert) was seen just below, from the edge of which the immense Mynydd Mawr reared his black and rugged sides. Beyond this was one of the Nantlle Pools, and near the latter, the small pool of Llyn Cwm Ffynnon. Extending from hence southwards, was a long range of mountain summits, and hollows, some verdant, and others totally destitute of vegetation, but the shades and colours of the whole were strikingly grand and beautiful. At some distance part of the yellow sands of Traeth Mawr, were seen beyond the rocks. The distant mountains of Merionethshire, closed the scene in this direction. On the south-east side of my station, I observed a dreary vale, with nearly perpendicular boundaries, called Cwm Dwythwch, *the hollow of the rapid burrowing river*, containing a small pool, in which the finest and best flavoured of all the Caernarvonshire trout are said to be caught. Beyond this, Snowdon is easily distinguished from his fellow-mountains, by his size and appearance. Part of the vale and lakes of Llanberis, with the castle of Dolbadarn, were visible, in a somewhat different direction. When I was here, Snowdon was covered with a dense black cloud, that seemed to rest on its sides and summit, and gave to it the terrible aspect of a volcano. Dusky intervening clouds passed on with considerable velocity, which rendered the scene as wild as imagination could paint. Heavy showers were pouring into some of the adjacent vales; and light vapours scudded with the wind along the hollows on all sides. Snowdon, and the immediately adjacent mountains, alone remained black and terrific. The intervening rocks received a yellow tinge from the refraction of the light of the sun through the mist; and various other tints and shades were thrown on the vallies and mountains' sides, by different refractions of the light through the more or less dense mediums.

I descended from this mountain, to the road not far from the romantic little village of *Bettws*, or, as it is sometimes called, for the sake of distinction, Bettws Garmon. Its church is dedicated to St. Germanus, who led on the Britons to the famous " *Alleluia*" victory obtained over the Saxons, at Maes Garmon, near Mold.

NANT MILL.

About half a mile beyond Bettws, are a beautiful little cascade and bridge, at a place called

R

Nant Mill. This waterfall would appear to much greater advantage, in almost any other situation than the present; for here the black and majestic mountain of Mynydd Mawr, on the right, and the more smooth and regular, though still lofty Moel Aelir, on the left of the vale, attract to themselves so much of the traveller's attention, that the little waterfall appears diminutive, amidst such surrounding grandeur.

Beyond the mill, Snowdon is seen on the left, rearing his pointed summit into the sky. His red and precipitous cliffs, and huge bulk, compared with the adjoining mountains, render him easily distinguishable from all the rest.

LLYN CWELLYN.

On the right of the road, this pool extends itself for about a mile and a half. During the winter season, the *Red char**, a species of fish, which is confined principally to Winander Mere, and Coniston water, two lakes in the north of England, were formerly caught here in considerable quantities. These fish are called by the Welsh Torgoch, or *Red belly*, and are in season only during the winter.

On the farther edge of the lake, just under, and forming part of the mountain of Mynydd Mawr, is

CASTELL CIDWM.

Cidwm's fort. This is a high and steep rock, on the summit of which, we are informed, there

---

* *Salmo alpinus* of Linnæus.

was once a fortification, one of the guards to the interior of the mountains. This is said to have been founded by the Britons, some time prior to the sixth century. Whether there are any remains of the fort now existing, I am not able to say: the difficulty of the ascent, and the small importance of the object, deterred me from attempting to examine it.—The Welsh people have a tradition respecting this rock, that its summit was formerly inhabited by a giant, or a warrior, called *Cidwm*. As Constantine, the son of Helen, was marching in the rear of an army, towards Merionethshire, he was distinguished from his soldiers, by the watchful Cidwm, who was on his station; and though the distance is many times as great, as our modern, degenerated bows, would twang their arrows, yet he aimed one, that, with instant celerity, proved fatal. The news of his death was soon carried, along the ranks, to his mother, who was in the van of the army, about ten miles distant. He was interred in the meadow at the lower end of the lake, in a place now called Bedd y mab, *the grave of the son*. On enquiring into the particulars of this unaccountable story, I could neither learn who this Cidwm was, (beyond what I have stated,) nor what the Welsh believe to have been the cause of his enmity to Constantine: in short, it is one of those traditionary legends, that defy all attempts at investigation.

LLYN Y DYWARCHEN.

Higher up, amongst the mountains on the right, I visited a small pool, about the size of a good horse-pond, called Llyn y Dywarchen, *The Pool of the Sod*, first celebrated by Giraldus Cambrensis in the account of his journey through Wales, in the twelfth century, as containing a floating island. This is yet in existence, but is not more than eight or nine yards in length; and evidently appears to have been a detached piece of the peat of which the bank is composed. There is a small willow tree growing upon it; and it is carried to and fro by the action of the wind and water. Sometimes it remains near the side of the pool for a considerable while; and it is so large and firm as to bear cattle upon it. When it has been disloged by the wind, a sheep or two have often been borne by it to the other parts of the bank.

I passed Llyn Cadair, *The Pool of the Chair, or Eminence*, and, shortly afterwards, crossing a bridge, descended through Nant Colwyn, *The Vale of Colwyn,* to

BEDDGELERT,

A village completely embosomed in mountains, whose rude sides form a fine contrast with the meadows of the vale below. Moel Hebog, *The Hill of Flight,* rises to a point just in front of the village. In a deep hollow high up the side of this mountain, there is a cave in which Owen Glyndwr, on one of his expeditions to harass the English forces, sought, for some time, a shelter from his enemies.—The houses of the village are few and irregular, but the church is one of the neatest of those among the wilds of Caernarvonshire. In the church-yard, among many Welsh inscriptions on the grave-stones, I was surprized by one in English:

> Thousand fates on death attends,
> Which *brings* poor mortals to their ends.

Llewelyn the Great, prince of Wales, is said to have had a hunting seat at this place. Among many others, he possessed one greyhound, a present from his father in law, King John, so noted for excellence in hunting, that his fame was transmitted to posterity in four Welsh lines, which have been thus translated:

> The remains of famed Gêlert, so faithful and good,
> The bounds of the cantred conceal,
> Whenever the doe or the stag he pursued,
> His master was sure of a meal.

During the absence of the family, tradition says, a wolf entered the house; and Llewelyn, who first returned, was met at the door by his favourite dog, which came out, covered with blood, to salute his master on his arrival. The prince, alarmed, ran into the nursery, and found his child's cradle overturned, and the ground flowing with blood. In this moment of his terror, imagining that the dog had slain his child, he plunged his sword into the animal's body, and laid him dead upon the spot. But, on turning up the cradle he found his boy alive, and sleeping by the side of the dead wolf. This circumstance had such an effect on the mind of the prince, that he erected a tomb over the faithful dog's grave; on the spot where afterwards the parish-church was built, called, from this incident, Bedd Gêlert, or *The Grave of Gêlert*. From this story was derived a very common Welsh proverb; " I repent as much as the man who slew his greyhound."

The following beautiful stanzas, which the author, the honourable W. R. Spencer, has obligingly allowed me to insert here, are founded on the above tradition. They were written at Dolmelynllyn, the seat of W. A. Madocks, Esq. after a perusal of the story as related in my *Tour round North Wales:*

> The spearmen heard the bugle sound,
>   And cheerly smil'd the morn,
> And many a *brach*, and many a hound,
>   Obey'd Llewelyn's horn.
>
> And still he blew a louder blast,
>   And gave a lustier cheer,
> " Come, Gêlert, come; wer't never last,
>   " Llewelyn's horn to hear.
>
> " Oh ! where does faithful Gêlert roam,
>   " The flower of all his race,
> " So true, so brave, a lamb at home,
>   " A lion in the chace ?"
>
> 'Twas only at Llewelyn's board
>   The faithful Gêlert fed ;
> He watch'd, he serv'd, he cheer'd his lord,
>   And sentinell'd his bed.
>
> In sooth he was a peerless hound,
>   The gift of royal John :
> But now no Gêlert could be found,
>   And all the chace rode on.
>
> And now as o'er the rocks and dells
>   The gallant chidings rise,
> All Snowdon's craggy chaos yells
>   The many mingled cries !
>
> That day Llewelyn little lov'd
>   The chace of hart or hare,
> And scant and small the booty prov'd,
>   For Gêlert was not there.

Unpleas'd Llewelyn homeward hied,
  When, near the portal seat,
His truant Gêlert he espied,
  Bounding his lord to greet.

But when he gain'd his castle door
  Aghast the chieftain stood,
The hound all o'er was smear'd with gore,
  His lips, his fangs ran blood.

Llewelyn gaz'd with fierce surprize,
  Unus'd such looks to meet,
His fav'rite check'd his joyful guise,
  And crouch'd, and lick'd his feet.

Onward in haste Llewelyn past,
  And on went Gêlert too,
And still where e'er his eyes he cast,
  Fresh blood gouts shock'd his view.

O'erturn'd his infant's bed he found,
  With blood stain'd covert rent,
And all around, the walls and ground
  With recent blood besprent.

He call'd his child, no voice replied,
  He search'd with terror wild,
Blood, blood he found on every side,
  But no where found his child.

" Hell-hound! my child by thee's devour'd,"
  The frantic father cried,
And to the hilt his vengeful sword
  He plung'd in Gêlert s side.

His suppliant looks, as prone he fell,
  No pity could impart,
But still his Gêlert's dying yell
  Pass'd heavy o'er his heart.

Arous'd by Gêlert's dying yell
  Some slumb'rer waken'd nigh :—
What words the parent's joy could tell,
  To hear his infant's cry !

Conceal'd beneath a mangled heap
  His hurried search had miss'd,
All glowing from his rosy sleep
  The cherub boy he kiss'd.

Nor scath had he, nor harm, nor dread,
  But the same couch beneath
Lay a gaunt wolf all torn and dead,
  Tremendous still in death.

Ah! what was then Llewelyn's pain!
  For now the truth was clear,
His gallant hound the wolf had slain
  To save Llewelyn's heir.

Vain, vain was all Llewelyn's woe,
  " Best of thy kind, adieu!
" The frantic blow whicn laid thee low,
  " This heart shall ever rue."

And now a gallant tomb they raise,
  With costly sculpture deck t,
And marbles storied with his praise
  Poor Gêlert's bones protect.

There never could the spearman pass,
  Or forester, unmov'd;
There oft the tear-besprinkled grass
  Llewelyn's sorrow prov'd.

And there he hung his horn and spear,
  And there as evening fell,
In fancy's piercing sounds would hear
  Poor Gêlert's dying yell.

And till great Snowdon's rocks grow old,
  And cease the storm to brave,
The consecrated spot shall hold
  The name of " Gêlert's Grave."

PRIORY.

On this spot there was formerly a priory of
Augustine monks, of a foundation so ancient,

that Anian, bishop of Bangor, who lived in the thirteenth century, asserts it to have been the oldest religious house in Wales, except one. Part of the south walls of the present church were evidently formed from the old building. In the year 1283, this priory was so much injured by fire, that, in order to encourage benefactors to contribute towards the rebuilding of it, the bishop gave notice that he would remit to all such persons (who sincerely repented of their sins), forty days of any penance inflicted on them.*

The *inn*, or rather public house, that I found at Beddgelert in both my journies, was one of the worst and most uncomfortable houses, in which necessity ever compelled me to take up my abode. In my first journey I found only one bed in the place that was not wretchedly bad. The room in which I slept for three nights (for the other two bed-rooms were occupied), was at the back of the house, and partly over the kitchen. The floor, the ceiling, and the boarded partition, were all so full of large holes, as to seem only an apology for separation from the rest of the house. I was so intolerably pestered by myriads of fleas, bred and harboured among the filth accumulated in every part, that had I not every night been fairly wearied out with my rambles during the day, it would have been altogether impossible for me to have taken any rest. After I had been here one night, I

---

* The name of this priory was " Abbey de Valle, S. Mariæ Snowdonia." — Its revenues, at the dissolution, amounted to about 70l. per annum.

complained to the servant of the inexcusable negligence that had suffered these animals to become so numerous, as now to defy all attempts at their destruction : " Lord, sir, (said she,) if we were to kill one of them, ten would come to its burying."—Nothing, in this state of the house, could possibly have induced a traveller to remain here through the night, but the exquisite scenery around the place. In my second journey I found several very material improvements, in consequence of Mr. Jones of Bryntirion having begun to build a comfortable house for the reception of travellers, on the other side of the river, at a few hundred yards distance. This now affords excellent accommodations. It is called the *Beddgelert Hotel.* The sign over the door is of a goat clambering among the mountains of Snowdon, and, underneath it, is the motto " *Patria mea petra.*"

PONT ABERGLASLLYN.

Beddgelert is the place to which travellers usually resort who wish to see Pont Aberglàsllyn, *The Bridge at the Conflux of the Blue Pool,* or, as it is usually called, *The Devil's Bridge.* It is about a mile and half distant, but, as all travellers must cross it in their journey to Tan y Bwlch, many content themselves with merely resting a little while in their progress.

About a mile beyond Beddgelert, the rocks on each side become incomparably grand. The road winds along a narrow stony vale, where the huge cliffs so nearly approach, as only just to leave width sufficient at the bottom for the road, and the bed of the impetuous torrent that rolls along the side of it. Here these lofty rocks, which oppose nothing to the eye but a series of the rudest precipices, " raised tier on tier, high piled from earth to heaven," seem to forbid all further access, and to frown defiance on the traveller:

Fled are the fairy views of hill and dale,
Sublimely thron'd on the steep mountain brow
Stern nature frowns: her desolating rage
Driving the whirlwind, or swoln flood or blast
Of fiery air imprison'd, from their base
Has wildly hurled the uplifted rocks around
The gloomy pass, where Aberglasllyn's arch
Yawns o'er the torrent. The disjointed crags
O'er the steep precipice in fragments vast
Impending, to the astonish'd mind recal
The fabled horrors by demoniac force
Of Lapland wizards wrought; who borne upon
The whirlwind's wing, what time the vext sea
Dash'd against Norwegia's cliffs, to solid mass
Turn'd the swoln billows, and the o'erhanging waves
Fix'd e'er they fell.

It was, probably, from this very scene, that Giraldus Cambrensis asserted of Merionethshire, that it was " the roughest and most dreary part of Wales, for its mountains were both high and perpendicular, and in many places so grouped together, that shepherds talking or quarrelling on their tops, could scarcely, in a whole day's journey, come together."*

In the bridge itself my expectations were, I must confess, considerably disappointed. I had somewhere read of an arch thrown across a narrow stream, one end resting on a perpendi-

* Itin. Cam. lib. ii. c. 5.

cular rock in Caernarvonshire, and the other on another in Merionethshire. Perhaps also in some measure confounding it, with what I had heard of the Devil's Bridge, near Hafod, in Cardiganshire, I had formed an idea that I should see an arch thrown across a deep narrow valley, and hanging, as it were, in mid air: but how disappointed to find it a bridge very little out of the usual form! The grandeur of all the surrounding scenery rendered it, indeed, an insignificant object; but even this does not prevent it from forming a beautiful addition to the mountain view.—Many of the ignorant people of the neighbourhood believe that this structure was formed by supernatural agency. They attribute it to the devil, who, they say, proposed to the neighbouring inhabitants, that he would build them a bridge across the pass, on condition that he should have the first who went over it for his trouble. The bargain was made, and very soon afterwards the bridge appeared in its place. But the people were too cunning to adhere to any other than the literal terms of so unequal a bargain; and they cheated the devil by dragging a dog to the spot, and whipping him over the bridge. This, say those who tell the story, was all the recompence this universal agent, in difficult undertakings, was able to obtain for his labour. Hence they account for this structure having the name of the " Devil's Bridge."

A few yards above the bridge, the river flows down a range of rocks, eight or ten feet from the surface of the lower water. This cataract is chiefly noted as a salmon leap. Salmon come up the fresh water streams to deposit their spawn on the sandy shallows, and, when impeded in their progress by rocks or dams across the water, they have the power of springing to an amazing height above the surface, in order to pass over them. This place being only a very few miles from the sea, is frequented by great numbers. In the course of an hour, I have seen twenty or thirty of them attempt to overcome this barrier; but, on account of a piece of netting which the renters of the fishery place there for the purpose of preventing them, they do not often succeed. Their extraordinary power of leaping out of the water is owing to a sudden jerk which the fish give to their body, from a bent into a straight position. At this place, when the fish are fatigued, from their vain attempts to gain the upper stream, they retire to the still waters below, where they are either taken in nets, or are killed with harpoons. In the latter mode the men are always so sure in their aim, that I have seen five or six fine fish killed by one person in the course of an hour. The general weight of the salmon caught near Pont Aberglàsllyn in August and September, is from one to eighteen pounds. About the month of October they become much larger.—This fishery, I was informed, is the property of Mr. Wynne, who lets it to the fishermen at the rent of twelve pounds a year. The fish, when sold on the spot, are generally thought worth three-pence or four-pence a pound.

I wandered several times from the bridge to the adjacent arm of the sea called Traeth Mawr, *The Great Sands,* and was often amused by the few goats kept in this vale, chasing each other,

in playful gambols, among the most dangerous
steeps of the rocks. I seldom saw more than
from twenty to forty at a time. The goats in
this country are all now private property, none
of them, as formerly, running entirely wild:
they all return regularly to their folds in the
evenings. The varied scene beyond the bridge
of wood, rock, and vale, is extremely fine.
From several stations

> The mountains huge appear
> Emergent, and their broad bare backs upheave
> Into the clouds; their tops ascend the sky;

And their rugged files seem here to close, and
oppose an invincible barrier into the interior of
the country.

Sir John Wynne of Gwydir conceived the
vast design of recovering for cultivation the two
arms of the sea, Traeth Mawr, and Traeth Bach,
by embanking out the water. For this purpose,
in the year 1625, he applied for assistance to sir
Hugh Middleton, who, in the Isle of Wight had,
not long before, gained upwards of two thousand acres of land from the sea. The affair,
however, probably from want of money to execute
it properly, was never carried into execution.
This object has, however, been in a great measure
attained by W. A. Madocks, esq. who, within
the last fourteen years, recovered above 1500
acres by embanking out the sea. The name of
the place is *Glandwr*, and the whole length of
the land recovered is about two miles.

MOONLIGHT SCENE AT PONT ABERGLASSLYN.

During the time I was at Beddgelert, I found myself one evening in want of employment; and as the moon shone beautifully bright, I was tempted to wander alone as far as the bridge. There never was a more charming evening. The scene was not clad in its late grand colours, but was now more delicately shaded, and arrayed in softer charms. The darkening shadows of the rocks cast a gloom around, and the faint rays, in some places faintly reflected, gave to the straining eye a very imperfect glimpse of the surfaces it looked upon; whilst, in others, the moon shot her silver light through the hollows, and brightly illumined the opposite rocks. The silence of the evening was only interrupted by the murmuring of the brook, and now and then by the shrill scream of the night-owl, flitting by me in search of food.

> The river rushing o'er its pebbled bed
> Imposed silence, with a stilly sound.

The bridge was deserted, and I hung over its rude battlements, listening to the hoarse fall of the water down the weir, and watching, as the moon ascended higher, the decreasing shadows of the mountains. The solitude gave rise to reflection, and I indulged almost too long; for, when I arrived at the inn, I found I had been absent near two hours, and from the countenance of the inn-keeper on my appearance, I suspect the family had believed that I should not again return.

EXCURSION INTO NANT HWYNAN.

I had not been long at Beddgelert before I strolled through this vale, called also sometimes Nant Gwynant, *The Vale of Waters*; and I found it more beautiful than any other amongst these mountains. It is about six miles long, and affords, in its whole length, such a variety of scenery, of wood, lakes, and meadows, bounded on each side by lofty mountains, that one can scarcely conceive it to be excelled. The vale of Llanberis is the only one that seemed to me to rival it; but the character of the two are so essentially different, and the beauty of each is so exclusively its own, that they cannot be put into comparison.

DINAS EMRYS.

On the left of the path, about three quarters of a mile up the vale, the guide pointed out to me a round high rock, with many trees growing from the clefts and shelves of its sides, called Dinas Emrys, *The Fort of Emrys, or Ambrosius,* where

> Prophetic Merlin sate, when to the British king
> The changes long to come auspiciously he told.

It was to this place that Vortigern retired to hide his shame, and provide for his security, when he found himself under the general odium of his subjects, and unable any longer to contend with the treacherous Saxons whom he had introduced into his kingdom. It is probable, that upon this insular rock he erected a temporary residence of timber (for the country at that time abounded with wood,) that lasted him till he went to his final retreat in Nant Gwrtheyrn, or *Vortigern's Valley*, not far from Nefyn, in the promontory of Llyn.*—Many of the ancient British and monkish writers assert, that, on his coming to Dinas Emrys, he attempted to erect a place of defence, but that, what was built in the day time always disappeared during the night. He therefore consulted his magicians, for such all the men of learning in those dark ages were esteemed, as to the manner in which he ought to act in this dreadful predicament. " They advise (says the author of the notes on Drayton), that he must find out a child which " had no father, and with his blood sprinkle the " stones and mortar, and then the castle would " stand as on a firm foundation." They no doubt considered this to be a tolerably secure mode of solving the difficulty ; but for once, as the story goes, they were disappointed ! Emissaries were sent in all directions through the kingdom, and one of these, as he was going along the streets of the town, since called Caermarthen, over-heard some boys quarreling at play, one of whom reproached his adversary with the epithet of " unbegotten knave." This was the very boy that he wanted : he ran up to them, took him from among the rest, and having found out his mother, brought them both to the king. The boy, whose name is Merlin, it is said, was or-

* Vortigern was king of Britain from the year 449, to 466.

S

dered to be sacrificed, but he obtained his liberty
by confounding all the magicians with his questions, and himself explaining the cause of the
failure of the work. " He being hither brought
" to the king (continues the above writer,)
" slighted that pretended skill of his magicians,
" as palliated ignorance; and with confidence
" of a more knowing spirit, undertakes to shew
" the *true cause* of that amazing ruin of the
" stone work. He tells them that in the earth
" there was a great water which could endure
" the continuance of no heavy superstructure.
" The workmen digged to discover the truth,
" and found it so. He then beseeched the king
" to cause further inquisition to be made, and
" affirmed, that in the bottom of it were two
" sleeping dragons, the one white and the other
" red, which proved so likewise. The white
" dragon he interpreted for the Saxons whom
" the king had brought over, and the red one
" for the oppressed Britons; and upon this
" event in Dinas Emrys, he began those pro-
" phecies to Vortigern, which are to this day
" common in the British storie."*

The only probable part of this story is, that
Myrddin Emrys, for so he is called by the Welsh
writers, may have been employed by Vortigern
to search out for him a secure retreat from the
just vengeance of his injured subjects; and that
being a skilful architect and mechanic, he su-

* Selden's notes on Drayton's Polyolbion. Matthew of
Westminster has given us a long account of the latter part
of Vortigern's life, and a full detail of all Merlin's pro-
phecies. p. 161—170.

perintended the building of a fortress in this place.*

A little farther in the vale is a pool, in a very charming situation, called

LLYN Y DINAS,

The Pool of the Fort, taking its name from its neighbouring rock of Dinas Emrys. It abounds in large and well-flavoured trout.—Two miles beyond this is *Cwm Llan*, a romantic hollow, extending into the mountains on the left towards Snowdon, the summit of which is visible from hence. The scene from this station is remarkably fine; there are here many trees about the foreground, and others are distributed among the rising steeps, exhibiting the rocks in various places, and thus elegantly varying the otherwise dull uniformity of the sides of the mountains.— Having passed the entrance into Cwm Llan, I soon afterwards came to another small pool, not even so large as that I had left, called *Llyn Gwynant.*

* There was another Merlin, frequently mistaken for this, a native of Caledonia, called *Myrddin ap Morvryn* and Myrddin Wyllt, who, in the year 542, when fighting under the banner of king Arthur, accidentally slew his own nephew. In consequence of this accident, he was seized with a madness which affected him every alternate hour during the rest of his life. He retired into Scotland, and in his lucid intervals composed some of the most beautiful pieces of poetry extant. This Merlin afterwards resided in North Wales, where he died: he was buried in the isle of Bardsey.

s 2

IMMENSE STONE.

Near the end of the vale, I observed two enormous masses of rock, that had once, no doubt, been loosened from some of the high precipices above by rain or frost, and had tumbled from thence into their present insulated situations. One of them was much larger than the celebrated *Bowdar stone* in Borrowdale, near Derwent water. On one side it has the appearance of the gavel end of a house. It projects so far over its base, that an immense number both of men and horses might take shelter under it.

WATERFALL.

I ascended the rocks on the left of the vale, to a considerable height, to see the cataract Rhaiadr Cwm Dyli, *The Waterfall of the Vale of Dyli.* There are two distinct falls one above the other. The rivulet that runs from the alpine pool, Llyn Llwydaw, in the mountains above, here breaks in foam and spray down the rugged fronts of the rocks. At the time I was here there had been a succession of dry weather for near a month, and the water was of course very inconsiderable in quantity. The rocks, however, had in themselves, sufficient grandeur to compensate for my trouble, and there was still water enough to render the scenes extremely picturesque.

The softened beauties of the vale of Gwynant,

or *Nant Hwynan*, are particularly pleasing to a tourist, who has lately visited the other more rude vales of Caernarvonshire. The present is varied by all the elegant features that meadows, woods, and corn fields can furnish: it contains two beautiful little pools, and it is bounded by high rocks and mountains. In some places the specimens of picturesque scenery were so perfect, that all the order and beauty of colouring, so well described by Mason, were to be traced in them.

> Vivid green,
> Warm brown, and black opake the foreground bears
> Conspicuous.   Sober olive coldly marks
> The second distance.   Thence the third declines
> In softer blue, or lessening still, is lost
> In faintest purple.

EXCURSION FROM BEDDGELERT TO THE SUMMIT OF SNOWDON.

As I had made a determination, soon after I first came into Wales, that I would ascend Snowdon by all the tracts that are usually pointed out to travellers, I, for the last time, undertook the task, along with a party of four others, from Beddgelert.

The distance from Beddgelert to the summit, being reckoned not less than six miles, and a lady being one of our number, it was thought most eligible for her to ride as far as she could without danger, and for the rest to walk he whole way. In this manner, therefore, we set out, commencing our *mountain* journey by turning to the right, from the Caernarvon road, at the distance of about two miles and a half from the village.—We left the horse at a cottage about half way up, from whence taking a bottle of milk to mix with some rum that we had brought along with us, we continued our route over a series of pointed and craggy rocks. Stopping at different times to rest, we enjoyed to the utmost, the prospects that by degrees were opening around us. Caernarvon and the isle of Anglesea, aided by the brightness of the morning, were seen to great advantage; and Llyn Cwellyn below us, shaded by the vast Mynydd Mawr, with Castell Cidwm at its foot, appeared extremely beautiful. In ascending, the mountains, which from below appeared of immense height, began now to seem beneath us; the lakes and vallies were more exposed, and all the little rills and mountain streams, by degrees became visible to us, like silver lines intersecting the hollows around.

Towards the upper part of the mountain, we passed over a tremendous ridge of rock, called Clawdd Coch, *the red ridge.* This narrow pass, not more than ten or twelve feet across, and two or three hundred yards in length was so steep, that the eye reached on each side, down the whole extent of the mountain. And I am persuaded, that in some parts of it, if a person held a large stone in each hand, and let them both fall at once, each might roll above a quarter of a mile, and thus, when they stopped, they might be more than half a mile asunder. The lady who accompanied us, to my great surprise, passed this ridge without the least apparent signs of fear or trepidation.

There is no danger whatever in crossing Clawdd Coch in the day-time, but I must confess, that I should by no means like to venture along this tract in the night, as many do who have never seen it. If the moon shone very bright, we might, it is very true, escape unhurt; but a dark cloud coming suddenly over, would certainly expose us to much danger. Many instances have occurred of persons who, having passed over it in the night, were so terrified at seeing it by day-light the next morning, that they have not dared to return the same way, but have taken a very circuitous route by Bettws. I was informed that one gentleman had been so much alarmed, that he crawled over it back again on his hands and knees.

In the hollow, on the left of the ascent, are four small pools, called *Llyn Coch*, the red pool; *Llyn y Nadroedd*, the adder's pool; *Llyn Glas*, the blue pool; and *Llyn Ffynnon y Gwas*, the servant's pool.

Soon after we had passed Clawdd Coch, we became immersed in light clouds, till we arrived at the summit of the mountain, when a single gleam of sun-shine, which lasted but for a moment, presented us with the majestic scenery on the west of our station. It served, however, only to tantalize our hopes, for a smart gust of wind again obscured us in the clouds. We now sheltered ourselves from the cold, under some of the projecting rocks near the top, and ate our dinners, watching with anxiety the dark shades in the clouds, in hopes that a separation might take place, and that we should be once more delighted with a sight of the grand objects around us. We did not watch in vain, for the clouds by degrees cleared away, and left us at full liberty to admire the numerous beauties in this vast expansive scene. The steep rock of *Clognyn y Garnedd*, whose dreadful precipices are, some of them, above two hundred yards in perpendicular height, and the whole rock, a series of precipices was an object which first struck one of my companions with terror, and he exclaimed, almost involuntarily :

> How fearful
> And dizzy 'tis to cast one's eyes so low !
> The crows and choughs that wing the midway air
> Shew scarce so gross as beetles.

We now stood on a point which commanded the whole dome of the sky. The prospects below, each of which we had before considered. separately as a grand scene, were now only miniature parts in the immense landscape. We had around us such a variety of mountains, vallies, lakes, and streams, each receding behind the other, and bounded only by the far distant horizon, that the eye almost strained itself with looking upon them. These majestic prospects were soon shut from our sight by the gathering clouds, which now began to close in much heavier than they had done before, and it was in vain that we waited near an hour for another opening. We were, therefore, at length obliged to descend, in despair of being any more gratified with these sublime prospects.

We again passed Clawdd Coch, and soon afterwards, turning to the left, descended into

the mountain vale, called *Cwm Llan*, which I
have mentioned in a preceding part of this
chapter. We followed the course of a stream,
which runs from thence into Llyn y Dinas, in
Nant Hwynan. This little rivulet entertained
us much in its descent, being, in many places,
thrown over low rocks, and forming small, but
sometimes elegant, cascades.—After a walk of
two hours, we arrived in Nant Hwynan, the vale
that I had traversed with so much pleasure a
day or two before ; and passing Llyn y Dinas,
and Dinas Emrys, soon afterwards reached
Beddgelert, not a little fatigued with our mountain ramble.

I observed near a cottage in Cwm Llan, that
several children were employed in gathering
the berries of the mountain ash (Sorbus aucu-
paria of Linnæus.) On enquiring of the guide
for what purpose this was done, he informed me
that the Welsh people brew from them a liquor,
which they call *Diod griafol.* This, he said,
was done by merely crushing the berries, and
putting water to them, which, after remaining a
fortnight, is drawn off for use   The flavour, as
I understood him, was somewhat like that of
perry.

CHAP. XX.

EXCURSION FROM CAERNARVON TO THE NANTLLE POOLS.

Nant Lle.—Dreary Mountain Pass.—Beautiful Views.— Slate Quarries.

In my visit to the Nantlle Pools, I proceeded along the road from Caernarvon to Beddgelert, till I had passed Llyn Cwellyn, when taking a route westward, between Llyn Cader and Llyn y Dywarchen, I entered a wild mountainous pass, that led me along a series of sheep tracts, into Nant Lle, *the Vale of Lle.* The mountains rose on each side to an immense height, those towards the north forming a long range of precipices, singularly marked by the innumerable gullies of the mountain storms. The whole scene was that of savage wildness, of nature in her most dreary attire. It is a narrow pass, encompassed by mountains, uncultivated, destitute altogether of wood, and unsheltered on all sides from the fury of the tempests.—As I proceeded, the scene by degrees began to extend its limits, and the mountains to attain more varied and elegant forms. At length the two Nantlle Pools, called by the Welsh *Llyniau Nantlle,* and the whole range of the vale, with the gradually declining mountains, became visible nearly to the sea. The prospect was exceedingly beautiful; and the number of trees in different parts, and particularly about the foreground, added greatly to the effect.—On turning round, to look towards the road that I had left, now about two miles distant, I observed that Snowdon closed up the end of the pass, and terminated the view in that direction: its upper parts were, however, so enveloped in clouds, as to render them invisible.—I continued my route along a tolerable good horse path, between hedge rows, among meadows and woodland, on the north side of the pools. The trees were chiefly old oaks, that had withstood the fury of probably a hundred winters; the limbs shattered, covered with moss, and bared of leaves. Several of the small farmers' cottages among these trees, presented, with the other objects around, scenes peculiarly picturesque. By an ancient over-shot mill, between the pools, I remarked a scene that exceeded all the rest. The mountain grandeur of the vale was broken by the wooded foreground; and the water of one of the lakes, from the rays of the sun, which shot obliquely upon it, glittered through the dark foliage of the trees. The mill, and its rude wooden aqueduct and wheel, with an adjacent cottage or two, overgrown with moss and lichens, and shattered in the walls and roofs, were the other component parts of the landscape. This was, however, by no means, the last of the elegancies of the vale; in almost every part of my walk, I had something to admire, some new object presented to me, that afforded sources both of reflection and delight. At some distance beyond the farthest lake, the road, which is here wide enough to admit carriages to the neighbouring slate quarries, led me to some little height above the vale. I again turned round to look along the vale in the direction I had come, and was surprised by a view so elegantly picturesque, that even my fancy had scarcely ever led me to imagine one equal to it. The dense clouds that had enveloped all the higher regions of Snowdon, were in a great measure driven away, and those that I now saw, floated below the pointed summit of the mountain, which was visible above. It bounded the end of the vale, and I never before observed this mountain in so much grandeur. A dusky haziness about it, threw it to appearance very distant, and added greatly to its effect in height. A gleam of sun-shine, passing the valley by Llyn Cwellyn, that crossed by its foot, and softening upwards, formed a fine light in the middle of the scene. The steep black rocks of Mynydd Mawr, on the left, and the craggy summits of the elegant and varied range of the Drws y Coed mountains, on the right of the vale, on whose side I stood, and appearing even still darker than usual, from the light on the mountain beyond them, formed a truly elegant middle distance. The expanse of the water of the two lakes, intersected by a narrow isthmus, appeared in the bosom of the vale. The rude trunks, and weather-beaten limbs of the old oaks around, not only added beauty to the foreground, but varied, by their intervention, the otherwise too uniform appearance of the meadows of the vale, and of some parts of the mountains' sides. This landscape is not exceeded in beauty by any in North Wales.

As the *slate quarries* were not far from this

station, I walked up to them, and found a chasm formed in the rocks that, from its peculiar appearance, surprized me almost as much as the excavations in the mountains of Nant Frangon, belonging to lord Penrhyn. This is very narrow, long, and deep, its sides being nearly all perpendicular; and to a stranger, unaccustomed to sights of this nature, it will be found very interesting. The mountain, in which these quarries are formed, is called Cilgwyn, *the white retreat*: it is in the parish of Llanllyfni.

CHAP. XXI.

EXCURSION FROM CAERNARVON INTO THE PROMONTORY OF LLYN.

The promontory of Llyn.—Account of Dinas Dinlle, and other ancient Forts dependant on it.—Clynog —Church.— Beuno's Chapel and Chest.—Superstitions.—Llanhaiarn.— Nevin.—Porthynllyn.—Pwellheli. — Criccieth. — Criccieth. Castle.—Story of Sir Howell y Fwyall, and his Battle-Ax.— Penmorfa.—Anecdote of Sir John Owen.—Ford at Penmorfa.

THE promontory of Llyn, or that division of Caernarvonshire which juts outs into the Irish sea, affords very little that can be interesting to the tourist. In the more northerly parts a considerable quantity of corn is grown; so much indeed as to supply nearly all the rest of the county. The farther extremity is, in general, bleak, open, and exposed.

DINAS DINLLE,

An ancient fort, about two miles west of Llandwrog, (a village near six miles south of Caernarvon,) was the first place of any consequence that I came to. This is situated on the summit of a green eminence, immediately on the coast. In a stream called Voryd, that runs not far from the place, there are two fords, which, to this day, retains the names of *Rhyd equestre,* and *Rhyd pedestre,* (Rhyd being the Welsh word for ford),

and are understood by these names, as the horse
and foot fords.—The mount on which the fort
was constructed, is supposed to have been artificial. It is so near the sea, that at high tides the
water comes entirely up to it: on the side towards the water, the bank is very steep.—The
fort was of a circular form, and about four hundred feet in diameter. On all sides, except towards the sea, it was defended by a deep foss
five or six yards wide. The principal entrance
was on the east side. This station not only
commanded the whole of Caernarvon bay, its
creeks and harbours, but great part of the county
of Caernarvon, and of the isle of Anglesea,
was also within sight of the garrison.—To this
great centre of observation and action (says the
late learned vicar of Llanwnda) correspond
several other forts, that lie diagonally across the
country, some towards the north, and others towards the south; which, like the wings of an
army, were of infinite service in time of danger,
for its safety and protection. The most considerable on the east are Dinorddwig, in the
parish of Llanddiniolen; and Yr Hên Gastell,
and Dinas Gorfan, both in the parish of
Llanwnda, and about three miles distant. Towards the south, one of the most rocky is Craig
y Dinas, on the river Llyfni, about a mile and
half distant.—Dinorddwig, or, as it is now
called, Pen Dinas, in the parish of Llanddiniolen,
is still entire and strengthened with a double
ditch and strong rampart. The excellence of this
fort has consisted in strength and compactness,
standing, as it were, on tiptoe above all the rest.
Yr Hên Gastell, *the old castle*, near the brook
Carrog, is a small entrenchment with a single

rampart, about fifty paces in length. Dinas
Gorfan, near Pont Newydd, *the new bridge,* has
merely the name remaining. But Craig y
Ddinas, *the rocky fort,* is a circular encampment,
about one hundred paces in diameter, very steep
towards the river that passes it on the south, as it
is also on every other side except the west. The
ramparts, with a treble ditch, are composed of
loose stones. The entrance is towards the north,
very narrow, and forty paces in length. This
fort is about a mile south-west of the great road
that leads from Caernarvon to Pwllheli, and
about a quarter of a mile from Lleiar, the ancient family of the Twistletons.—Farther on,
towards the extremity of the diagonal line, as
the foot of Llanhaiarn mountain, and not far
from that place where that parish joins upon
Llan Gybi, there is a small fort upon the top of
a high rock called *Caer·* This was a fort of
observation, to guard not only the passes of the
mountains, but to overlook Llyn, the ancient
division of Caernarvonshire, called Evionedd,
and St. George's channel.—There are other
smaller forts, interspersed about the country (connected, no doubt, in some shape or other with
Dinas Dinlle.) These were either the residences of generals, as Gad-lys, in the parish of
Llanwnda, or places of observation for some
peculiar military uses, as Dinas y Prif, in the
parish of Llanwnda, where there is one deep
ditch and a western entrance, looking towards
the principal fort Dinas Dinlle.—The disposition and economy of these head quarters, savour
of the wisdom and sagacity that seem to run
through the whole, being situated, (if the expression may be used,) at proper intervals in the

base of a triangle, which the two diagonal lines form, by meeting with the base, in a point at Dinas Dinlle.*

On the left of the road, about half a mile beyond the village of Llandwrog, I passed the grounds of *Gllynllivon*, the seat of lord Newborough. The views were over a country in a tolerably good state of cultivation, and on the whole were interesting. At a little distance to the right was the sea; and on the opposite side, a few miles off, were the mountains around Snowdon.

As I approached the *Rival* or *Eifl* (forked) mountains, they began to assume a very grand aspect. Their conical summits, all nearly of equal height, were obscured by light clouds. They seemed to oppose an impassable barrier, to the still extensive country beyond them. The mountain next the sea, presents a perpendicular precipice to the waves.

CLYNOG

Is a small village, which, with its elegant gothic church appearing among the trees, and the mountains in the background, forms, at the distance of about half a mile from the place, an highly picturesque scene. The houses are half hidden by the foliage, and the tower of the church rises very beautifully from among

* Letter of the Rev. R. Farringdon, vicar of Llanwnda, near Dinas Dinlle.

T

them. The sea, on the right, forms an essential part of the view.

The *church*, differing in that respect from every other parish church in North Wales, is a large gothic building, with some of the windows of painted glass. In different parts of it, I observed the tombs of several persons of a Yorkshire family of the name of Twisleton, who retired into Wales, and lived chiefly in this parish. A passage called Yr heinous, *the heinous*, (from its having been used as a place of confinement for disorderly persons), leads from the church to a small gothic building, called Eglwys Beuno, *the chapel of Beuno*, supposed to have been originally founded about the year 616. This Welsh saint was the son of one of the kings of Powys, and uncle to Wenefred, the celebrated virgin of Holywell. He is reported to have been interred in the chapel, and an ill wrought stone figure, now placed in the belfry, headless and mutilated, was supposed to have covered his grave. In consequence of this opinion, lord Newborough, in the year 1793, ordered the ground to be examined for his remains, but nothing could be discovered.—In the south east corner of the church, near the altar table, there is an old wooden chest, belted with iron, and fastened to the floor, called Cyff Beuno, *Beuno's chest*. It has a slit in the cover, to receive the offerings of money from the devotees of the saint. If a person was affected with any disorder, he made his offering into this chest, usually a fourpenny piece, if such could be obtained, and having sat down on Bueno's grave, and addressed his prayers to the saint, he expected immediate relief. This custom is even yet continued by a

few ignorant persons.   On Trinity Sunday,
bread and cheese were usually offered to Beuno;
and the church formerly claimed all the calves
and lambs that were cast with a slit in their
ear.

The other curiosities in the neighbourhood of
Clynog are, the *well* dedicated to St. Bueno,
inclosed in a square wall on the left of the road,
about a quarter of a mile beyond the village; a
cromlech, which is to be seen from the road,
a little further on in a field near the sea; and a
waterfall called *Rhaiadr Dibbin Mawr*, in the
mountains about two miles distant.   The latter
I had not heard of when I was here.

From Clynog I directed my route towards the
Rivals, and in passing the foot of a smooth and
conical mountain called Gyrn Goch, *The Red
Point*, observed several women and children
busily employed in rolling large bundles of heath
down the sides, to save themselves the labour of
carrying them.—The road led me, up a tolerably
steep hill, to *Llanhaiarn*, whose white-washed
church on its elevated site, affords a land-mark
to the distant mariner.   I now wound my way
along the hollows of the Rival mountains, and
for a considerable distance through a country
as desolate and barren as can be well imagined.
Emerging from these dreary wilds, I not long
afterwards arrived at a small and insignificant
borough town, governed by a bailiff and corporation, called *Nevin*, surrounded by mountains,
and appearing altogether separated from the
world.

I descended from hence to the shore, at
Porthynllyn, *The Harbour in Llyn*, about a

T 2

mile distant. Here are three or four houses situated at the foot of a small semicircular range of low mountains, with, in front, a large and extensive bay. This place is even more secluded from the world than Nevin; it cannot be seen except from the edges of the hills that immediately surround it. The extent of all the land betwixt the hills and the sea is so small, as scarcely to be more than a mile and a half across, and a quarter of a mile deep. The harbour is chiefly frequented by coasting and Irish vessels.

As I had already seen nearly as much of this uninteresting part of Caernarvonshire as I wished, and as I had previously determined, in the course of a few days, to sail in the cutter belonging to the hotel at Caernarvon, from that place entirely round the promontory, I now cut short my journey by crossing directly over from hence to

PWLLHELI.

This is a small market town supported principally by its coasting trade. Vessels are here built of a tolerably large size; one that I saw on the stocks, I was told, would be registered as of about six hundred tons burthen, but this was the largest that had ever been constructed here. The harbour is a pretty good one, but at the ebb of the tide it is left nearly dry. Pwllheli is the principal town in the promontory, and has in its neighbourhood the seats of several families of **great respectability.** The surrounding country is more cultivated than in most other parts of

Llyn ; and it is in many parts varied with wood.
The town itself is very unpleasant, from the extreme irregularity of the houses and streets.

CRICCIETH

Is situated at the north corner of Cardigan bay,
about nine miles from Pwllheli. It is an insignificant borough town contributory to Caernarvon ; and, except in the few remains of its
castle, affords nothing which can claim attention
from the traveller. This is situated on a rising
ground, at the end of a long neck of land that
juts into the sea. The entrance to it is betwixt
two round towers, which are square within : all
the other towers are entirely square. There
have been two courts, but neither of them was
very large, nor indeed has the whole castle been
a building of any other than small extent. At
present it is in a very ruinous condition.—From
the eminence on which it stands, there is a
beautiful view across the bay towards Harlech.

From the architecture of Criccieth castle, it
appears undoubtedly to have been of British
origin; and its reputed founder Edward I.,
seems only to have cased the two towers at the
entrance, their exterior workmanship being
very different from that of the interior. It is
conjectured by Rowlands to have been in existence before the sixth century*.—The constable
appointed by Edward was allowed a salary of a
hundred pounds a year, but out of this it was
stipulated, that he should maintain a garrison of

* Rowlands, 149.

thirty men, a chaplain, surgeon, carpenter, and
mason.

SIR HOWELL Y FWYALL,

A native of the adjoining parish of Llanstyndwy,
was constable of this castle. This valiant officer
attended the Black Prince in the battle of
Poictiers, where, although on foot, and armed
only with a battle-axe, he performed several
acts of the utmost bravery and heroism. The
principal of his services was the cutting off the
head of the French king's horse, and taking him
prisoner. As a recompence for his valour he
received the honour of knighthood, and was
allowed to bear the arms of France, with a
" battle-axe in bend sinister;" and to add to his
name y Fwyall, *the battle-axe* In further commemoration of his services, it was ordered that
a mess of meat should, at the expence of the
crown, be every day served up before the axe
with which he had performed these wonderful
feats. This mess, after it had been brought to
the knight, was taken down, and distributed
among the poor. Even after Sir Howel's death
the mess continued to be served as usual, and
for the sake of his soul, given to the poor till so
lately as the beginning of the reign of Queen
Elizabeth. Eight yeomen attendants, called
yeomen of the crown, were appointed to guard
it, who received each eight-pence a day con-
stant wages.—The present parish clerk of Criccieth informed a gentleman of my acquaintance,
that in digging a grave in the church-yard, about
ten years ago, he found a human skull of enor-

mous size, holding in the cavity for the brain more than two quarts of water. He used it for some time, in the place of a more convenient implement, to throw water out of newly opened graves; and supposed it to have been the skull of this renowned hero, probably, however, without any other reason, than from its enormous size: for the ignorant generally associate the idea of gigantic stature with the character of a valiant man.

From Criccieth I proceeded about three miles to

PENMORFA,

The Head of the Marsh, a wood-clad village, romantically situated on the western bank of Traeth Mawr. The church contains a small monument to the memory of *Sir John Owen,* a valiant commander in the army, and a staunch supporter of Charles I. This hero, after the execution of his royal master, with several of the nobility, was condemned by the parliament to lose his head. During his trial he exhibited a spirit of intrepidity worthy so brave a man; and, after his condemnation, he bowed to the court, and expressed his thanks for the honour they intended him. One of the members asked what he meant, and he replied loud enough to be heard by most of the persons present, " I think it a great honour for a poor gentleman of Wales to lose his head with such noble lords :—by G—, I was afraid they would have hanged me." By great good fortune, however, and by the interest of Ireton, who became his advocate, he was set

at liberty, and restored to his friends, after only
a few months imprisonment.*

There is a ford from Penmorfa, across the two
sands, Traeth Mawr and Traeth Bach, to the
roads leading to Tan-y-bwlch and Harlech : this
saves a very circuitous route to those who wish
to go from hence by Beddgelert. Passing this
ford is, however, sometimes attended with danger, owing to the tide's not leaving the same
level, but sometimes washing deep holes in the
sand : and it is never proper for a stranger to
attempt to cross it without the attendance of a
guide.

* Pennant, i. 279.

CHAP. XXII.

VOYAGE FROM CAERNARVON TO THE ISLE OF BARDSEY, AND THENCE TO PWLLHELI.

Llanddwyn Rocks.—View of the Caernarvonshire Mountains from the Sea.—Island of Bardsey.—Gatherers of the Eggs of Sea-fowl.—Account of the Inhabitants and Productions of the Island.—Account of the Visit of Lord Newborough, and a large Party.—History of Bardsey.—Singular Legend.—The dangerous Bay of Hell's Mouth.—Description of this Part of the Welsh Coast.—Studwal's Islands.—Arrival at Pwllheli.

HAVING victualled the Flora cutter, belonging to the Hotel at Caernarvon, with provisions for a week's voyage, I went on board one morning in August, on the first of flood, with the intention of sailing to the island of Bardsey, (distant about twelve leagues,) and round the promontory of Llyn, to Pwllheli.

In the first tide, from want of wind, we only just cleared what is called the bar, a range of sand banks a little beyond the gap of Abermenai. At low water, we were, therefore, under the necessity of coming to anchor off the Llanddwyn rocks. And in order to amuse myself for a few hours, I landed on this point of the island of Anglesea.—As I had examined the place before, I now passed my time in searching

for plants and shells ; of the former I took away
with me several specimens of *Euphorbia Portlan-
dica*, and the bulbs of *Scilla verna*. Of the shells,
besides those already mentioned, I found only the
Limpet, Periwinkle, *Buccinum capillus*, and
Nerita littoralis, adhering to the rocks; and
Buccinum reticulatum, *Cyprœa pediculus* (gow-
ries), *Turbo terebra*, and *Solen siliqua* (common
razor-shell), and *Nerita glaucina*, amongst the
rubbish thrown up by the tides.

The moment the tide became again in our
favour, we weighed anchor, and to catch the
faint breeze over the island, crowded every inch
of our canvass.—In a short time we came into
a situation that afforded me a most beautiful and
extensive view of the whole range of the Caernarvonshire mountains, from Penmaen Mawr
towards the north, to an extreme point of the
promontory of Llyn. In this range, which in a
direct line occupies upwards of fifty miles, all
the primary mountains were visible, namely
Snowdon, Glyder, Llyder, Garn, Carnedd
Ddafydd, Carnedd Llewelyn, Carnedd Elain,
and Penmaen Mawr northwards; and on the
south of Snowdon, Mynydd Mawr, Drws y
Coed, Barra dû, the Rivals, Carn Madryn, and
Cefn Amlwch. We were proceeding sufficiently
slow and steady to allow me to make a tolerably
good sketch of their appearance from the sea.—
It is perhaps the finest range of mountain scenery
that this kingdom affords.

Towards sun-set we found ourselves off Clynog,
about six miles from the coast, and as the wind
had now entirely failed us, we thought it best to
come again to an anchor. When it was nearly
dark, I had a fire lighted in the cabin, and re-

tired to rest. I slept till near five o'clock in the morning, when, as we had still a dead calm, I got up and determined to amuse myself with fishing. It was not long after putting out my line, that I caught an immense skait, and after that a dog-fish. I was interrupted in this employment, by a breeze springing up, just at the turn of the tide, and was not displeased at lying aside my line, to assist in weighing anchor..

We passed the harbour of Porthynllyn, and in return for the late calm, the weather now became so boisterous, that it was necessary, for our safety, to hold out to sea. We soon approached the island of Bardsey, on which I was desirous to land ; but till the wind abated, this was altogether impracticable.

The sudden change in the weather, which at first augured in every respect favourable, was now become worse to us than the preceding calm. We suffered ourselves to be driven about during the rest of the day, and all the next night, by the fury of the elements ; but in the morning we determined, at all hazards, to enter the strait between the island and the main land, and if possible, get into shelter under the south-east side of the island. In the sound we had, in addition to our heavy gale of wind, to encounter the fury of a violent tide. Our boltsprit several times dipping into the tide, threw the whole spray of the divided wave upon us. I was completely wet through two great coats, and the cabin floor at one time was two or three inches deep in water. We made several tacks to accomplish the object of our voyage, but, after beating about nearly twelve hours, we were at length compelled to abandon all further thoughts

of it, and to make the best of our way into
harbour at Pwllheli.—The reader will, however,
experience no disappointment in my not having
been able to effect a landing, since the letters
of the Rev. Mr. Jones, the worthy vicar of
Aberdaron, to whose parish it belongs, have given
me a better account of the

ISLAND OF BARDSEY

Than my own observations could possibly have
furnished.

This island, which is the property of lord Newborough, is somewhat more than two miles long,
and one in breadth; and contains about three
hundred and seventy acres of land, of which
nearly one third is occupied by a high mountain,
that affords feed only for a few sheep and rabbits.
Its distance from the main land is about a
league. Towards the south-east and south-west
it lies entirely open, but, on the north and north-
east, it is sheltered by its mountain, which to
the sea presents a face of perpendicular, and in
some parts even of overhanging rocks. Among
these precipices the intrepid inhabitants, in the
spring of the year, employ themselves in collecting the eggs of the various species of sea-fowl
that frequent them. This is usually done bare-
footed, to prevent them from slipping from
heights whence they must be dashed to pieces;
and their concern for their safety, while seizing these eggs, is infinitely less than that of the
beholder, sitting securely in the boat below:

Nor untrembling canst thou see
How from a scraggy rock, whose prominence
Half o'ershades the ocean, hardy men,
Fearless of dashing waves, do gather them.

These poor fellows do not often meet with accidents, except by the giving way of pieces of the
rock. In this case they are irrecoverably lost.
The men who venture without ropes are accounted by the natives the most bold climbers:
those who are more cautious fix a rope about
their middle, which is held by some persons on
the top of the rock. By this they slip down to
the place where they think the most eggs are to
be found. Here, untying it from their body,
they fasten it to the basket that is to contain
the eggs, which they carry in their hand. When
this is filled, they make a signal to their companions to draw them up. In this manner they
proceed from rock to rock, ascending or
descending as they find it necessary. They
adopt the same modes in collecting samphire,
with which the rocks also abound.

On the south-east side of the island, the only
side on which it is accessible to the mariner,
there is a small, but well sheltered harbour,
capable of admitting vessels of thirty or forty
tons burthen. In this the inhabitants secure
their own fishing-boats.

The soil is principally clayey, and produces
excellent barley and wheat: vetches, peas, and
beans, are said to succeed sufficiently well, but
to oats it is not so favourable. Trees will not
grow here, the keen westerly winds immediately
destroying the young plants. Indeed, except
a small quantity of fine meadow land, all the
lower ground of the island is of little value.—

No reptile is ever seen in this island, except the common water lizard. None of the inhabitants ever saw in it a frog, toad, or snake of any kind. —Till about fourteen years ago, no sparrows had been known to breed here : three nests were, however, built during the same spring, and the produce have since completely colonized the place.

There are here but eight houses, although the number of inhabitants is upwards of seventy. Two or three of the principal of these rent the island of lord Newborough. They pay for it a hundred guineas a year, and have their land tythe free, and are also freed from taxes and rates of every description. They keep about twenty horses, and near thirty cows. All the former, though greatly overstocking so small a place, are absolutely necessary, on account of the great labour required in carrying up the seaweeds from the coast for manure.

The sheep are small, and, on the approach of a stranger, as Mr. Jones informs me, they squall not much unlike hares. Their activity is very remarkable. In the year 1801, Mr. Jones had one of them on his farm at Aberdaron, that had twice ventured through the sea, though the channel is three miles across, and regained the island. The inhabitants train their dogs to catch them, but if the sheep once gain the rocks, they bid defiance to every attempt for the time, as, rather than suffer themselves to be seized, they will plunge from thence into the sea. At the time of the year when the females usually drop their offspring, the inhabitants watch them every day, and before these are able to follow their dams, they mark them in the ears : they then suffer them to range at liberty. Without this attention, from the extreme wildness of the animals, the owners would never be able to distinguish their respective property. Some few of the sheep of the island, from having been rendered tame when young, are more easily managed. These alone submit to be folded in the evenings.

Curiosity induces many persons to visit this island almost every summer; but the grandest sight the present inhabitants ever witnessed, was at a visit of the proprietor, lord Newborough, about eighteen years ago, accompanied by lady Newborough, and several persons of distinction, in the whole to the number of about forty. This company embarked in fishing-smacks from Porthor, near Carreg Hall, in the parish of Aberdaron. On their arrival in the island, marquees were immediately pitched. The whole company dined in the open air; and, at the conclusion of their repast, all the inhabitants were assembled. The ensuing scene reminded a gentleman of my acquaintance, who was present, of what he had read respecting the inhabitants of some of the South-Sea islands. They were drawn up into a circle, and lady Newborough adorned the heads of the females with caps and ribbons, whilst lord Newborough distributed hats among the men. The nominal king and queen of the island were distinguished from the rest by an additional ribbon. Part of the day was occupied in strolling over the island, examining the creeks, and picking up shells, and the rest was spent in mirth and pleasantry. On the embarkation it was intended, being in the heat of summer, that the whole party should

continue in the island till the next day. The
ladies, however, in the evening suddenly changed
their resolution, and judiciously ordered the
boats to be got ready. The rest of the company
followed the example, and the night was spent,
under the hospitable roof of Mr. Thomas of
Carreg, much more agreeably than could have
been done in the island.*

* *History of Bardsey.*—The Welsh name of this place is
Ynys Enlli. During the violent struggles between the
Welsh and English, it was stiled by the poets the Sanctuary,
or Asylum of the Saints, and it was sometimes denominated
the Isle of Refuge. Some of these poets assert that it was
the cemetery of *twenty thousand saints!* The reputed
sanctity of this island induced the religious to resort to it
from many very distant parts of the country.

It has been asserted by several writers that Roderic
Moelwynog, prince of North Wales, first founded here a
monastery some time in the eighth century. He might
perhaps rebuild or enlarge it, but there are good grounds,
from Welsh manuscripts, for supposing that there was a
religious house in this island of a much more early date.

There is an old legend yet extant, written in Monkish
Latin, which assures us that the Almighty had entered
into a particular covenant with Laudatus, the first abbot of
Bardsey, in return for the piety of his monks. This granted
to all the religious of the monastery of Bardsey, the peculiar
privilege of dying according to seniority, the oldest always
going off first. By this privilege it is stated, that every one
knew very nearly the time of his own departure. The following is a translation of it;—" At the original foundation
of the monastery of this island, the Lord God, who attendeth
to the petitions of the just, at the earnest request of holy
Laudatus, the first abbot, entered into a covenant with that
holy man, and miraculously confirmed his promise, unto him
and his successors, the abbots and monks, for ever, while
they should continue to lead holy and religious lives, that
they should die by succession, that is, that the oldest should
go first, like a shock of corn ripe for the sickle. Being thus
warned of the approach of death, each of them, therefore,
should watch, as not knowing at what exact hour the thief
might come; and, being thus always prepared, each of them

After these observations, I resume the narrative of my voyage to Pwllheli. The wind, as I have already observed, continued still boisterous; it was therefore necessary for us to be very cautious in the management of our little bark. We therefore held off from the Welsh coast, for some distance, towards the south, that we might weather the eastern point of the extensive, but dreadful bay, called

HELL'S MOUTH.

I never saw a place which presented so favourable an appearance, and that was at the same time so much dreaded by the mariners, as the

by turns should lay aside his earthly form. God, who is ever faithful, kept this covenant, as he formerly did with the Israelites, inviolable, until the monks no longer led a religious life, but began to profane and defile God's sanctuary by their fornications and abominable crimes. Wherefore, after this, they were permitted to die like other men, sometimes the older, sometimes the younger, and sometimes the middle-aged first : and being thus uncertain of the approach of death, they were compelled to submit to the general laws of mortality. Thus, when they ceased to lead a holy and religious life, God's miraculous covenant also ceased : and do thou therefore, O God, have mercy upon us."

The ancient building is now entirely destroyed ; but, about the ground where the monastery stood, a great number of graves have even very lately been discovered, lined with white stone or tile, and distant about two feet from each other.

All the religious duties of the inhabitants are now performed in the parish-church of Aberdaron. Sometimes, however, in stormy weather, they are under the necessity of interring their own dead in the island.

present. It is at the very end of the promontory, and from point to point is supposed to measure about eight miles: it is also nearly semicircular. None but strange vessels, even in the most boisterous weather, ever seek for shelter here, and when these are so unfortunate, they are soon stranded, and never again return. " We remember (says Mr. Jones, in one of his letters) more misfortunes to have happened in this bay, and more inhumanity shewn to the sufferers. than we have ever heard of any where else on the Welsh coast." My pilot, who had been long acquainted with every part of these coasts, informed me, that, from whatever point of the compass the wind blew, out at sea, on account of the surrounding high rocks, it always came into the mouth of this bay; and from whatever quarter the tide flowed, the upper current here always sets inwards! From these circumstances the common tradition is, that the place obtained the appellation of *Hell's Mouth*.

The whole coast, from the Rivals round the end of the land, nearly to Pwllheli, is terminated only by high and steep rocks, inhabited in the summer by a variety of sea-fowl.

Passing the eastern point of Hell's Mouth, we kept as close to the wind as we could, and soon afterwards came in sight of St. Tudwal's, or, as they are usually called, *Studwal's Islands*, of which a considerable sum of money is annually made, as puffin warrens. After a difficult navigation of several hours, we at length sailed round the rock of Carreg, at the mouth of the harbour of Pwllheli, and came to anchor in the river just opposite to the town. This was about eight o'clock in the evening of our third day.

From Pwllheli I chose the next morning to make a short passage back, by crossing over the land to Clynog, and walking from thence to Caernarvon. This journey I performed in about five hours. The cutter did not arrive till two days afterwards.

CHAP. XXIII.

EXCURSION FROM CAERNARVON BY CAPEL CURIG, TO LLANRWST; AND FROM THENCE, BY THE VALE OF FFESTINIOG, AND TAN-Y-BWLCH AGAIN TO CAERNARVON.

ACCOMPANIED by my worthy friend the rector of Llanrûg, I went from Caernarvon, by way of Nant Frangon and Capel Curig, to Llanrwst.

THE VALE OF CAPEL CURIG

(For I have described all the former part of our route in a previous chapter) is bounded by the British Alps, Snowdon and his adjacent moun-

tains, and affords some of the most picturesque
landscapes of the whole country.

> Here hills and vales, the woodland and the plain;
> Here earth and water seem to strive again :
> Not chaos-like, together crush'd and bruis'd,
> But, as the world, harmoniously confus'd.

In this vale there is that variety both of wood
and water, which most of the other Welsh vales
so much want to add to their picturesque effect.
Here are two tolerably large pools. Near one
of these lord Penrhyn has erected, from a design
of Mr. Benjamin Wyatt, a small, but very
comfortable

INN.

Those tourists who, like myself, have visited this
vale some years ago, when the only place of public
accommodation was a mean pot-house, considerably allied to those at Llanberis, and who shall
now visit it with the present accommodations,
(with which for a mountain country, I was
greatly surprized), will be able with some justice to appreciate the spirited conduct, and truly
patriotic exertions of the noble proprietor, who
has not only constructed for them an inn, but
who was the first to make this part of the country passable in carriages.

The name of the vale is derived from its
chapel, dedicated to a Welsh saint called Curig.
He is mentioned in an old Welsh poem, which,
however, only intimates his order; and nothing
more is at present known of him.

" A certain friar to increase his store,
  Beneath his cloak, *grey Curig's* image bore ;
  And to protect good folks from nightly harm,
  Another sells St. Seiriol as a charm."

When we left Capel Curig, we proceeded about two miles on the road to Llanrwst, and then leaving it, went about three miles southward to see

DOLWYDDELAN CASTLE,

A fortress, some centuries ago, of considerable importance to the Welsh princes. Its mountainous situation rendered it difficult to find, and it was not till after numerous inquiries that we could get into the track that led us immediately up to it.

This castle stands on a rocky steep, nearly perpendicular on one side, and in a vale entirely closed round by mountains. The original import of the name seems to have been the castle in *the meadow of Helen's wood ;** for the ancient military road called Sarn Helen, or *Helen's Road,* from Helen, the daughter of Octavius, duke of Cornwall, passed through the country not far from hence, to the sea-coast of Merionethshire. —It has never been a large building, but it occupied the entire summit of its mount. It formerly consisted of two square towers, each three stories high, having but one room on a floor, and a court-yard, which was betwixt them.

* Dol Gwydd Elen; or the name may have been Dol Gwydd Elain, *The Meadow of the Wood of the Doe.*

The largest of these towers measures within no more than twenty-seven feet in length, and eighteen in width, and the walls are about six feet thick. The walls of the court are entirely destroyed, and very little is now left of the other parts of the building.*

This place was, for many years, the residence of the eldest son of Owen Gwynedd, Iorwerth Drwndwn, or *Edward with the broken nose*. On the death of his father, Iorwerth claimed the crown of Wales as his hereditary right, but was unanimously rejected, and merely from the blemish in his face : so whimsical and indecisive, was, at that time, the mode of succession to the Welsh throne. He had, assigned to him, as part of his parental inheritance, the hundreds of Nan Conwy and Ardudwy, and he retired to this sequestered spot to spend the rest of his life. It was in Dolwyddelan castle that his son was born, who, afterwards, in the beginning of the thirteenth century, reigned in Wales under the title of Llewelyn the great.

---

* Who the founder of this fortress was, or what purpose it was originally intended to answer, we have not at this time any documents left to inform us. Most probably, when the feudal system prevailed in Wales, and petty chieftains were engaged in perpetual war with each other, Dolwyddelan castle, and others similar to it, may have been erected by some of them as places of retreat and refuge, where they could reside in security, attended by their vassals and adherents, in case they should be compelled by superior force to relinquish the plains and more cultivated parts of the country. These castles also answered the double purpose of guarding the passes and defiles of the mountains.

It is a conjecture of Rowland, that this castle was erected prior to the sixth century. What his grounds for this supposition are, he does not state.*

* Rowland, 149.

Meredith, the son of Jevan ap Robert, purchased the lease of this castle, and of the inclosures belonging to it, in the reign of Henry the Seventh.

About this period the whole of the surrounding country was one entire forest overrun with thieves and outlaws. The castle had itself been previously possessed by Howell, ap Evan, ap Rhys Gethin, one of the most noted of those, against whom David ap Jenkin rose in arms. David, who was likewise an outlaw, contended with him long for the sovereignty of the mountains, and at length, by stratagem, took him in bed, but spared his life, on condition that he should immediately seek refuge in Ireland. In that country he scarcely remained a year, but returned in the ensuing summer with some select adherents. He clothed himself and his followers entirely in green, that they might be the less distinguishable among the forests, and in this disguise, appearing abroad only in the nights, they committed the most dreadful depredations.

The friends of Meredith ap Jevan, were greatly surprised that he should think of changing his habitation near Penmorfa, for this castle thus surrounded by multitudes of freebooters. He gave, as a decisive reason, that he chose rather to fight with outlaws and thieves, than with his own immediate relatives. "If (says he) I live in my own house in Evionedd, I must either kill my own kinsmen, or submit to be murdered by them."—He had not been here long before he built the house at Penanmen, and removed the church from the thicket in which it formerly stood, to its present more open situation: the church, his house, and the castle, thus forming the points of a triangle, each a mile distant from the other. Whenever he went to the church, he took with him as a guard, twenty stout archers; and he had a centinel placed on a neighbouring rock called Carreg y Big (from whence the church, the house, and the castle could be seen) who had orders to give immediate notice of the approach of banditti. He never mentioned before-hand when he intended to go out, and always went and returned by different routes through unsuspected parts of the woods. He found it necessary, to his perfect security, to increase the number of his adherents; he therefore established colonies of the most tall and able men he could procure, occupying every tenement, as it became empty, with such tenants only as were able to bear arms. His force, when complete, consisted of a hundred and forty archers, ready to assemble, whenever the sound of the bugle from the castle, echoed through the woods, to call for their assistance. These, says sir John Wynne, were each arrayed in a " jacket, or armolet coate, a good steele cap, a short sword and dagger, together with a bow and arrows. Many of them had also horses and chasing slaves, which were ready to answer the crie on all occasions, whereby he grew soe strong that he began to put back, and to curb the sanctuary of thieves and robbers, which, at times, were wont to be above a hundred, well horsed and well appointed."*—Such was the state of Wales in these unhappy times, when every one claimed

* Wynne, 429. The sanctuary here alluded to, was the hospital which will be hereafter mentioned, at y Spytty Evan, of the knights of St. John of Jerusalem.

by a kind of prescriptive right, whatever he had power to seize; and when lives or property were considered of no other value than interest or ambition chose to dictate. Meredith ap Jevan, to enjoy a quiet life, threw himself into the bosom of a country infested with outlaws and murderers, and, comparatively with the state of society about his former residence near Penmorfa, attained his end. He closed his useful life in the year 1525, leaving to survive him twenty-three legitimate, and three natural children.

DOLWYDDELAN.

The village of Dolwyddelan is about a mile from the castle, and, from its mountainous situation, it is altogether secluded from the world. Its inhabitants seemed extremely simple, and in their manners they exhibited signs of great shyness and timidity, probably, however, arising from the unaccustomed appearance of strangers among them. None of them are acquainted with any other language than that of their country: and hemmed in as they are with mountain barriers, it is very probable that three fourths of them never in their lives wandered half a dozen miles from their dwellings.—The village itself is composed of little else than small cottages; for I could only observe one house of any tolerable size in the place.

PONT Y PAIR.

We left Dolwyddelan, and came into our former road near Pont y Pair, *the Bridge of the Cauldron*, a singular structure of five arches, not far from the village of Bettws y Coed, *the Station in the Wood.* This bridge, whose arches are irregular and very lofty, is built over the river Llugwy, and has, with the adjoining scenery, a very singular effect. Both above and below it, the bed of the river is covered with such strange masses of rock, as, when the quantity of water is considerable, to exhibit a most pleasing and picturesque scene.

From Pont y Pair, we returned for about a mile, along the road leading towards Capel Curig. Then leaving it three or four hundred yards to the left, and passing over some meadows, we came to the celebrated

WATERFALL OF THE RIVER LLUGWY.*

called Rhaiadr y Wenol, *the Cataract of the Swallow.* This fall and the scenery around it, are altogether grand. The water is thrown in a single sheet down a rock nearly perpendicular; but below, its course is changed, by its direction over a smooth and slanting bed. The high and wooded banks were enlivened by the various tints of the oaks, birch, and hazels, which hung from the rocks. Had there been more water in the river, we should have seen this cataract to

* This cataract is about five miles from Llanrwst.

greater advantage than we now did, but the
dry weather had diminished all the mountain
streams to mere rills. The station on the side
of the stream opposite to that on which we
stood, appeared as if it would take in more of
the fall: I made several attempts to get across,
but from the rapidity of the current found it
impossible. When the river, after a heavy fall
of rain, assumes a more impetuous form than at
this time, the cataract must certainly be very
grand, as the bed of the stream is at least
twenty yards wide; and the innumerable masses
of rock, which have at different times been carried along with it, and lodged here, opposing
its fury, must throw it foaming into all directions.

At a little distance below the bridge Pont y
Pair, the rivers Llugwy and Conwy unite. The
latter rises from *Llyn Conwy,* a large pool about
three miles beyond the village of Penmachno.
Both these streams before their junction, are
furious and broken torrents, they are each a
truly " foaming flood," but from hence they
assume a placid form, and glide, in one tranquil
current, silently through the vale.

We stopped awhile at Bettws y Coed, to see
an ancient monument in the church, in memory
of Griffith, the son of David Goch, who was a
natural son of David, brother to Llewelyn, the
last prince of Wales. He died in the fourteenth
century, and is here represented by a large
armed recumbent figure in a recess in the north
wall. On one side of the figure, there is yet
left this inscription: " *Hic jacet Gruffydd ap
Davydd Goch, agnus Dei misere me.*"

VALE OF LLANRWST.

The road now led us into the luxuriant vale of Llanrwst, where the gay tints of cultivation once more beautified the landscape, for the fields were coloured with the rich hues of ripened corn and green meadows. Many gentlemen's seats interspersed around, gave an air of civilization to this valley. We had not long enjoyed the beauties of this prospect before we entered the gloomy woods of *Gwydir*, which afforded a fine contrast to the luxuriance of the vale. The Conwy runs at a little distance from the road, and the silvery reflection of its water through the dark foliage of the trees, gave an additional interest to the scene. On emerging from hence, we had again the same open vale, in which the town of Llanrwst, now before us, formed a conspicuous feature; and the extensive landscape, thus completed, heightened by the dreary rocks, bounding it on each side, has been justly admired by all the lovers of nature, as one of the finest scenes her pencil ever traced.

GWYDIR.

About a quarter of a mile from Llanrwst, we passed by Gwydir, the old family residence of the Wynnes. This mansion was erected about the year 1558, by John Wynne ap Meredith, as appears by the date and initials over the gateway. It is an extensive but irregular building.

At a little distance, among the woods above this mansion, was *Upper Gwydir*, a house erected by Sir John Wynne, in 1604, apparently for the purpose of enjoying from thence the numerous beauties of the vale, which is here seen in a broad and elegant expanse, nearly as far as Conwy. The house was taken down some time ago, but the family chapel is still left. This is a small building in the gothic stile, sufficiently neat on the outside, but the roof and various other parts within, are decorated with paintings of scriptural figures, most miserably executed.

Both these places are at present the property of Lord Gwydir, in right of his Lady Priscilla, Baroness Willoughby, the eldest sister of Robert late Duke of Ancaster. They passed into this family in the year 1678, by the marriage of Mary, daughter and heiress of Sir Richard Wynne, with Robert, Marquis of Lindsey.

LLANRWST BRIDGE.

Betwixt Gwydir and Llanrwst, is the celebrated bridge over the river Conwy, constructed by Inigo Jones. This bridge was directed to be built by an order of the privy council, in the ninth year of the reign of Charles the First. The expences, which were estimated at a thousand pounds, were paid by the two counties of Denbigh and Caernarvon. It consists of three arches, the middle one of which is near sixty feet wide. One of the other two has been rebuilt since Jones's time, and the inferiority of the workmanship is very visible. The inhabitants of Llanrwst *boast*, that their bridge is formed on such nice principles, that if a person thrust against the large stone, over the centre of the middle arch, the whole fabric may plainly be felt to vibrate: though one cannot, from conviction, be inclined to concur with them in this assertion, yet allowing it true, would not the bridge have been better built, if it was entirely firm? So many persons have tried the experiment, that the stone is now become quite loose. We attempted it, but, except that stone, found the whole bridge as firm as a rock.

THE TOWN OF LLANRWST

Is finely situated on the eastern bank of the river Conwy. In itself, it has nothing to recommend it to notice: the streets are narrow, and the houses very irregular.

THE CHURCH

Is a plain, ill-looking structure; but adjoining to it is a *chapel*, built in 1633, by sir Richard Wynne, from a design of Inigo Jones, which has a considerable degree of elegance.

Against the wall of the chapel, there are five brasses, four of them engraved by Sylvanus Crew, and one by William Vaughan, that are remarkable for the excellence of their execution. Each of these, besides an inscription, contains a portrait of the person to whose memory it was finished. They are the work of the seventeenth century. That on Sarah Wynne, by Vaughan, is much superior to the rest.

The carved work of the roof of the chapel is said to have been brought from the neighbouring

Abbey of Mænan.*—Into this chapel has lately been removed, an ancient monument of Hoel Coytmor, which lay before among the rubbish, under the stairs leading into the gallery of the church. It is an armed recumbent figure, with the feet resting on a lion. The inscription upon it is: *Hic jacet Hoel Coytmor ap Gruff. Vychan ap Gruff. Amn"* Hoel Coytmor possessed the estates of Gwydir, which were sold by his son David, to Meredith ap Jevan, Welsh nephew, or first cousin once removed to the renowned John ap Meredith, and ancestor to the Wynnes of Gwydir. Hoel was the grandson of David Goch of Penmachno, whose monument we had just seen in the church of Bettws.

Near this monument is placed a large stone coffin, supposed to have been that of Llewelyn ap Iorwerth, denominated from his valiant actions, Llewelyn the great. He was interred in the abbey of Conwy, in the year 1240, but after the dissolution of monasteries in the reign of Henry VIII. as appears from a brass plate affixed to it, this coffin was removed from thence to this place, where it has ever since remained.

Besides these, there are no other monuments in this chapel worth notice, except one, which bears a singularly long and curious inscription, containing a pedigree of the Wynne family, from Owen Gwynedd, prince of Wales, to sir Richard Wynne, who died about the middle of the seventeenth century.

---

* This abbey stood about three miles north of Llanrwst. On its scite was erected a house, at present the property of Lord Newborough. It was founded by Edward I. after he had fortified the town of Conwy, for the purpose of removing into it the religious of the Cistertian abbey there.

The river Conwy runs close past the church-yard of Llanrwst, from whence there is a fine prospect of the bridge, and the high woods of Gwydir behind it. In this river salmon are frequently taken, and during the months of February and March, great numbers of smelts. The tide reaches no farther than to the village of *Trefriew*, about a mile and half from Llanrwst, to which place only the river is navigable.

In the fifteen years of civil discord during the insurrection of Owen Glyndwr, such were the ravages committed in these parts of Wales, that this place was so entirely forsaken by its inhabitants, that grass grew in the market-place, and the deer from the mountains fled for refuge into the church-yard.

INN.

The Eagles inn at Llanrwst, the only one where post horses are kept, is in general found a very comfortable house; but during the summer season it is often so much crowded by company, as to render it very unpleasant to the wearied tourist. From this house guides may be had to accompany the traveller to any of the curiosities of the neighbourhood.

About five miles from Llanrwst, leaving the road to Penmachno on the right, we passed over some fields, to see a small *w. terfall on the river Conwy*. Its height is not very considerable, being only twelve or fourteen yards. The scene was clad with wood, and the bed of the river excessively rugged.

x

Somewhat more than half a mile beyond this
we stopped at a fulling mill, near a bridge called
Pont y Pandy, *the bridge of the fulling mill.*
Here is a

CATARACT,

Called *Rhaiadr y Craig Llwyd,* truly romantic
and picturesque.   It is not very lofty, and the
river, from want of water when we were here,
flowed in two streams, but the black and rugged
rock which separated them, rendered the scene,
though not perhaps quite so tremendous, yet
much more beautiful than if the whole had been
concealed by the water.   The high banks on
each side are ornamented with pendent shrubs,
and a mill, and rude wooden aqueduct (which
conveys water to an old overshot wheel), overgrown with mosses and grass, completed this
elegant landscape.   The descent to the bottom
was steep and difficult, but my trouble in scram-
bling down was well repaid in seeing the fall to
much greater advantage than from above.   From
hence it seemed increased in height, and many
of the prominent and pointed rocks, before hidden, came, from this situation, into the view.

The river accompanies the road to some distance beyond this waterfall.   Where they parted
we left the road, and wandered along the banks
of the stream for some time, till we came to a
most wild scene of wooded and projecting rocks,
overhanging the black and dismal torrent.   A
grassy ledge on the opposite side, at some height
above the water, reminded me very forcibly of

the scene where Gray has placed his bard; and
all the accompanying features were well suited
to such a scene.

> High on a rock, whose haughty brow
> Frowns o'er old Conwy's foaming flood,
> Rob'd in the sable garb of woe,
> With haggard eyes, the poet stood
> (Loose his beard, and hoary hair
> Stream'd like a meteor to the troubled air),
> And with a master's hand, and prophet's fire,
> Struck the deep sorrows of his lyre.

From hence we returned to the road, and proceeded onward over a mountainous, though not
either very romantic or interesting country, till
we reached Penmachno. *The Head of the
Machno*, a village singular in its appearance,
the houses being built almost in a circle round
the church.

At the distance of about four miles from Penmachno, in the road leading from thence to
Corwen, is *Yspytty Evan*, now a small village,
but so called, it hás been conjectured, from
its having formerly contained a house belonging
to the knights hospitallers, or knights of St.
John of Jerusalem*. This had the privilege of
a sanctuary, and the place of course became a
receptacle for thieves and murderers. It wis,
says sir John Wynne, "a wasp's nest, which
troubled the whole country,—a sanctuary of
robbers, which at times were wont to be above
a hundred, well horsed and well appointed†."

* The word *spytty* being probably derived from *hos-
pitium*.
† Wynne, 420, 429.

Being here beyond the reach of invaders, the place was always fully peopled; and extending their plundering excusions on all sides to the distance of twenty or thirty miles, they rendered themselves the terror of the adjacent country. Such were indeed the ravages they committed, that nearly all the inhabitants of the neighbourhood were driven to seek for refuge and security beyond their reach.

From Penmachno, for we did not think it worth our while to visit Yspytty Evan, we continued our journey, over a still mountainous but dreary country, till we came to the village of

FFESTINIOG,

The Place of Hastening. This little place, and the vale near it, have been justly celebrated by the elegant pen of lord Lyttleton, who made a tour through Wales in the year 1756.

It happened to be during the fair that we were here, and as we chose to suffer any inconvenience rather than be pestered with the vociferous curiosity of a set of drunken fellows, we were taken from the inn into an adjoining building, and shewn up stairs into a bed-room, even worse than that I had slept in at Beddgelert. After we had satiated our thirst as well as we could with what was called brandy and water, but which might indeed have been as easily mistaken for Burgundy as brandy, we went by a foot-path which passes through the

field, opposite to the end of the house, to see
the

FALLS OF THE CYNFAEL.

These are situated, the one about three hundred yards above, and the other three hundred yards below a rustic stone bridge over
the river, to which the path led us.—The upper cataract consists of three steeps, over which
the water foams into a deep black bason, shadow-
ed by the adjacent rocks.—The other, which I
think nearly as beautiful as this, is formed by
a broad sheet of water, precipitated down a
slightly shelving rock, about forty feet high, and
darkened by the foliage around it, which closes
in almost to the edge of the stream. After
the water has reached the bottom of the deep
concavity, it rushes along a narrow rocky chasm;
then

> Raging still amid the shaggy rocks,
> Now flashes o'er the scatter'd fragments, now
> Aslant the hollow channel rapid darts,
> And falling fast from gradual slope to slope,
> With wild infracted course and lessen'd roar,
> It gains a safer bed, and steals at last,
> Along the mazes of the quiet vale.

Betwixt this cataract and the bridge there
is a tall columnar rock, which stands in the
bed of the river, called *Pulpit Hugh Lloyd
Cynfael*, or Hugh Lloyd's pulpit, the place
from whence, the peasantry say, a magician
of that name used to deliver his nightly incan-
tations.

THE VALE OF FFESTINIOG.

From the village of Ffestiniog we descended into Cwm Maentwrog, *The Vale of Maentwrog.* (improperly called by tourists the vale of Ffestiniog,) and wandered leisurely along, enjoying all the way the most sublime pleasure in contemplating the beauties of the scene before us. There are few vales in this country that afford such lovely prospects as this. Many of the high mountains bounding its sides are shaded with lofty oaks; and the silver Dwyryd, *Two Fords,* serpentines placidly and silently along the bottom, amidst the richest cultivation. The sea, at a distance, closes the view; and Traeth Bach, a wide arm of it, is seen to receive the Dwyryd, a little below Tanybwlch hall, which is situated on a rising ground, and embowered in woods, at the north west extremity of the vale. The little village of Maentwrog, from whence it takes its name, is seated nearly in the middle. The character of the vale of Ffestiniog is very different from that either of Llanberis or Nant Hwynan: the former is majestic, grand, and sublime; Nant Hwynan bears a middle character, its bottom is varied by insulated rocks, and clad with trees; this is simply elegant, and principally affords charms to the admirer of nature in her most chaste and delicate attire. The bottom is open, and cultivated from end to end, with trees scattered along the walls and hedge-rows. The thick woods on the mountains to the north soften very beautifully what would be otherwise a bleak and dreary feature in the scene. " With the woman one loves, with the friend of one's heart, and a good study of books, (says lord Lyttleton to his friend Mr. Bower,) one might pass an age in this vale, and think it a day. If you have a mind to live long, and renew your youth, come with Mrs. Bower, and settle at Ffestiniog. Not long ago there died in that neighbourhood an honest Welsh farmer, who was 105 years of age. By his first wife he had *thirty* children, *ten* by his second, *four* by his third, and *seven* by two concubines: his youngest son was *eighty-one* years younger than his eldest; and 800 persons, descended from his body, attended his funeral." —I can add another instance of age and fecundity in this vale, which, though far short of this in point of numbers, is still sufficiently great to prove the healthiness of the place. Jane Price, who died in the year 1694, had at the time of her death *twelve* children, *forty-seven* grand-children, and *thirteen* great grand-children.

We ascended, along with the road, the mountains forming the northern boundary of the vale, on the heights of which stand Tanybwlch inn. Here we dined, and from hence we went the same evening, through Beddgelert, again to Caernarvon*.

---

* Tanybwlch will be described in the ensuing chapter.

CHAP. XXIV.

CAERNARVON, THROUGH BEDDGELERT, TO HARLECH.

Pont Aberglásllyn.—Mountain Road, and New Road from Beddgelert to Tanybwlch.— Tanybwlch.—Vale of Ffestiniog.—Maentwrog. Twrog.—Waterfall, called Rhaiadr Dú.—Impending Scenery.—Llyntecwyn Ucha.—Llantecwyn. — Beaut ful Vale. — Harlech. — Harlech Castle. — Extensive View.—Mephitic Vapour.—Inn.

EXCURSION FROM HARLECH TO CWM BYCHAN.

Cylch Cyngrau, or Druidical circles.—Cwm Bychan.—Bwlch Tyddiad.—Drws Ardudwy.— Cwm Nancoll.—Cataract. — Sarn Badrwyg.—Cantref Gwalod, or Overflowed Hundred. Cardigan Bay.

Having remained at Caernarvon a length of time fully sufficient to enable me to visit and examine all the places deserving of notice within a circle of about thirty miles on every side of it, I now proceeded towards Beddgelert and Harlech, in my journey to the other parts of North Wales.—The road to Beddgelert, together with the scenery around that place, have already been described. I shall, therefore, in this chapter,

suppose myself proceeding southward, immediately from

PONT ABERGLASLLYN.

From this celebrated bridge there are two
roads to Tanybwlch the low or *new road,* and
the *mountain road,* the former of which occupies
about ten, and the latter eight miles.   Till
within the last two years, carriages were usually
taken along the mountain-road a series of rocky
steeps, which were considered so dangerous,
that most persons preferred walking for at least
five of the eight miles: and several people, to
avoid it, have even gone more than forty miles
round.   From one very elevated situation, I had
a most delightful view of all the fine and mountainous country around me : Harlech and Criccieth castles were both in sight, and the long
extent of ground forming the promontory of
Llyn, was visible even to its extremity.

Beyond the bridge, on the *new road,* which is
formed through the more flat and level country
towards the sands, the varied scene of wood,
rock, and mountain, is uncommonly fine.   In
some situations the view is confined to the immediately surrounding rocks, whilst in others the
eye wanders over a vast expanse of mountains.
On one elevation I observed no fewer than six
ranges of mountain, one above another, the uppermost at a great distance.   I passed on the
left two conspicuous and conical summits called
Moelwyn.

Tanybwlch,

Below the Pass, so called from its being situated on the brow of the hill overlooking the *Vale of Ffestiniog,** consists only of a small but comfortable inn, and an elegant mansion embowered in woods, the property of ———— Oakley, esq. This vale, watered by the little river Dwyryd, which meanders along its bosom, contrasted with the bleak and dreary mountains on the opposite side, from hence affords a most delightful prospect. A former traveller, H. P. Wyndham, esq. was so highly gratified with the scene, as to make the singular remark, " That if a person could live upon a landscape, he would scarcely desire a more eligible spot than this."

The inn is small, but good.

On the other side of the vale stands the church of Maentwrog, *The Stone of Twrog,* so denominated from a large stone in the church-yard, at the north-west corner of the church. Twrog was a British saint, who lived about the year 610, and was the writer of Tiboeth, a romantic record belonging to St. Bueno, that was formerly kept in the church of Clynog in Caernarvonshire.

I left Maentwrog, and inquiring the road to Harlech, proceeded on my journey. At the distance of about half a mile, I crossed a small bridge. From hence, leaving the road for a while, I wandered along a foot path up a wooded

* Or more properly the vale of Maentwrog.

valley for about a mile and a half, in search of a

WATERFALL

That had been described to me, called Rhaiadr Du, *The Black Cataract.* It was not without some difficulty and after much trouble in ascending and descending the sides of the hills, that I found it. In this cataract, which is surrounded with dark and impending scenery, the water is thrown with vast impetuosity over three black and smooth rocks, each in a different direction. Of its height I could form no idea, for the top of the upper fall, by the winding of the rocks, was not visible from below. The rock that immediately overhangs the cataract, from its great height and rude form, was a fine object in the landscape: and the whole of the hollow, to some distance below the cataract, was extremely grand. I attempted to climb to the upper part, but the rocks were too perpendicular, and too slippery, to suffer the attempt without danger. Therefore contenting myself with seeing as much as I could from below, I crossed the water, and crept along, but not without difficulty, on the shelving rocks, by the side of the stream, for near half a mile. Here the banks closed over my head, leaving but a narrow chasm, from which the light was altogether excluded by the dark foliage from each side, and I found myself entering, to appearance, the mouth of a deep and horrid cavern. The sides were too steep for me to entertain any idea of clambering up, and unless I chose to scramble back again to the cataract, I had no alternative, but to penetrate the place. The darkness, fortunately, did not extend far, and I soon found myself in a place where the bank was sufficiently sloping to to admit of my ascending to the meadows above.

Regaining the road I had left, it led me along the side of Llyntecwyn Ucha, *The Upper Pool of Tecwyn,* where I found the scenery pleasant, though less mountainous than what I had passed. This pool is larger than many of those in Wales, and its waters are beautifully clear. On one side there is a range of low rocks, composed of a shivery kind of slate, which had mouldered in many places to the bottom, in small sharp pieces, almost resembling needles.

Afterwards passing the village of Llantecwyn, and Llyntecwyn Isa, *The Lower Tecwyn Pool,* I came to a most lovely little vale, about three miles distant from Harlech, called (if I understood the guide right) *Dol Orcal.* After the late uncouth scenery, I here enjoyed in the utmost the pleasing effect of the green woods and meads of the vale, and the purple heath which concealed and softened the harsh colouring of the adjacent rocks.

The whole of the walk from Beddgelert to Harlech I found exceedingly pleasant. From the continual varying of the scenery, the attention was fully occupied during every part of the journey.—The road from Tanybwlch is scarcely passable for carriages, but there is another from Beddgelert, at the ebb of the tide, over the sands: a guide, however, must be taken who is acquainted with the track, as it is unsafe for strangers to venture alone.

HARLECH,

Once the principal town in Merionethshire, is now dwindled into an insignificant village, containing not more than four or five hundred inhabitants. It is in the parish of Llanfair, and on the sea coast, near Cardigan Bay : the houses and castle are built on a cliff that immediately overhangs the marsh. Not far from the castle, there is a roofless building, once the town hall; in which, however, the members of parliament for the county continue still to be elected.

HARLECH CASTLE.

This venerable structure is in tolerable preservation. It is a square building, each side measuring about seventy yards; and has at every corner a round tower. From each of these issued formerly a circular turret; nearly all now destroyed. The entrance is betwixt two great rounders. The principal apartments appear to have been over the gateway, in a building which projected into the court; and at each angle of this building there is yet left a round tower. The castle was defended on the east side by a deep foss; and its situation, on the verge of an almost perpendicular rock, rendered it impregnable in nearly every other part.—From the marsh, it is said, except in size, to bear a considerable resemblance to the castle of Belgrade in Turkey.

On the evening that I arrived at Harlech, the

atmosphere was so perfectly clear, that I could plainly distinguish the peaked summit of Snowdon, elevated high above all the other mountains. The promontory of Llyn was visible in almost every part; Criccieth castle seemed scarcely a mile distant; and the fine, though dangerous bay of Cardigan, lay entirely before me.*

* *History of Harlech Castle.*—The ancient name of this fortress was Twr Bronwen, *Bronwen's Tower;* so called from Bronwen, *the white necked,* sister to Bren ap Llyr, duke of Cornwall, and afterwards king of Britain. She lived in the third century, and was the wife of Matholwch, an Irishman. Her husband one day, *unfortunately,* struck her a violent blow in the face, and she resented the outrage by inciting an insurrection among the people, and causing a civil war. This blow is called, in the ancient Triads, one of the three evil blows of Britain; two others, of a nature nearly similar, being there said to have produced similar commotions. Bronwen is supposed by some to have resided here; and the highest turret of the present castle, though for what reason I know not, since this building was altogether founded many centuries after her time, goes yet by the name of Bronwen's tower.

In the eleventh century this place took the name of Caer Collwyn, *Collwyn's Fort,* from Collwyn ap Tangno, lord of Eivonedd and Ardudwy, who repaired the ancient castle, and took it for his own residence. The present name of Harlech is probably derived from the British words hardd, *beautiful,* and llech, *a rock,* indicating its situation.

According to some of the ancient British historians, Harlech castle was originally built, about the year 350, by Maelgwn Gwynedd, prince of North Wales; and it is generally believed that Edward I. founded the present fortress on the ruins of the old castle; some parts of which are yet distinguishable from the more modern work of that monarch.

In the year 1404, this castle, along with that of Aberystwyth in Cardiganshire, was seized by Owen Glyndwr, during his rebellion against Henry IV. They were both retaken about four years afterwards, by an army which the king had dispatched into Wales against that turbulent chieftain.

Margaret of Anjou, the queen of Henry VI., after the king's defeat at Northampton in 1456, fled from Coventry,

MEPHITIC VAPOUR.

In the winter of 1694, this neighbourhood was much alarmed by a kind of fiery exhalation, which came from a sandy and marshy tract of land, called Morfa Bychan, *The Little Marsh,*

and, narrowly escaping the hands of lord Stanley, who discovered and seized her jewels and baggage, found in this fortress an asylum from her enemies. She resided here but a little while, when she proceeded into Scotland, where, collecting her friends, she marched towards Wakefield. At the latter place she made an attack on the army of her enemy, the duke of York, which she routed; and she further succeeded in destroying the leader.

Soon after Edward IV. attained the English throne, he found means to make himself master of every part of the kingdom, except this castle and two or three others in Northumberland. These he did not think it necessary immediately to attack, in the expectation, probably, that when their governors saw the whole country continue in quiet possession, they would of their own accord submit. The idea, however, proved groundless, for David ap Ivan ap Einion, a staunch friend to the house of Lancaster, held out in this castle for nine years afterwards, till 1468. The king finding him still determined to resist, was at length compelled to send an army against him under the command of William Herbert, earl of Pembroke. The men with incredible difficulty marched over the heart of the British Alps to the attack. On being summoned to surrender, David returned for answer: " Some years ago I held a castle in France against its besiegers so long, that all the old women in Wales talked of me : inform your commander that I will defend this Welsh castle till all the old women of France shall hear of it." The besieging army found the place altogether impregnable, except by famine, and sir Richard Herbert (brother to the earl), who had commanded during the siege, was at last obliged to compound for the surrender, by promising the heroic Welshman that he would intercede with the king for his life. It was therefore given up, and with it upwards of fifty gentlemen of rank who had adhered

across the channel eight miles towards Harlech. This so much injured the grass as to
kill the cattle; and it set hay and corn-ricks
on fire for near a mile from the coast. It
is represented to have had the appearance of a
blue lambent flame, which by any great noise,
such as the firing of guns, or the sounding of
horns, was easily extinguished. All the damage
was done in the night; and, in the course
of the winter, no fewer than sixteen hay-
ricks, and two barns, one filled with hay, and
the other with corn, were entirely destroyed by
it. It did not seem to affect any thing else, and
men could go into it without receiving the least
injury. It was observed much more frequently

to the Lancastrian cause. These were all committed close
prisoners to the tower; and when David was brought to the
king, sir Richard intreated that he might receive an uncon-
ditioned pardon, on the ground that it had been in his power,
if he had chosen it, to retain the castle considerably longer,
even in spite of all the efforts of the English army. The
king refused. " Then, Sire, (said sir Richard,) you may, if
you please, take my life instead of that of the Welsh
captain : if you do not, I will most assuredly replace David
in his castle, and your highness may send whom you please
to take him out again." The king knew too well the value
of a hero like Sir Richard, to carry his denial any further.
David ap Ivan was pardoned, but his friend received no
other reward for this perilous service.

In the civil wars of the reign of Charles I., Harlech
castle was the last in North Wales that held out for the
king, being surrendered in March 1647, to general Mytton,
on honourable terms. At this time Mr. William Owen
was the governor, and the garrison consisted but of twenty-
eight men.

The *town* of Harlech was made a free borough by
Edward I., who confirmed to it several grants of lands and
other emoluments.

during the first three weeks than afterwards, yet it was seen, at different intervals, for at least eight months. The occasion of this singular phenomenon is not exactly known. It appears most probably to have arisen from some collections of putrid substances, the vapour issuing from which might have been directed towards this place by the wind; and yet it is singular that, although the prevailing winds here are from the south-west, which ought to have blown it in a very different direction, it should not have been observed in other parts north of Harlech. Bishop Gibson conjectured that it might have proceeded from the corrupted bodies of a great number of locusts which visited this kingdom about that time, and were destroyed by the coldness of the climate. He says that a considerable number of them had been seen lying about the shores of Aberdaron, in Caernarvonshire.

The *public house* at Harlech, for such it can only be denominated, was kept, when I was last there, by a very civil man of the name of Anwyl. The provisions were homely, but the beds (only two, and those in the same room) were clean and comfortable.

Y

EXCURSION FROM HARLECH TO CWM BYCHAN.

Conducted by a guide, I went from Harlech to explore an obscure vale, about four miles distant, called Cwm Bychan, *The Little Hollow.*

About a mile from the town, on a large elevated moor, he pointed out to me a circle of small stones near thirty yards in diameter, with another at some distance, surrounding it. From its form and appearance, I am inclined to suppose that this was one of those

DRUIDICAL CIRCLES

In which were formerly holden the *Gorseddau,* or bardic meetings. These meetings were always in some place set apart in the open air, in a conspicuous situation, and surrounded by a circle of stones, having in the centre a larger one, by which the presiding bard or druid stood. There was here no relic of the middle stone. This kind of circle was called *Cylch Cyngrair,* or the circle of congress. At these meetings, candidates were admitted to the different degrees of bardism, and on these occasions it was that all the oral bardic poems and traditions were recited, and their laws settled. During these ceremonies all the bards stood within the circle, with their heads and feet bare, and clad in their unicoloured robes.

CWM BYCHAN

Is a grassy dell, about half a mile in length, surrounded by scenery as black and dreary as imagination can paint. On the right of its entrance there is a small pool called *Llyn y Cwm Bychan,* from whose edge, Carreg y Saeth, *The Rock of the Arrow,* (from its being the station where the ancient British sportsmen watched and killed the passing deer,) towers the blackest of all the vale.—I rested myself for a while on a rock above the pool, in a situation whence I could at ease observe the rugged beauties of this romantic hollow. From hence the landscape extended in all its magnificence: the vale was seen embosomed in stupendous rocks, black and barren, and enlivened only by the patches of meagre vegetation lodged on their shelving precipices.

We descended into the hollow, and passing an ancient mansion, ascended on the other side till we came to a deep mountain hollow called

BWLCH TYDDIAD.

Here the rocks close, and oppose a series of shattered precipices, forming a scene of desolation and barrenness throughout. A few grasses,

liverwort, and heath, constitute all the vegeta
tion of this place. We wandered on this rocky
cleft, for such it only seemed, until we got beyond the higher mountains, when, on a sudden,
a fine open prospect of all the country eastward
was extended before us. Here we were treated
with a pastoral landscape, bounded by high distant mountains, which formed a majestic barrier around : amongst these, Cader Idris, and
the two Arrennigs, were particularly conspicuous.

DRWS ARDUDWY.

From hence we made a turn to the right, still
continuing our journey over a wretched horse-
path, and soon afterwards turning again to the
right, we entered another deep glen called
Drws Ardudwy, *The Pass of the Maritime Land,*
a place well calculated to inspire a timid mind
with terror. The sides and bottom were
almost covered over with loose fragments
of stone, once detached by the force of frost,
or the irresistible rushing of torrents, after
storms and heavy rain, from the heights
above.

After this dreary scene, we entered a more
wide and fertile valley, called Cwm Nancoll,
The Hollow of the sunken Brook. From hence
the guide took me, out of the usual track, to
see a *cromlech,* in a farm called Gwern Einion.
This cromlech is about two miles south of
Harlech. It is at present made to form the
corner of a wall, and is, on two sides, built up

with stones, to prevent the sheep from getting through. There are six supporters, three about six feet, and the other three about four feet in height. The stone that rests upon these is large, flat and slanting.

CATARACT.

A little while before we came to this crom-lech, I heard, from the side of the hill on which we were walking, the falling of water, in a wood on the opposite mountains, and apparently about half a mile from us. I could also, notwithstanding the distance, plainly perceive a silver line among the trees, formed by the rushing of water down a precipice. The guide in answer to my questions respecting it, said that it was a cataract of no great height or beauty, and if it had a name he was not acquainted with it. My walk of this day had been very long and laborious, near twenty miles, over the most stony paths that I had yet seen in the country, and I was almost fainting from want of refreshment : I was therefore under the necessity of being satisfied with his account. In almost any other case I should have crossed the vale to examine it, for I am convinced, from its appearance at so great a distance, that it must have been a cataract of very considerable height and beauty.

Betwixt the cromlech and the town of Har-lech, I passed another druidical circle, some-what smaller than the one I have before mentioned, but surrounded with a similar distant circle.

As it happened to be about the ebb of the tide when we returned, the guide pointed out to me part of a long stone-wall, which runs out into the sea from Mochras, a point of land a few miles south of Harlech, in a west-south-west direction for near twenty miles. This is called

SARN BADRWYG,

The Shipwrecking Causeway. It is a very wonderful work, being throughout about twenty-four feet in thickness. *Sarn y Bwch* runs from a point north-west of Harlech, and is supposed to meet the end of this. The space betwixt these formed, some centuries ago, a habitable hundred belonging to Merionethshire, called

CANTREF GWAELOD,

The Lowland Hundred. The Welsh have yet traditions respecting several of the towns, as Caer Gwyddno, Caer Ceneder, &c. These walls were built to keep out the sea. About the year 500, when Gwyddno Garan Hîr, *Gwyddno with the high Crown,* was lord of this hundred, one of the men who had the care of the dams, got drunk and left open a flood-gate. The sea broke through with such force, as also to tear down part of the wall, and overflow the whole hundred, which, since that time, has been always completely flooded.—Thus is *Cardigan Bay*, (a principal part of which Cantref Gwaelod formerly occupied,) for many miles so full of shoals, as to render it extremely dangerous for a vessel of any burthen to venture at all near the Merionethshire coast.

CHAP. XXV.

HARLECH TO BARMOUTH.

Upright Stones.—Cromlechs.—Ancient Barrows, the Mode of forming, and the Utility of them.—Barmouth.—Houses singularly situated.—Inn.—Beach, and River.—Uncommonly beautiful Scene.—Trade of Barmouth.

THE road from Harlech to Barmouth (ten miles) is even and good; but lying over a flat and disagreeable country, it is beyond measure dull and uninteresting. At a distance towards the sea there are nothing but turfy bogs and salt marshes; and, on the other side, the mountains are low and stony, and in every respect devoid of picturesque beauty.

In a field by the road-side, near Llanbedir, I observed two upright stones standing near each other, the one ten, and the other about six feet in height. These were without inscriptions, and are what the Welsh call *Meini Gwyr*, " stones of the heroes;" or the funeral monuments of celebrated warriors slain in battle.

A few hundred yards beyond the fifth mile

stone, and at a little distance on the left of
the road, two *cromlechs* were pointed out to
me. They were near each other, and placed
on barrows, or heaps of loose stones. These
barrows or *carnedds,* as they are usually called, from the circumstance of the cromlechs
being erected on them, are evidently of high
antiquity.—The mode of forming the carnedd
in this country was somewhat singular. When
it was considered as the honourable tomb of
a warrior, every one that passed by threw on
it an additional stone as a mark of respect;
but when this heap became disgraced by
shielding the body of the guilty, it was still
the custom of every one that passed to fling
his stone, but, in this case, it was done in
token of detestation.—The original intention
of heaping stones over the dead, was doubtless to defend the bodies from being dug up,
and devoured by the wolves, with which the
wild and mountainous parts of Britain formerly abounded. It was a necessary precaution, to prevent the friends of the deceased from
being shocked by the horrid sight of their car-
cases mangled by these rapacious animals.

I passed *Cors y Gedol,* the ancient family
seat of the Vaughans, but now the property
of sir Thomas Mostyn, bart., and continuing
my journey by Llanaber, soon afterwards arrived at

BARMOUTH.

This town is situated in one of the most unpleasant places that could have been chosen for

it, near the conflux of the river Maw, or Mawddach*.—Some of the houses are built among
the sand at the bottom, and others, at different
heights, up the side of a huge rock, which entirely shelters the place on the east. The situations of the latter are so singular, that it is
really curious for a stranger to wind up along
the narrow paths among the houses, where, on
one side, he may, if he please, enter the door
of a dwelling, or, on the other, look down the
chimney of the neighbour in front. The inhabitants might almost cure their bacon in some
parts of this town by the simple process of
hanging it out of their windows. The houses
at the foot of the rock are nearly choaked up
with sand, which fills every passage, and is blown
into every window that is for a moment left
open. In rainy weather this sand, on the contrary, renders the place very dirty and unpleasant. The buildings are exceedingly irregular,
and in most instances very bad. Notwithstanding all these disadvantages, Barmouth is frequented during the summer season by many gen-
teel families from Wales, and the west of England, as a sea-bathing place. Its origin, as the
resort of invalids, has been attributed to persons
frequenting the banks of this part of the river
for the sake of the scurvygrass, which grows
there in great abundance.

The company must necessarily find it a most
uncomfortable place, for the inn (the Corsygedol
arms) is at times almost buried in sand, and
no person can possibly walk many yards with-

---

* From this river the town is sometimes called Aber Maw,
The Conflux of the Maw. This has been shortened into
'Bermaw, and corrupted to Barmouth.

out having it over his shoes. Were it not for the civility and friendly attention of Mrs. Lewis the inn keeper, Barmouth would fail in its principal attraction.—I was beyond measure surprized, on being introduced into the dining-room, to find, in this secluded corner of the kingdom, upwards of thirty persons, most of them of fortune and fashion. I found also on inquiry, that this was by no means all the company at that time in the town; another large and good building, which Mrs. Lewis had in her own hands as a lodging-house, being also quite full. To be thus suddenly introduced, as it were, into the world, after my solitary rambles among the wilds of the country, was a very grateful incident; and I enjoyed the general cheerfulness and affability that prevailed, perhaps the more from its being entirely unexpected.

The lodging-houses in the town are many of them dirty and miserable places.—There are on the sands three bathing machines, but these are altogether appropriated to the use of the ladies, the gentlemen bathing on the open coast —The amusements seem to consist principally in going out in parties on the water, and in promenading on the beach or the sands. The beach is one of the most delightful walks I ever beheld. The wide river Mawddach winds amongst the mountains, forming many, and elegant promontories. These rise to great heights on each side, some clad with wood, and others exhibiting their naked rocks, scantily covered with the purple heath. The summit of the lofty Cader Idris is seen to rise high above the other mountains, in the back ground. Had the town been built here, scarcely half a mile from its present situation, instead of one of the most unpleasant, it might have been rendered one of the most delightful retirements in the kingdom.

Barmouth is the port of Merionethshire. Mr. Pennant, however, informs us, that prior to the year 1781, flannels to the value of 40,000l., and stockings to the value of 10,000l., had been exported from hence in the course of a year.—The number of ships at present belonging to this port is about a hundred : and the population of the place is estimated at fifteen hundred.

CHAP. XXVI.

BARMOUTH TO DOLGELLE.

The River Mawddach.—Beautiful Scenery.—Dolgelle.—. Whimsical Description of Dolgelle.—Fuller's Enigmatical Description.—Trade.—Inn.—Fortified in the Reign of Charles I.—Account of Places worth visiting in the Neighbourhood of Dolgelle.

EXCURSION FROM DOLGELLE TO KEMMER ABBEY AND THE WATERFALLS.

Y Vanner, or Kemmer Abbey.—Cataract at Dolmelynllyn.— Distant Waterfall.—Cataract of the Mawddach.—Cataract of the Cain.

I HAD already been highly gratified in my ramble along the beach for about a mile and a half from Barmouth; and, in my walk to Dolgelle, I retraced my steps with additional pleasure. The Mawddach, usually called Avon Vawr, *The Great River,* forms in this place a wide arm of the sea. It was now high water, and from the whole bed of the river being filled, the various scenes that presented themselves for some miles were truly picturesque. The two first miles, at the end of which I was compelled to leave the bank of the river, and proceed along the road, were, however, more interesting than any other part of the journey. In the composition of the views, scarcely any thing appeared wanting : there was every requisite of a fine landscape, mountain and vale, wood, water, meadows, and rocks, arranged in beautiful order. The numerous heaps of peat spread along the green bottom, were the only unpleasing objects in the scene, and these were easily overlooked where every other object was so beautiful.—Beyond the beach the road winds among the low mountains, at a little distance from the river. From the openings or eminences I frequently saw the water, partly hidden by the intervening mountains, in which situations it several times assumed the appearance of a beautiful lake.

From the village of Llanelltyd, about two miles from Dolgelle, there is a road which winds along a dark and gloomy vale towards Tanybwlch ; and at a little distance a stile is seen, from whence a footpath will lead the inquiring tourist, over the meadows, to the ancient monastic ruin called by the Welsh Y Vanner, and by Tanner *Kemmer Abbey*. This will be described in the ensuing chapter.

Many persons prefer making the excursion from Barmouth to Dolgelle by water. To sit at ease, and enjoy without interruption the pleasures afforded by the picturesque scenes along the Mawddach, must doubtless be highly gratifying to an admirer of nature. The voyage, however, must end at the distance of about a mile from Dolgelle, for here the river becomes so greatly diminished, as not even to admit a pleasure boat any farther. The company must therefore be contented to walk from thence to the town.

DOLGELLE,

The Holme of the Groves, is a market town, in a commercial view, of some importance, seated in a wide and fertile vale, between the rivers **Arran** and **Wnion**, and surrounded on all sides by high, and in many parts wooded, mountains.

A student of **Jesus College, Oxford**, who was a native of **Dolgelle**, was one afternoon drinking wine with a party of collegians, when, in a bantering stile, they asked what kind of a place it was that had been honoured in giving him birth : —" There," says he, flinging on the table a handful of nuts, and setting up a cork in the middle, " suppose each of these nuts a house, and that cork the church,—you will have some tolerable idea of **Dolgelle**."

The analogy holds good, for the streets are as irregular as it is possible to imagine them. The houses in general are low, and ill built. The *church*, which is by much the neatest structure in or about the place, has in itself nothing that can attract particular attention.   From various points of view on the outside of the town, the painter will, however, acknowledge, that it is not without its beauty.

We have a singular enigmatical account of **Dolgelle**, written by Fuller somewhat more than a century ago.

" 1. The walls thereof are three miles high.
  2. Men go into it over the water; but
  3. Go out of it under the water.
  4. The steeple thereof doth grow therein.
  5. There are more ale-houses than houses."*

These five enigmas he solves in this manner: the *first*, he says, is explained by the mountains that surround the place. The *second* implies, that on one side of the town there was a bridge over which all travellers must pass; and the *third*, that on the other side, they had to go under a wooden trough, which conveyed water from a rock, at a little distance, to an overshot mill. For the *fourth*, he says, the bells (if plural) hung in a yew tree; and the *last*, that " tenements were divided into two or more tipling-houses, and that even chimney-less barns were often used for that purpose."—I presume in this he alludes to the time in which some fair was held, for the sale and exchange of the manufactures of the place. None of these remarks will apply at present except the two first.

There are at Dolgelle very considerable manufactories of flannel, which, from the number of hands' necessarily employed, have rendered the place very populous, comparatively with other Welsh towns. The principal market for the goods is Shrewsbury, but so great a portion has of late been bought on the spot, that the inhabitants have had little occasion to send to a market at such a distance.

The best *inn* is the Golden Lion, called likewise Plas Isa, *The Lower House.* The provi-

---

* Fuller's Worthies of Wales, p. 43.

sions, except the wine, I found good; but the bed into which I was put was intolerable.

During the civil wars of the reign of Charles I., about a hundred of the king's troops attempted to raise a fortification around this town. Mr. Edward Vaughan, however, at the head of a small party of the parliament's forces, attacked and routed them, taking prisoners the captain and several of the men.

The neighbourhood of Dolgelle affords many interesting objects to the tourist. The summit of *Cader Idris*, the celebrated Merionethshire mountain, is not much more than six miles distant. A few miles towards the north, and at a little distance from each other, are the three cataracts *Rhaiadr Dú*, *The Fall of the Cain*, and *The Fall of the Mawddach*. To all these places guides may be taken from Dolgelle.—The whole of the vale in which the town is situated is remarkable for its picturesque scenery, and beautiful views.

EXCURSION FROM DOLGELLE TO KEMMER ABBEY, AND THE WATERFALLS.

In my excursion to the above mentioned waterfalls, I proceeded near a mile and a half along the road, when, (a few hundred yards before I reached the bridge at Llanelltid,) I

z

left it, and went on a foot-path to the right.
This led me over some meadows, for about a
quarter of a mile, to an avenue of sycamores,
and thence to the remains of an abbey, not
visible from the road, called by the Welsh, Y
Vanner, and by the old writers, Kemmer
abbey.*

> Where pious beadsmen, from the world retir'd,
> In blissful visions wing'd their souls to heav'n,
> While future joys their nobler transports fir'd,
> They wept their erring days, and were forgiv'n.

The present remains of this monastery have
little interest for any but the antiquary : they
are altogether devoid of ornament or elegance,
and from no point of view are in any degree
picturesque. Part of the church only is left,
and the space of ground it occupies is very inconsiderable. The ruins of the refectory and
the abbot's dwelling, form part of the walls of
an adjoining farm house. The other parts are
much shattered, and the farmer, in whose ground
the building stands, has patched them in many
places with modern masonry, to render them of
use in his business. The length of the church
is betwixt thirty and forty yards, and the width
not more than eight or nine. The east end is
more perfect than any other part, and, through
its thick covering of ivy, I could discern three
small lancet-shaped windows. Against the south
wall there are a few small gothic pillars and
arches ; and in the wall an aperture where pro-

* Or variously, Cymmer, Cymner, Cwmner, Kinner,
Kinmer, and Kymmer Abbey. *Kymer*, in the ancient British language, signified the meeting of two or more rivers.

bably the holy water was kept. In this part of the building, opposite to two small arches, there has also been a semi-circular door; and, near this, there is the mutilated head of a human figure. A large plane-tree is now growing from among the ruins of the west-end of the building, whence it should seem to have long been in a ruined state. From the obscurity of its situation, and the want of that kind of elegance which is usual in monastic ruins, this abbey is scarcely known even at Dolgelle. The tourist will inquire for it in vain as Kemmer abbey, for the Welsh people in general know it by no other name than that of Y Vanner.*

* This abbey was founded about the year 1200 for some monks of the Cistercian order, from Cwm Hir Abbey in Radnorshire, by Meredith and Griffith, the sons of Cynan ap Owen Gwynnedd, prince of North Wales. This seems, (says a Welsh writer) to have been a colony of monks, sent off by that monastery, as bees do when the hive is too full.†

About thirty years after the supposed period of its foundation, Kemmer abbey appears to have been in a flourishing state. At this time, when Henry III. was marching against the Welsh, who had risen, under their prince, Llewelyn ap Iorwerth, and attacked the castle of Montgomery, one of the monks of Kemmer happened to be near, and was questioned as to the situation and strength of the Welsh army. He considered it a duty to befriend his country, rather than assist the enemy, and therefore deceived them so much by his report of the state of the opposing forces, that Henry determined on an immediate attack. The Welsh, at the first onset, feigned a retreat to a neighbouring marsh. The English soldiers, incumbered as they were with their armour, plunged, without hesitation, after them, and as soon as the enemy saw that the greater part were in the marsh, and unable either to act offensively or to retreat, they returned

† Letter of Lewis Morris. Cam. Reg. ii. 493. This seems to account for Dugdale's mistake in confounding this abbey with that of Combehire, or Cwm Hir, in Radnorshire.

On a bank not far distant, there was formerly a British fortress called Castell Cymmer, *The Castle of the Conflux*. This was demolished about the year 1113, not along after its erection, by the sons of Cadwgan ap Bleddyn, on some disagreement with the founder; and it is supposed to have never been rebuilt.

Returning from the abbey to the road, I crossed the bridge at Llaneltid, and proceeded along the vale leading towards Tanybwlch. The first waterfall the guide brought me to was

RHAIADR DU,

The Black Cataract. This, as I have before said, is in the grounds of **W. A. Madocks, esq.** at Dolmelynllyn, whence it is often called the *Dolmelynllyn Fall.*—The water foams, with thundering noise, down two rocks about sixty feet high. The scene has a singular appearance from the black adjacent and uncouth rocks being in many places covered with a pure white lichen. The trees on one side of the stream

upon them with so much fury, as, after a short conflict, to come off victorious.—This deception enraged the king, and, not long afterwards, as he passed the abbey with his army, he ordered the monastery to be set on fire and destroyed. All the out-offices were consumed, but the abbot saved the rest of the building by his entreaties to the king, and paying down a fine of three hundred marks.

At the dissolution of abbies, the revenues of Kemmer were estimated at betwixt fifty and sixty pounds a year. The site remained in the crown till the reign of queen Elizabeth, who, about the year 1578, granted it to Robert, earl of Leicester.

had been lately cut down, but the lively and varied green and brown tints of the other were beautifully contrasted with the almost jet black rocks with which they were intermixed. The torrent rolls into a small deep bason, from whence it dashes along the rugged channel to the river Mawddach, which flows at no great distance. Mr. Madocks has been at the expence of making a good foot-path, both to the bottom, and to the upper part of this cataract, by which the traveller is enabled with comfort to see it to the greatest advantage.

I went about a mile farther on the road, from whence I had a walk of near two miles, along a foot-path to the right, to the remaining water-falls, which are within a few hundred yards of each other. From the side of an eminence about half a mile from these, I could observe the river Mawddach rolling down a steep, in a woody vale above, and its hoarse murmuring just reached my ear. Beyond it, at some distance, there was a rude arch, which crossed the glen, and from my station gave a pleasing and romantic cast to the scene.

> Descending now (but cautious lest too fast),
> A sudden steep upon a rustic bridge,
> We pass a gulph in which the hazels dip
> Their pendant boughs.————

This was a perfectly alpine bridge over the river Cain, formed by the rude trunk of an oak which hung frightfully over the black torrent, that roared amongst the rocks many feet beneath. I had not passed this bridge far, before I found myself at the foot of Rhaiadr y Mawddach,

THE CATARACT OF THE MAWDDACH.

The river here forces itself down a rock betwixt fifty and sixty feet in height, whose strata, lying in parallel lines several degrees inclined from the horizon, give to the scene a singularly crooked appearance. The stream is thrice broken in its descent, and the bason into which it is precipitated is very large. The rocks and trees form an amphitheatre around, and the foreground was finely broken by the large pieces of rock that had been once loosened from above. I had to cross the stream before I could see the upper part of the fall, which was hidden by intervening rocks. In this station the scene appeared complete, and it was certainly picturesque.

PISTYLL Y CAIN,*

The Spout of the Cain, is by far the highest and most magnificent cataract of the three. A narrow stream rushes down a vast rock, at least a hundred and fifty feet high, whose horizontal strata run in irregular steps through its whole breadth, and form a mural front. These, indeed, are so regular, as in a great measure to destroy

* The word *Pistyll,* in the Welsh language, signifies a narrow stream of water, somewhat resembling that which issues through a spout.

the picturesque effect of the scene, unless they ar enearly hidden by a much greater volume of water than usual. Immense fragments of broken rock at the foot of the cataract, scattered in every different direction, communicate a pleasing effect ; and the agreeable mixture of tints of the dark oak and birch, with the yellower and fading elm, formed altogether a highly pleasing scene.

My guide to the waterfalls was an English-man, who keeps a small public house near Dol-melynllyn. His name is Bartlet. He has re-sided in Wales only a few years, and is yet scarcely able to speak the language of the country,

CHAP. XXVII.

DOLGELLE TO MACHYNLLETH.

View of the Country around Dolgelle.—The Pool of the three Pebbles ; and tradition respecting the enormous Giant Idris.—The Blue Lion, and Edward Jones.—Ascent to the Summit of Cader Idris.—Account of Idris.—Cascades.— Llyn y Cae.—Prospect from the Summit of Cader Idris. —Cataract near the Blue Lion.—Machynlleth.—Mr. Aikin's Description of the Devil's Bridge, near Havod in Cardiganshire.

From the road leading to Machynlleth, and at the distance of about two miles, the town of Dolgelle is seen to greater advantage than from most other points of view. It appears in the midst of a vale replete with pastoral beauty. The wide river Mawddach in the distance, reflects its silvery whiteness in the bosom of high and dreary mountains. The intervening space exhibits luxuriant woods, meadows, and cornfields, intersected by the river Wnion, which serpentizes along the vale.

The road now passes over high and swampy moors, and for some miles the scenery is wild, dreary, and comfortless. The lofty Cader Idris, its summit obscured in clouds, formed the entire boundary of these wilds towards the south-west.

THE POOL OF THE THREE PEBBLES.

This is a small pool on the left of the road about five miles from Dolgelle. The Welsh call it *Llyn Trigrainwyn.* It has its name from the three huge fragments of rock that are seen by its side, which the traditions of the peasantry assert to have been what the giant Idris called three pebbles. This huge man, from whom the adjacent mountain had its name, was one day walking round his possessions in these mountains when, says tradition, he found something had fallen into his shoe that began to hurt his foot. He pulled it off, and threw out these three pebbles, after which he experienced no further inconvenience! One of these *pebbles* is about four and twenty feet long, eighteen broad, and twelve high. — So much for tradition!

The pool is believed to be bottomless; but though this is not the case, its depth for so small a surface of water is uncommonly great, being, as I was informed, upwards of fifty fathoms.

I had not proceeded far beyond this pool, when I found the prospect become somewhat interesting. A pleasing vale now presented itself, which incloses a pool about a mile in length, called Llyn Mwyngil, *The Lake of the Pleasant Retreat.* This is bounded by hills.

THE BLUE LION.

As I was anxious to ascend **Cader Idris**, and, although the weather had become very unfavourable, as I should lose all opportunity of doing it if I proceeded any farther at present, I stopped at the Blue Lion, a small public house, a little beyond the pool of the Three Pebbles. It had begun to rain very hard a little before my arrival, and, as it was then late in the day, I determined to remain here all night, in the hope that before morning the weather might clear up. Not having yet dined, I enquired what I could have to eat, but found, as **Dr.** Johnson did at Glenelg, in the Highlands of Scotland, that, " of the provisions, the negative catalogue was very copious." I could have no meat (except bad bacon,) no eggs, no wine, no spirits. It was needless to inquire further into what I could *not* have, I therefore directed the good woman of the house to bring me any thing that was eatable. Bread and butter, and new ale, taken evidently from the tub in which it was fermenting, constituted therefore my principal fare at this cottage for two days.

The landlord of the Blue Lion, if I may dignify him with that appellation, is a school-master, a guide, and a cutter of grave-stones, and to his various other qualifications, he adds a very considerable taste for—ale, as the following memoranda of my cheap living at this house will shew:

	s.	d.
Two dinners (N. B. bread and butter),	1	6
Tea, supper, and breakfast, - - -	1	0
Ale, - - - - - - - - - - -	2	6
	5	0

This man, whose name is Edward Jones, I found somewhat too talkative, particularly on the subject of his own qualifications. I obtained from him much of the news of the neighbourhood, but little information on which I could rely respecting the country.

This house is situated by the road side, immediately under Cader Idris, and is a very convenient place from whence travellers, coming from Machynlleth, may ascend that mountain. If it be not found inconvenient, on account of carriages or horses, they may pass over the summit, and down the other way to Dolgelle: this they would do in nearly as short a space of time as it would require to descend again to the Blue Lion.—The bed I slept in was not a very bad one, nor was I here, though in a smaller house, so pestered with fleas, as I had before been at Beddgelert.

ASCENT TO THE SUMMIT OF CADER IDRIS.

The morning proved more favourable than I expected; and although it was still cloudy, I was determined to venture on an excursion to the summit of the mountain, under the hopes that the weather might entirely clear up before I arrived at the top. About nine o'clock, therefore, in company with my loquacious host, I commenced my expedition.

I have said that this mountain had its name from a person called Idris, supposed by tradition to have been an enormous giant. The old bardic writings, however, rather represent him great in mind than stature: in these he is said to have been a poet, an astronomer, and philosopher. He is supposed also to have been a prince of these parts; but the period is so remote, that little more than his name and talents are now to be ascertained. *Cadair Idris,* or the seat of Idris, is thought to imply that he had an observatory, or study, on the summit of the mountain. These suppositions, however, seem founded on a very insufficient basis.

There had been much rain during the night, in consequence of which the guide took me along the side of a rivulet, which flows from one of the hollows above, to see a small cataract. The torrent was thrown down the face of a steep rock in a white sheet of foam, thrice broken in its descent. It might perhaps be more properly denominated a cascade, for, although it was extremely pretty, it was on so small a scale, as to be devoid of much of the grandeur that is usual in waterfalls which boast any degree of picturesque beauty.—Above this, on the same stream, another still more small and contracted was pointed out to me. The height of the latter rock was not more than seven or eight yards, and the whole scene would have appeared very trifling, had it not been ornamented by three majestic oaks, whose branches, whilst they almost concealed the stream, added greatly to its beauty.

Crossing the rivulet, I went for a little way along its bank, and was much pleased with several other cascades that were formed in its descent. After a while I arrived in the mountain hollow, that contains the waters of

LLYN Y CAE,[*]

The inclosed Pool, from the west side of which rises a stupendous, black, and precipitous rock, called *Craig y Cae,* that casts a gloomy shade on every thing below it, and throws upon the water its own dismal hue. Its sullen and majestic front was enlivened only with patches of the moss saxifrage, and a few goats, that were seen skipping carelessly among its dangerous steeps. From its spiry points and deep precipices, it has assumed an appearance that somewhat resembles the age-worn front of a massy cathedral. The whole of the scene, from near the edge of the pool, was truly picturesque and grand.

Whilst I was gazing at the rock, a shower of rain so smart came on, that in a short time my clothes were wet through. Soon after this the clouds rose above the lower parts of the mountain, and the highest peak alone was clouded.— The summit is called Pen y Cader, *The Head of*

---

[*] " Some travellers have mentioned the finding of lava, and other volcanic productions here : upon strict examination, however, we were unable to discover any thing of the kind; nor did the water of the lake appear to differ in any respect from the purest rock water, though it was tried repeatedly with the most delicate tests." *Aikin's Tour through North Wales,* p. 62.

the Seat. This, like that of Snowdon, is conical,
and covered with loose stones. With the utmost
patience and composure, I waited on this point,
enveloped in mist, for more than half an hour,
when, for about ten minutes, the mountain became perfectly cleared. I had from hence a
view, if not more extensive, I think more varied,
than that from Snowdon. On one side the mountain formed an abrupt and deep precipice, at the
bottom of which a small lake or two were
lodged. The distant views were of Bala Pool,
and its adjacent mountains, and beyond these
of the long range of Ferwyn mountains, headed
by Cader Ferwyn. Towards the south lay the
county of Montgomery, which, with its celebrated mountain Plinlimmon, seemed almost
immediately under the eye. On the west side I
had the whole curve of Cardigan Bay, from St.
David's entirely round to Caernarvonshire. I
had scarcely looked round, when the gathering
clouds swept over me in deeper folds, and all was
again concealed from my sight.

The ascent to the summit of Cader Idris is
much more easy than that of Snowdon; and I
am confident that from Jones's house I could
attain the highest point in about two hours.—
The perpendicular height of this mountain, mea-
sured from the green near Dolgelle, is but 950
yards.*—Cader Idris has three high points, the
most lofty is called *Pen y Cader;* the next in
height *Mynydd Moel;* and the other *Craig y Cae.*

In descending I took a direction eastward of
that in which I had gone up, and proceeded
along that part of the mountain called *Mynydd*

* Pennant, ii. 99.

Moel. The path in this direction is sufficiently sloping to allow a person to ride even to the summit. A gentleman, mounted on a little Welsh poney, had done this a few days before I was here.

At the bottom of a hill on the right of the road leading to Machynlleth, and about half a mile from the Blue Lion, I saw another small cataract, which, although scarcely more than seven or eight yards high, was by no means destitute of beauty. The rock is five or six times as wide at the top as it is below, which gives to the scene a very singular effect. In dry weather I should think this would be in want of water: after a heavy shower of rain it may, however, be always seen in perfection.

The road from Jones's cottage to Machynlleth is level and good; but as I had rain nearly the whole way, and as it lies along a narrow hollow, between a series of wooded mountains, without much variety of character, even this short journey was rendered very unpleasant. The murmuring of the rivulet, which accompanied me for some miles, and here and there a picturesque cottage, seated in the woods, chiefly occupied my attention, till I had arrived within two miles of Machynlleth. Towards evening the rain ceased, the clouds dispersed, and the fine vale in which the town stands appeared exceedingly beautiful. Machynlleth is hidden from the observer in this direction, by intervening mountains, till he is arrived within about a mile of it; and it is first seen on a sudden turn of the road at a little distance from the river.

MACHYNLLETH.[*]

I crossed the Dovey, and shortly afterwards arrived at Machynlleth, a neat, and much more regularly built town than most in Wales. The town-hall is a plain unadorned structure; and the church (a common fault in this country) is white-washed. From the church-yard there is a pretty view along a green and meadowy vale. Machynlleth is a place of some trade, and it has an air of greater opulence than most of the Welsh towns.

An ancient building, constructed of the thin shaly stone of this country, and now converted into stables, was pointed out to me as that in which Owen Glyndwr summoned the chieftains of Wales in the year 1402. He was here acknowledged their prince, and as such proclaimed and crowned.

It is highly probable that this town was the site of *Maglona*, the principal Roman station in Montgomeryshire. Near Penallt, about two miles distant, there is a place called Cefyn Caer, *The Ridge of the City*, where Roman coins have frequently been found, and where there has once been a small circular fort.

When on the point of setting out from Machynlleth to Llanydloes, I was informed of a lofty cataract, near a pool called Llyn Pen Rhaiadr, *The Pool at the Head of the Cataract*, about six miles distant; but, as the road lay

---

[*] This word implies *the place near the river Cynllaeth*, which was the ancient name for the Dovey.

entirely over the mountains, and I was desirous
to reach Llanydloes as soon as possible, I did
not take the trouble of visiting it.

If I had not (in order that I might confine
my attention altogether to North Wales, and
give to it all the time I had to spare) entered
into a resolution not even to set my foot in the
southern division of the principality, I should
have gone from Machynlleth to

ABERYSTWYTH,

The Conflux of the Istwyth, distant about nine-
teen miles. This is now a celebrated sea-bathing place, frequented by much company.—It
has the remains of a castle, founded at the
commencement of the twelfth century by Gilbert
Strongbow, but about two centuries afterwards
rebuilt by king Edward I.

From hence I should have proceeded to an inn,
about twelve miles off, called the Havod Arms,
not far from which is the celebrated bridge called
Pont ar Monach, *The Bridge over the Monach*,
and by the English, *The Devil's Bridge;* and
from this place I should have returned into North
Wales near Llanydloes.—The excursion altogether would not have been .more than fifty
miles, and the twenty miles of unpleasant road
betwixt Machynlleth and the Llanydloes I
should by this means have avoided.

THE DEVIL'S BRIDGE.

As, however, it may be useful to some future traveller in this country, I shall transcribe the short description of the Devil's Bridge, and the deep glen over which it is built, from an interesting journey through North Wales by Mr. Aikin. It is the only account on the accuracy of which I could rely.*

" After a long, and rather tedious walk (from Aberystwyth,) we came suddenly to a most singularly striking spot.   The valley of the Rhydol contracts into a deep glen, the rocky banks of which are clothed with plantations, and at the bottom runs a rapid torrent.   This leads soon to the spot that we were in search of, which is full of horrid sublimity.   It is formed by a deep chasm, or cleft, between two rocks, which just receives light enough to discover at the bottom, through the tangled thickets, an impetuous torrent, which is soon lost under a lofty bridge.   By descending an hundred feet, we had a clearer view of this romantic scene. Just above our heads was a double bridge, which has been thrown over the gulph; the inferior bridge was built by a monastery, and hence called Pont ar Monach ; this growing to decay, and being thought insecure, another arch was thrown directly above, and resting on the ancient one, and which now supports a good road across the precipice.   The water below has scooped out several deep chasms in the rock,

* Journal of a Tour through North Wales, and part of Shropshire.   Crown 8vo, Lond. 1797

through which it flows before it dives under the
bridge. A large beech has flung its boughs
horizontally over the torrent, as if to hide it
from the spectator; and the whole banks of this
wild spot are rough with fern, moss, and native
thickets, except on one side, where a perpendicular naked slate-rock lets in the light to the
inmost recesses. Having sufficiently admired
this tremendous scene, we walked along the
cliffs overhanging the deep glen, which receives
the mingled waters of the Rhydol and Monach,
whose luxuriant woods almost concealed the
numerous rapids and falls occasioned by the
ruggedness of its rocky bottom.   After a trou-
blesome, and rather a hazardous descent, forcing
our way through the trees, and across two or
three headlong little streams, we arrived at a
rocky bank, a few feet above the river, commanding a fine view of the junction of the
Rhydol and Monach, which seem to vie with
each other in the turbulence of their waters,
and the frequency of their cascades. Immediately above the union of the two torrents, rises
a perpendicular rock, on the crags of which we
saw several kites perched; the summit of the
rock is crowned with wood, equal in luxuriance
to that which clothes the lofty sides of the glen."

CHAP. XXVIII.

MACHYNLLETH TO LLANYDLOES.

Account of the Mountain Plynlimmon.—The Source of the Severn.—Cataract.—Llanydloes.

THE distance from Machynlleth to Llanydloes is about twenty miles, and the road lies over a series of dreary and barren moors. The mountains here have no one character of beauty, and during my whole walk I scarcely saw a single tree. The only pleasing objects were a few patches of corn, sparingly scattered in different parts of the adjacent bottoms.—I had proceeded about five miles, when I arrived at the foot of a lofty hill, along which the road continues on an ascent for near three miles. From the top I had an ample view of all the country around me; but its beauties were very few, it seemed little more than one dismal waste of hill and vale.

Proceeding on my journey, the Montgomery-shire mountain

PLYNLIMMON

Became visible at the distance of four or five miles on the right. From the various accounts that had reached me respecting this mountain, there did not appear any probable compensation for my trouble in going so far out of my road to ascend its summit, I therefore continued my route, and only passed it at a distance.—The adjacent mountains being all low, render Plynlimmon much higher in appearance than it really is: from this, and its giving birth to three noted rivers, the Severn, the Wye, and the Rhydol, it seems not improbable that it originally obtained its celebrity. In perpendicular height it is far exceeded by Snowdon, Cader Idris, and many other mountains of the principality.

THE HEAD OF THE SEVERN.

The manuscript journal of an intelligent friend has furnished me with the following short account of the source of this celebrated river. The Severn rises from a small spring on the south-east side of Plynlimmon, and nearly at its summit. The water issues from a rock at the bottom of a kind of large hole, whose sides are formed of peat. The ground around the edges is somewhat elevated. A stream so small issues from this place, that a child four years of age might stride across it. The water, which is of a red colour, is unpleasant to the taste.—Those persons who wish to trace the Severn to its source, are directed to keep the right-hand stream all the way up the mountain.

In the flat country, betwixt Plynlimmon and the road, I observed a small unadorned pool called Glâs Llyn, *The Blue Pool.*

CATARACT.

Having proceeded about half way to Llanydloes, I was directed to leave the road, and go a
mile and a half south, to see a cataract called
Frwd y Pennant, *the Torrent at the Head of
the Vale.* The rock was nearly perpendicular,
and the water, then in plenty, from the late
rains, roared down its lofty front with a deafen-
ing noise. The shrubs hanging from the adjacent
rocks added to its beauty. This waterfall is
exceeded in height by few in North Wales.

About four miles from Llanydloes, the appearance of the country began to change, and the
woody vales in front, with the little Llyn yr
Avangc, *Beaver's Pool,* at a distance among
them, formed on the whole a pleasing scene.

LLANYDLOES.

The entrance into Llanydloes, *the Church of
St. Idlos,* is over a long wooden bridge across
the Severn. This was such as not to prepossess
me in favour of the town. The streets are wide,
but the houses are principally formed by means
of timber frames, with their intermediate spaces
closed with laths and mud. These in general are
very irregular, and I found a greater scarcity of
good houses in this place than in any of its size
and consequence that I had yet visited.—The
town house is a wretched building, constructed
much in the manner of the dwelling houses.
The width of the streets of Llanydloes is

(very singularly) a great inconvenience, for the inhabitants throughout the town, taking advantage of it, accumulate all their ashes and filth in great heaps before their doors. These heaps are, indeed, so large, that in a hot day the exhalation of noxious vapours from them must be an abominable nuisance to every person accustomed to cleanliness.

The town is built in the form of a cross, having the market house nearly in the centre.—The *church* is remarkable only for having six arches, with columns surrounded by round pillars, ending in capitals of palm leaves. The inhabitants assert that these were brought, some time after the dissolution, from Cwm Hir abbey in Radnorshire.

In Llanydloes there is carried on a considerable trade for yarn. This is manufactured into flannels, and sent to Welsh Pool for sale.

CHAP. XXIX.

LLANYDLOES TO NEWTOWN.

View of the Country.—Anecdote of Edward Herbert, Esq.—
Newtown.—Cataract.—Castell Dolforwyn.—History of this
Fortress.

On my leaving Llanydloes, I soon began to
find myself in a kind of country that plainly indicated an approach towards England. The
road winds along a vale much flatter, and more
highly cultivated, than any in the interior of
Wales.—I now wandered

On the gentle Severn's sedgy bank.

The river was here but a few yards across,
and it glided silently and smoothly along, reflecting brightly the green impending foliage of
its banks.

Fields, lawns, hills, vallies, pastures, all appear
Clad in the varied beauties of the year.
Meand'ring waters, waving woods are seen
And cattle scatter'd in each distant green.
The curling smoke, from cottages ascends,
There towers the hill, and there the valley bends.

I passed *Llandinam,* a small village, about
seven miles from Llanydloes, which I mention

only for the purpose of relating an anecdote of the valour of Edward Herbert, Esq., the grand-father of the celebrated lord Herbert of Chirbury. This gentleman was a strenuous opposer of the outlaws and thieves of his time, who were in great numbers among the mountains of Montgomeryshire. In order to suppress them, he often went with his adherents to the places which they frequented. Some of them having been seen in a public house at Llandinam, Mr. Herbert, and a few of his servants, proceeded thither to apprehend them. The principal outlaw aimed an arrow at him, which struck his saddle, and stuck there. Mr. Herbert, with his sword in his hand, and with undaunted courage, galloped up to him, and took him prisoner. He pointed to the arrow, requesting the fellow to observe what he had done. " Ah! (replied the man,) had not my best bow been left behind, I should have done a greater deed than shoot your saddle." He was tried for the crime, found guilty, and hanged.

NEWTOWN.

In Newtown, or, as it is called by the Welsh, *Tre-Newydd*, I found nothing remarkable. It is a clean, and rather neat place, and the surrounding country is fertile and pleasant.—The manuscript journal of my friend, quoted in the last chapter, contains the following memorandum respecting the church. " This building has a screen, said to have been brought from some neighbouring abbey. It may be antique, but

its gilded ornaments rendered it very unsightly.
There is also here a small altar piece, said to
have been painted by Dyer the poet. The subject is the last supper, but it is in part a copy from
Poussin, and is bad."

A glen about a mile from the town, on the
right of the road leading to Builth, was pointed
out to me as containing a *cataract*, and some
beautiful scenery. I was, however, greatly disappointed in finding these scarcely worth notice.
The face of the rock had much the appearance
of a shattered wall, thrown a slaunt by one end
sinking into the ground. The water scarcely
trickled down it, and if I might judge from the
muddy pool at the foot, it very seldom descends
in quantity sufficient to entitle the scene to the
appellation of a cataract.

Returning to Newtown, I crossed the river
and walked along its banks about three miles
and a half to

CASTELL DOLFORWYN,

The Castle of the Virgin's Meadow. The remains of this fortress are to be found upon a
lofty hill, on the north-west bank of the Severn,
a situation that commands the whole of the
adjacent country. From hence I had a lovely
and extensive prospect of the vale of Severn,
through which the river was seen to glide in
elegant curves, blackened by its high and shady
banks. The landscape was enlivened by the
luxuriance of woods and meadows; and the

towns and villages around lent their aid to decorate the scene.

The castle has been a four-sided building, of no great strength, about fifty yards long, and twenty-five wide; and the exterior walls appear to have been about four feet in thickness. A small part of the north wall, with some trifling remains of the interior of the building, are yet left. The south and the east walls are entirely demolished, and the other parts that are yet standing are greatly shattered.

* There have been various conjectures respecting the founder of this castle. Dugdale attributes it to David ap Llewelyn, prince of North Wales, about the middle of the thirteenth century. Stowe says it was the work of Llewelyn; and Mr. Evans, who is now generally thought to be right, that it was indebted for its origin to Bleddyn ap Cynvyn, some time betwixt the years 1066 and 1073*.

In the sixth year of the reign of Edward I., Bogo de Knovill was made governor; and, in the following year, the castle was granted to Roger Mortimer, earl of March, to hold to himself and his heirs by the service of one knight's fee. His son was attainted of high treason, but afterwards, on the reversal of the attainder, it was restored to the family in the person of his grandson. By the marriage of Anne, the sister to the last earl of March, with Richard Plantagenet, earl of Cambridge, this, and some other Welsh castles, became the property of the house of York, and thence descended to the crown.

These are all the memoranda of any importance that I have been able to collect respecting this fortress.—How it first took the name of Dolforwyn, or *The Meadow of the Virgin*, cannot now be ascertained.

* Evans Dissertatio de Bardis, 92. from the Institutiones Linguæ Cymraecæ, of John David Rhys.

CHAP. XXX.

NEWTOWN TO MONTGOMERY.

View near Abermule.—Montgomery.—Church.—History of the Town.—Montgomery Castle.—Leland's Description of the Town.—The Cucking Stool, formerly in use here.

FROM Newtown I had a fine cultivated country all the way to Montgomery. The infant Severn accompanies the road nearly half the distance, in some places approaching, and in others receding from it, and hidden by intervening trees and hedges.

The few houses at Abermule, *The Conflux of the River Mule*, about five miles from Newtown, were delightfully situated on the bank of the Severn, surrounded by hills, and decorated by woods, in all the luxuriance of foliage. From hence the road gently ascends, and from the eminence a view so extensive and beautiful bursts on the sight, as to defy the utmost expression of the pencil to represent it. A vale in high cultivation is seen to extend for several miles, the Severn appearing in different parts from among the trees and meadows: The whole scene was bounded by distant hills. The descent continues still beautiful; and, near the town of Montgomery, the fine ruins of its castle formed a very interesting addition to the prospect. —The road is so much elevated immediately above the town, as to afford the traveller a bird's eye view into almost every street.

MONTGOMERY,

From the neatness of its houses, seemed to me to be inhabited principally by persons of small fortune, who had settled here to lead a life of retirement. It is clean, and well built; and seems capable of affording the comforts and conveniences, without any of the bustle and noise of a large town. All the adjacent country is decorated with the most lively and luxuriant scenery.

The *church* is an elegant cruciform structure, dedicated to St. Nicholas, and contains an ancient monument, to the memory of Richard Herbert, Esq. (the father of the celebrated lord Herbert of Chirbury,) and his lady. The two figures are recumbent, under what has once been a magnificent and much ornamented canopy. In an adjacent corner of the church, I observed a large collection of legs, arms, heads, and trunks of other monumental figures, but all of them so much shattered, that I could make nothing out of them. On the gravestones in the church-yard I remarked more epitaphs than I had usually seen together before. Among such a number, many were of course absurd.

MONTGOMERY CASTLE.

The castle is situated upon an eminence on the north side of the town, and appears to have once been a grand and majestic building. It is, however, at present so much demolished, that it is impossible to trace its extent with any degree of accuracy. It stood on a rock precipitous on one side, and so elevated as to overlook all the immediately adjacent country. The present remains consist of a small part of a tower at the south-west angle, and a few low and shattered walls. This fortress seems to have been defended by four fosses, cut in the rock, each of which had formerly its draw-bridge*.

* *History of Montgomery Castle.*—Montgomery was built and fortified with a castle during the reign of William the Conqueror, by Baldwyn, lieutenant of the Marches; and in 1092, the place was fortified afresh by its then owner, Roger de Montgomery, earl of Shrewsbury. In the following year, the Welsh mustering all their force, rose in arms, seized and ransacked the castle. William Rufus marched with an army to the relief of the English, retook and repaired the castle; but, in his encounter with the Welsh, having lost a great number both of men and horses, he was compelled to return into England for the purpose of recruiting his forces. Montgomery castle was at this time believed to be the strongest fortress in Wales, and the Welsh, after William's retreat, took it by storm, and after putting the whole garrison to the sword, levelled it with the ground. The English struggled ineffectually against this hardy people for near four years. At length they obtained a decisive victory. The castle was immediately rebuilt by the earl of Shrewsbury; but in little more than a century afterwards was again destroyed.

In the year 1231, a party of Welshmen having made an excursion into the lands adjoining the castle, they were intercepted by the English, and many were taken prisoners, and beheaded. Prince Llewelyn ap Iorweth, in retaliation for this injury, assembling an enormous force, laid waste all the English borders. During the general consternation, Hubert de Burgh evacuated the castle; on which it was immediately seized by the Welsh, who set fire to and destroyed it.

THE TOWN OF MONTGOMERY

Was formerly defended by a circumambient wall, strengthened with towers. Leland, in the sixteenth century, thus describes it: " The soyle of the ground of the towne is on mayne slaty

In a conference held at Montgomery, in the year 1268, a peace was established betwixt Llewelyn ap Griffith, then prince of North Wales, and king Henry III.

From an inquisition taken on the reversal of the attainder of Roger Mortimer, earl of March, in the year 1345, it appears that he had been possessed of Montgomery castle at the time of his death. It was in consequence restored to the family, and passed, with his other castles and property, by the marriage of Anne, the sister of the last earl, into the house of York, and thence to the crown.

This fortress was held by the immediate ancestors of lord Herbert of Chirbury, as stewards for the crown, and it was their principal place of residence*.

In the civil wars of the reign of Charles I,. lord Herbert was made governor. On the arrival of the army of the parliament in 1644, under the command of sir Thomas Middleton, he declared himself of that party, and on treaty permitted the men to enter the castle. Not long after this transaction, lord Byron advanced with the king's forces, consisting of about four thousand men, on which sir Thomas Middleton was compelled to flee to Oswestry, leaving his foot-soldiers with lord Herbert to defend the castle. The royalists commenced their attack ; but, sir Thomas having been joined by sir John Meldrum, sir William Brereton, and sir William Fairfax, returned with about three thousand men to the relief of the place. Lord Byron brought forward his men to engage them, but. after a dreadful conflict, which lasted more than eight hours, the parliament's army obtained a complete victory. The routed troops fled towards Shrewsbury, and the pursuit was continued near twenty miles. In this battle betwixt three and four hundred of the king's party were slain, and above a thousand taken prisoners. Sir William Fairfax, major Fitzsimons, and about

* Life of Lord Herbert. 5.

rocke, and especially the parte of the towne hillinge toward the castell, now a late re-edified, whereby hathe been a parke. Great ruines of the waulle yet apere, and the remains of foure gates, thus called, Kedewen Gate, Chirbury Gate, Arthur's Gate, and Kerry Gate. In the waulle yet remayne broken tourets, of the which the white tower is the most notable."

King Henry III. granted to Montgomery the privileges of a free borough.—The town is now governed by two bailiffs, and twelve burgesses, or common-council men; and it sends one member to parliament, who is elected by the burgesses, and returned by the bailiffs.

CUCKING-STOOL.

In Blount's Ancient Tenures and Jocular Customs, I find that this singular instrument of justice was once in use at Montgomery. Whenever any woman was found guilty, in the judgment of the free burgesses of the town, of causing strifes, fightings, defamations, or other disturbances of the public peace, she was adjudged to the goging-stool, or cucking-stool, there to stand, with her feet naked, and her hair dishevelled, for such a length of time as the burgesses should think proper, as a public warning to all who beheld her. This is the same kind of instrument which was used among

sixty men belonging to the parliament, were killed, and about a hundred others dreadfully wounded.—The castle met the fate of all others, in being dismantled by order of the Commons. Lord Herbert, however, received from the parliament a satisfaction for the the loss of his property.

the Saxons. It was called by them scealfing, or scolding stool, that is, a chair in which they placed scolding women as public examples; but in addition to this, if the enormity of the case required it, this people also plunged them over the head in water. The engine in general consisted of a long beam, or rafter, that moved on a fulcrum, and extended towards the centre of a pond: at its end was fixed the stool, or chair, on which the offender was made to sit. It was called by the Welsh Y Gadair Goch, *The Red Chair.*

CHAP. XXXI.

MONTGOMERY TO WELSH POOL.

Welsh Pool.—Church.—Powis Castle.

LEAVING Montgomery, I went over a rich champaign country, about ten miles, to Welsh Pool. I passed on the left Powis castle, situated on the narrow ridge of a rock, about a mile from Pool. For three or four miles of the road this building is a striking object in the scene.

WELSH POOL

Is a large and populous place, and from its vicinity to England, it has assumed much the appearance of an English town. The houses are in general well built, and principally of brick. There is one long and handsome street, in which stands the county hall, an elegant structure, erected by subscription a few years ago. The inhabitants of this town are so completely English, that even the language of the country seems scarcely known here. An air of opulence unusual in Wales may be observed throughout the place, owing to the trade in Welsh manufactures, which is carried on to a great extent. It is principally resorted to as a market for Welsh flannels, which are manufactured here, and in various adjacent parts of the country: from hence these are sent into England, and principally to Shrewsbury and Liverpool.—The Severn is navigable to a place called Pool Stake, within a mile of Welsh Pool, although upwards of two hundred miles from its mouth in the Bristol channel.

The *church*, apparently a modern structure, is singularly situated at the bottom of a hill, and so low, that the upper part of the church-yard is nearly on a level with its roof. This church has a chalice which was presented to it by Thomas Davies, some time governor-general of the English colonies on the western coast of Africa. It is formed of pure gold brought from Guinea, and is valued at about a hundred and seventy pounds. Notwithstanding the evidence of its inscription to the contrary, the sexton informed me, with much assurance, that this chalice had been given to the church by a transported felon, who, from industry and application during his banishment, had returned to his country the possessor of considerable wealth.—I was somewhat surprised in observing in the choir a few branches of ivy that had penetrated the roof, and were permitted to hang entwined round each other in a cylindrical form, to a length of more than eighteen feet. The neatness of the place was not in the least injured by them, and I presume their singularity was the cause of their preservation.

POWIS CASTLE,

Has been originally built of a reddish stone, but in order to keep the structure in repair,

this has of late years been so plaistered over
with a coat of red lime, that at present very
little of the stone is visible. This red coating
gives to the building so much the appearance of
brick, that it was not until I almost touched it,
that I was undeceived in supposing it such.
The antique grandeur of this castle is much
injured by the great number of chimnies, and
by the striking and harsh contrast betwixt the
walls and the modern sash windows.

The ascent to the castle is up a long and laborious flight of steps, much out of repair when
I was there; and the principal entrance is a
gateway betwixt two large round towers. The
edifice is kept in repair as an habitable mansion,
but its owner very rarely visits it. The apartments have a heavy and unpleasant appearance,
from the great thickness of the walls; and the
furniture is chiefly in the ancient stile of elegance. In some of the chambers the old and
faded tapestry is yet left. There are, in different rooms, several portraits, chiefly of the
family, the best of which are the work of Cor-
nelius Janson. Among them there is one of
king Charles II. painted by sir Peter Lely, two
of the earl of Strafford, one of lord Herbert of
Chirbury, and others of various other celebrated
characters. In the gallery, which is near a
hundred and twenty feet in length, there is a
small collection of antiques, some of which are
supposed to be valuable.

The gardens were laid out in the wretched
French taste, but in 1798, when I saw them,
they were greatly out of repair.

The prospects from the terrace are very extensive, this situation commanding all the beautiful and spacious country eastward, intersected by the Severn, and the Breiddin hills; with much of the cultivated and well wooded county of Salop*.

* *History of Powis Castle.*—Leland informs us that there were formerly at this place two castles included in the same walls. " Welsch Pole had (he says) two lord's marcher's castles within one waulle, the lord Powys, named Greye, and the lord Dudley, caullid Sutton; but now the lord Powys hath bothe in his hand. The Welsch Pole castle is in compass almost as much as a little towne. The lord Dudley's part is almost fallen downe: the lord Powys part is meatly good*."

Whether these castles were erected at the same, or at different times, I have not been able to learn, nor what were their distinct names. None of the writers, except Leland and Camden, mention more than one castle. This was anciently called *Pool Ca·tle*, from its vicinity to Pool; and *Castel Coch*, the Red Castle, from the hue of its stone. Its name of Powis Castle, which is more modern, it seems to have obtained from its having been the principal place in that division of Wales called Powisland.

Cadwgan ap Bleddyn ap Cynvyn, a Welshman who had rendered himself eminent in the reign of Henry the first by his services and bravery, began, about the year 1110 to erect here a castle with an intention of making this the place of his residence, but before the work was finished, he was murdered by one of his relations. The castle appears to have been completed before the end of the same century; for in 1191, on various depredations having been committed by the Welsh in the marches, Hubert, archbishop of Canterbury, in the absence of Richard I., on the crusades, hastened here, and with a powerful army besieged the castle, at that time in the hands of the Welsh. As soon as the archbishop had obtained possession he fortified it afresh, and he left it with a very strong garrison. The Welsh, however, soon again attacked and retook it.

It changed owners again not long afterwards, for in 1233, it was attacked and seized by prince Llewelyn ap Iorwerth.

* Leland's Itinerary.

It descended to Llewelyn's grandson, Owen ap Griffith, and on his death to his daughter Hawys Gadarn, who was afterwards married to John de Charlton. It continued in their posterity for several generations.—In the reign of Henry the eighth it was purchased by sir Edward Herbert, the second son of William earl of Pembroke, who died in the year 1594.

In October 1644, Powis castle was attacked and taken for the parliament by sir Thomas Middleton. Its owner, Percy lord Powys, was taken prisoner, all his estates were sequestered, and he was obliged to compound for them. During the siege the castle is said to have received much damage in its outer walls from the enemy's cannon.

CHAP. XXXII.

WELSH POOL TO OSWESTRY.

The Breiddin Hills.—Llanymynech.—Llanymynech Hill and Cavern called Ogo.—Lime Quarries.—Prospect from the Hill.—Offa's Dyke.—Oswestry.—Account of the Death of Oswald — Monastery —Oswald's-well.— Oswestry castle.— Fires.—Siege in the civil wars.—Privilege and trade.

ABOUT six miles from Welsh Pool I passed a group of three lofty mountains called the

BREIDDIN HILLS.

The highest and most conical of these has the name of *Moel y Golfa;* the second *Craig Breiddin ;* and the third *Cefyn y Castell.* On one of them an obelisk was erected a few years ago, from a subscription of several of the neighbouring families, in commemoration of lord Rodney's defeat of the French fleet, under the command of the Count de Grasse.

Just before I arrived at Llanymynech, I had to cross the furious little river *Virnwy* by a ferry.

LLANYMYNECH,

The Village of the Miners, is a small whitewashed village, standing on the northern bank

of the Virnwy. Its name was evidently derived
from the mines in which the neighbourhood formerly abounded, and which were worked in
the adjoining hill, called *Llanymynech Hill*,
even so early as the time of the Romans. Of
this there are undeniable proofs. One vestige
of their work is a large artificial cave, of immense length, called Ogo, from whence they
obtained considerable quantities of copper.—
The windings of this cavern are very numerous
and intricate. Some years ago, two men of
the parish, endeavouring to explore it, were so
bewildered in its mazes, that, when they were
discovered by some miners who were sent in
search of them, they had thrown themselves on
the ground, in despair of ever again seeing the
light.—Previously to this period, some miners
who were searching for copper, found in the recesses of the cavern several skeletons; and near
them some culinary utensils, a fire-place, and
a small hatchet. These too plainly indicated
that the unfortunate wretches had for some time
dragged on a life of misery in this gloomy mansion. One of the skeletons had a battle-axe by
his side, and round his left wrist there was a
bracelet of glass beads. About fifteen years
after this first discovery, other miners found human bones, and in one instance a bone of the
arm clasped by a golden bracelet. Several Roman coins of Antoninus, Faustina, and others,
have also been discovered in this cavern.

The hill, besides copper, affords zinc, lead,
calamine, and so much lime, as to supply the
whole county of Montgomery, and a great part
of Shropshire. In the summer of 1795, upwards

of eight thousand tons were exported from hence to different parts of the adjacent country.

From the summit of Llanymynech hill I had an extensive view over the plains towards Shrewsbury on the east; and, on the other side, of the rough and uncultivated parts of Montgomery-shire, in which I either could, or fancied I could, discern the lofty cataract called Pistyll Rhaiadr, lighted by the beams of the morning sun, and glittering like a stream of light down the black front of its rock. Below me was the Virnwy, sweeping in elegant curves along the meadows; and towards the south of the Breiddin hills, I had a view in Montgomeryshire of a series of wooded and pleasant vales.

OFFA'S DYKE.

Under the west side of this hill runs the rampart constructed by Offa, king of Mercia, for the purpose of dividing his country from Wales, called Clawdd Offa, *Offa's Dyke*. This commences from the river Wye, near Bristol, and extends along Herefordshire, Radnorshire, part of Shropshire and Denbighshire, and ends near Treyddin chapel in Flintshire. From the time of its formation, till nearly the conquest, Offa's dyke was considered as the dividing line betwixt England and Wales.

OSWESTRY

Is a considerable market town in Shropshire, and a place that during the Saxon times was much celebrated.—At a little distance from the town I passed a large and elegant brick building, a *house of industry*, erected a few years ago by the joint subscription of several of the adjacent parishes, for the use of their poor.

This town was anciently called *Oswaldstre*, a name which it is said to have obtained from the following event: In the year 642, the contending armies of Oswald, king of Northumberland, and Penda, the ferocious king of Mercia, met here: the former was routed, and Oswald fell on the field of battle. Penda, with unexampled barbarity, caused the breathless body of Oswald to be cut in pieces, and stuck on poles, as so many trophies of his victory. Thus the place was called *Oswald's Tree,* and some time afterwards Oswestry.*—In a manuscript account of the town, written in 1635, I find the following note: " There was an old oake lately standing in Mesburie, within the parish Oswestry, whereon one of king Oswald's armes hung, say the neighbours by tradition."†

Oswald had been a great benefactor to various monasteries, and his character was so much revered by the monks, that a short time after his death he was canonized; and the field in which he was slain became celebrated for the numerous miracles that were believed to have been wrought in it.

On the place of martyrdom, as the monks have termed it, a *monastery* was founded, dedicated to St. Oswald; but there are no evidences

* *Oswaldstre,* as a Welsh word, signifies only *Oswald's town.* Previous to the death of Oswald, this place was called Maeserfelth, or Maeserfield, in the kingdom of Mercia.

† Harleian MSS. in the British Museum, No. 1981.

at present extant of the time either of its foundation or dissolution. In the reign of Henry the Eighth no part of the building was left; for Leland, who then visited this place, says that the cloister only was standing within the memory of persons then living.

This accurate writer likewise informs us, that when he was here, the houses of the town were principally formed of timber, and slated.—Not far from the church there was a fine spring of water, surrounded by a stone wall, (having a chapel over it,) called *Oswald's Well*. Of the origin of this well, the inhabitants had a tradition, that when Oswald was slain, an eagle tore one of the arms from the body, and making off with it, fell and perished on this spot, whence a spring of water immediately gushed up, which has remained ever since a memorial of the event.—The town was defended by walls, and was moated round, but in the walls there were no towers except those of the four gates.—This place, he says, was also principally supported by its trade in woollen cloth.[*]

OSWESTRY CASTLE.

On an artificial mount, at the outside of the town, are the remains of this fortress; but they are at present little more than a confused heap of shattered walls and rubbish.[†]

[*] Leland's Itin. v. 37, 38.
[†] According to the Welsh historians, it was founded in 1148 by Madoc ap Meredith ap Bleddyn, prince of Powis, an ally of Henry II. The English records, however, assign

The town of Oswestry has thrice suffered dreadfully by accidental fires in the space of thirty years. In 1542, two long streets were thus consumed; two years afterwards there was a fire more destructive than this; and in 1567 two hundred houses were burnt to the ground, namely, a hundred and forty within the walls, and sixty in the suburbs, in only two hours, betwixt two and four o'clock in the morning.

This town, in the reign of Charles I, was in

to it a more ancient date. They inform us that it was in being before the Norman conquest, and that William the Conqueror, shortly after that event, bestowed it on Alan, one of his Norman friends.

In the year 1214, a complaint was laid to the archbishop of Canterbury by Llewelyn ap Griffith ap Madoc, against the constable of Oswestry castle, for compelling him to put to death two young noblemen, in derogation of their birth and extraction; " which disgrace (he states) their parents would not have undergone *for three hundred pounds sterling!*"† He alleges also, that the constable had twice imprisoned sixty of his men, when each man was compelled to pay ten shillings for his liberty; and that when the Welsh people came to Oswestry fair, the constable had frequently seized their cattle, by driving them into the castle, and refused to make any satisfaction.

Two years after this period the town was destroyed by order of king John, on account of Llewelyn, prince of Wales, having refused to aid him in the contentions with his barons. It experienced a similar disaster in the reign of Henry III., in being burned during an insurrection of the Welsh.

In the subsequent reign, that of Edward I., Oswestry was surrounded with walls, that it might be less liable to suffer from the plundering excursions of this people.

These, however, do not appear to have altogether restrained them, for during the rebellion of Owen Glyndwr, in the beginning of the fifteenth century, it was again plundered and burnt.

---

* This is a singular valuation of parents of the lives of two children.

possession of the royalists till June 1644. When
it was besieged by general Mytton and the earl
of Denbigh with a force consisting of two
troops of horse, and two hundred foot soldiers.
The attack was so furious, that in the short
space of an hour, and with the loss of only one
or two men, a breach in the wall was effected,
by which they entered the town. The inhabitants, in consternation, fled for shelter to the
castle; but an attack was immediately commenced on it by cannon. A daring youth, of
the name of Cranage, was persuaded by some of
the parliament's officers to fasten a *petard** to
the castle gate. Being well animated with sack,
he undertook the desperate enterprize. With
the engine hidden, he crept unperceived from
one house to another, till he got to that next the
castle, whence he sprang to the gate : he fixed
his engine, set fire to it, and escaped unhurt.
This, by the force of its explosion, burst open
the castle gate, and the place was immediately
taken. The deputy governor, four captains,
and about three hundred soldiers, were made
prisoners. From hence the parliament's soldiers hastened into Lancashire to other service
there.

Previously to the attack, the governor pulled
down the tower and part of the body of the
church which stood without the walls, lest the

* A petard is an engine made of copper and brass, somewhat in the shape of a high crowned hat. Its use was to
break down gates, barricades, drawbridges, &c. After being
loaded with gunpowder, it was fastened to the place to be
forced, and then lighted by a match, which burnt sufficiently
long, before the explosion, to allow the soldier to escape.

enemy should use them to the annoyance of the garrison.

About a fortnight after its surrender, the king's forces, consisting of about three thousand foot, and fifteen hundred horse, under the command of colonel Marrow, attempted to retake this place. Intimation of their approach was immediately sent to Sir Thomas Middleton, who hastening to the assistance of the garrison, attacked the king's troops, and completely routed them. After the death of the king the castle was demolished.

Oswestry has at different times been favoured with many privileges from its lords. Its most extensive charter was however granted in the year 1406, by Thomas earl of Arundel, at that time owner of the place. From this the inhabitants derived several advantages which they had not before enjoyed. The chief of these were, that neither the lord nor his heirs should seize on or confiscate the effects of any person in the corporation that died without making a will; and that none of the inhabitants of the lordships of Oswestry, Melverley, Kinardsley, Egerley, Ruyton, and eleven adjacent villages, at that time called the *eleven towns*, should convey cattle or goods to any other fair or market without having previously exposed them for sale in the town of Oswestry, under the penalty of six shillings and eight-pence for each offence.

Till about the end of the sixteenth century there was a very considerable market at Os-

westry for Welsh flannels: Shrewsbury, however, soon after this period, deprived it of the
principal part of this trade.

Oswestry and its hundred, at the making of
Domesday, formed a part of Wales. They
were taken thence, and annexed to England in
the eighth year of the reign of Edward the
First.

CHAP. XXXIII.

OSWESTRY TO RUABON.

Chirk.—Aqueduct.—Church.—Chirk Castle, and extensive View.—Anecdote respecting a whimsical Painting of Pistyll Rhaiadr.—History of Chirk Castle.—Memoranda of Sir John Trevor.—Beautiful Scene at New Bridge.—Ruabon.— Church and Monuments.—Dr. David Powell.

EXCURSION FROM RUABON TO BANGOR ISCOED.

Wynnstay.—Beautiful Scene at Nant y Bele.—Overton.— Bangor Iscoed, the most ancient Monastery in Britain.

THE village of *Chirk* is situated on the brow of a hill; and from the numerous coal works and other undertakings in the neighbourhood, it appears to be a place of some business.

The Ellesmere canal passes within half a mile of the village, and is carried over the river and vale of Ceiriog by a long aqueduct.

In the *church* at Chirk there are several marble monuments in memory of the Middletons of Chirk castle: the best of these was erected for sir Thomas Middleton, one of the commanders in the army of the parliament during the civil wars.

CHIRK CASTLE

Is about a mile and half from the village. This building, like that of Powys, still retains a mixture of the castle and mansion. It stands in an open situation, on the summit of a considerable eminence, and commands an extensive view into *seventeen* different counties. On the exterior it retains much of its primitive aspect. It is a quadrangular structure, having five towers, one at each corner, and the fifth for the gateway, in front. The entrance is into a spacious court yard, a hundred and sixty feet long, and a hundred broad; and on the east side of this there is a handsome colonnade. The principal apartments are a saloon, a drawing room, and gallery; in the latter of which there is a large collection of paintings, consisting, however, almost entirely of family portraits.

In a room adjoining to the gallery I observed a singular landscape, in which *Pistyll Rhaiadr,* the waterfall in Montgomeryshire, is represented as falling into the sea. I asked the cause of this strange impropriety, and was informed that the painter was a foreign artist; he had been employed by one of the Middletons to take a view of that cataract, and when the piece was nearly finished, it was hinted that a few *sheep,* scattered in different parts, would probably add to its beauty. The painter mistook the suggestion, and nettled that a person whom he judged ignorant of the art should presume to instruct him, replied with considerable tartness, " You want some *sheeps* in it? Well, well, I will put you some *sheeps* in it!" He soon dashed out

C c

the bottom of the picture, and introduced the
sea, and several *sheeps*, (ships) some of which
are represented as lying at anchor close to the
rocks.

There is a dungeon to this castle, as deep
as the walls are high: it is descended by a flight
of forty-two steps.—The building is on the whole
low and heavy, and wants magnitude to give
consequence to its appearance.*

* *History of Chirk Castle.*—The present structure was the
work of Roger Mortimer, the son of Roger, baron of Wigmore, and founded on the site of a very ancient fortress,
called *Castell Crogen.*

John, earl of Warren, and Roger Mortimer, were appointed guardians to the two sons of Madoc ap Griffith, a
strenuous partisan of Henry III. and Edward I. They
murdered their wards, and appropriated the estates to their
own use. Mortimer's share in the robbery consisted of the
lands at Nan-heudwy and Chirk, which belonged to the
youngest boy. At the latter of these places he found it
politic to erect a place of defence. This he was suffered
to enjoy with impunity till his death, which took place in the
tower of London, after an imprisonment of four years and
a half, for the commission of some other crime. The property was even suffered to continue in the family, and his
grandson sold the castle to Richard Fitz Alan, earl of
Arundel, whose son, in the seventh year of Edward III., was
made governor, with a confirmation of his father's grant.
The Fitz Alans possessed it for three generations, after
which it passed to Thomas Mowbray, duke of Norfolk, in
right of his wife, the eldest sister of Thomas, earl of Arundel.
On the duke's disgrace and exile in 1397, it was probably
resumed by the crown; for it was afterwards granted to
William Beauchamp, earl of Abergavenny, who had married the other sister of the earl of Arundel. On the marriage of the grand-daughter of this nobleman with Edward
Nevil (afterwards lord Abergavenny), it was, in the reign
of Henry VI., conveyed into that family. After this it
became the property of sir William Stanley, and on his
execution it escheated again to the crown. It was bestowed
by queen Elizabeth on her favourite, Dudley, earl of Lei-

MEMORANDA OF SIR JOHN TREVOR.

About a mile from the village of Chirk is Brynkinallt, the family seat of the Trevors, descendants of Tudor Trevor. This was the dwelling of Sir John Trevor, master of the rolls, and speaker of the house of commons, in the reigns of James II. and William. Being a man of considerable talents, he found means to ingratiate himself with king James, and during his reign obtained some popularity. He was, however, too fond of money, and this was the cause of his expulsion from the house in 1695. An act was passed for creating a fund towards repayment of the debt due to the orphan charity from the city of London, and Sir John received from the city a purse of a thousand guineas, for his services in influencing the house in their favour. He would have been impeached by the house of commons for this offence, had the parliament not been unexpectedly prorogued. He therefore escaped with no further punishment than his dismissal and disgrace.

Sir John Trevor is said, among his other qualifications, to have been an economist. Of this we have a whimsical anecdote: he one day dined by himself at the Rolls, and was drinking his wine quietly, when his cousin, Roderic Lloyd,

cester. On his death it became the property of lord St. John of Bletso, whose son sold it in 1595 to sir Thomas Middleton, knight, in whose family it yet continues.

In the civil wars sir Thomas Middleton revolted from the parliament, and defended his castle, till one side, and three of the towers, were thrown down by the enemy's cannon. These he, however, rebuilt within twelve months, but at an expence of not less than eighty thousand pounds.

was unexpectedly introduced to him by the side
door. " You rascal, (said Trevor to his servant,)
and you have brought my cousin Roderic Lloyd,
esquire, prothonotary of North Wales, marshal
to baron Price, and so forth, and so forth, up
my *back stairs.* Take my cousin, Roderic Lloyd,
.esquire, prothonotary of North Wales, marshal
to baron Price, and so forth, and so forth; you
rascal, take him instantly back, down my *back
stairs,* and bring him up my *front stairs.*"
Roderic in vain remonstrated; and whilst he
was conveying down one, and up the other
stairs, his honour had removed the bottle and
glasses.

Sir John Trevor died in 1696.

About two miles from Chirk, in the road to
Ruabon, I was much pleased with a view down
a woody dell, in the bottom of which ran the
river Dee. It was the first time that I had seen
this stream surrounded by those romantic features for which it is so justly celebrated.

This scene was interesting, but at

NEW BRIDGE,

About half a mile farther on, it was greatly
exceeded. Out of the road, about a hundred
yards above the bridge, such a scene presented
itself, that with the pencil of a Claude, I could
have sketched one of the most exquisite landscapes the eye ever beheld. The river here
dashed along its rugged bed, and its rocky banks
clad with wood, where every varied tint that
autumn could afford added to their effect, cast a

darkening shade upon the stream. With the green oak, all the different hues of the ash, the elm, and the hazel, were intermingled. Above the bridge arose a few cottages surrounded with foliage. The evening was calm, and the smoke, tinged by the setting sun, descended upon the vale, whilst the distant mountains were brightened by his beams into a fine purple. I sat down on the bank of the river, and contemplated these beauties till the declining sun had sunk beneath the horizon, and twilight had begun to steal over the landscape, and blend into one every different shade of reflection, and to cover the whole face of nature with its sober grey.—I forced myself away, and pursued my journey to Ruabon, my intended residence for the night.

RUABON

Is a village pleasingly situated on a rising ground, and has around it the residences of several persons of fortune. I spent two or three days very agreeably in little excursions around the neighbourhood.

The *church* is a good building: it contains an organ, an instrument very unusual in Welsh churches, which was given by the late sir Watkin Williams Wynne.—At its east end I observed a table monument of marble, with the date of 1526, in memory of John ap Elis Euton, and Elizabeth Clefeley, his wife:

A tombe, it is right rich and stately made,
Where two do lye, in stone and auncient trade.

The man and wife with sumptuous solemne guise.
In this rich sort before the aulter lies.*

His head on crest, and warlike helmet stayes,
A lion blue, on top thereof comes out :
On lion's necke along his legges he layes,
Two gauntlets white are lying there about.
An auncient squire he was, and of good race,
As by his armes appeeres in many a place :
His house and lands, not farre from thence do show
His birth and blood were great, right long ago.†

Besides this, there are four other marble monuments, two of which deserve particular attention. One of these is in memory of the late sir Watkin Williams Wynne, and the other of his wife, lady Henrietta Williams Wynne. The latter is represented by a beautiful figure of Hope, reclining on an urn : the inscription is on a pedestal, within a serpent with its head and tail united, expressive of eternity. If I am not deceived in the recollection, they are both the workmanship of Roubiliac.

DR. DAVID POWELL,

The Welsh historian, was instituted to this vicarage in the year 1571, and lies buried here. He was born about the beginning of the reign of queen Elizabeth ; and after he left Oxford, obtained the living of Ruabon, and was made a prebendary of St. Asaph. Thus rendered easy and independent in his circumstances, he studied with great assiduity the ancient history of Bri-

---

* Not at present.   † Churchyard.

tain. For this he was well qualified by his extensive acquaintance with the Welsh and other languages. He translated into English the History of Wales, written in Welsh by Caradoc of Llancarvan; and edited the writings of Giraldus Cambrensis, which he illustrated, and corrected by many learned and valuable notes. He died in 1590, leaving behind him a large collection of ancient manuscripts.

EXCURSION FROM RUABON TO BANGOR ISCOED.

From Ruabon I wandered into the grounds of sir Watkin Williams Wynne, baronet, at

WYNNSTAY.

These grounds extend to the village; they are well wooded, and about eight miles in circumference. I observed in them some immensely large oak, ash, and birch trees; the trunk of one of the oaks was near fifty feet in girth in the smallest part.

I ascended, by its well-staircase, to the top of a handsome, lately erected stone column, of very considerable height. I had entertained hopes that from thence I should have had a fine view of the surrounding country, but was dis-

appointed : the prospect was sufficiently extensive, but in no degree interesting.

At a little distance from the column there is a
tolerably large pool. The rivulet that supplies
it is thrown over some artificial rock-work, and
forms not an inelegant cascade.

The house is deficient both in elegance and
uniformity, having been erected at different
periods, and in different styles of architecture.—
From the ancient rampart called Watt's Dyke,
which passes through the grounds, this place
was formerly called Wattstay : but, on the marriage of sir John Wynne with Jane, the daughter of Eyton Evans, and heiress of this property, he changed its name to Wynnstay.

It was anciently the property and residence
of Madoc ap Griffith Maelor, the potent lord
of Bromfield, and founder of Valle Crucis abbey,
near Llangollen.

NANT Y BELE,

The Dingle of the Martin, within the grounds
of Wynnstay, is a deep and wooded hollow.
The sides are precipitous and rocky; and the
waters of the Dee, which roll along the bottom,
are blackened by the shady banks, and for the
most part concealed from the eye of the observer,
by the thickness of the foliage. In the distant
background, I observed Chirk Castle, and the
country around it, clad in lively colours ; whilst,
to the westward, I had a view of Castell Dinas
Brân, crowning the summit of its steep. The
whole vale of Llangollen, as far as the town, lay

nearly in a strait line, and was richly varied with wood, rock, and pasture.—The scene was closed in the horizon by the far distant British Alps, which bounded the sight.—From this station I proceeded along the bank of the Dee, clambering over hedges and ditches, till I found myself at Pen y Llan, the seat of Mr. Lloyd, whence I had another charming view of the country.

I returned to Ruabon, and rambled from thence to Bangor Iscoed, *Bangor under the Wood*, a village about ten miles distant. In this excursion I passed through

OVERTON,

A picturesque little village, seated on an eminence at a small distance from the Dee. Near the bridge I had another fine prospect along this romantic stream.

In the churchyard I saw several fine old *yew trees*. These, from their size and beauty, have been accounted among the wonders of Wales.

BANGOR ISCOED

Is somewhat more than two miles beyond Overton. It is situated on the banks of the Dee, which here flows under an elegant stone bridge of five arches.

This place has its chief celebrity from having been the site of the most ancient monastery in Britain, founded, as the old writers assert, by

Lucius, the son of Coel, and first Christian king
of Britain, somewhat prior to the year 180.
Lucius formed it as an university, for the increase of learning, and the preservation of the
Christian faith in this realm; and it produced,
for an age so unenlightened, many learned
men. It is said by some writers to have been
converted into a monastery about the year 530
by 'Cynwyl or Congelus, who was created the
first abbot. Others say that Pelagius the
monk, a native of Wales, who had studied
here in his youth, after having travelled
through France, Italy, Egypt, Syria, and various other countries, was made a bishop,
and on his return to England converted this
house.

At the arrival of Augustine, who was missioned about 596, from pope Gregory I., to
convert the English Saxons to Christianity,
this monastery appears to have been in a very
flourishing state. There were at this time as
many as 2400 monks: a hundred of these, in
turns, passed one hour in devotion, so that the
whole twenty-four hours of every day were
employed in sacred duties. Bede says there
were just so many, that being divided into
seven parts, each of these contained three hundred men, which, with their proper rulers,
passed their time alternately in prayer and
labour.

The monks of Bangor were dissenters from
the Romish church; and on a conference
betwixt Augustine and its governors, the im-
perious monk demanded of them that they
should keep the feast of Easter at the same

time the papists did; that they should administer baptism according to the ceremonies of the church of Rome; and " preach the word of life with him and his fellows." In other things, he said, they would be allowed to retain their ancient customs, insolently concluding, that " if they would not accept of peace with their brethren, they should receive war from their enemies, and by them, without reserve, should suffer death." They refused obedience to his injunctions, and resolutely maintained the original rites of their church. Shortly after this period followed the dreadful massacre of above twelve hundred of the monks by Ethelfrid, king of Northumbria, at the memorable battle of Chester.— This unmanly slaughter the British annals and songs ascribe to the instigations of Augustine.

Not long after this event the monastery became neglected, and went entirely to decay. William of Malmsbury, who lived shortly after the Norman conquest, asserts, that even in his time, there remained only some relics of its ancient magnificence : there were, he says, so many ruined churches, and such immense heaps of rubbish, as were not elsewhere to be found. —Leland says of it, in the reign of Henry VIII., that its site was in a fertile valley on the south side of the Dee; but that the river having since changed its course, then ran nearly through the middle of the ground on which it stood. The extent of its walls, he says, was equal to that of the walls round a town; and the two gates, the names of which had

been handed down by tradition, had been
half a mile asunder. Within the memory of
persons then living, the bones of the monks,
and pieces of their clothes, had been ploughed
up, in the cultivation of the ground, as well
as pieces of squared stones, and some Roman
money.*

* Leland's Itin. v. 30.

CHAP. XXXIV.

RUABON TO WREXHAM.

Erddig.—Wrexham.—Church and Monuments.—Anecdote of Elihu Yale.—Wrexham Fair.—Trade and Manufactories.

EXCURSION FROM WREXHAM TO HOLT.

Village of Holt.—Castle.

I LEFT Ruabon, and proceeded on my journey towards Wrexham. In order to pass through the grounds of *Erddig*, belonging to Philip Yorke, esq. the author of a valuable History of the Five Royal Tribes of North Wales, I left the carriage-road, and went along a foot-path, over the meadows on the right. I observed considerable taste displayed at Erddig, but all the efforts of art are so infinitely inferior to the majestic operations of nature, which I had lately seen in so great a variety, that I cannot say I derived much pleasure from these grounds.— Watt's Dyke runs through them ; and not far distant is the fragment of a wall, conjectured to have been part of a Roman fort.

WREXHAM

Is a populous market town, and of such size
and consequence as to have obtained the appellation of the metropolis of North Wales.
The streets and buildings are in general good;
and the adjacent country is so beautiful, as to
have induced many families to fix their residence in its vicinity.   The centre street, in
which the market is held, is of considerable
length, and of unusual width for an ancient
town.   A few centuries ago it was noted as the
resort of buckler, or shield makers.

The *church* was formerly collegiate, and is
yet a most elegant structure.   On the exterior
it is richly ornamented with gothic sculpture.
The tower, which is about a hundred and forty
feet in height, is particularly beautiful.   On
three of its sides there have been statues as
large as life, of no fewer than thirty saints:
two have been destroyed by falling from their
niches.   Miss Seward, in her verses on Wrexham, has finely expressed the elegance of this
building:

> Her hallow'd temple there religion shews,
> That erst with beauteous majesty arose,
> In ancient days, when gothic art display'd
> Her fanes in airy elegance array'd,
> Whose nameless charms the Dorian claims efface,
> Corinthian splendor and Ionic grace.

The interior of the church is plain, but exceedingly neat, being devoid of the load of orna-

ments common in gothic churches. It contains, among other monuments, two of the elegant workmanship of Roubiliac. One of these, having the date of 1747, was erected to the memory of Mary, the daughter of sir Richard Middleton. A female figure is represented in the act of bursting from the tomb: the countenance is truly angelic, and the mixture of surprize and admiration is so delicately, and at the same time so firmly expressed, that after gazing for some moments stedfastly on the face, I could almost have fancied it more than stone. The sainted maid,

—— Amid the bursting tomb
Hears the last trumpet shrill its murky gloom,
With smile triumphant over death and time,
Lifts the rapt eye, and rears the form sublime.

Against the wall, an ancient pyramid, a building, from its solidity, calculated to resist the efforts of time, is represented as falling into ruin. The ridiculous little figure blowing the trumpet might have been omitted without any derogation from the merit of the sculpture. On the whole, however, it is so uncommonly beautiful, as to demand the admiration of every lover of the art.—The other piece of Roubiliac's performance, is a medallion containing two profile faces of the reverend Thomas Middleton, and Arabella his wife.—Nearly opposite to the former of these monuments there is a recumbent figure of *Hugh Bellot*, of the ancient family of Morton in Cheshire. He was bishop of Bangor, was afterwards translated to the see of Chester, and died in the year 1596. There is under the belfry an antique monument, which was some years ago discovered in the ground by the workmen who dug for a foundation for the iron gates of the church-yard. The figure is of a knight in complete armour; his feet rest on some kind of animal, and round his shield there has been an inscription, but this is at present illegible.

The altar-piece is a fine painting of the institution of the sacrament. It was brought from Rome, and given to the church by Elihu Yale, esq. a native of America, who went on speculation to the East Indies. Of this person, it is recorded by one of the travellers in India, that he ordered his groom to be hanged for having ridden his horse on a journey of two or three days for the sake of his health: he was tried for this crime in the English courts, and escaped with a high pecuniary punishment. He died in London in the year 1721, but was interred in this church-yard with the following inscription on his tomb:

Born in America, in Europe bred,
In Afric travelled, and in Asia wed;
Where long he liv'd and thriv'd—in London dead.
Much good, some ill he did, so hope all's even,
And that his soul through mercy's gone to Heaven!
You that survive and read this tale, take care
For this most certain exit to prepare,
Where blest in peace, the actions of the just
Smell sweet, and blossom in the silent dust.

The present church at Wrexham was finished, except the tower, before the year 1472: the latter, from a date there is upon it, does not seem to have been completed till about thirty-four years afterwards. In 1647, during the civil wars, this venerable building was used for some time as a prison, and several of the committee-men were confined in it by the parliament's soldiers, who had mutined for want of pay.

At this town there is a noted annual fair, held in the month of March, which lasts nine days. This is frequented by traders from various, and even very distant parts of the kingdom. The commodities brought by the Welsh people are chiefly flannels, linen, linsey-wolsey, and horses and cattle in abundance. Traders from other parts bring Irish linen, Yorkshire and woollen cloths, and Manchester and Birmingham goods of all kinds. For the accommodation of those who have goods to sell, there are two squares, or areas, furnished with little shops or booths.

The two principal inns are the Eagles and the Red Lion, both good houses. At the former I had excellent accommodations, and experienced the most obliging treatment.

In the neighbourhood of Wrexham there are several manufactories of military instruments; and in particular a large cannon foundery not far from the town.

EXCURSION FROM WREXHAM TO HOLT.

From Wrexham I made an excursion to *Holt*, an obscure village on the west bank of the Dee, about six miles distant. This was once a market town, and a place of some consequence; and it still continues to be governed by a mayor and aldermen. The former is usually some gentleman of respectability who resides in the neighbourhood.—The town was incorporated in the year 1410, by a charter of Thomas earl Arundel, which, however, restricts the burgesses from being Welshmen:—the charter runs in this singular form: "To the burgesses of our town, and to their heirs and successors, being *Englishmen.*" This arose, no doubt, from the hatred which the lords marchers entertained towards the Welsh people, on account of the insurrection of their hero Glyndwr, at that time scarcely suppressed*.

This place has also the name of *Lyons*. The castle was anciently called Castrum Leonis, which appellation Camden conjectures to have been derived from the Roman twentieth legion having been stationed at a little distance higher up, and on the other side of the river.

The two villages of Holt and Farndon are divided only by the river Dee, and have a communication by a very ancient bridge of ten arches.—All the scenery of this neighbourhood is flat and unpleasant. The Dee flows through meadows, without any of the beauty or grandeur of rocks, or foliage, that adorn its banks in the more mountainous parts of the country.

* Pennant, i. 210.

HOLT CASTLE

Was situated close to the river, and defended on three sides by a moat forty or fifty yards wide, cut out of the solid rock : the present remains consist of little else than rock, for this originally formed the basis of the castle to the depth of eight or ten yards. The stone used in the building appears to have been the same as that which was obtained from the moat.—The fortress consisted of five bastions, of which four were round, and the remaining one, facing the river, square. The entrance was by a draw-bridge on the west side. So little of the masonry is left, that in the present state it is impossible to form any idea of its ancient strength. The site is by no means extensive ; and as it stood on a piece of ground level with the town, it must have had its principal strength in the deep and perpendicular sides of its moat.*

* The lands of Holt and Chirk, in the reign of Henry III., and the commencement of the reign of Edward I. were the property of Madoc ap Griffith, a native of Wales who had espoused the English cause. On the death of Madoc, two sons were left, both of them under age ; and Edward gave one of them to the guardianship of John, earl of Warren†, and the other to the care of Roger Mortimer, the son of lord Mortimer of Wigmore. To the former boy belonged the lordship of Bromfield and Yale, in which stand Holt castle and that of Dinas Bran ; and to the other the property of Chirk and Nanheudwy.—The guardians, in order to disburthen themselves of their charge, and get possession of the estates of the children, caused them both to

† Camden is wrong in stating that John earl of Warren was guardian to " Madoc, a British prince;" as it was the *son* of Madoc that had been entrusted to his protection.

D d 2

The inhabitants of Holt contribute with those of Ruthin and Denbigh, towards sending a member to parliament.

be murdered. Their inhumanity, so far from meeting its just reward, was freely pardoned by Edward, who came in for a share of the spoil. He confirmed to Warren the castle of Dinas Bran, and the lordship of Bromfield and Yale; to Mortimer he gave the property of Chirk; and the castle and demesnes of Caergwrle, or Hope, he reserved to himself. Warren and Mortimer immediately began to secure their possessions by erecting on them places of defence. The latter built Chirk castle, and the former commenced this fortress, but dying soon afterwards, it was finished by his son.

In the ninth year of Edward II., John earl Warren, the grandson of the founder, having no issue, gave this castle, with that of Dinas Bran, and the lordship of Bromfield, to the king. He was soon afterwards divorced from his wife, and he obtained a regrant of them to himself, and Matilda de Nereford, his mistress, for life, with remainders to his illegitimate children, and their heirs. Matilda was the last survivor, and therefore at her death, in the following reign, the property reverted to the crown. It was, not long afterwards, given to Edward Fitz Alan, earl of Arundel, who had married the sister of the late owner. In this family it remained for three generations; but on the execution of Richard it appears to have been forfeited to the crown. When, in 1399, after this event, Holt castle was delivered to the duke of Hertford, there were found in it jewels to the value of two hundred thousand marks, and a hundred thousand marks in money. These had been deposited there, as a place of safe custody, by the unfortunate Richard II, previously to his expedition into Ireland.

The estates and title were restored in the succeeding reign, and they once again escheated to the crown. Henry VII. granted them to sir William Stanley; but on his execution resumed them, and took in this castle plate and money to the value of above forty thousand marks, which Stanley had obtained from the plunder of Bosworth Field.

The lordship of Bromfield and Yale afterwards became the property of Henry Fitzroy, duke of Richmond, the natural son of Henry VIII.: and in the reign of Edward VI., of Thomas Seymour, brother to the protector

Somerset who formed here a magazine of military stores. On his execution it once more fell to the crown.

During the civil wars Holt castle was garrisoned for the king, but in 1643 was seized by the parliament. It was afterwards retaken, and in February 1645-6 was again besieged by the parliament's forces. The governor, sir Richard Lloyd, defended it for more than a month with the utmost bravery, but was at length compelled to surrender. Towards the end of this year Holt castle, with four others, was dismantled by order of the parliament.

The lordship of Bromfield and Yale is at present the property of the crown; and sir Watkin Williams Wynne, bart. is the steward.

CHAP. XXXV.

WREXHAM TO MOLD.

Romantic Glen.—Caergwrle.—History of Caergwrle Castle.— Mold.—Church.—History of Mold Castle.—Account of Maes Garmon, and the " Alleluia" Victory.

ABOUT five miles from Wrexham I passed through a romantic glen, which would have had considerable picturesque effect, had not this been destroyed by several white-washed cottages obtruding themselves on the sight from among the trees. A little beyond this scene I passed a neat bridge of a single arch, which appeared very beautiful, accompanied by the rustic cottages overshadowed with trees on the bank of the stream.—The country I now journied through was somewhat mountainous; but beyond this vale it became again flat and uninteresting.

CAERGWRLE.

Caergwrle, like Holt, was once a flourishing town, but it is dwindled into an insignificant village.—Its parish church is about a mile distant.

There is good reason for supposing that this was a Roman station, probably an outpost to Deva. Camden discovered here an hypocaust hewn out of the solid rock, six yards and a quarter long, five yards broad, and somewhat more than half a yard in height. On some of the tiles were inscribed the letters LEGIO XX., which seem to point out the founders. This is further corroborated by the name of the place. Caer gawr lle, *the camp of the great legion;* Gáwr lle being the name by which the Britons distinguished the twentieth legion.

The *castle* stood on the summit of a high rock. Its present remains are very inconsiderable; they are, however, sufficient to indicate that it could never have been a fortress of any great importance*.

* The founder has not been ascertained; but from its construction it has been evidently of British origin.—In the reign of Edward I. we find it possessed by the English crown, for that monarch bestowed it, along with the lordship of Denbigh, on David, the brother to prince Llewelyn. Whilst in his hands, Roger de Clifford, justiciary of Chester, cut down the adjacent woods, and endeavoured to wrest the castle from its owner: this, however, he was prevented from doing by the timely interference of the king.—When David, in 1282, insidiously took up arms with his brother against his former benefactor, he left a garrison of some strength in the castle; but it was besieged by a division of the English army, and was shortly afterwards surrendered to them.

In the preceding account of Holt I have remarked that Caergwrle castle was excepted from the grant which was made to John earl of Warren of the property of one of the children of Madoc ap Griffith. Edward annexed it, with the tract of land in which it is situated, to Flintshire: it continued to form a part of this county till Henry VIII. separated, and added it to the county of Denbigh. It was, however, not long afterwards restored to its proper county.

Edward I. after the surrender of the garrison that David

MOLD

Is a small market town, consisting principally of one long and wide street.

The *church* is a neat building, ornamented all round the top of the outside walls with gothic carvings of animals. The body was erected in the reign of Henry VII., but the tower is of more modern date. The pillars in the interior are light and elegant, and its whole appearance was exceedingly neat. There is a good monument of Richard Davies, esq. of Llanerch, who died in the year 1728. He is represented in an upright attitude, but, unfortunately, the figure has lost its nose from an accidental stone thrown through the window.— The epitaph on Dr. William Wynne of Tower,

left in it, gave the castle to his consort, Eleanor, from whom it acquired the name of *Queen Hope.* She lodged here in her journey to Caernarvon ; and either during her abode in the castle, or very shortly afterwards, it was by some accident set on fire, and burnt.

In the first year of the succeeding reign, this castle and manor were granted to John de Cromwell, on condition that at his own expence he should repair the castle.— Some years afterward they were given to sir John Stanley.

The town of Hope received its first charter from Edward the Black Prince, in the year 1351. By this charter it is directed that the constable of the castle for the time being should also be the mayor, and he was to choose annually from the burgesses two persons as bailiffs.—All the privileges which the inhabitants enjoyed from this charter were afterwards confirmed by Richard II.—Caergwrle and Hope, in conjunction with Flint, Caerwys, Rhyddlan, and Overton, send a member to parliament.

some time fellow of All Souls College Oxford, who died in the year 1776, deserves a place here, not from its eccentricity, so much as its recording an example of an express direction against interment within the walls of the church, which ought to be generally followed :

In conformity to ancient usage ;
from a proper regard to decency,
and a concern for the health of his
fellow-creatures, he was moved to give
particular directions for being buried
in the adjoining church-yard,
and not in the church.
And as he scorned flattering of others
while living, he has taken care to prevent
being flattered himself when dead,
by causing this small memorial to be
set up in his life time.

God be merciful to me a sinner.

MOLD CASTLE.

From the church-yard a lofty mount called the Bailey Hill, was pointed out to me as the site of the castle*. Of the building there are not not now, I believe, the smallest remains. The hill was planted on its summit, and round the bottom, with larches, firs, and other evergreens†.

* " At the north end of Byly streate, appere ditches and hilles, yn token of an auncient castel, or building there.   It is now called Mont Brenebyly.'   Leland's Itin. v. 35.

† This castle appears to have been founded during the reign of William Rufus, by Robert Montalt, the son of the high steward of Chester.   From him the place received its name of Mont Alt, or De Monte Alto.

MAES GARMON.

About a mile west of Mold, and not far from Rhual, the seat of the Griffiths, is a place which to this day retains the name of Maes Garmon, *The Field of Garmon, or Germanus.* On this spot, in Easter week 448, was fought the celebrated battle between the joint forces of the Picts and Scots against the Britons, headed by the bishops Germanus and Lupus, who had about two years before been sent into this kingdom. Previously to the engagement, Germanus instructed the soldiers to attend to the word given them by the priests on the field of battle, and

In the year 1144 it was seized and demolished by Owen Gwynedd, prince of Wales, and in little more than a century it appears to have several times changed owners. At length in 1267, Griffith ap Gwenwynwyn wrested it from the hands of the English, and again destroyed it. It was soon rebuilt, and restored to the barons of Montalt.—In 1327, the last baron having no issue, conveyed it to Isabel, the queen of Edward II., for life, with remainder to John of Eltham, a younger brother of Edward III. But on his death, without issue, it reverted with his possessions to the crown.

The lordship became some time afterwards the property of the Stanley family. The earls of Derby possessed it till the execution of James, after which it was purchased, along with the manor of Hope, by some persons whose names I have not been able to learn, who enjoyed them till the Restoration. At the conclusion of the civil wars, the earl of Derby agreed to pay eleven thousand pounds for these manors; but afterwards retracting, the king ordered the former purchasers to be confirmed in their possession. The Derby family, however, by some means regained the manor of Hope, but that of Mold was lost to them for ever*.

* Pennant, i. 426.

to repeat it with energy through the whole army.
When the forces were prepared for the critical
onset, that was to decide the important fate
of the day, Germanus pronounced aloud ALLE-
LUIA! The priests repeated it thrice, and it was
afterwards taken up by the voices of the whole
army, till even the hills reverberated the sound.
The enemy, confounded, affrighted, and trem-
bling, fled on every side. The Britons pursued, and left few alive to relate the dismal story.
Most of them fell by the sword, but many threw
themselves into the adjoining river, and perished
in the flood*. This victory has been called by
all the historians *Victoria Alleluiatica.*—A pyra-
midal stone column, erected on the spot in 1736
by Nathaniel Griffith, Esq. of Rhual to comme-
morate the event in the following inscription.

Ad annum
ccccxx
Saxones Pictique bellum adversus
Britones junctis viribus susciperunt
In hac regione, hodieque MAES GARMON
Appellata: cum in prælium descenditur,
Apostolicis Britonum ducibus *Germano*
Et *Lupo*, CHRISTUS militabat in castris ;
Alleluia tertio repetitum exclamabant,
Hodie agmen terrore prosternitur ;
Triumphant
Hostibus fusis sine sanguine ;
Palmâ fide non viribus obtentâ.
M. P.
In victoriæ Alleluiaticæ memoriam.
N. G.
MDCCXXXVI†.

* The river is at present so very shallow, that it would
scarcely drown a dog: this battle might have taken place during
an overflowing of the water in consequence of heavy rains.
† The date of this battle seems to have been mistaken
both by Mr. Griffith and Mr. Pennant, who each fix it in the

year 420. Matthew of Westminster, from whose work the preceding account is extracted, says expressly that it took place in 448, and that Germanus and Lupus did not arrive in this kingdom till about two years before this time*. He mentions nothing of the Saxons having any share in the business; nor indeed does it appear very probable that they should, since their army was not introduced by Vortigern till the following year. What has been said, that the Saxons here engaged might have been such as came over on some predatory excursion, prior to the invitation of Vortigern, can have little validity when such evidence both direct and circumstantial is to be adduced to the contrary. The arrival of the Saxons prior to that period, seems however of much less importance in the proof than the arrival of the bishops, for they evidently were not in the kingdom till twenty-six years after the generally supposed time of the event.

---

* Matt. West. 152—154. In Rymer, i. 443, it is said to have taken place about the year 447.

CHAP. XXXVI.

MOLD TO RUTHIN.

Vale of Clwyd.—Llanrhaiadr.—Church.—Epitaph.—The Well at Llanrhaiadr.—Ruthin.—Church.—Castle.

From Mold I went again to Denbigh, in order to pursue a regular track through the remainder of North Wales to Shrewsbury, which was the place I had fixed as the termination of my pedestrian ramble, and from whence I intended to take coach immediately to London.

I was highly delighted with my walk along the vale of Clwyd, from Denbigh to Ruthin. The views all the way were of the elegant, rich, and here picturesque vale, bounded by the distant Clwyddian hills. The day was peculiarly favourable to this kind of scenery ; it was dark and hot, and the rolling clouds that hung heavily in the atmosphere, tinged the mountains with their sombre shade, which gave an indescribable richness to the scenes.

LLANRHAIADR.

I arrived at Llanrhaiadr, *The Village of the Cataract**, which is situated on a small eminence in the midst of this fertile vale.

---

* This is the literal translation of the Welsh word : whence the name can have been derived I know not, as there is no cataract near the place.

The *church* is a handsome structure, with a
large and somewhat elegant east window, containing a representation of the genealogy of
Christ from Jesse. The patriarch is painted
upon his back, with the genealogical tree growing from his stomach —I was wandering carelessly about this building, when I cast my eyes
on a tombstone containing the·following inscription, which affords a memorable instance of
the pride of ancestry which is inherent in the
Welsh character :

> Heare lyeth the body of
> John, ap Robert of Porth, ap
> David, ap Griffith, ap David
> Vaughan, ap Elethyn, ap
> Griffith, ap Meredith,
> ap Iorworth, ap Llewelyn,
> ap Ieroth, ap Heilin, ap
> Cowryd, ap Cadvan, ap
> Alawgwa, ap Cadell,
> the
> KING OF POWIS,
> who departed this life the
> xx day of March, in the
> year of our Lord God
> 1643, and of
> his age xcv.

About a quarter of a mile distant there is a
a celebrated spring called Ffynnon Dyfnog,
The Well of Dyfnog. There was on this spot
a bath, and formerly a chapel dedicated to this
Welsh saint.

RUTHIN.

I proceeded on my journey, and found the scenery all the way to Ruthin, *The Red Fort*, ex-

tremely beautiful.—This place, like St. Asaph
and Denbigh, is pleasantly situated on a considerable eminence nearly in the middle of the
Vale of Clwyd. At a little distance behind the
town, the mountains seem to close up the end
of the vale. From different situations in the
outskirts of the town I had several fine prospects
of the adjacent country. The little river Clwyd
runs through this place, and is here scarcely
three yards across.—Ruthin is a large and tolerably populous town having two markets in
the week, one on Saturday for meat, and the
other on Monday principally for corn. The
county-gaol for Denbighshire is here : it is a neat
and well-constructed building.

The *church* was originally conventual, belonging to a house of Bon-hommes, a species of Augustine monks. It was made collegiate in 1310
by John, the son of Reginald de Grey, lord of
Dyffryn Clwyd, who endowed it with upwards
of two hundred acres of land, granted to it many
privileges, and established seven regular priests,
one of whom was to serve the chapel of the
garrison. In this state it probably continued
till the dissolution, although neither Dugdale nor
Speed have mentioned its valuation.—The apartments of the priests were joined to the church
by a cloister, part of which is built up, and
now serves as the mansion of the warden.—The
tower is of a much later date than the rest of
the building.

It is believed that there was formerly a *house
of white friars* in this place : but of this there is
nothing left except the name.

RUTHIN CASTLE

Was situated on the north side of the town, and
on no great elevation. Its present remains are
a few foundations of the walls, and the fragments of a tower or two. Some parts of the
building appear to have been of vast strength
and thickness. The stone of which it was
formed was of a brick red colour, whence the
place had the name of Rhudd Ddin (or Dinas,)
The Red Fort. On the area of the castle there
is at present a meadow, and in another part a
fives court, and bowling-green. The walls afford a fine prospect of the vale.—The following
is a description of this fortress during the sixteenth
century, previously to its demolition :

This castle stands on rocke much like red bricke,
The dykes are cut with tool through stony cragge,
The towers are high, the walls are large and thicke,
The worke itself would shake a subject's bagge,
If he were bent to build the like againe.
It rests on mount, and lookes o'er wood and playne,
It hath great store of chambers finely wrought
That tyme alone to great decay hath brought.

It shews within by double walls and wayes,
A deep device did first erect the same ;
It makes oure worlde to think on elder dayes
Because one worke was form'd in such a frame.
One tower or waull the other answers right,
As though at call each thing should please the sight ;
The rocke wrought round where every tower doth stand
Set forthe full fine by head, by heart, and hand*.

* The town and castle of Ruthin appear to have been
founded by Reginald Grey, second son to lord Grey de
Wilton, to whom Edward I. had given nearly the whole of
the vale of Clwyd, as a reward for his active services against

the Welsh. His posterity, who received the title of earls of Kent, resided here, until earl Richard, having dissipated his fortune by gambling, sold the whole property to king Henry VII.—From this time the castle, being unroofed, fell into decay, till, along with large revenues in the vale, it was bestowed by the bounty of queen Elizabeth, on Ambrose earl of Warwick. By him it was repaired, and again rendered tenable.

During a fair that was holden at Ruthin in the year 1400, the soldiers of Glyndwr suddenly entered the town. They set it on fire in various places, plundered the merchants, and again retired in safety to the mountains.

In the civil wars the castle was retained by the royalist party till February 1645 6 : it was then attacked, and, after a siege of near two months, was surrendered to general Mytton. Colonel Mason was made governor; but in the same year it was ordered by the parliament to be dismantled.

CHAP. XXXVII.

The Vale of Crucis.—The Pillar of Eliseg.—Valle Crucis Abbey —Singular Explanation of an Inscription.—Llangollen.—Llangollen Bridge and Church.—Plâs Newydd, the Seat of Lady Eleanor Butler and Miss Ponsonby.— Castell Dinas Brân.—Craig Eglwyseg.—Excursion round the Vale of Llangollen.—Aqueduct near Pont y Cyssyllte. —Views.—The Inn at Llangollen.

I LEFT Ruthin early in the morning. The clouds began to collect, and a drizzly rain came on, which lasted without intermission till I arrived within four miles of Llangollen. I thus lost several probably fine views from the high mountains that form the eastern barrier of the vale of Clwyd, over which the road winds. During the greatest part of this journey I was so enveloped in clouds and mist, that I could not, literally, discern objects that were twenty yards distant from me.

VALE OF CRUCIS.

About ten miles from Ruthin I descended into this, one of the most charmingly secluded vales that our kingdom can boast, surrounded by high mountains, and abrupt rocks towering rudely into the sky. The bottoms of these were, in many places, clad with wood and verdure. In this vale are seated the venerable ruins of Llan Egwest, or Valle Crucis abbey; and from the road, at a little distance, the fine gothic west end, embowered in trees, and backed by the mountain, on whose summit stand the shattered remains of Castell Dinas Brân, form a scene finely picturesque. The adjacent precipices were enlivened by the browsing flocks, which were scattered along their sides, and by

> Kites that swim sublime
> In still repeated circles, screaming loud,

whilst from below **I** was entertained with

> The cheerful sound
> Of woodland harmony, that always fills
> The merry vale between.

The rugged and woody banks of the Dee, upon my proceeding onward, soon added a fresh interest to the scenery of this beautiful retreat. —The vale extends nearly to Llangollen; and at the distance of about a mile, the town, with its church and antique bridge, romantically embosomed in mountains, whose rugged summits pierced the clouds, became additional features in the landscape.

PILLAR OF ELISEG.

The vale of Crucis is indebted for its name to this cross, or pillar, which is to be found in a meadow near the abbey; and just opposite to the second mile-stone from Llangollen.* This pillar is very ancient. It appears to have been erected upwards of a thousand years ago, in memory of Eliseg (the father of Brochwel Yscithroc, prince of Powis, who was slain at the battle of Chester in 607,) by Concenn, or Congen, his great grandson. The inscription is not at present legible.† The shaft was once above twelve feet long, but having been thrown down and broken some time during the civil wars, its upper part, only about seven feet in length, was left. After these commotions it was suffered to lie neglected for more than a century. At length, in 1779, Mr. Lloyd, of Trevor Hall, the owner of the property on which it now stands, caused this part of it to be raised from the rubbish with which it was covered, and placed once again on its pedestal.

VALLE CRUCIS ABBEY.

Or, as it is called by the Welsh, Llan Egwest abbey, is about a quarter of a mile from the pillar of Eliseg. It is a grand and majestic ruin, affording some elegant specimens of the pointed stile of architecture. Miss Seward has

---

* Buck says the vale took its name from the circumstance of the abbey having possessed a piece of the true cross. This, we are informed, was given to Edward I., who, in return for so valuable a present, granted to the abbey several immunities. Buck's Antiquities. Matt. Westm. 371.

† Mr. Edward Lhwyd copied it when it was in a more perfect state. See Gough's Camden, ii, 582.

addressed this abbey in language finely poetical
and descriptive:

Say, ivy'd Valle Crucis, time decay'd,
Dim on the brink of Deva's wandering flood,
Your riv'd arch glimmering thro' the tangled glade,
Your gay hills, towering o'er your night of wood,
Deep in the vale's recesses as you stand,
And desolately great the rising sigh command.

There are still remaining of the church the
east and west ends, and the south transept. In
the west end there is an arched door-way, that
has been highly and very beautifully ornamented:
over this, in a round arch, there have been three
lancet windows; and above these a circular,
or marigold one, with eight divisions. The east
end, from its stile of architecture, appears of
higher antiquity than the other; and its three
long, narrow, and pointed windows, give it a
heavy appearance. The cloister on the south
side, which a century ago was only a shell, is
now converted into a dwelling house, the residence of the person who farms the adjacent
land. Three rows of groined arches, on single
round pillars, support the dormitory, which is
now a loft for containing corn, approached by
steps from without. The floors are here so thick,
from their being arched beneath, that when the
doors are shut, and the threshers are at work,
even in that part directly over the present kitchen,
they cannot be heard below.—Part of a chimney in one of the bed chambers is a relic of
a sepulchral monument. The ornaments to the
pillars and arches are of free-stone, and many
of them are perfectly fresh and beautiful. The
area of the church is overgrown with tall ash

trees, which hide from the sight some parts of
the ruin, but contribute greatly to its picturesque
beauty.

> I do love these auncient ruynes,
> We never tread upon them but we set
> Oure foote upon some reverend historie;
> And questionless here, in this open courte
> (Which now lies naked to the injuries
> Of stormy weather) some men lye interred
> Who lov'd the church so well and gave so largely to't,
> They thought it should have canopied their bones
> Till dombesday : but all things have their end;
> Churches and cities (which have diseases like to men)
> Must have like death that we have.

> This sober shade
> Lets fall a serious gloom upon the mind
> That checks but not appals.   Such are the haunts
> Religion loves, a meek and humble maid,
> Whose tender eye bears not the blaze of day.

Valle Crucis was a house of Cistertian monks,
dedicated to the virgin mother. It was indebted
for its foundation, about the year 1200, to Madoc
ap Griffith, a prince of Powis, who, after various
successes, and acquiring much booty by the
reduction and ruin of English castles, dedicated
a portion of his plunder to the service of religion! He was interred here. At the dissolution the revenues appear to have amounted to
about two hundred pounds *per annum*.

I shall conclude my account with a singular
passage from Mr. Grose's work on the Antiquities of Great Britain. It contains the explanation by Mr. Griffiths of the Navy Office, of an
inscription found on the ruins, and is as good
a specimen of antiquarian *ipse dixit* as I have
ever met with:

" Most of these houses were founded by an

injunction from the popes, by way of penance, upon some great lords of those times, for what the holy church judged infringements on her prerogative; or for some crime which those fathers of the church knew full well how to avail themselves of.—Taking the matter in this light, and from the Welsh name of the place, the inscription upon the ruins will be intelligible. The characters are maso-gothic, and franco-theotiscan mixt.—MD H OO HR BMSPOE aᷓ hⴱ aPO u S ⹀ PRO BHQV OES CM G RQO.—The first double letters I take to be MAD, or Madocus; H. hoc; OO. monasterium; HR. honori; B. beatæ; M. Mariæ; S. sanctæ, P. pœnitens; OE. Œdificavit; ac, et; h ⴱ. hoc; a P. appropriavit; Ou S. opus; PRO. pro; B. bono; HQV. hospitioque; OES. ejusdem; CM. centum marcas; GR. gratis; Q. quoque; O. ordinavit.—In English, *Madoc, a penitent, erected this monastery to the honour of the blessed and holy Virgin, and appropriated for this work, and for the better maintenance thereof, an hundred marks, which he freely settled on them!*"

LLANGOLLEN.

From these elegant and beautiful scenes I wandered into the dirty, ill built, and disagreeable town of Llangollén. The streets are narrow, and all the houses are formed of the dark shaly stone so common in North Wales. The situation of this place is, however, truly delightful to an admirer of nature: it stands on rocks that overlook the Dee, and is surrounded by high and bold mountains.

The *bridge*, which consists of five narrow and pointed arches, was originally erected about the middle of the fourteenth century, by John Trevor, bishop of St. Asaph. It is built on the rock, and in a place where it would almost seem impossible to fix a foundation sufficiently firm to withstand the furious rapidity of the current, which has worn the shelving masses to a black and glossy polish. During late years it has undergone considerable repairs.

In the *church* I found nothing deserving of attention. The name of the patron saint, who has left behind him a legend worthy even of the Koran, is pretty enough, and of no great length! *Coilen, ap Gwynawc, ap Clydawc, ap Cowrda, ap Caradawc Freichpas, ap Llyr Meirim, ap Einion Urth, ap Cunedda Wledig!*—From the church-yard the lofty mountains, on one of which stands Castell Dinas Brân, and the woody banks of the Dee, whose rapid stream winds along the valley, form a scene by no means inelegant.

PLAS NEWYDD.

About a quarter of a mile south of Llangollen is Plâs Newydd, the charming retreat of lady Eleanor Butler and Miss Ponsonby, which, however, has of late years been probably too much intruded upon by the curiosity of the multitudes of tourists who every summer visit Llangollen. Lady Eleanor Butler was, I am informed, the youngest sister of the late, and is consequently aunt to the present earl of Ormond. —Miss Ponsonby is the grand-daughter of general Ponsonby, who was slain in the battle of Fontenoy. Her father, Mr. Chambre Ponsonby, married Miss Louisa Lyons, a most elegant and accomplished woman, the second daughter of captain John Lyons, clerk of the council in Dublin. This lady lived but a few years after their marriage, and left the present Miss Ponsonby, her only child.—These two females, delighted with the scenery around Llangollen, when it was little known to the rest of the world, sought here a philosophical retirement from the frivolities of fashionable life, erected a dwelling that commands a fine mountain prospect, and have resided here ever since.

CASTELL DINAS BRAN

Is situated on a high, and somewhat conical hill, about a mile from Llangollen. This hill is so very steep on all sides, towards the summit, as to render the walk to the castle not a little fatiguing.—The building has been about a hundred yards long, and fifty in breadth; and it formerly occupied the whole crown of the mountain. From its extremely elevated situation it must have been a place of vast strength. On the side which is least steep it was defended by trenches cut through the solid rock. The present remains consist of nothing more than a few shattered walls. The views from hence on every side are very grand. Towards the east I could look along the whole vale of Llangollen, through which the Dee was seen to foam over its bed of rocks; and, beyond the vale, I could see all the flat and highly cultivated country that extended for many miles. Just beneath me lay the town of Llangollen. Towards the west I overlooked the vale of Crucis, and the mountains beyond it were all exposed, their dark sides agreeably varied with wood and meadow. On the north west I was much struck with the singular appearance of a vast rock called Craig Eglwyseg, *The Eagle's Rock*, from a tradition that formerly a pair of eagles had their nest, or aery, here. Leland has mistaken this rock for that on which the castle stands, where he says, " there bredith every yere an egle. And the egle doth sorely assault hym that destroyeth the nest; going down in one basket and having another over his hedde, to defend the sore stripes of the egle."—For upwards of a mile this rock lies stratum upon stratum, in such a direction as to form a kind of horizontal steps, denominated by naturalists *saxa sedilia.*—The inhabitants of Llangollen assert, that in one part of the rock there is an opening, whence a long arched passage leads to the foundation of the castle. The latter part of this assertion is evidently false from the situation of the building; and I could scarcely even credit the report of a cavern in the rock, for, though such is generally believed to exist, I was not able on frequent inquiry either to find any person who had himself seen it, nor could any one point out its situation to enable me to examine it.*

---

* *History of Castell Dinas Bran.*—This fortress, from the stile of its architecture, was evidently the work of the Britons. It is supposed by some writers to have been founded by Brennus, the Gaulic general, who is reputed to have come into this country to contend with his brother Belinus. The similarity of names seems, however, the only

VALE OF LLANGOLLEN.

In order that I might see the beauties of the vale of Llangollen to as great an advantage as possible, I determined to walk round it. This led me through a circuit of about eleven miles. —I crossed Llangollen bridge, and went along the road leading to Ruabon and Wrexham, on

foundation for the conjecture, and the most accurate historians believe it to have originated at a much later period — The mountain river Brân runs at the foot of the hill, but whether the fortress derived its name from the stream, or the stream from the fortress, would be no easy matter to decide at the present day : Mr Edward Lhwyd, a justly celebrated antiquary, who lived upwards of a century ago, considers the former to have been the case.

Castell Dinas Brân was the principal residence of the lords of Yale, and probably was founded by one of them.— In the reign of Henry III., Griffith ap Madoc resided here. He had married the daughter of James lord Audley, by which his affections were alienated from his own country; and he took part with the English against the Welsh prince. This induced a persecution, which compelled him to seek for security in this aerial retreat, and confine himself to the walls of his castle. The Welsh writers say that grief and shame, not long afterwards, put an end to his life. His son possessed the property; and, after his death, the guardianship of his two children was given by Edward I. to John earl of Warren, and Roger Mortimer. In the account of Holt castle, I have stated that the iniquitous guardians caused the boys to be murdered, and then seized the estates to their own use. Castell Dinas Brân was part of Warren's share in the plunder.

In the ninth year of Edward II., the grandson of the earl of Warren having no issue, surrendered this and other fortresses to the king. Being, however, afterwards separated from his wife, he obtained a regrant of the estates to himself, and his mistress, Matilda de Nereford, for life, with remainder to their children. Matilda was the last survivor, and therefore on her death, in the thirty-third year of Edward III., they reverted to the crown.—Not long after-the north side of the river. The scenery in this direction was pretty, but from the lowness of the road it had nothing particularly interesting. The most beautiful prospects were those that I had by looking back towards the town. In these the castle, from its great elevation, formed a very conspicuous feature; and in many places the Dee added considerable beauty to the scene. —I passed Trevor Hall, the family seat of the Lloyds, seated on an eminence above the road.

I had proceeded somewhat more than four miles when I turned to the right, along a road

wards they were given to Edward Fitz Alan, earl of Arundel: and from him they seem to have followed the succession of the lords of Bromfield.*

In 1390, Castell Dinas Brân was the habitation of Myfanwy Vechan, a very beautiful and accomplished female, a descendant of the house of Tudor Trevor. She was beloved by Howel ap Einion Lygliw, a Welsh bard, who addressed to her an ode full of sweetness and beauty :†

'Mid the gay towers on steep Din's Branna's cone,
  Her Hoel's breast the fair Myfanwy fires,
Oh! harp of Cambria, never hast thou known
  Notes more mellifluent floating o'er the wires,
Than when thy bard this brighter Laura sung,
And with his ill starred love Llangollen's echoes rung.

Thus consecrate to love in ages flown,
  Long ages fled, Din's Branna's ruins shew,
Bleak as they stand upon their steepy cone,
  The crown and contrast of the vale below,
Than screen'd by mural rocks with pride displays
Beauty's romantic pomp in every sylvan maze.

At what period this castle was demolished, we have no information. Churchyard, who visited it in the sixteenth century, calls it " an old and ruynous thing."

* See the account of Holt castle.   † Pennant, i. 298.

which led over the Dee at Pont y Cyssyllte. Near this bridge I saw the columns of the famous *aqueduct* formed for conveying the water over the river Dee and the vale of Llangollen. At the time I was here there were eleven erected, and the two that stood in the bed of the river were each about a hundred and twenty feet high. From a tablet on one of them I copied the following inscription, which will sufficiently explain the nature of the undertaking :

The Nobility and Gentry of
the adjacent counties
having united, their efforts with
the great commercial interest of this country,
in creating an intercourse and union, between
England and North Wales,
by a navigable communication of the three rivers,
Severn, Dee, and Mersey,
for the mutual benefit of agriculture and trade,
caused the first stone of this aqueduct of
Pont Cysyllty,
to be laid, on the 25th day of July, MDCCXCV.
when Richard Middleton, of Chirk, Esquire, M. P.
one of the original patrons of the
Ellesmere Canal,
was Lord of this manor,
and in the reign of our sovereign
GEORGE THE THIRD,
when the equity of the laws and
the security of property,
promoted the general welfare of the nation,
while the arts and sciences flourished
by his patronage, and
the conduct of civil life, was improved
by his example.

I returned to Llangollen by the Oswestry road on the south side of the river. This is considerably elevated above the bottom of the vale, and from hence all the surrounding objects

are seen to great advantage. From these steep
banks the Dee's transparent stream is seen to
wind in elegant curves, along the wooded meadows beneath. The mountains on the opposite
side of the vale are finely varied in shape and
tints; and Trevor Hall, seated on its eminence,
embosomed in woods, lent its aid to decorate the
scene. From hence Castell Dinas Brân, and
its conical hill, seem to close up the end of the
vale, and imperiously to hold in subjection all the
surrounding country. This sylvan vale, justly
celebrated for its numerous beauties, affords
many picturesque and highly romantic scenes.

The Hand is the only tolerably good *inn* in
Llangollen, but in the summer time I have more
than once found it very unpleasant, from the
crowd of travellers that are constantly passing
on the great roads to and from Ireland, and
from the number of Welsh tourists that visit
Llangollen. I never yet heard any one say that
he received either civility, or good accommodation, at this house: I have often heard, and I
have experienced, the contrary.

CHAP. XXVIII.

LLANGOLLEN TO CORWEN.

The Vale of the Dee.—Llandysilio Hall.—Extensive Pro-
spect.—Memoranda of Owen Glyndwr.—Corwen.—Church.
—Picturesque Scene.—Cefyn Creini.—Excursion to Glynn
Bridge.

ALL the country betwixt Llangollen and Corwen
is exceedingly beautiful. The road, for about a
mile, extends along the picturesque vale of
Crucis, which through its whole length, is
adorned with woods, and in many places enlivened by neat little cottages peeping from
among the trees.—I had not passed this vale
far before I entered *the valley of the Dee*, Glyn
Dyfrdwy, celebrated as, some centuries ago, the
property of the Welsh hero, Owen Glyndwr.
The mountains are high, and their features bold
and prominent. From the winding of the river,
and the turnings of the vale, almost every step
presented a new landscape.

I passed Llandysilio hall, the family seat of
the Jones's, seated on a woody flat, near the
opposite edge of the Dee. From its situation in
the bosom of the mountains, it is secluded
from the world, but there is so much elegance
around it, that it appeared to me a charming
retreat.

Looking back upon the country I had left, I saw Castell Dinas Brân, and its accompanying rock, Craig Eglwyseg, at the head of the vale. The latter forms from hence a very conspicuous object.

About half a mile beyond Llandysilio, I clambered to the top of a lofty hill on the left of the road. I was considerably deceived in its height. I fancied that it extended no higher than the ridge visible from the road; but had no sooner attained this, than I had another eminence before me: I persevered, and found two others equally high beyond.

From the summit of this eminence I had a view of the whole vale and its various windings, with its still more serpentizing river, immediately beneath me. Castell Dinas Brân was very evidently lower than my present station. I could carry my eye along the entire vale of Llangollen, and over the flat country for many miles beyond, to the far distant mountains on the verge of the horizon.

I descended to the road, and continued my journey.—Beyond the fourth mile-stone, the vale began to change its appearance. The road, instead of winding amongst mountains, now lay in a direct line.

About three miles farther on, an oak wood on the left, and a small clump of furs on an eminence on the right of the road, mark the place near which the palace of " the wild and irregular" Owen Glyndwr once stood. There are at present no other remains of it than a few scattered heaps of stone. Iolo Goch, Owen's bard, about the year 1390, wrote a poem con-

taining a description of this palace. He says
that it was surrounded by a moat filled with
water, and that the entrance was by a costly
gate over a bridge. The stile should seem to
have been of gothic architecture, for he com-
pares one of the towers to a part of Westminster
abbey. It was a Neapolitan building, containing eighteen apartments, " a fair *timber* structure, on the summit of a green hill."

MEMORANDA OF OWEN GLYNDWR.

This celebrated hero, whose actions make so
conspicuous a figure in the English history at the
commencement of the fifteenth century, was
the son of Griffith Vychan, a descendant of Meredith, prince of North Wales. He received a
liberal education; and when of proper age, was
admitted a student in one of our inns of court,
and was afterwards regularly called to the bar.
It is probable that he soon quitted the profession
of the law, and adopted that of arms, which,
as it afterwards proved, was much more con-
genial with his disposition. He warmly espoused
the cause of Richard II., to whom he was sincerely attached, He adhered to his royal
master till the last, having been taken prisoner
with him in Flint castle; and when the king's
household was dissolved, retired to his patrimony
in Wales, with full resentment of his sovereign's
wrongs. During the reign of Richard the second he had received the honour of knighthood.

F f

He married a daughter of sir David Hanmer,
of Hanmer in Flintshire, one of the justices of
the court of King's Bench; and had by her several children.

In the beginning of the reign of Henry IV.
Reginald lord Grey, of Ruthin, taking advantage of the deposal of Richard, and Glyndwr's
attachment to his cause, wrested from him a
considerable part of his possessions. Glyndwr
applied to the parliament for redress, but in
vain. His ambitious spirit, conspiring with a
sense of his wrongs, and a detestation for the
usurper Bolingbroke, determined him to throw
off, if possible, the English yoke, and to obtain
by force the government of Wales. He revolved in his mind his own genealogy, a descendant from the ancient British princes: his superstitious notions attached to himself many of
the prophesies of Merlin, and other bards of
former years. These, with the dreadful omens
that he believed had taken place at his birth,
confirmed him in the opinion that he was des-
tined to be the redeemer of his country from
the tyranny and oppression of the English
throne.

He first appeared in arms in the year 1400;
and commenced his warlike career, by attack-
ing his chief enemy, lord Grey. He was so far
successful as to take this nobleman prisoner;
and he compelled him to marry one of his
daughters. By this success his estates were
recovered. Glyndwr now meditated, and soon
afterwards performed more extensive exploits.
Aided by the inaccessible mountains of Wales,
and soldiers on whose valour he had the utmost

reliance, he sat at defiance the whole power of England. After a series of engagements which lasted more than twelve years, he proved himself so formidable an enemy to Henry **IV.** that at length the English monarch thought it politic to make him an offer of accommodation. Death, however, prevented him from accepting it. He died in September 1415, as it is supposed, at the house of one of his daughters at Monnington in Herefordshire ; and he probably was buried at that place, but there is no memorial whatever of the spot where his body was deposited.

About two miles before I arrived at Corwen the vale completely changed its aspect. It was here destitute of wood, and the low and verdant mountains were cultivated nearly to their summits. The river Dee assumed a placid form, and glided silently and smoothly within its flat and meadowy banks.

CORWEN,

The White Choir, is a disagreeable little town, with a white-washed church. Its situation is under a rock at the foot of the Berwyn mountains.—It is a place much resorted to by anglers, who come here for the advantage of fishing in the Dee, which abounds in salmon, trout, and various other species of esculent fish.

The church contains an ancient monument

F f 2

to the memory of Iorwerth Sulien, one of the vicars. In the church-yard there is an ancient square stone pillar, that has once had much carved work upon it, but from the effects of time and weather, this is now nearly obliterated.

A mill on a stream at the back of the inn I found a picturesque object; and some of the cottages near it are rude, and singularly built. The young artist would find here a good study or two.

Corwen is celebrated as having been a place of rendezvous to the Welsh forces under their prince Owen Gwynedd; who from hence, in 1165, put an end to the invasion of Henry II.

CEFYN CREINI.

Near the summit of a hill on the opposite side of the river, called Cefyn Creini, *The Mountain of Worship*, there is a vast circle of loose stones, which bears the appearance of having once been a British fortification. This is called Caer Drewyn and Y Caer Wen *The White Fort*. It is near half a mile in circumference, but the walls are at present in such a state, that at a distance they appear like huge heaps of stones piled round the circumference of a circle. Owen Gwynedd is believed to have occupied this post, whilst Henry the second had his men encamped among the Berwyn mountains, on the opposite side of the vale. It is also related that Owen Glyndwr made use of this place in his occasional retreats.—The whole circle is perfectly visible from the road leading to Llanrwst, at the distance of about two miles from the town.

GLYNN BRIDGE.

From Corwen I made an excursion of six miles to Pont y Glynn, *The Bridge of the Glen,* on the road leading to Llanrwst. The scenery along the whole walk had numerous beauties; but from one situation I had a delightful view along the beautiful vale of Edeirnion, bounded by the lofty Berwyn mountains, and adorned with the most pleasing cultivation.—The woody glen, at the head of which stands Pont y Glynn, with its prominent rocks, nearly obscured by the surrounding foliage, after a while presented itself; and then, almost in a moment, on a sudden turn of the road, appeared the bridge, thrown over the chasm. Beneath it was the rugged and precipitous bed of the river, where, amongst immense masses and huge fragments of rock, the stream foamed with the most violent impetuosity. The transition to this romantic scene was so momentary, as to seem almost the effect of magic. The cataract is not very lofty, but from its being directly under the bridge, where the foam and spray were seen dashing among the dark opposing rocks, and having the addition of pendant foliage from each side, a scene was formed altogether

finely picturesque and elegant. The bridge
rests on two nearly perpendicular rocks,
and appears to be at least fifty feet above
the bed of the stream. The view from thence
down the hollow was grand and tremendous.

CHAP. XXXIX.

CORWEN TO BALA.

THE distance from Corwen to Bala, along
the usual road, is about eleven miles; but as
there was another that for some miles accompanied the Dee, I was induced to prefer it.
This road, as I had imagined from my map,
extended along the *vale of Edeirnion*, which I
had so much admired in my late ramble to
Glynn Bridge. I found it so bad as in some
places to be nearly impassable. From its very
low situation I had few opportunites of seeing
the elegancies of the vale ; but whenever the
road passed over an eminence, I found much
to admire.

WATERFALL OF CYNWYD.

At the village of Cynwyd, *The Source of
Mischief*, (probably so called says Mr. Pennant,

in consequence of the courts which formerly were held there by the great men of the
neighbourhood, to settle the boundaries of the
adjacent commons, and to take cognizance of
encroachments,) I left the road about half a
mile, and proceeded along a deep glen that led
me to Rhaiadr Cynwyd, *The Waterfall of
Cynwyd.* The water dashed from precipice to
precipice, among the wood and rocks, in the
wildest and most romantic manner imaginable.
The scene was so varied from the confusion of
the water foaming in every direction, and partly
hidden by the shrubs and trees growing on the
ledges of the rocks, that the pen cannot describe
it with justice, and even the efforts of the pencil
could only give a faint conception of its elegance. Many detached parts of it afford excellent studies to the admirers of picturesque
beauty.

I resumed my journey, passed Llandrillo,
The Church of St. Trillo, and afterwards crossing the river, arrived at *Llanderfel,* another
small village, whose church is dedicated to a
British saint, called

DERFEL GADARN.

The church once contained a vast wooden
image of this, its patron saint, which was held
in such superstitious veneration, that people
from very distant parts made pilgrimages to it,
and on these occasions offered not only money,
but sometimes even horses or cattle. The

Welsh people believed that Derfel Gadarn had the power of once rescuing each of his votaries from the torments of hell. On the 5th of April 1537, the festival day of this saint, no fewer than betwixt five and six hundred persons, some of them from a great distance, came to Llanderfel to make the accustomed offerings. —The letter from Elis Price, commissary-general of the diocese of St. Asaph, to Cromwell the vicar-general, of which the following is a copy, was the first cause of this very lucrative antique being destroyed, to the great displeasure, no doubt, of the monks, who rioted in the produce of its coffers:

"Right honorable, and my syngular good lorde and mayster, all circumstanncys and thankes sett aside pleasithe yt yowre good lordeshipe to be aduisid that where I was constitute and made by yowre honorable desire and commaundmente comissarie generall of the dyosese of Saynte Asaph, I haue done my diligens and dutie for the expulsinge and takynge awaye of certen abusions supersticions and ipocryses usid withyn the saide dyosese of Saynte Assaph accordynge to the kynges honorable rules and injunctions therein made, that notwithstandinge, there ys an image of *Darvell Gadarn* withyn the saide diosese in whom the people have so greate confidence hope and truste that they come daylye a pillgramage unto hym some withe kyne, other withe oxen or horsis, and the reste withe money in so muche that there was fyve or syxe hundrethe pillgrames to a mans estimacon that offered to the saide image the fifte daie of this presente monethe of Apll; the innocente people hathe ben sore aluryd and entisid to worshipe the saide image in so muche that there is a comyn saynge as yet amongist them that who so ever will offer auie thinge to the saide image of Darvell Gadarn, he hathe power to fatche hym or them that so offers once oute of hell when they be dampned. Therfore for the reformacon and amendmente of the premisis I wolde gladlie knowe by this berer youre honorable pleasure and will, as knowithe God; who euer preserue your lordeshipe longe in welth and honor.—Written in Northe Wales the vi. day of this presente Aprill (1537.)— Youre bedeman and dayelie orator by dutie.

" ELIS PRICE*."

The Welsh people had extant a prophesy concerning this image, that it shold " make a *forest* blaze," and in the ensuing year an opportunity occurred not only of depriving them of the cause of their superstition, but even of completing the prophesy, in a manner, however, that they little expected. A friar observant, whose name was *Forest*, was condemned to the stake for having denied the supremacy of the king. The name was thought by the heads of the church a fortunate occurrence, and it was advised that the image should be immediately brought to London to consume this wretched friar. To the stake on which he suffered was affixed the following elegy :

David Darfel Gatheren,
As sayth the Welshmen,
   Fetched outlawes out of hell.
Now is he come, with spere and shield,
In harnes, to burne in Smithfield,
For in Wales he may not dwell.

And Forest the friar,
That obstinate lyar,
   That wilfully shall be dead,
In his contumaciè,
The gospel dothe deny
   And the king to be supreme head†.

---

* Cotton MSS. in the British Museum; CLEOPATRA, E. IV. fol. 55.
        † Hall's Chronicle, ccxxxiii.

At Llanfawr, *The Great Village*, two miles from Bala, is the supposed place of interment of

THE WELSH BARD, LLYWARCH HEN,

Who flourished in the seventh century. He was nearly allied to the Welsh princes, and to his bardic character united that of a warrior. His whole life was spent in a series of vicissitudes and misfortunes, and he died about the year 670, at the great age of a hundred and fifty years. Somewhat more than a century ago an inscription was found upon the wall, near which his remains were supposed to have been deposited: this wall is now covered with plaster.—Not far from hence there is a circle of stones called Pabell Llywarch Hên, *The Tent of old Llywarch*, where it is probable he had a house, and spent the latter part of his days. He had been one of king Arthur's generals, and a member of his council. In his activity in opposing the encroachments of the Saxons and Irish, he was deprived of his whole patrimonial possessions, and lost every one of his four-and-twenty sons. Having now no friends, he retired to a hut at Aber Cuog (now Dôlguog, near Machynlleth,) to soothe with his harp the remembrance of misfortune, and to vent in elegiac numbers the sorrows of old age in distress. One of his poems, particularly, describes his misfortunes, and his deplorable situation, in the most simple and affecting language. It opens with the representation of an aged prince, who once ruled in magnificence, now robbed of his possessions, and wandering in a strange country, oppressed with wretchedness and poverty. Overcome with fatigue and hunger, he is supposed to rest his wearied limbs on the top of an eminence, and to contemplate there the varied and unhappy events of his life. This elegy has appeared in an English dress : what follows is a selection from it, as the whole would be too long for insertion here :

> Hark! the cuckoo's plaintive note
> Doth thro' the wild vale sadly float;
> As, from the rav'nous hawk's pursuit,
> In Ciog rests her weary foot,
> And there, with mournful sounds and low,
> Echoes my harp's responsive woe.
> Returning spring, like opening day,
> That makes all nature glad and gay,
> Prepares Andate's fiery car,
> To rouse the brethren of the war;
> When as the youthful hero's breast
> Gloweth for the glorious test,
> Rushing down the rocky steep,
> See the Cambrian legions sweep,
> Like meteors on the boundless deep.
>
>   Old *Mona* smiles
> Monarch of an hundred isles.
> And *Snowdon* from his awful height,
> His hoar head waves propitious to the fight.
>
> But I—no more in youthful pride,
> Can dare the steep rock's haughty side;
> For fell disease my sinews rends,
> My arm unnerves, my stout heart bends;
> And raven locks, now silver-grey,
> Keep me from the field away.
>
> But see!—He comes, all drench'd in blood,
> *Gwên*, the Great, and Gwên, the Good;
> Bravest, noblest, worthiest son,
> Rich with many a conquest won;

Gwên, in thine anger great,
Strong thine arm, thy frown like fate ;
Where the mighty rivers end,
And their course to ocean bend,
There, with the eagle's rapid flight,
How wouldst thou brave the thickest fight!
Oh, fatal day ! Oh, ruthless deed !
When the sisters cut thy thread.
Cease, ye waves, your troubled roar;
Nor flow, ye mighty rivers more ;
For *Gwên,* the Great, and *Gwên,* the Good,
Breathless lies, and drench'd in blood !
Four and twice ten sons were mine,
Us'd in battle's front to shine ;
But——low in dust my sons are laid,
Nor one remains his sire to aid.

Hold, oh hold, my brain thy seat ;
How doth my bosom's monarch beat !
Cease thy throbs, perturbed heart ;
Whither would thy stretch'd strings start !
From frenzy dire, and wild affright,
Keep my senses thro' this night*.

BALA,

The Outlet of the Lake, is a market town containing about two thousand inhabitants. It consists principally of one long and wide street, and is situated at the bottom of a pool, the largest in the country, called Llyn Tegid, *The Fair Pool.* It is principally noted for its manufacture of woollen stockings, and as the autumnal resort of grous shooters.

Near the town I passed a lofty artificial mount

* See the preface to Owen's translation of the Elegies of Llywarch Hên. Jones's Welsh Bards. Vaughan' Merionethshire. Camb. Reg. i. 192.

called Tommen y Bala, *The Tumulus of Bala.*
This is supposed to have been of Roman origin,
and to have been formed here, with a small
castle on its summit, to secure the pass toward
the sea, and to keep the mountaineers in subjection. The Welsh taking advantage of it,
made it one of their chain of fortresses which
extended through the country to the coast of
Flintshire*. On the eastern bank of the Dee,
not far distant, there is another mount called
Castell Gronw Befr o Benllyn, *The Castle of
Gronw the Fair of Penllyn,* a Welsh chieftain
who lived in the sixth century.

BALA LAKE,

Llyn Tegid, or Pimblemere, for this pool has
these various names, is about a quarter of a
mile south of the town of Bala. It is by much
the largest of the Welsh lakes, being about four
miles long, and in many parts near a mile in
breadth. The scenery around it is mountainous,
but not sufficiently rude to render it very picturesque. It reminded me of the low mountain-scenery surrounding Winandermere, in the
north of England. From the bottom, however,
the diversified shores present a pleasing scene.
On the west are seen the summits of the lofty
Arrenigs. Arran Benllyn, beyond the upper
end of the pool, stretches his black and rocky

* The history both of this place and of the town is little
known. I only find that the mount was fortified in the year
1202 by Llewelyn ap Iorwerth, prince of North Wales.

front into the clouds; and in the extreme distance, in fainter colours, are seen the three
summits of Cader Idris.

This pool is well stocked with fish of various
kinds, but in particular with trout, eels, and a
species found only in alpine lakes, called, from
the whiteness of its scales, *Gwyniadd**. These
fish which are gregarious, and from three to
four pounds in weight, usually reside at the
bottom of the water, where they feed on small
shells and aquatic plants.—It is generally believed by the inhabitants of the neighbourhood,
that although the Dee runs directly through this
pool, the gwyniadds are never to be caught in
the river; nor, on the contrary, are the salmon
with which the river abounds, ever taken in the
pool. Hence old Churchyard,

> A poole there is thro' which the Dee doth passe,
> Where is a fish that some a whiting call:
> Where never yet no salmon taken was,
> Yet hath good store of other fishes all.
> Above that poole, and so beneath that flood
> Are salmons caught, and many a fish full good,
> But in the same there will no salmon bee,
> And neere that poole you shall no whiting see.

The overflowings of this pool are at times
very dreadful. These, however, seldom take
place, except when the winds, rushing from
the hollows of the mountains at the upper end,
drive the waters suddenly along. In stormy
weather great part of the vale of Edeirnion
will sometimes be overflowed. By the united
force of the winds and mountain torrents, the

* *Salmo lavaretus* of Linnæus.

water towards the bottom of the pool has been known to rise six or eight feet in perpendicular height. On the contrary, in calm and settled weather, it is always very smooth. There have been some instances, in severe winters, of its being entirely frozen over; and when covered with snow, it has been mistaken by travellers for an extensive plain.

EXCURSION ROUND BALA LAKE.

In this excursion, of about ten miles, I crossed the bridge over the Dee, and proceeded along the eastern bank of the pool. From near the church of Llangower, a pleasing vale was seen to open on the opposite side, bounded by mountains, and closed at the end by one of the Arrenigs.

I had passed the head of the pool somewhat more than half a mile, when I found the narrow lane which leads to Llanwchllyn, *The Church above the Lake.* I left the road and soon afterwards entered the *Vale of Twrch.* Nature is seen in all her majesty here; but as lord Lyttleton observed of the Berwyn mountains, " it is the majesty of a tyrant frowning over the ruins and desolation of a country." There were no marks of habitations or culture; and heath, moss, lichens, and a few grasses, seemed the only vegetation. The surrounding mountains were as rude as description can paint. the most prominent of these was Arran Benllyn, which here presented only a series of naked crags and precipices.—From hence I crossed the river Twrch, *The Burrower.*

PHENOMENON CALLED DAEAR-DOR.

My guide now pointed out a piece of land, of considerable extent, nearly covered with innumerable masses of broken rocks. These, he said, had all been conveyed thither in the summer of 1781, by what the inhabitants of the mountains call Daear-Dor, *a breaking of the earth.* The daear-dor is a dislodgement, by means of water, of a vast quantity of the surface of the ground, or, as in the present instance, of a considerable part of some of the rocks among the higher mountains. An unusual volume of water descending suddenly from the clouds becomes lodged in some confined situation : by degrees it penetrates the earth, and this loosening, the whole mass is swept along before the torrent, till it meets with resistance in some of the vales below, where it is therefore deposited. The accident near Llanwchllyn happened after a violent storm of thunder. The banks of the Twrch were overflowed, and the torrent carried every thing before it that was not actually embedded in the rock. Seventeen cottages, ten cows, and a vast number of sheep, besides the soil of all the meadows and corn-fields along its course, were overwhelmed and destroyed. This meadow, in which the river deposited its chief contents, was rendered totally unfit to be any more cultivated. The dimensions of some of the pieces of rock borne here by the fury of the torrent, are almost inconceivable. Two of

G g

the stones each near twenty feet in length, eight broad, and six deep, came in contact, and by the collision one of them was split. Eight other stones, about half this size, were carried near nine hundred yards beyond. Five bridges were swept away; and had not the inhabitants of Llanwchllyn, providentially, received timely alarm, they would all have been destroyed.

Whilst speaking of the neighbourhood of Llanwchllyn, I must digress a little from my subject to relate a whimsical adventure which happened to a gentleman of my acquaintance, Mr. D., an artist, and his friend, whilst at this village some years ago.—These gentlemen, in a pedestrian excursion round Bala lake, found themselves, on their arrival at Llanwchllyn, fatigued and hungry. As neither of them could speak a word of Welsh, they were compelled to have recourse to signs in order to make themselves understood. These so far answered their purpose, that a man whom they met in the village exclaimed in answer, " eze" (intended doubtless for " yes"), and pointed with his finger to a kind of hut, from the rafters of which two or three dirty candles, and a few bits of bacon were suspended. On entering they again made the signs of eating and drinking, and the woman conducted them to what they conjectured to be the public-house. Here their attention was fixed upon some fragments of bacon, which had hung so long, that all the strings had nearly cut their way through. They explained by signs as well as they were able, what it was they wanted, and the female of the house brought out *three* eggs. This was but a slender supply for two hungry men. They both called out " *more*," the woman answered " eze," but brought out the frying-pan. They shook their heads, she fetched a sauce-pan. Here they found a difficulty which they knew not how to encounter. A bright thought suddenly came into the other gentleman's head : —" D., you can draw, *ask the woman for a piece of chalk*, and *draw* an egg." The absurdity of the idea was such, that Mr. D. could not refrain from a loud and hearty laugh. It was, however, at last agreed, that the woman should be suffered to boil the three eggs, but that when she brought them to the table, **D.** was to snatch them from her, and pretend to eat them all himself. The plan succeeded ; the woman laughed immoderately at the contest, and running out with a cry of " eze, eze, eze," soon afterwards brought in four eggs more. There was no difficulty in making the payment for this rude cheer : Mr. **D.** held out some silver in his hand, from which the honest Welshwoman took a sum fully sufficient for the seven eggs, and a quart of ale !

On the summit of a high and craggy rock, at some distance from the road, and about a mile from Llanwchllyn, are the remains of *Castell Corndochon*, an ancient British fort. It was of a somewhat oval form, and has consisted of a square tower, and another oblong, but rounded at the extremity. I have met with no historical data whatever respecting this fortress.

In my return I observed an eminence on the west side of the head of the pool, which the guide informed me was called Caer Gai. There was on this spot a fort that belonged to Cai Hir

ap Cynyr, or, as Spencer has called him, Timon :
he was the foster-father of king Arthur, who
during his youth resided here. The Romans
are supposed to have had a fortress on this spot;
and many of their coins have been dug up in
the neighbourhood. This place of defence was
doubtless constructed to guard the pass through
the mountains. Of its history I am altogether
ignorant.

THE RIVER DEE.

The source of the Dee is under one side of
Arran Benllyn, the high mountain at the head
of Bala pool.—Its name is thought to have been
derived from the Welsh word Dwy, which signifies something *divine*. Some centuries ago
it was held in superstitious veneration by the
inhabitants of the country, from what was
then believed the miraculous overflowing of its
banks at times when there had been no preceding heavy rain : and from its being believed to
have foretold some remarkable events by changing its channel. History informs us, that when
the Britons, drawn up in battle array on its
banks, have been prepared to engage with
their Saxon foes, it was their custom first to
kiss the earth, and then for every soldier to
drink a small quantity of the water.—The name
is certainly not derived, as many have supposed,
from Dû, *black ;* for, except when tinged by
the torrents from the mountain morasses, its
waters are perfectly bright and transparent.
In Spencer's description of Caer Gai, the
dwelling of old Timon, the foster-father of Ar-

thur, the colour of the Dee is considered very
different from black :

—Lowe in a valley green,
Under the foot of Rawran, mossie o'er,
From whence the river Dee, as *ilver clene*,
His tumbling billows rolls with gentle roar.

That lover of the marvellous, Giraldus Cambrensis, informs us very gravely, that the river
Dee runs through Bala lake, and is discharged
at the bridge near the town, without their
waters becoming mixed. He doubtless means
to say that the river might be traced by its appearance from one end of the lake to the other.
Giraldus believed every thing that the inhabitants chose to impose upon him.

454

CHAP. XL.

BALA TO SHREWSBURY.

Cascade at Pont Cynwyd.—Rhiwedog.—Trûm y Sarn.—The Berwyn Mountains.—Llangynog.—Slate Quarries.—Hazardous Mode of conveying Slates from the Mountain into the Vale.—Lead Mines.—Llanrhaiadr.—The Cataract of Pistyll Rhaiadr.—The Vale of Langedwin.—Knochin.—Account of the singular Discovery of a Murderer.—Kynaston's Cave in Ness Cliff.—Montford Bridge.—Shrewsbury.

Leaving Bala, I turned my steps towards England, and occupied two days in the journey from hence to Shrewsbury. These, from severe rain that set in when I had got about ten miles from Bala, and lasted with little intermission till I arrived at Shrewsbury, were rendered two of the most unpleasant days I had spent in the country.—At my outset the morning was, however, very serene. The sun, in exhaling the dews, gave a delightful air of freshness to all the surrounding objects. The whole scene was enlivened by the music of birds, whose various tones and elegant strains would have interested less ardent admirers of the works of nature than myself. Every thing seemed to partake of a general sprightliness. The thrilling tones of the sky-lark were heard on every side: the notes of the black-bird echoed from among the distant foliage,

Whilst now and then sweet Philomel would wail,
Or stock-doves plain, amid the forest deep,
That drowsy rustled to the sighing gale;
And still a coil the grass-hopper did keep.

These rural objects continued, however, for very few miles; for I then entered on a succession of dreary and open moors, which might have charms for the sportsman, but they had none for me.

About a mile and a half from Bala, I passed a bridge called *Pont Cynwyd.* The bed of the turbulent little stream is here crowded with huge masses of rock, deeply excavated into circular hollows by the furious eddying of the water. In one situation these rocks, with the stream rushing down amongst them, form a small but pleasing cascade.

A little beyond the bridge stands Rhiwedog, *The abrupt Ascent.* This was an ancient family seat; and a vale in its neighbourhood was the scene of that severe battle betwixt the British and Saxon forces, in which the aged Llywarch took an active part, and lost his only surviving son.

From the side of a steep, on the edge of the moors, I was presented with a distant view of the vale of Edeirnion, whose verdure and fertility formed a striking contrast with my bleak and dreary situation.—The road now led me over Trûm y Sarn, *The Causeway of the Ridge,* a place that has its name from being near a lofty heath-clad mountain, which I passed at a little distance towards the south. It is one of that immense range of mountains which extend fifteen or sixteen miles, and are called

Berwyn Mountains. The two most elevated summits are Cader Ferwyn, and Cader Fronwen.—I arrived at a noted bwlch, or pass, which divides the counties of Merioneth and Montgomery, called Milltir Gerig, *The Stony Mile.*

LLANGYNOG.

I had now a view into the curious and romantic *vale of Llangynog,* a hollow so completely inclosed on all sides by mountain barriers, as apparently to afford no outlet to the residents in its bosom. The mountains seemed in many places perpendicular, and their cliffs too steep to be scaled by any other than those most active of all British animals, the sheep and goats. These I observed browsing along the sides with the utmost unconcern. The bottom was entirely in a state of cultivation, but principally as meadow land: it was interspersed with the houses of the farmers and their labourers.

A tolerably good road took me from the edge of this vale by a descent, somewhat steep, first into the hollow, and then to the small and comfortless village of Llangynog, *The Church of St. Cunog.*

SLATE QUARRIES.

From a stupendous rock, which rises on the north side of the village, are obtained those slates for which this neighbourhood is celebrated through all the adjacent counties. The quarries are situated high up in the mountain. I observed that the mode of conveying them to the vale was different from that practised near Llanberis, which I have already described, but it appeared much more dangerous. The slates are loaded on small sledges, which are to be conveyed down the side of the mountain, along winding paths formed for the purpose. Each of these sledges has a rope by which it is fastened to the shoulders of a man who has the care of conveying it. He lays firmly hold with his hands, and thus, with his face towards it, begins to descend. The velocity which the sledge acquires in its descent is counteracted by the man's striking forcibly against the prominences with his feet. This manœuvre, since he goes backward, and has at the same time some attention to pay to the sledge in order to keep it in the track, must be difficult to attain, and long practice alone can render it easy. The danger to an observer seems very great: on enquiry at the village, I was, however, informed that a serious accident had scarcely ever been known to occur from it.

LEAD MINES.

At Craig y Mwyn, about two miles and a half from Llangynog, somewhat more than a century ago, a vein of lead ore was discovered, so valuable as to yield to the Powis family, for forty years, a clear revenue of at least twenty thousand pounds a year. It had been worked to the depth of about a hundred yards, when on a sudden the water broke in, and became so powerful, that the proprietor was compelled to

abandon the undertaking.*   Ever since that
time the mines have continued nearly filled with
water, but some gentlemen a few years ago
determined to attempt their recovery, and for
this purpose levels were to be driven in various
parts of the mountain, if possible, to drain off
the water. Whether they have proceeded in the
attempt, or given it up, I have not the means of
being informed.—Besides these there are some
mines, but of less importance, near the village,
which were worked when I was at Llangynog.
The produce of these I was informed was very
trifling.

On my leaving Llangynog, the clouds ga-
thered round the summits and sides of the mountains, and the rain soon afterwards began to
descend in torrents. This village appeared, however, so wretched a place for a wearied traveller,
that I had no inducement to return for shelter.
In the greatest misfortunes we are generally able
to find some object on which we can rest with
satisfaction : it soon occurred to me that the
drenching of my clothes would be amply compensated by the increased volume of water at
the cataract of *Pistyll Rhaiadr,* which I intended to visit in the morning.   The idea of
this gave me so much pleasure, that when I
became fairly wet to the skin, I was altogether
careless as to personal comfort ; and now the
faster and more heavily the rain descended, the
better a great deal I was pleased with it.

* Pennant, ii. 347.

LLANRHAIADR,

In this state it was, that after about two hours slippery walking, and my clothes dripping with wet, I arrived at Llanrhaiadr, *The Village of the Cataract*, situated, like Llangynog, in a deep hollow, surrounded on all sides by mountains, whose summits were now entirely obscured by clouds. This hollow is called Mochnant, *The Vale of the rapid Brook*. The houses, or rather cottages, of the village are irregular; but, as most of them were old and overgrown with vegetation, it had from many points of view an appearance highly picturesque.

I found very tolerable accommodations, even for the night, at the *Coach and Horses*, an inn, or rather public-house, whose exterior does not bespeak the good opinion of the traveller.

Dr. William Morgan, who first translated the Bible into the Welsh language, was vicar of this place. He was afterwards rewarded with the bishopric of Llandaff, and in 1601 with that of St. Asaph.

PISTYLL RHAIADR,

The Spout of the Cataract, the most celebrated waterfall of this country, rushes down the front of an almost perpendicular rock, that terminates a vale at the distance of about four miles from the village. The vale is narrow and well wooded; it is watered by the little river Rhaiadr, which here constitutes the boundary line betwixt the counties of Denbigh and Montgomery, and

it affords many pleasing and beautiful scenes.
The upper part of the cataract, when the sun
shines upon it, is visible to a great distance;
and along this hollow its silvery and linear
appearance give an air of singularity to many
of the views.—Pistyll Rhaiadr is upwards of
two hundred and ten feet high; and for near
two thirds of this height, the water is thrown
down the flat face of a bleak, naked, and barren
rock; from thence it rages through a natural
arch, and betwixt two prominent sides into the
small bason at its foot.   The whole scene is destitute of wood, but it has so much simple grandeur, that trees would injure, rather than
heighten the general effect.   When visited after
very heavy rain, a singular occurrence is to be
remarked.   The water in its descent is ob-
structed by the mass of rock, through which it
seems by time to have forced a passage, and it
is said to burst through it with a vast quantity of
spray, appearing like smoke from the explosion
of a cannon.—I was told that the late worthy
vicar of Llanrhaiadr, the Rev. Dr. Worthington, with a view of gratifying the curious, had
a pair of flood gates fixed on the stream, above
the cataract, occasionally to obstruct the passage of the water: when a sufficient quantity
had been collected behind them, they were suddenly thrown open, and the rushing down of the
flood is said to have afforded one of the grandest
spectacles imaginable. — This gentleman also
erected a small building at the foot of the rock,
for the accommodation of visitors, which is found
very convenient to those who bring refreshments
along with them.

On my return from the cataract, I left Llan-rhaiadr, and proceeded along the road which leads through part of the vale of *Llangedwen*. I passed Llangedwen hall, a handsome stone edifice, the property of Sir Watkin Williams Wynne. This place was a favourite residence of the late baronet, but it is seldom visited by the present owner.

I once again arrived at *Llanymynech*. Be-twixt this village and Shrewsbury the rain poured down in such torrents as to render my journey in every respect dreary and uncom-fortable. Through the thickness of the mist I could but just discern the *Breiddin Hills*, at the distance of a few miles on the right: their summits were perfectly obscured in clouds.

KNOCHIN,

A village about five miles from Llanymynech, has once been a place of some celebrity. The hall was the residence of the family of L'Estrange, who built the town. They had on its site a castellated mansion so early as in the reign of Henry II. The last of the family was Joan, who married George Stanley, the eldest son of the first earl of Derby. The following occurrence is said to have taken place, some years ago, in the neighbourhood of Knochin:

A man of the name of Elkes was left guar-dian to his brother's son. This boy was very young, and the only obstacle to Elkes becoming possesssed of considerable property. He had long revolved in his mind the manner in which he could rid himself of this incumbrance, and at length hit upon the following inhuman expedient: a poor child of the village was directed to take the boy to a distant corn-field to play and gather flowers. Elkes met them near the spot, and directed the other child to return immediately home. He then took his ward unto his arms, walked with him to the end of the field, where he knew there was a tub nearly full of water, and forcing his head into it, held him in that position till the child was suffocated. The neighbours soon observed that the boy was missing; the *poor* boy who had accompanied him to the field told his simple story, and a party of the inhabitants, on searching the place, discovered the body. Information soon reached them that Elkes had fled towards London. Two horsemen were therefore immediately dipatched in pursuit of him. These men were riding along the road near South Mims in Hertfordshire, when they were surprized by the singular actions of two ravens, that were perched on a cock of hay in an adjoining field. The birds made an unusual noise, and furiously pulled about the hay with their beaks. Curiosity alone, the men said, induced them to alight, and see what could be the cause of such singular actions. They threw down the heap of hay, and were astonished to discover beneath it the man of whom they were in search. He asserted that these two birds had followed him incessantly, from the time that the murder had been committed. This unhappy victim of avarice was conveyed to Shrewsbury, tried, condemned, and afterwards hung in chains on Knochin heath.*

* Phillips's History of Shrewsbury, App. 233.

KYNASTON'S CAVE.

A few miles from Knochin I passed under a high rock of red free-stone, called Ness Cliff. In the south-east side of this rock there is a cave, which has the name of Kynaston's Cave. This was a place of occasional retreat to Humphrey, the son of sir Roger Kynaston, constable of Harlech castle, and a party of his mad companions. He was outlawed in the sixth year of the reign of Henry VII., was pardoned in the year following, and died in 1534. He is remembered by many strange pranks, and still continues the talk of the neighbouring peasantry.

Leaving this rock, I soon afterwards saw, by the road-side, a small building, from which several boys were issuing. An inscription over the door arrested my steps for a moment:

> God prosper long this public good,
> A school erected, where a chapel stood.

I crossed the Severn at Montford bridge; and in about an hour afterwards ended my pedestrian excursion at Shrewsbury.

CHAP. XLI.

SHREWSBURY.

SHREWSBURY is a town of considerable magnitude and importance, situated on a sloping
ground, and nearly surrounded by the Severn.
The streets are irregular, and many of the
buildings very ancient —This place once formed
the capital of Powisland, and was, for some
years, a seat of the Welsh princes.

CASTLE.

In my tour through the town and suburbs I
first visited the castle. This is built of a red
stone, and situated on an eminence above the
river, just in that part of the town where the
river leaves it undefended. Its foundation has
been ascribed to Roger de Montgomery, the
great earl of Shrewsbury, who lived in the
reign of William the Conqueror, but of the

ancient structure there is not at this time much remaining. It is the property, and forms one of the residences of Sir William Pulteney, in right of his lady, Henrietta, baroness of Bath. The owner, however, very seldom visits the place. —The *keep* stood on a large artificial mount, which seems to prove it of Saxon or British origin.

The castle continued in possession of the two sons of the founder till the reign of Henry I., when that monarch chose to take it into his own hands. After the restoration of Charles II. it was granted to Francis, Lord Newport, afterwards earl of Bradford; and some time consequent to this grant it became the property of the Pulteney family.

WALLS.

Robert de Belesme, son to Roger de Montgomery, was the first who attempted to defend the town by walls. This he did, by building from the castle along each side of the river for a considerable distance; and thus he secured himself for a while from the attacks of his enemy, Henry the First. The remaining part of the walls was erected in the reign of Henry the Third, at the request of the inhabitants, to fortify the place against the inroads of the Welsh. So great, however, was the want of money for the completion of the undertaking, that thirty two years elapsed before they could be finished.—A very small portion of the walls is now left. From one situation near them I had a good prospect of part of the suburbs of the town.

COUNTY GAOL.

At a little distance beyond the castle, and, situated like that building, on the elevated bank of the Dee, I saw the county gaol, a large and handsome structure. It is constructed of brick, and in a situation that cannot be surpassed for the purity, and consequent healthiness, of its atmosphere. In a niche over the entrance there is a bust of Howard. The outer walls were begun in the year 1789, and some of the apartments were ready for the reception of prisoners in 1796.

I proceeded along a pleasant terrace walk to the end of the building, whence descending to the river, I found a foot-path which led me to the English bridge. From hence the castle, the river, and the town, partly hidden by trees, with the spires of St. Mary's and St. Alkmund's churches, formed a beautiful and picturesque scene.

THE STONE BRIDGE,

Called also the East bridge, the English bridge, and the new bridge, is an elegant structure, of seven arches, which was erected about forty years ago. — Near the middle of it are the water-works, from which the town receives its supply of that very essential article of life.— On the west side of the town, in a direction nearly opposite to this, is the other, called the

Welsh bridge. This is a late erection. The ancient bridge had a gate, and towers at each end, a necessary defence against the turbulent neighbours on that side of the water.

SHREWSBURY ABBEY

Is situated in the suburbs of the town, a little beyond the stone bridge. The present remains consist of only the west part, from the transept to the west tower. The choir, the cloister, and chapter-house, are entirely destroyed. Of the side aisles, the arches are yet left, and the east end of the present church is a modern wall that has been run up betwixt two of the ancient columns. This church is supposed to have been made parochial in the reign of Queen Elizabeth. The great tower is still left, and contains a fine gothic window, over which is a statue, supposed to represent the founder, Roger de Montgomery. The whole building is of the same kind of red stone as the castle, and, except the west window, is in the Norman stile of architecture, with plain arches, and massy columns.—On the south side of the altar there is a recumbent figure, in a coat of mail, and in the act of drawing a sword. This is believed to have been the monument of Montgomery. An inscription intimates that it was discovered among the ruins of the abbey, and that, in 1622, it had been directed by the heralds at arms to be carefully preserved, in consequence of which it was placed in its present situation.*

* The history of the abbey is short.—It was founded by Roger de Montgomery, and his Countess Adelissa, in the

H h 2

In the garden of Sir Charles Oakely, on the south side of the church there is a small but elegant octagonal building, the remains of an *ancient oratory* belonging to the abbey, now called St. Wenefred's Pulpit.

CHURCHES.

The remaining churches in Shrewsbury are,

St. Giles's,	St. Julian's
St. Alkmund's,	and
St. Mary's,	St. Chad's.

St. Giles's church is situated on the skirt of the suburbs, about a mile east of the abbey. It is an ancient, small, and inelegant, but somewhat picturesque building. It boasts a higher origin than the abbey, and in the domesday survey is called " the parish of the city." It is at present annexed to the church of Holy Cross, or the abbey. The bones of St. Wenefred, when they were removed from Denbighshire to

year 1083, and dedicated to St. Peter and St. Paul. Its monks were of the Benedictine order, and first brought over from Seez, in Normandy ; and the earl, by permission of his lady, became himself one of the religious of his own abbey. He endowed it largely, and encouraged all who were dependant on him to become benefactors. At his death, about nine years afterwards, he received here an honourable interment.—Robert, the fourth abbot, procured, though with much difficulty, the bones of St. Wenefred, and had them enshrined here.—The property of the abbey at the dissolution was valued by Speed at about five hundred pounds *per annum.*—On the church being made parochial by Queen Elizabeth, it received the name of St. Crux, or the *Holy Cross*, in the abbey of Shrewsbury, which name it still retains.

Shrewsbury, are said to have been first, for a time, deposited in this church.— In the church-yard, but now almost obliterated, there is an inscription to the memory of William White, a quarter-master of horse, in the reign of William the Third :—

In Irish wars I fought for England's glory;
Let no man scoff at telling of this story.
I saw great Schomberg fall, likewise the brave St. Ruth,
And here I come to die, not there in my youth.
Through dangers great I have pass'd many a storm,
Die we all must, as sure as we are born.

St. Alkmund's church is remarkable for its handsome spire. It contains an east window of stained glass, the workmanship of Eginton of Birmingham. This was put up in the year 1795, and, as I was informed, cost about two hundred pounds. Its execution was infinitely superior to any thing that I had before seen in glass. A figure representing Faith is in the attitude of kneeling on a cross. Her arms are extended towards a crown, which appears from the clouds; and the countenance bears an interesting expression of mingled adoration and wisdom. " Be thou faithful unto death, and I will give thee a crown of life," is the motto. The lights appeared to me well disposed, and the drapery good. The colours are so managed as to prevent any glaring effect from the passage of light through a transparent medium; a fault too often observable in paintings on glass.

This church is said to have been founded by the heroine Elfleda, the daughter of King Alfred. The body of the structure is modern, but the tower and spire appear of considerable antiquity.

In the year 1621, about four yards of the top
of the spire were taken down, and rebuilt by a
man of the name of Archer, who came from St.
Alban's. His fool hardy feats are yet in the
mouths of the inhabitants. On Saturday, the
22d of February, he climbed up the outside of
the spire to the top, and brought down the
weather-cock, notwithstanding its size and
weight were such that he could with difficulty
hold it. On the 3d of March he climbed up
again, and put the weather-cock in its former
place, turning it about several times, standing
upright on the iron cross, and shaking both his
hands and legs. In the following week he
climbed up, taking with him a drum, and a
long bow and arrows. He stood upright on the
cross, beat the drum, and shot an arrow from
the bow On the 13th of March he again went
up, and turned the weather-cock round like a
wheel: he shook about his hands and legs, and
continued hallooing and shouting there for
more than two hours. In every one of these
daring exploits the man was in a state of intoxi-
cation.

If we may believe a manuscript written by the
Reverend Dr. Taylor, and deposited in the
Free School Library, the devil appeared in St.
Alkmund's church in the year 1533, as the
priest was at high mass. During a great
tempest and darkness he passed through the
church, mounted up the steeple, and, tearing
away the wires of the clock, left the print of
his claws on the fourth bell; and in his way out
took off one of the pinnacles! This is a singular
mode of accounting for a violent thunder-storm,
and it will appear the more remarkable when

the reader is informed, that the prince of darkness on this occasion appeared clad in the habit of a grey friar!

St. Mary's church bears the appearance of great antiquity. The south and west entrances are beneath arches of Norman architecture. This church was founded by King Edgar, and it formerly had a dean and seven prebendaries. Before the foundation of the abbey, it was esteemed the principal church *in* the town. It is a donative, and in the nomination of the mayor, and the head master of the Free School.

From the elevated situation of the building, and the great height of its spire, the latter has frequently suffered from high winds. In 1739, the weather-cock was blown on one side, when a person of the name of Cadman engaged to take it down, which he soon afterwards did, and then put it in its place again. This man was an adventurer on church steeples of a different description from the man I have just mentioned. He fixed a rope from the top of the spire to a tree in a field on the opposite side of the river, and to various other places; and for a few times slided from thence without injury : but on Candlemas day in the same year, after beating a drum, firing pistols, &c. he attempted to slide down the rope across the river, but it broke soon after he had trusted his weight upon it, and he was consequently dashed to pieces. — He was buried on the same day, the 2d of February 1739, at the foot of the steeple, and a plain slab was fixed to the wall over his grave, with this quaint inscription, now scarcely legible :—

Let this small monument record the name
Of Cadman, and to future times proclaim
How by'n attempt to fly from this high spire,
Across the Sabrine stream, he did acquire
His fatal end. 'Twas not for want of skill,
Or courage to perform the task, he fell,
No, no, a faulty cord, being drawn too tight,
Hurried his soul on high to take a flight,
Which bid the body, here beneath, good night.

St. Julian's church. The body of this building is of brick, and the tower of stone ; the
former is of modern erection. When or by
whom the church was founded is not known : it
was formerly stiled a Royal Chapel.

St. Chad's church has very lately been erected,
at some distance from the ancient building of
the same name. Of the latter, part of the
chancel it yet standing, and is kept in repair as
a chapel to the burying-ground. This building
(old St. Chad's) stood on the site of a palace of
the Princes of Powis, which was destroyed by
fire during the Saxon wars. The church was
probably erected not long afterwards. In the
year 1393, the first structure was burnt down
by the carelessness of one of the workmen who
was mending the leads. The fellow observing
the mischief he had done, and that the flames
had become too powerful for him to extinguish
them, ran home, put some money in his pocket,
and attempted to escape, but was drowned in
fording the river. On an inquisition before the
coroners of the town of Shrewsbury, the jury
found, " That John Plomer, working upon the
leads of St. Chad's church, and perceiving the
same in flames through his neglect, ran to his
own house in the High street, put five marks,
four shillings and sixpence in his pocket, and

fled; and when he came to the ford at the
Stone Gate, endeavouring to make his escape,
he was drowned in the river Severn."—In
order that this loss might be retrieved, King
Richard II. granted to the bailiffs and com-
monality of the town, for three years then
following, a quittance from their fee-farm, and
likewise from their arrears of taxes then lately
granted by the parliament 'to the king. The
fabric erected from this indulgence is that of
which the ruins are still left.

The *New St. Chad's* is built near the ground
called the Quarry. It is highly ornamented.
The principal entrance is through the west door,
into a circular vestibule that contains the stairs
leading to the galleries. The body of the
church is circular, and in its appearance rather
like a place of amusement, than a place of
sacred worship. The blue and white rails in
front of the galleries, remind us too much of
theatrical decoration. The supporting pillars
both above and below are out of all proportion.
The upper ones are in the Corinthian order, and
though the intention may have been to give
an appearance of lightness to the building, they
are inexcusably too long for their diameter: one
cannot always shut out an odd association of
ideas, and these columns, the moment I entered
the church, reminded me of a range of long
mould candles. The columns that support the
galleries are of a different order, and, I presume, by way of contrast, are as short and
thick as the others are long and small. In addition, their bases are made level with the tops
of the pews, giving an appearance of want of
security and firmness to the galleries. These

pillars correspond exceedingly ill with the other parts of the building. All circular churches must also rest under one very material inconvenience; they are all, it is true, well calculated for *seeing,* but the articulation of the minister, which ought to be the principal object attended to, is, in buildings of this nature, generally destroyed by the reverberation of sound.

THE QUARRY.

From this building I descended immediately to the Quarry, a most delightful walk, along an avenue of limes, which led me to the Severn, and then a considerable distance each way along its bank. The trees are large and old, and even in the hottest days of summer afford a sheltered and pleasant retreat. The ground is the property of the corporation; the part appropriated to pasturage is let to the inhabitants, and the profits are distributed among the burgesses.

THE HOUSE OF INDUSTRY

Is the large brick building which is seen from hence on the opposite lofty bank of the Severn. I crossed the river by the ferry with one of the directors, and was shewn every thing within it that I was desirous of seeing.

The erection of this elegant structure was begun in the year 1760, for the purpose of receiving part of the foundlings from the great hospital in London. These were to be put out

to nurse in the country; and when of proper
age were to be brought into the house, and
instructed in sewing, knitting, carding, spinning,
&c. till they were old enough to be put out
apprentices. The hospital in London discontinued sending children, and in consequence
the building became useless as to its original
purpose.— The expences of its erection amounted
to more than twelve thousand pounds.—It was
afterwards made a place of confinement for
prisoners of war.

An act of parliament was obtained by the
inhabitants of Shrewsbury to enable them to
form a house of industry for the poor of their
several parishes, and this building was purchased
and opened for the reception of its objects in
December 1783. The buildings, necessary
alterations, furniture, &c. cost seven thousand
pounds.

Such of the inhabitants of these parishes as
are rated and assessed, and possessed of property to the amount of thirty pounds *per annum*,
or are rated at fifteen pounds, are incorporated
as *guardians* of the poor. From them there are
chosen twelve *directors*, each of whom serves
his office for three years; and to the board of
directors the management of the whole business
of the house is entrusted. They meet, in a
room appropriated to their use, twice a week.

The number of men, women, and children in
the house when I was there, amounted to about
four hundred. Their employment consists principally in preparing their own clothing, which
they do from the raw material to its finished
state. The necessary machines and implements
are arranged in different apartments; and per-

sons versed in scribbling, carding, and spinning
wool, are employed to instruct the paupers.
Weavers were likewise engaged, and a shop
was allotted for their accommodation. Working rooms are also set apart for shoe makers,
taylors, &c. where the paupers who have been
brought up in these occupations are employed,
and where one division of the boys are taught
to work. The largest apartments are allotted
to the carding and spinning rooms. The girls
are by rotation employed and instructed, as
much as possible, in cooking, managing the
affairs of the kitchen and laundry, and in washing, scouring, and such other work as may best
qualify them for service.—The usual hours of
working are from six o'clock in the morning to
six in the evening, from the 1st of March to
the middle of October; and from seven in the
morning to such an hour at night as the directors
choose to appoint during the remainder of the
year. They are allowed half an hour at breakfast, and an hour at dinner. No work is done
on Sundays; Saturday afternoons, from four
o'clock; Good Friday; Christmas day, and the
two following days: Monday and Tuesday in
Easter and Whitsun weeks; and on Shrewsbury-
show day.

To encourage the exertions of the poor, the
directors make them an allowance of the sixth
part of their earnings, as a gratuity; and this
measure has been crowned with the happiest
success.

The punishments of the idle and refractory
are inflicted in various ways. For smaller
offences they are clothed in sack-cloth, have a
clog fastened to them, or are deprived of the

above gratuity. For more flagrant misconduct they are confined to a cell where they are kept apart from all the rest, and fed only with bread and water. If they are mutinous, and endeavour to excite a spirit of sedition among their companions, they undergo corporal punishment. The latter has, however, been seldom found necesary; but, whenever it is inflicted, it is done in the presence of all the persons of the house, and, as might naturally be expected, has never failed to produce a very striking and useful effect.

The persons who manage the concerns of the house, are a steward and matron, who are answerable for their conduct to the board of directors.

At a little distance from the house there are two ranges of building that run parallel with each other. The one contains apartments to which the poor are sent, on their admission, to be stripped and washed; and, if found to have any cutaneous, or other infectious disorder, they remain there till they are cured: there are, of course, separate wards for the women and the men. Adjoining to this, there is an apartment to which the dead are immediately conveyed, to remain till their interment. In the same range is another apartment, called the Fever Room. In the opposite range is the house infirmary, with separate wards for the men and women; where the sick and infirm are lodged under the care of nurses, and attended by the apothecary of the house. In surgical cases the patients are generally sent to the county infirmary.

The advantages of this institution became apparent in a very short time after it was commenced. Notwithstanding the heavy expences necessarily attending an establishment of this nature, the inhabitants of the different parishes found that even during the *first* year, the sum required for the maintenance of the poor was near two thousand pounds less than the sum raised for that purpose in the preceding year: and they now derive a most important pecuniary advantage from this establishment. The aged and infirm are comfortably provided for, and the young are trained in habits of industry and virtue. A complete stop has been put to the great frauds and abuses that prevailed in the parochial expenditure; and even those poor who have laboured under temporary distress or disability, have been more liberally assisted and relieved *in their own dwellings*, than had before been found practicable. Thus, while the poor have derived these important benefits from the institution, the inhabitants have also been greatly relieved in their parochial taxes. The amount of the reduction in the term of twelve years was very near twenty thousand pounds.

But a still greater advantage is derived to society in general, and to the immediate objects in particular, by the seeds of virtue and happiness that are carefully sown in the minds of the younger branches of this little community. Children thrown upon the parish from their birth are put out to nurse, where they remain till they are of age sufficient to be admitted into the house. The nurses are occasionally required to bring them before the directors, that these may observe that care is taken of them, and that the children may be identified, and those frauds

guarded against which have not unfrequently
been practised. When taken into the house,
the children are put under the care of the house
nurses, the boys in one nursery, and the girls in
another. As soon they are capable, they every
morning and afternoon attend the school room,
where proper instructors are provided. Here
they are taught to read. Soon after they are
five years old they are taken into the factory, or
spinning room, and begin to spin yarn at the
long wheel, under the tuition of a spinning mistress; and then they attend the evening school,
after the working hours are over. — They
amuse themselves after their meals, and at some
other times, in a large piece of ground behind
the house, and inclosed by a sunk fence. By
habit their daily employment soon ceases to
become irksome. They see their little companions around them, all engaged like themselves;
and from their cheerful countenances and general vivacity, it is apparent that they are contented and happy.

Mr. Howard once went through the house;
and not only the apartments, but the paupers
themselves, particularly the children, underwent
a very critical inspection. He obliged many of
the latter to take off their shoes and stockings,
and shew him the soles of their feet. He expressed much pleasure and satisfaction as to the
mode in which the affairs of the house were
managed.

The situation is one of the most healthy that
could have been chosen, and at the same time
uncommonly beautiful. The front of the building commands a fine view of the town and

suburbs of Shrewsbury. The trees of the Quarry form the appearance of a wood in front of the houses, above which the churches of St. Mary, St. Alkmund, and St. Chad, are particularly conspicuous. Beyond these objects is seen the round hill of the Wrekin, and others of the Shropshire mountains.—At a little distance from this station, and in an opposite direction, the Breiddin hills are visible, and an extensive tract of country towards Wales.*

Recrossing the Severn, from the House of Industry to the Quarry, by the ferry-boat, I was soon afterwards shewn a few ancient walls of the house of Austin, or *Augustine Friars.* This stood close to the river, at a short distance from the Quarry. It is supposed to have been founded by some one of the Stafford family.

The Grey, or *Franciscan Friary,* was situated a little to the south of the stone bridge. Its ruins now form part of a dwelling house. It is supposed to have been founded some time prior to 1353.

The Black, or *Dominican Friary,* stood near the river, between the castle and the stone bridge, at the bottom of St. Mary's Water Lane. Its foundation is ascribed to Maud, the wife of Jeffry, lord Genevil, about the 1265. The two sons of Edward the Fourth, who are believed to have been murdered in the Tower by order of Richard, duke of Gloucester, afterwards king

* For a very minute and interesting account of the House of Industry at Shrewsbury, with many valuable observations on the subject, see the work of Mr. Wood, published by Longman and Co. 8vo. price 3s. 6d.—1800.

Richard the Third, are said, with what truth I know not, to have been born in this friary.

PUBLIC BUILDINGS.

The Free School stands in a street leading to the castle. It is a large antique stone building, with a square tower, and contains, besides a good school-room, a dwelling house, chapel, and library. In the latter there is a valuable collection of books, and several natural and artificial curiosities. This school was founded in 1552 by king Edward VI.; and the original building was constructed of timber. The present edifice was erected about forty years afterwards.

The Infirmary stands near St. Mary's church-yard. It was opened in the year 1745. It is supported by voluntary benefactions, and its benefits extend not only to the town and county, but to all proper objects, without distinction of place. The average number of in-patients is about five hundred, and of out-patients seven hundred.

Millington's Hospital is situated on an eminence above Frankwell, a suburb beyond the Welsh bridge. It is a handsome brick building, and was founded in 1734, under the direction of the will of Mr. James Millington, formerly a draper of Shrewsbury. It maintains twelve decayed house-keepers (single persons), and a charity-school, for twenty boys and twenty girls, from the district of Frankwell, if such are to be found, and if not, from the nearest part of the parish of St. Chad. No dissenters of any denomination can have relief from this charity: it is

I i

confined to persons of orthodox principles of the church of England.

St. Chad's Alms-Houses, for decayed old men and women, were founded in 1409 by Bennet Tupton, a brewer of Shrewsbury. They are situated in old St. Chad's church-yard.

St. Mary's Alms-houses, in Ox-lane, near St. Mary church, were founded about the year 1460, by Digery Waters, a draper. He is said to have lived here among the poor people. They are confined principally to old persons, and those from St. Mary's parish only. The people have clothes, and a small salary allowed them.

The Charity School in Back-Lane was founded in 1724, under the will of Mr. Alderman Bowdler. This is intended for poor children of the parish of St. Julian, and if such are not found, of the parish of Holy Cross.

The Subscription Charity School, for instructing and clothing poor children, is situated by the road-side, leading to the abbey. It was begun in the year 1708. The boys are taught to read, and the girls to read, sew, and knit.

Besides these may be mentioned *the Town Hall,* in which the assizes are holden, and where the magistrates transact public business ; and *the Market House,* where the drapers hold their market for Welsh cloths and flannels.*

* *History of Shrewsbury.*—The town of Shrewsbury boasts a very remote origin, but the exact date of its foundation cannot at this day be ascertained. It is supposed to have been first built from the ruin of the Roman *Uriconium,* or the *Vreken Ceaster* of the Saxons, whose site has been discovered at Wroxeter, a village on the bank of the Severn, about four miles distant. The Welsh name for Shrewsbury

was Pen Gwern, *The Head of the Alder Groves;* and the Saxons called it Scrobbes Byrig, on account of the eminence on which it was situated being covered with wood. I have before related that it was once the capital of Powisland, and a seat of the Welsh princes.

In the reign of William the Conqueror, Shrewsbury was granted to Roger de Montgomery, who shortly afterwards founded the castle and abbey. At this time it was called a city, and had two hundred and fifty-two citizens. Whenever the king passed through the place, twelve of the highest order of these were compelled, whether he was sleeping or waking, to attend on his person; and as many, with horses and arms, were also to attend him whenever he took the recreation of hunting in the neighbourhood. These services were imposed as a punishment; for, not many years before the conquest, Edric Streon, duke of Mercia, having, near this place, lain in wait for, and murdered prince Afhelm, as he was returning from the chace.

The burgesses of Shrewsbury had many privileges even before the conquest; and Henry I. on the forfeiture of Robert de Belesme, son to Montgomery, seized the town into his own hands, and granted the burgesses their first charter. By various grants and charters in this and subsequent reigns, the burgesses, amongst others, were allowed the following privileges :—To hold all pleas except those of the crown :— to receive toll and custom from all the Welsh that traded in the town.—They were exempted from pontage, toll, and all exactions of burgesses throughout the kingdom, except London.—Their goods could not be seized for any forfeiture made by their servants.—They could in no case be summoned to appear before any others than burgesses, their peers.—No sheriff, or other officer, could distrain within the liberties of the town; and no burgess could be arrested, nor have his goods seized. In the reign of Elizabeth the town was incorporated; and the charter of the incorporation was afterwards confirmed by Charles I. and James II. The corporation consists of a mayor, twenty-four aldermen, forty-eight assistants, and inferior officers. The town returns two members to parliament.

Several parliaments have been holden in Shrewsbury. The first that was summoned formally by writ, met in September 1283. By this, David, the brother of Llewelyn, prince of Wales, was tried for high treason, and condemned : he was the first person who suffered the death of a traitor, in the form of the sentence now in use. Another parliament

I i 2

was holden here in 1397, which, on account of the great number of people that were assembled in it, was called the Great Parliament. By a strange concession of this parliament, Richard II. obtained an unexampled stretch of power, that the whole government of a nation should devolve on the king, twelve peers, and six commoners. A bull from the pope was thought necessary to confirm so irregular a proceeding.

Of the military transactions relative to this place, the most important was the battle fought here in July 1403, best known by the name of *The Battle of Shrewsbury*, between king Henry IV., and the soldiers commanded by Henry Percy, surnamed Hotspur. It had been the design of the insurgents from the north, to make themselves masters of this town and castle, and then to strengthen their forces by a junction with Owen Glyndwr and his countrymen. The activity of Henry prevented this junction, and saved his crown. Coming up with Percy's army at this town, the high spirit of that hero would not suffer him to wait the arrival of Glyndwr, who was encamped near Oswestry, but he hazarded a contest even with his inferior force. The fight commenced early in the morning, and after a violent struggle of three hours, Percy's party was completely routed, and himself, and about five thousand of his men, were slain. The earls of Worcester and Douglas were taken prisoners, the former of whom was soon afterwards beheaded at Shrewsbury. The scene of this contention was a place since called Battlefield, in the parish of Albrighton, about three miles distant.

One of the ordinances made by Alcock, bishop of Worcester, and Anthony, earl Rivers, in April 1478, for the government of Shrewsbury, was as follows:

" First that the bayliffs for the time beinge iustly, truly, endifferently shall execute their offices, according to their liberties and laudable customes, without any corruption favor or parcialitie. And that they see yf any person come into the towne there abydinge two days suspiciously, without any lawfull errand or occupacion, that then he the third daye be putt in prison there to remayne till he have founde surety of his good abearing; or els to auoyde the towne." Any person so committed by the warden, and four men, was not to be declared out of ward by the bailiffs without consent of the same warden and four men. These injunctions were to be obeyed, under the penalty of a hundred pounds, half to be paid to the king, and the remainder to the town.

In the year 1485, Henry earl of Richmond, afterwards

king Henry VII., arrived at Milford Haven, from Bretagne, and he had so far paved the way for his reception in this country, as to meet with little opposition till he came to Shrewsbury. Here, however, the gates were shut against him. He sent messengers to demand that the gates be opened to admit the rightful sovereign of England. The head bailiff, whose name was Mytton, appeared at the gate, and answered, " I acknowledge no sovereign but king Richard III., whose servants I and my townsmen are. *I solemnly swear, that before any other enter this town, he shall first make his way over my body.* By this expression he meant that he would suffer himself to be slain, rather than admit any but his acknowledged monarch. The messengers returned to Henry, and they were again sent on the following morning, to request that the earl of Richmond might be suffered to pass. They pledged themselves for the earl, that no injury whatever should be done to the town, or its inhabitants, and that Mytton himself should also be saved from the guilt of perjury. The bailiff having in some measure changed his mind since his last interview with the messengers, did not object to these lenient terms. Henry entered the town *by stepping over the body of Mytton, who laid down for the purpose in the gateway.*—From hence he passed on to Bosworth Field, where the decisive battle was fought in which Richard III. was slain.

It is affirmed of this entry of the army of Henry VII., that a malady unknown before was introduced into England, called the *sweating sickness.* It raged for upwards of sixty years in the kingdom, carrying off many thousand people, and at last ended in this town, in the year 1551. A short time before this period it was so violent here, as to take off no fewer than nine hundred and ninety persons in the course of a few days. The disease began with a violent perspiration, which continued till either the death or recovery of the patient. It seldom lasted more than twenty-four hours, so that those who happened to be taken ill in the day time, were put to bed with their clothes on to wait the event; and those who were seized in the night were ordered to remain in bed, but on no account to sleep. This singular and dreadful malady seems to have originated among the levies that Henry had raised on the continent, which had been raked out of hospitals and gaols, buried in filth, and, without any attention to their health or comfort, immediately crowded on board the transports.

In the civil wars, Shrewsbury was garrisoned for the king, and sir Michael Earnly was made governor. General Mytton made two unsuccessful attempts upon it, but in February 1644 the place was surrendered to him. Crowe, the lieutenant, was afterwards hanged for his treachery, or cowardice. The governor, and several persons of rank, were made prisoners; and the town was plundered.— Mytton, soon after the siege, was made governor, and he received the thanks of the House of Commons for his good services.

In a chronological list of remarkable events at Shrewsbury, are recorded the following singular occurrences :

1282. This year the sheriffs of Salop and Stafford were compelled to provide two hundred wood cutters, to cut down timber and other obstructions, in order to make way for the king's army to enter into Wales.

1427. A bye law was made against swine wandering about the town: the penalty was cutting off an ear for each of the two first offences, and forfeiture for the third.

1519. The brewers were ordered by the corporation not to use that *wicked and pernicious weed*, hops, in their brewings, under the penalty of 6s. 8d.

1547. This year Adam Mytton and Roger Pope, the bailiffs, ordered the picture of our lady to be taken out of St. Mary's church; and the pictures of St. Mary Magdalen, and St. Chad, out of St. Chad's church, and burned.

1552. The magistrates of Shrewsbury were restrained by act of parliament from licensing any more than three persons to sell wine within the town.

1585. On the 15th of May, lord Robert Devereux, earl of Essex, came through the town, before whom the free-school scholars made several orations, as he passed through the castle gates ; they standing in battle array, with bows and arrows in their hands.

1618. It was in this year ordered by the corporation, that two persons should be constantly stationed in each street to search for vagrants.

CHURCHYARD, THE POET.

As I have so frequently had occasion to quote the writings of Churchyard, it is but proper that he should have a place at the end of this chapter. Very little is, however, known of his life. He was born at Shrewsbury, a descendant, as he says himself, " of right good race," and flourished in the reigns of Henry VIII., Edward VI, Mary, and Elizabeth. His verses are neither elegant nor smooth, but they are generally supposed to abound in faithful description. His Worthiness of Wales was his principal work, but he also wrote in verse, " A Description and Discourse of Paper, and the Benefit it brings, with the setting forth of a Paper Mill near Dartford."—He died about the year 1570; and his epitaph, written by himself, is preserved in Camden's Remains:

Come Alecto, and lend me thy torch,
To find a Churchyard in a church porch;
Poverty and poetry his tomb do enclose,
Wherefore good neighbours be merry in prose.

CHAP. XLII.

THE MANNERS AND CUSTOMS OF THE WELSH.

Impositions sometimes practised on English Travellers.—Iras-cibility. — The Welsh Cottages.—Women. — Curiosity.—Superstitions.—Account of a supposed Kind of aërial Beings called Knockers.—Witches.—Coelcerth.— Yr Eryr. Offering of Enemies.—Wells of Saints.—Plygain.—Leeks on St. David's Day. — Terming.—Mode of Courtship called Bundling.—Customs at Weddings.— Funerals.—Offer-ings at Funerals.—Reason for not interring on the North Sides of Churches.—Planting the Graves.

Wɪᴛʜ respect to the habits of life and man-ners of the Welsh people, it is to be observed, that in those mountainous and secluded parts of Wales, as the interior of Caernarvonshire, Merionethshire, and Denbighshire, that are yet scarcely known to the English tourist, they differ very essentially from what will be observed near any frequented road. The people seem there to have an innocence and simplicity of character, unknown in the populous parts of our own country. Among these it is that we are to search for those original traits, and that native hospi-tality, so much the boast of the Welsh writers. Wherever the English have had uninterrupted

communication, the money of which they have
been so lavish has afforded an irresistible temptation for the lower classes of the inhabitants to
practise impositions: in such situations the people differ little from the like class amongst us.
On all the great roads, they seem to pride themselves in being sufficiently expert to over-reach-
their Saxon neighbours in any of their little
bargains. A Welsh gentleman of undoubted
veracity informed me, (and in various instances
I have myself experienced its truth,) that it is
a common practice amongst his countrymen, to
ask for any article they have to offer for sale
nearly double the sum they will take: those
persons who are acquainted with these prac-
tices never give them the full price for what
they purchase. I have good authority for as-
serting that at some of the inferior inns, if an
Englishman sits down at table with Welshmen,
the charge for his eating will be at least one
third more than that of each of the rest of the
company. This is a provoking imposition.

A rustic bashfulness and reserve seem to be
general features in the character of the Welsh
people, and strangers, unaccustomed to their
manners, have often mistaken these for indications of sullenness.—It is usual to say of them
that they are very irascible. This may be the
case, but from what I have myself seen, I am
inclined to think, that the natural rapidity of
their expression in a language not understood,
has often been construed into passion, without
any other more certain grounds. Persons who
form their ideas from the opinions of others,
without being at the trouble of making observations for themselves, are often deceived and

misled. Such, 1 am confident, has been the case à thousand times in the judgments formed on the present subject.

The lowest classes bear indications of extreme poverty, yet they seem to enjoy good health. Their dwellings are cottages, or rather huts, built of stones, whose interstices are closed with peat or mud. They are in general so dark, that, on first entering, the glare of light down the chimney alone takes the attention. The following is a good picture by Mr. Hutton of one of the better kind of cottages made uncommonly neat for the celebration of a wedding dinner:

Arriving, I crept through a hole in the door,
Some stones were laid down, and some not, on the floor,
The whole was one dark room, with three windows so small,
That the light down the chimney quite outstript them all,
But this great relief came to soften their cares,
Neither sober or drunk could they tumble down stairs.
Two beds grac'd the mansion, which made it appear
That cleanliness, prudence, and order reigned there.
The tables and cupboards, which, opened to view,
Shew'd the hand of industry had polished their hue.
The shelves and their crockery, both china and delph,
Were clean, and were orderly rang'd on the shelf.
Dad, mam, and nine children, which fortune bestow'd,
In harmony liv'd in this darksome abode;
Nor can we consent to call those people poor,
Where prudence steps in, and bars want from the door.

The usual food of the labouring Welsh is bread, cheese, and milk; and sometimes what they call *flummery*, a composition of oatmeal and milk. Animal food and ale are by no means among their usual fare.

The women of the mountainous parts of the country are generally of a middle size, though more frequently below that than above it.

Their features are often very pretty, but in
point of figure they are in general uninteresting,
and their long, and thickly matted hair, crowned with hats similar to those worn by the men,
affords the unpleasant idea of a due want of
cleanliness. They wear long blue cloaks that
descend almost to their feet. These they are
seldom to be seen without, even in the hottest
weather; owing to the frequency of showers in
a country surrounded with mountains. On their
legs they have blue stockings without any feet
to them : they keep them down by means of a
loop fastened round one of the toes. In the
more unfrequented parts the women seldom wear
any shoes, except on a Sunday, or the market-
day, and even on those days they often carry
them in their hands as they go along the roads.
I have sometimes seen six or eight of them,
after their journies from the adjacent villages,
seated on the bank of a rivulet, in the act of
washing their feet previously to their entering
the towns. During these journies they often
employ their time in knitting, and a heavy
shower of rain will not sometimes compel them
to give up their work. Their employment within doors, besides their family duties, is chiefly
in spinning wool.

What has been repeatedly asserted of the
Welsh people, that they are naturally inqui-
sititive and curious respecting strangers is certainly true, but it is a circumstance by no means
peculiar to this country. In all wild and unfrequented parts of the world it is the same,
and it is in such parts of Wales that this dis-

position is chiefly observable. It is easily accounted for when we consider their manners of life, and general ignorance. Surprize on the appearance of strangers, where in their limited ideas there could seem no inducement to repay the trouble or expence of a journey, would naturally excite their wonder, and this as naturally leads to the questions, " Where do you come from?"—" Why do you come here?"— and, " Where do you go to from hence?"— Unsatisfied with my answers, that I was an Englishman come to visit the mountains and waterfalls, I have often and often been asked, with the utmost simplicity, " Are there then no mountains nor rivers in England?" In all accounts of travels through unfrequented countries we find this disposition to curiosity very common, and a slight acquaintance with the nature of the human mind is sufficient to allay any surprize that may be excited in discovering that it is prevalent in Wales.

They are much inclined to superstition, but in all countries we find that there are multitudes of weak and foolish people. In England, most of the peasantry swallow with credulous avidity any ridiculous stories of ghosts, hobgoblins, and fairies. There is, however, in the Welsh, certainly a greater inclination to credulity than what an Englishman can discover among our own people. There are few indeed of the mountaineers of Wales, who have not by heart a string of legendary stories of those disembodied beings.—The cavern in Llanymynech hill, not far from Oswestry, has been long noted as the residence of a clan of fairies, of whom the neighbouring villagers relate many surprizing and mischievous pranks. Whilst they have stopped to listen at the mouth of the cave, the people state that they have sometimes even heard the little elves in conversation, but this was always in such low whispers, that (with the reverberation along the sides and roof of the cavern) the words were rendered indistinguishable. The stream that runs across a distant part of this cavern, is celebrated as the place where the fairy washerwomen and labourers have been heard frequently at work.

Considerably allied to the fairies is another species of supposed aërial beings, called by the Welsh *knockers*. These the Welsh miners say, are heard underground, in or near mines, and by their noises generally point out to the workmen a rich vein of ore. The following are extracts from two letters on this extraordinary subject, written in the year 1754 by Mr. Lewis Morris*, a man eminent for his learning and, in many respects, his good sense.

" People who know very little of arts or sciences, or the powers of nature, (which, in other words, are the powers of the author of nature,) will laugh at us Cardiganshire miners, who maintain the existence of *knockers* in mines, a kind of good-natured impalpable people, not to be seen, but heard, and who seem to us to work in the mines; that is to say they are the types, or forerunners of working in mines, as dreams are of some accidents which

---

* To his brother, who at that time resided at Holyhead.

happen to us. The barometer falls before rain
or storms. If we did not know the construction
of it, we should call it a kind of dream, that
foretells rain ; but we know it is natural, and
produced by natural means, comprehended by us.
Now how are we sure, or any body sure, but
that our dreams are produced by the same natural
means ? There is some faint resemblance of this
in the sense of hearing ; the bird is killed before
we hear the report of the gun. However this is,
I must speak well of the *knockers*, for they have
actually stood my very good friends, whether they
are aërial beings, called spirits, or whether they
are a people made of matter, not to be felt by
our gross bodies, as air and fire, and the like.

" Before the discovery of *Esgair y Mwyn*
mine, these little people, as we call them here,
worked hard there day and night ; and there
are abundance of honest, sober people, who have
heard them, and some persons who have no
notion of them or of mines either ; but after
the discovery of the great ore they were heard
no more.

" When I began to work at *Llwyn Llwyd,*
they worked so fresh there for a considerable
time, that they frightened some young workmen out of the work. This was when we
were driving levels, and before he had got
any ore ; but when we came to the ore,
they then gave over, and I heard no more
talk of them.

" Our old miners are no more concerned at
hearing them *blasting,* boring holes, landing
deads, &c. than if they were some of their own
people ; and a single miner will stay in the
work, in the dead of the night, without any

man near him, and never think of any fear, or of any harm they will do him. The miners have a notion that the *knockers* are of their own tribe and profession, and are a harmless people who mean well. Three or four miners together shall hear them sometimes, but if the miners stop to take notice of them, the knockers will also stop; but, let the miners go on at their own work, suppose it is *boring*, the *knockers* will at the same time go on as brisk as can be in landing, *blasting*, or beating down the *loose*; and they are always heard a little distance from them before they come to the ore.

" These are odd assertions, but they are certainly facts, though we cannot, and do not pretend to account for them.—We have now very good ore at *Llwyn Llwyd*, where the *knockers* were heard to work, but have now yielded up the place, and are no more heard. —Let who will laugh, we have the greatest reason to rejoice, and thank the *knockers*, or rather God, who sends us these notices."

The second letter is as follows :

" I have no time to answer your objection against *knockers;* I have a large treatise collected on that head, and what Mr. Derham says is nothing to the purpose. If sounds of voices, whispers, blasts, working or pumping, can be carried on a mile underground, they should always be heard in the same place, and under the same advantages, and not once in a month, a year, or two years. Just before the discovery of ore last week, three men together, in our work of *Llwyn Llwyd*, were ear-witnesses of *knockers* pumping, driving a wheelbarrow, &c.; but there is no pump in the work,

nor any mine within less than a mile of it,
in which there are pumps constantly going.
If they were these pumps that they heard,
why where they never heard but that once in
the space of a year? And why are they not
now heard? But the pumps make so little
noise, that they cannot be heard in the other
end of *Esgair y Mwyn* mine when they are at
work.

" We have a dumb and deaf taylor in this
neighbourhood, who has a particular language
of his own, by signs; and by practice I can
understand him, and make him understand me
pretty well; and I am sure I could make him
learn to write, and be understood by letters
very soon, for he can distinguish men already
by the letters of their names. Now letters
are marks to convey ideas, just after the same
manner as the motions of fingers, hands, eyes,
&c. If this man had really seen ore in the
bottom of a sink of water in a mine, and
wanted to tell me how to come at it, he would
take two sticks like a pump, and would make
the motions of a pumper at the very sink
where he knew the ore was; and would make
the motions of driving a wheel-barrow. And
what I should infer from thence would be, that
I ought to take out the water and sink, or
drive in the place, and wheel the stuff out.
By parity of reasoning, the language of the
knockers, by imitating the sound of pumping,
wheeling, &c. signifies that we should take out
the water, and drive there. This is the opinion
of all old miners, who pretend to understand
the language of the *knockers*. Our agent and

manager, upon the strength of this notice, goes on and expects great things. You, and every body that is not convinced of the being of *knockers*, will laugh at these things, for they sound like dreams; so does every dark science. Can you make any illiterate man believe that it is possible to know the distance of two places by looking at them? Human knowledge is but of small extent, its bounds are within our view, we see nothing beyond these; the great universal creation contains powers, &c. that we cannot so much as guess at. May there not exist beings, and vast powers, infinitely smaller than the particles of air, to whom air is as hard a body as a diamond is to us? Why not? There is neither great nor small, but by comparison. Our *knockers* are some of these powers, the guardians of mines.

" You remember the story in Selden's Table-Talk, of Sir Robert Cotton and others disputing about Moses's shoe. Lady Cotton came in, and asked, " Gentlemen, are you sure it *is* a shoe?" So the first thing-is to convince mankind that there is a set of creatures, a degree or so finer than we are, to whom we have given the name of *knockers*, from the sounds we hear in our mines. This is to be done by a collection of their actions well attested: and that is what I have begun to do, and then let every one judge for himself."

These letters are curious, though the reasoning is far from conclusive. When I was in the country, I was very desirous of seeing a copy of the remarks on these supposed aërial sprites, that Mr. Morris refers to in the second letter,

K k

but was not able to meet with such.—In endeavouring to account for the noises, for we
must believe that such noises have taken place,
it has been remarked that they might perhaps
have proceeded from the echo of the miners at
work, or from the dropping of water in some
hollow places in or near the mine. These conjectures are, however, very insufficient, if we are
to credit Mr. Morris's assertion that whilst the
miners are engaged in one kind of work, the
knockers, as they are called, are carrying on
another: while for instance, as he says, the
miners are *boring,* the *knockers* are *blasting,*
the former conjecture must fall to the ground;
and the droppings of water could in no case
produce an effect that might be mistaken for
blasting. I am acquainted with the subject
only from report, but I can assure my readers
that I found few people in Wales that did not
give full credence to it. The elucidation of
these extraordinary occurrences must be left to
those persons who have better opportunities of
inquiring into them than I have. I may be
permitted to express a hope that the subject
will not be neglected, and that those who reside in any neighbourhood where the noises are
heard, will carefully investigate their cause, and,
if possible, give to the world a more accurate
account of them than the present.

The lower class of the Welsh yet continue
to believe in the existence of witches. Many
old women, therefore, only because they are
old, and perhaps deformed, have to bear the
odium of preventing the cows from yielding

milk, and butter from forming in the churn. They are also believed to possess the power of inflicting disorders both on men and cattle, and that they seldom neglect to do it when they have been offended. This will well account for the notion of witches having been strenuously maintained some centuries ago, even by the most enlightened persons of the age. Old women, on whom the generally odious epithet of witch has been once fixed by the popular voice, have found it their interest, and in Wales to this day find it their interest, to deny nothing that is alledged of them. They become thus held in superstitious fear by the people, and in many instances obtain an easy livelihood from the supposed extent of their power. Where-ever they ask alms, it would be (say the common people) the death of a cow or horse, or perhaps even of one of the family, to refuse them; and the neighbouring peasantry, much as they hold them in detestation, believe it their own interest to keep them always in good humour. The old women thus live, in some measure, in affluence, with little other trouble than feeding and training up three or four cats, and attending minutely to the concerns of their neighbours.

On the eve of All Saints, the Welsh people, as soon as it is dark, kindle great fires near their houses, which they call *coelcerth*, or bonfires. This custom has been supposed, though probably without any foundation, to have originated with the druids, and to have been intended by them as an offering of thanksgiving for the fruits of the harvest. Sometimes fifty or a hun-

K k 2

dred of these fires may be seen at once, and round each the people dance, hand in hand, at the same time singing and shouting in the most riotous and frantic manner imaginable. In many places a custom is retained of each person throwing a few nuts into the flame, by which they pretend to foretell the good or ill fortune that will attend them during the ensuing year. If, by the expansion of air within them, the nuts burst, they immediately conclude that they are doomed to die within twelve months. —On the day after All Saints the poor children go about the towns and villages to beg bread and cheese.

On the eve of St. John the Baptist, they place little bundles of the plant called St. John's wort over their doors, or windows. These they believe will purify their houses, and drive away all fiends and evil spirits. The druids had a custom similar to this, in which they used sprigs of vervain.

The young people have many pretended modes of declaring their future lovers. Most of these are, however, common to the peasantry of our own country, which renders it needless to repeat them here.

I have been informed that a disorder somewhat resembling St. Anthony's fire, which the Welsh people call *Yr Eryr*, the eagle, is supposed to be at any time cured by the following kind of charm. A person, whose grandfather, or great grandfather, has eaten the flesh of an eagle, is to spit on the part affected, and rub it for a little while with his fingers. This is

esteemed an infallible remedy. A maid-servant
of a gentleman of my acquaintance who resides
in Caernarvonshire, declared, in my hearing,
that she had been cured of this complaint by an
old man whose grandfather had eaten of an
eagle. She said that he at the same time used
some words, to aid the charm, which she could
not comprehend.

A strange custom prevails in some obscure
parts of North Wales, which, however, the
clergy have now almost abolished. This is
termed the " offering of an enemy." When a
person supposes himself highly injured by any
one, he repairs to some church dedicated to a
celebrated saint, or one who is believed to have
great power over the affairs of men ; here kneeling on his bare knees before the altar, and
offering a piece of money to the saint, he utters
the most virulent and dreadful imprecations,
calling down curses and misfortunes on the
offender and his family even for generations to
come. Sometimes the offended persons repair
for the same purpose to some sacred well, dedicated to a saint. Mr. Pennant was threatened
by a man, who fancied he had been injured by
him, " with the vengeance of St. Elian, and a
journey to his well, to curse him with effect.*"
Some of these wells are held in great repute
for the cure of diseases ; and the saints are also
occasionally applied to for the recovery of stolen
goods.—In the parish of Abergeley, in Caernarvonshire, there was formerly a well dedicated
to St. George, who was the Welsh tutelary

* Tour in Wales, ii. 337.

Saint of horses. All these animals that were distempered were brought to the well, sprinkled with water, and received this blessing : *Rhad Duw a Saint Siors arnat,* " the blessing of God and St. George be on thee." It was the custom for those who kept a great number of horses, at certain times to make an offering of one of them to the saint, in order to secure his blessing on all the rest.—If a well of any saint was near the church, the water for baptism was always fetched from thence; and, after the ceremony, the old women would frequently wash their eyes in the water of the font.

Some years ago it was a custom in the churches of North Wales, whenever the name of the Devil occurred, for every one of the congregation to spit upon the floor. This was done to shew their contempt of the evil spirit. Whenever the name of Judas was mentioned, they expressed their abhorrence of him by striking their breasts.

On the morning of Christmas-day, about three o'clock, the inhabitants used formerly to assemble in the churches ; and, after the prayers and sermon were concluded, they continued their singing psalms and hymns with great devotion till daylight. Those who through age or infirmity were disabled from attending the church, invariably read the prayers in their own houses, and sang the appropriate hymns. This act of devotion was called *plygain,* " the crowing of the cock.*" It has been a general belief among the superstitious, that instantly

* Pennant, ii. 340.

At his warning,
Whether in sea, or fire, in earth, or air,
Th' extravagant and erring spirit hies
To his confine.

But, during this holy season, the cock was supposed to exert his power throughout the night :

Some say, that ever 'gainst that season comes
Wherein our Saviour's birth is celebrated,
The bird of dawning singeth all night long :
And then, they say, no spirit walks abroad ;
The nights are wholesome ; then no planets strike ;
No fairy takes ; no witch hath power to charm :
So hallow'd and so gracious is the time.

The Welsh yet retain the custom of wearing leeks in their hats on St. David's day. On the first of March 640, the Welsh forces under command of King Cadwallo obtained a signal victory over the Saxons. The battle happened near a large piece of ground in which this vegetable was cultivated, and the soldiers put leeks into their hats in order to distinguish themselves. Since this period the leek has been retained as a badge of honour. " The Welshmen (says Fluelin to Henry V.) did goot service in a garden where leeks did grow, wearing leeks in their Monmouth caps; which, your majesty knows, to this hour is an honourable padge of the service.*"

The middle and lower classes of the people were formerly much addicted to *terming*, that is, brewing a barrel of ale at some favourite ale-house, and staying there till it was all drunk

* Shakspere's Henry V., act. iv.

out. They never went to bed, though the *term* should even last a whole week. They slept in their chairs, or on the floor, as it happened, and the moment they awoke they renewed their jollity. At length when the barrel was exhausted, they reeled away home. The hero of this Bacchanalian rout always carried off the spiggot in triumph.

The peasantry of part of Caernarvonshire, Anglesea, and Merionethshire, adopt a mode of *courtship*, which till within the last few years was scarcely even heard of in England. It is the same that is common in many parts of America, and termed by the inhabitants of that continent *bundling*. The lover steals, under the shadow of the night, to the bed of his fair one, into which (retaining an essential part of his dress) he is admitted without any shyness or reserve. Saturday or Sunday nights are the principal times when this courtship takes place, and on these nights the men sometimes walk from a distance of ten miles or more to visit their favourite damsels.—This strange custom seems to have originated in the scarcity of fuel, and in the consequent unpleasantness of sitting together, in the colder parts of the year, without a fire. Much has been said of the innocence with which these meetings are conducted. This may be the case in some instances, but it is a very common thing for the consequence of the intercourse to make its appearance in the world within two or three months after the marriage ceremony has taken place. The subject excites no particular attention among the neighbours, provided the marriage be made good before the living witness is brought to light.—Since this custom is entirely confined to the labouring classes of the community, it is not so pregnant with danger as on a first supposition it might seem. Both parties are so poor, that they are necessarily constrained to render their issue legitimate, in order to secure their reputation, and with it a mode of obtaining a livelihood.

Their *weddings* are usually attended by all the neighbours, sometimes to the number of thirty or upwards. After the ceremony, the day is dedicated to festivity, and is chiefly spent in drinking and singing. At a wedding in the little village of Llanberis, I observed in the church as many as twenty or five-and-twenty attendants. A collection is made on their return to the house to defray the expences of the occasion, to which of course every one contributes. A good idea of the rest of the business may be collected from a pleasant account of a wedding-feast in Cwm y Clo, near Llanberis:

A fire of square peat, and sufficiently dried,
Was spread on the hearth, and at least four feet wide;
Over which took their station six kettles or more,
Which promised a feast, when they opened their store;
And round this flat furnace, to keep them quite hot,
Were plac'd twelve more vessels, which held—God know's
  what.
Four cooks, in short bed-gowns, attend by desire,
Like the witches in Macbeth, to stir up the fire.

Forty trenchers, with dull knives, and forks made no
  brighter,
Were spread on some napkins, which once had been whiter,
Supported by planks, forty feet long, or more,
Completely were rais'd on the grass out of door.
But here we are bound the word *table* to offer,
That our verses' great dignity never may suffer.

The table prepar'd, and the cooking completed,
'Twas perfectly needful the guests should be seated.
Loose boards were erected on stones with great art;
But proving too hard for a certain broad part,
A number of cushions were instantly made,
But not with a needle—no; formed with a spade.
The finest of ling, root and branch, from the common,
Par'd off, prov'd a cushion for man and for woman.

Now folks, male and female, came in by whole dozens,
Of neighbours, acquaintance, of friends, and of cousins.
It excited surprise, from a region of rocks,
That orderly people should issue by flocks.
Black stockings, blue cloaks, and men's hats, all admire,
Which appear'd to be every female's attire.

While many a longing eye glanc'd at the board,
The word *dinner* sounded—acceptable word!
Five butts of boil'd beef of a gigantic size,
On the board took their station, with joy and surprise;
On these close attended, as guards rang'd for pleasure,
As many mash'd pease as would heap a strike measure;
With cabbage a pyramid, much like a steeple:
All these were surrounded with—thirty-eight people.

The moment arriving when dinner was o'er,
The places were taken by thirty-eight more;—
And then a third set, nearly equal to these,
Sat down to the cabbage, the beef, and the peas;
Besides about fifty remaining behind,
Who stuck to the tankard, for none of them din'd.

And now an old dish open'd wide at each sinner,
As if it would say—" Pay a shilling for dinner."

Eight strike of brown malt, which Caernarvon had seen,
And cost the bride's father two pounds and fourteen,
Was brew'd into drink, that would make one man mad,
But given a second would make his heart glad.
Each quart brought back sixpence, and that pretty soon,
His *cot* was a public house that afternoon.

The glass going round—no—the mug I would say,
The lads and the lasses began to look gay,
To smile on each other, to toy and to joke;
I *was* an observer, but not a word spoke.

The *bard*, in a rapture, his harp handled soon,
And twang'd with his fingers, to try if in tune';
The people selected and pairing began,
Each lass was indulged with the choice of her man ;
Than *Amazons* more than like fairies were seen,
Full thirty gay couple to dance on the green.
Joy held his firm station till morning was come ;
When each swain had the pleasure to lead his nymph home.

In South Wales, previous to the weddings of the peasantry, a herald with a crook or wand, adorned with ribands, sometimes makes the circuit of the neighbourhood, and proclaims his *bidding*, or invitation, in a prescribed form ; but the knight-errant cavalcade on horseback, —the carrying off the bride,—the rescue,—the wordy war in rhyme between the parties, which once formed a singular spectacle of mock contest at the celebration of nuptials, is now almost, if not altogether laid aside, throughout every part of the principality*.

The *funerals* are attended by greater crowds of people than even their weddings. In the funeral that I attended at Llanberis, which has been described in a preceding chapter, there were at least a hundred attendants.—A custom prevails in this country of each individual of the congregation making some *offering* in money on these occasions, which, if done in the church, is paid as a mark of respect to the clergyman. This custom, which is at present confined to North Wales, has doubtless been retained from the Romish religion, where the money was intended as a recompence to the priests for their trouble in singing mass for the

* Cam. Reg. vol. ii.

soul of the deceased. In some cases, where the clergyman is not respected by his parishioners the *offerings* are made on the coffin at the door of the house where the deceased resided, and are distributed amongst the poor relatives. When, however, the offerings are made in the church, (and the other mode very rarely occurs), the whole of the morning or evening prayers for the day, and the usual part of the burial service in the church, are first read : the next of kin to the deceased then comes forward to the altar table, and if it is a poor person, puts down sixpence or a shilling, but if he be sufficiently opulent, half a crown or a crown, and sometimes even so much as a guinea. This example is followed by the other relatives, and afterwards by the rest of the congregation whose situation in life will afford, it, who advance in turns, and offer. When the offering of silver is ended, a short pause ensues, after which, those who cannot spare any larger sum, come forward, and put down each a penny (a half-penny not being admitted). Collections on these occasions have been known to amount to ten or fifteen pounds, but where the relatives are indigent, they do not often exceed three or four shillings. In cases where families are left in distress, this money is usually given by the clergyman to them. When the collection is entirely finished, the body is taken to the grave, the remainder of the burial-service is read, and the awful ceremony is there closed.—The offerings at Llanbublic, the parish church of Caernarvon, sometimes amount to fifty or sixty pounds a year.

It is usual in several parts of North Wales, for the nearest female relation to the deceased, be she widow, mother, sister, or daughter, to pay some poor person, of the same sex, and nearly of the same age with the deceased, for procuring slips of yew, box, and other evergreens, to strew over and ornament the grave for some weeks after interment; and in some instances for weeding and adorning it, on the eves of Easter, Whitsuntide, and the other great festivals, for a year or two afterwards. This gift is called *Diodlys*, and it is made on a plate at the door of the house, where at the same time the body is standing on a bier. It had its name from the custom, which is now discontinued, of the female relative giving to the person a piece of cheese with the money stuck in it, some white bread, and afterwards a cup of ale.—When this previous ceremony is over, the clergyman, or, in his absence, the parish clerk, repeats the Lord's prayer; after which they proceed with the body to the church. Four of the next of kin take the bier upon their shoulders; a custom which is considered as expressive of the highest mark that even filial piety can pay to the deceased. If the distance from the house to the church be considerable, they are relieved by some of the congregation; but they always take it again before they arrive at the church.—I have been informed that in some parts of the country it is usual to set the bier down at every cross-way, and again when they enter the church-yard, and at each of these places to repeat the Lord's prayer.

In some parts of Wales it was formerly

customary for the friends of the dead to kneel on the grave, and there to say the Lord's prayer for several Sundays subsequent to the interment, and then to dress the grave with flowers.—It was also reckoned fortunate for the deceased if a shower of rain came on while they were carrying the body to church, that his coffin might be moistened with the tears of heaven.

I have observed that in most parts of North Wales, the same practice prevails which is common in England, of crowding all the bodies into that part of the church-yard which is south of the church. The only reason that I have heard the Welsh people give for this custom is, that the north is the *wrong side*. The true reason, however, is, that formerly it was customary for persons, on entering a church-yard, and seeing the grave of a friend or acquaintance, to put up to heaven a prayer for the peace of his soul; and since the entrances to churches were usually either on the west or south side, those persons who were interred on the north escaped the common notice of their friends, and thereby lost the benefit of their prayers. Thus the north side becoming a kind of refuse spot, only paupers, still-born infants, or persons guilty of some crime, were buried there.*

In Mr. Pratt's Gleanings through Wales, I observe a charmingly animated description of the neatness and elegance of the Welsh church-yards, and of the attention that is bestowed by the surviving relatives, to the graves of their kindred : but I am sorry to say, if this gentle-man has stated facts, that the custom is not

* Grose's Olio, 222.

general, as he has asserted: it must be completely local. During the seven months that I
spent in visiting and examining North Wales,
I never saw, nor could I ever hear, of an
instance of the graves being weeded every
Saturday ; " of their being every week planted
with the choicest flowers of the season," or that,
if a nettle or weed were seen on the Sunday
morning, the living party to whom the grave
belonged, " would be hooted, after divine service, by the whole congregation."

SHORT DIRECTIONS

FOR THE

TOURIST

THROUGH

NORTH WALES,

IN THE ROUTE OF THE PRECEDING TOUR.

☞ At the inns marked with an asterisk*, post-chaises and horses
are kept.

THE DISTANCE FROM CHESTER TO CAERNARVON, ALONG
THE USUAL ROAD, (NOT GOING BY FLINT,) IS ABOUT
72 MILES.

AT Chester the tourist may find it worth his while
to visit and examine the castle and walls, with the
courts of justice, the cathedral, St. John's church,
and the rows. If he be an antiquary, he will derive
entertainment from examining the remains of the hypocaust, near the Feathers inn; and some other relics
of antiquity in the neighbourhood.

2 L

About 2 miles from Chester cross the Ellesmere canal, and soon afterwards enter the county of Flint. —At $4\frac{1}{2}$ miles pass the little village of Bretton. The mountain on the left is called Warren mountain.— At $7\frac{1}{2}$ miles, pass Hawarden castle, by the road side, and then enter Hawarden, a village containing a neat church, but little else deserving of notice.—2 miles beyond Hawarden, cross New Inn bridge. In a copse about a quarter of a mile to the right of this bridge, are the poor remains of Euloe castle, not visible from the road.—$10\frac{1}{2}$ miles from Chester, cross Pentre bridge; and 12 miles, enter the village of Northop. In Northop church there are two or three ancient monuments.—At this place the tourist who is desirous of visiting Flint, must leave the great Irish road, and proceeded along a road in a direction nearly north for about three miles†.

At Flint there is little worth seeing besides the re-mains of its castle, the county gaol, and a large smelting-house for the lead ore obtained in the neigh-bourhood. The inn is the Royal Oak, by no means a good one. No post-horses are kept here.

FROM FLINT TO HOLYWELL, $5\frac{1}{2}$ MILES.

Two miles from Flint is Bagillt;—$3\frac{1}{2}$, Wallwine turnpike;—and $5\frac{1}{2}$, Holywell. This is a very unplea-

† On the regular road, the following are the distances:—12 miles from Chester, pass the hamlet of Halkin;—and $18\frac{1}{2}$, enter the town of Holywell.

sant road, notwithstanding its lying along the bank of the river Dee, here almost three miles across.

At Holywell the tourist will of course visit St. Wenefred's well, from which the place derives its name. In several mills on the stream that proceeds from this well, he may see the different processes in the preparation and manufacture of lead, calamine, copper, brass, and cotton. About a mile and a quarter north of the town, are the ruins of Basingwerk abbey.—The principal inn at Holywell is the White Horse. Post-chaises and horses may be had here, as this town is stage-town from Chester.

FROM HOLYWELL TO ST. ASAPH, 10 MILES.

About a mile beyond Holywell, on an extensive common, are the lead mines.—At $2\frac{1}{2}$ miles see on an eminence, at a distance towards the right, a high circular tower, somewhat like an old windmill; this is supposed to have been a Roman pharos.—About 7, or $7\frac{1}{2}$ miles, descend into the *vale of Clwyd*. From the side of the hill there is a very extensive and beautiful prospect;—Denbigh, at a distance on the left, St. Asaph in front, and Rhyddlan castle on the right, with all the varied scenery of the vale.—10 miles, St. Asaph.

At St. Asaph are a cathedral, bishop's palace, and deanery.——The tower of the cathedral commands an extensive view along the vale. The inn is the White Lion*, a good house.

If the tourist wishes it, he may make the two follow-

516 GUIDE THROUGH NORTH WALES.

ing excursions from this place; in the latter, however, he will have but little amusement.

1. *Excursion from St. Asaph to Denbigh*, 6 *Miles.*
—The road lies entirely along the vale of Clwyd, but it is so low, as to afford few good prospects.—At three miles pass a woody dell that presents a picturesque scene on the right of the road.—6 miles, Denbigh.

See the castle, a fine ruin.—The antiquary would visit Whitchurch, the parish church, about a mile distant, to see the monuments of Humphrey Llwyd, the antiquary, and some of other celebrated personages. —There are two principal inns at Denbigh, the Crown and the Black Bull*. The latter is by much the most comfortable house of the two.

2. *Excursion from St. Asaph to Rhyddlan*, 3 *Miles.*
—This road lies also along the vale of Clwyd, and, about a mile from St. Asaph, affords a good view of the little city.

At Rhyddlan there is the shell of a castle.. No accommodations are to be had at this place, but what a very paltry public house can afford.

FROM ST. ASAPH TO CONWAY, 18½ MILES.

Four miles from St. Asaph, on the right of the road is Kinmael, the seat of the reverend Edward Hughes, one of the proprietors of the Anglesea copper mines. —At 4¼ miles pass the village of Llan St. Siôr, or St. George's; and 6¼, Abergeley. At

Abergeley there is a tolerably good inn, at which post-horses are kept.—At 9¼ miles pass Llandulas; and at 18 miles arrive at Conwy ferry-house*. The river is somewhat more than half a mile across, and must be passed in a boat.

At Conwy the tourist may examine the castle,—an ancient mansion, called Plàs Mawr,—the poor remains of the abbey,—and the church. The most comfortable inn is the Harp*.

From Conwy the two following very pleasant excursions may be made.

1. *Excursion from Conwy round the Creiddin, in the whole about* 18 *Miles.*—This excursion cannot be performed any way so well as on foot. Cross the ferry, and proceed to Teganwy, the seat of Mrs. Williams, near which are the poor remains of Diganwy castle, about a mile and half north of the ferry-house.—Continue the route along the west side of the promontory to Gogarth, a ruined palace of the bishops of Bangor, about 6 miles from the ferry. —Examine the high rocks that form the northern extremity of the Great Ormes Head,—and return by Gloddaeth and Bodscallon, two elegant seats belonging to sir Thomas Mostyn, bart.

2. *Excursion along the Vale of Conwy to Caer Rhûn, and the Waterfall, about* 8 *Miles.*—A mile from Conwy pass the village of Kyffin.—At 5½ miles is Caer Rhûn, where there are considerable remains of the *Conovium* of the Romans. In a mountain west of the road, and visible from thence,

13 miles beyond Caer Rhûn, is the grandest cataract perhaps in Great Britain. It is near a bridge called Pont Porthllwyd, and is called by the country people Rhaiadr Mawr.

FROM CONWAY TO BANGOR FERRY, 16½ MILES.

About 3 miles from Conwy, descend along the tremendous hollow of Sychnant; and about 5 miles, pass the Mountain Penmaen Mawr.—At 7 miles is the village of Llanfair Vechan ; and 9 miles, that of Aber. Near the bridge at Aber there is a mound on which once stood a house belonging to the princes of Wales ; and, at the distance of about two miles, at the extremity of a highly romantic vale, is a cataract well worth visiting. At Aber there is a small, but comfortable inn.—13 miles from Conwy is the village of Llandygai. The church contains a monument to the memory of Archbishop Williams.—13¼ miles in Penrhyn castle, the seat of lord Penrhyn.— 15 miles is the city of Bangor;—and 16½ Bangor Ferry.

At Bangor the cathedral is worth visiting.

The inn at Bangor Ferry* is a very good one.

From Bangor Ferry a very pleasant *excursion may be made to lord Penrhyn's slate quarries ;* the romantic vale called Nant Frangon; the waterfalls of Benglog ; Lyn Ogwen, and Llyn Idwel. The whole route would be about 26 or 28 miles, but the greatest part of it may be performed in carriages, or on horseback.—There is through Nant Frangon a carriage road through the village of Capel Curig to Llanrwst.

FROM BANGOR TO CAERNARVON, 9 MILES.

The road affords some fine views of the straits of Menai, and the surrounding country.

At Caernarvon the tourist will of course visit the castle.—From the rock behind the hotel, and from the Eagle tower of the castle, are very extensive views.— Half a mile south of Caernarvon is Llanbublic, the parish church, near which are to be seen some remains of the Roman *Segontium*.—The Hotel* at Caernarvon is, without any exception, the best and most comfortable inn in North Wales.

From Caernarvon, as a centre, various excursions may be made.

1. *To the village and lakes of Llanberis*, about 10 miles distant.† Here is one of the most romantic vales in the kingdom; and about three miles beyond it, one of the rudest mountain passes that imagination can paint. Near Llanberis are the old tower of Dolbadarn castle, and a fine cataract called Caunant Mawr; and, on the bank of the upper lake, a copper mine. On the left of the village are the mountains Glyder Vawr and Glyder Bach, in whose vicinity nearly all the Welsh alpine plants are found. On the right of the vale (and the summit about $4\frac{1}{2}$ miles distant from Dolbadarn castle), is Snowdon. From hence the ascent is so

† This excursion cannot be performed in carriages further than Cwm y Clo, the foot of the lower lake, whence a boat may be had to take the tourist up the lakes. This boat should be ordered the preceding day.— A pedestrian may perform the journey without the aid of a boat, as may also a person on horseback.

gradual, that a person, mounted on a strong Welsh poney, may ride very nearly to the summit.

From Llanberis the excursion may be varied by going through the above romantic pass called Cwm Glàs, into the beautiful vale of Nant Hwynan, and thence to Beddgelert; but, as this excursion would occupy in the whole near 30 miles, it could not conveniently be performed in one day on foot; on horseback, however, there would be little difficulty. This excursion, in its series of grand and romantic scenery, is scarcely exceeded in any other parts of Great Britain.

From Llanberis there is a horsepath to Capel Curig, whence the tourist will find a tolerably good carriageroad to Llanrwst.

2. *From Caernarvon to the Summit of Snowdon,* by Dolbadarn castle, the distance is about 12 miles. The chief part of this excursion may be performed on horseback.—There is another track somewhat nearer by Llyn Cwellyn, in the road to Beddgelert.

3. *From Caernarvon to Llanrwst, returning by the Vale of Ffestiniog, Tanybwlch, and Beddgelert; the Distance in the whole about* 70 *Miles.* This excursion cannot be conveniently performed except on horseback. The tourist may go either by Llanberis, or the vale called Nant Frangon, to Capel Curig, where he will find another beautiful vale, and two lakes. The inn at this place affords excellent accommodation, considering that it is situated in the interior of the mountains. Many persons remain here a few days to enjoy the fine scenery of the neighbourhood, and to amuse

themselves in angling for trout, with which the lakes and all the streams of the vallies abound. In his journey from Capel Curig to Llanrwst, the antiquary would probably choose to visit Dolwyddelan castle, a British ruin, three miles on the left of the road.—About 5 miles from Llanrwst is the celebrated cataract of the Llugwy, *Rhaiadr y Wenol*. A mile beyond this is the picturesque bridge called *Pont y Pair*, near the village of Bettws y Coed.

Near Llanrwst is the ancient mansion of Gwydir, once the family seat of the Wynnes, and now the property of the Right Honourable Lord Gwydir.—Llanrwst is chiefly celebrated for its fine bridge, built under the superintendance of Inigo Jones. The church, or rather the chapel adjoining to the church, is well worth a visit from the tourist. The inn is the Eagles*, a good house.

In his return to Caernarvon, on the prescribed route, the tourist, at $3\frac{1}{4}$ miles from Llanrwst, will repass the village of Bettws, from whence leaving the former road, for that leading to Penmachno, he will at 5 and 6 miles pass two cataracts of the river Conwy,- the former, however, not a very considerable one : the latter, which is called *Rhaiadr y Craig Llwyd*, is a little to the left of the road, near a small fulling mill, *Pandy*, in Welsh.—8 miles from Llanrwst he will pass through the village of Penmachno, and 8 miles farther, after a very uninteresting ride over mountainous moors, will enter the village of Ffestiniog. Here there is a very uncomfortable public-house. Near Ffestiniog are the cataracts of the Cynfael. A mile from the village he will enter the vale of Ffestiniog, and pass along it nearly to Tanybwlch, which is about 20 miles from Llanrwst. From Tanybwlch to Caernarvon, the distance is 22 miles farther. The inn at Tanybwlch* is a very comfortable house.—8 miles, cross Pont Aberglàslly :—10 miles, enter Beddgelert :—14, pass Llyn Cwellyn :—17, Bettws Garmon : and 22, enter Caernarvon.

4. *An excursion* may be made on foot or on horseback, about 23 miles, *from Caernarvon to the Pools called Llyniau Nantlle,* and the slate quarries near Llanllyfni. This part of the country is very fine.

5. Or *from Caernarvon to Pwllheli,* distant 20 miles, returning by Criccieth and Beddgelert, in the whole about 58 miles. This, however, may not be interesting to many tourists ; and very few would think their trouble repaid in visiting the extreme parts of the promontory.

6. *Excursions on the water* may be made, with a fair wind, to any of the adjacent parts of Anglesea. The sail up the straits of Menai, to Priestholme island, is êxtremely pleasant in fine weather. A small decked cutter, capable of accommodating ten or twelve persons, may be had of the innkeeper of the hotel. The charge, with two persons to manage it, is a guinea a day.

7. *Excursion from Caernarvon to Holyhead, the copper mines, and Beaumaris, in the whole about 90 Miles.*—Cross the Menai at Moel y Don ferry, 5

miles from Caernarvon.—About a mile from the ferry-house, on the Anglesea side, is Plàs Newydd, the beautiful seat of the Earl of Uxbridge. Near the house are two cromlechs, and an ancient tumulus.—At 8 miles from Caernarvon pass the village of Llandaniel; —11, Llanvihangel;—14½, Llangefni; and 20, arrive at Gwyndy*. Here there is a good inn, the end of the first stage from Bangor to Holyhead.—From Gwyndy it is 3½ miles to Bodedern;—5 to Llanygenedl;—8¼ to the Holyhead island;—and 12 to Holyhead.

There is little remarkable in Holyhead, except the situation of the church and church-yard.

The distance from Holyhead to Amlwch is about 20 miles. The copper mines are about a mile from Amlwch. There is no good inn at this place. Ty Mawr, appeared the best, but the accommodations were only tolerable.—Two miles east of Amlwch is the singular church of Llanellian.

From Amlwch to Beaumaris the distance is about 20 miles. Six miles from Amlwch pass the extremity of Dulas bay.—At 12 miles pass Red Wharf bay.—And 13, the village of Pentraeth. The church of this village Mr. Grose thought so picturesque as to deserve a place in his work on the Antiquities of Britain. Near Pentraeth is Plàs Gwynn, the residence of Paul Panton, Esq. but chiefly known for its excellent library of Welsh MSS.

The only object worth notice in Beaumaris, is the castle. Three quarters of a mile westward is Baron hill, the seat of the Right Hon. Lord Bulkeley.— About a mile north is Friars, the seat of Sir Robert Williams, Bart. ; and near it a barn built from the ruins of Llanvaes abbey.—Three miles beyond Friars, are the remains of Penmon priory ; and just off this corner of Anglesea, is the island of Priestholme, celebrated as the resort of various species of sea-fowl.—The principal inn at Beaumaris is the Bull's Head, a comfortable house.

In his return to Caernarvon, the tourist may either cross from Beaumaris immediately over to the village of Aber, in Caernarvonshire, or he may cross the Menai at Bangor ferry. The latter is preferable.

FROM CAERNARVON TO BEDDGELERT, THE DISTANCE IS
12 MILES.

Half a mile from Caernarvon, pass the remains of Segontium, and Llanbublic church.—Three miles on the left the woods of Glangwnna, the house of T. Lloyd, Esq. Five miles the village of Bettws.—Six and a quarter on the left Plàs y Nant, a house belonging to Sir Robert Williams, Bart. ; and on the right a small cascade at Nant mill. The high mountain on the right is called Mynydd Mawr, and that on the left, Moel Aelir.—Seven miles, Llyn Cwellyn. See Snowdon on the left; its summit may be ascended from hence. The tourist who wishes to visit Llyn y Dywarchen, the pool containing a small floating island, must ascend to the mountain hollow on the right, soon after he has passed Llyn Cwellyn.

At Beddgelert there is a very comfortable inn called the Beddgelert Hotel. The distance from Beddgelert to Pont Aberglàsllyn (the devil's bridge)

is about a mile and a half. — From Beddgelert
the tourist may ascend to the summit of Snowdon :
the distance about. 6 miles. He should by all
means visit the vale called *Nant Hwynan*, one of
the most beautiful in Wales. In this vale, one mile
and a half on the left, is Dinas Emrys, the place from
whence the prophesies of Merlin are supposed to have
been delivered. Two miles, Llyn y Dinas.—Four and
a half Llyn Gwynant : in a mountain on the left of the
path a little beyond this pool, is a cataract called
Rhaiadr y Cwm Dyli. There is a horse-path through
this vale to Capel Curig, and Llanrwst.

FROM BEDDGELERT TO TANYBWLCH, 10 MILES.

One mile and a half, Pont Aberglâsllyn. The new
road from hence is exceedingly good, and affords many
very beautiful prospects.

The inn* at Tanybwlch, is a small but comfortable
house, standing on an eminence that overlooks the vale
of Ffestiniog. Not far from the inn is Tanybwlch
hall, the seat of ——— Oakley, esq. The village of
Ffestiniog is about 3 miles distant, near which are the
cataracts of the Cynfael : the road to the village lies
along the vale.

FROM TANYBWLCH TO HARLECH, 10 MILES.

Cross the vale of Ffestiniog.—One mile the village
of Maentwrog.—One mile and a half, having crossed a
small bridge, there is, about a mile and a half on the
left of the road, a cataract called *Rhaiadr du*.—4

miles Llyn Tecwyn ucha.—5 miles Llantecwyn.—5¼ Llyn Tecwyn isa.—7 Pont y Crudd;—and 10 Harlech.

At Harlech are the remains of a castle. The public house is very small.

From Harlech a guide may be had to the romantic hollow, 4 miles distant, called Cwm Bychan ; and from thence round the still more romantic Bwlch Tyddiad, and Drws Ardudwy, in the whole about 18 miles.

FROM HARLECH TO BARMOUTH, 10 MILES.

One mile and a half, the village of Llanfair.—2½ miles Llanbedir. In a field on the right, near this village there are two upright stones, probably what the Welsh of former times erected in memory of some celebrated warriors.—5¾ Llanddwye.—8¼ miles, Llanaber, the parish church of Barmouth ; and 10 miles, Barmouth.

There is a charming walk along the beach of the river near Barmouth. This place is singular on account of many of its houses being built up the side of a lofty rock. The Corsygedol arms* is an excellent inn.

FROM BARMOUTH TO DOLGELLE, 10 MILES.

The 2 first miles are along the beach, one of the most beautiful rides in Great Britain.—8 miles, Llanellid turnpike.—10 miles, Dolgelle.

The Golden Lion* at Dolgelle is a tolerably good inn. From Dolgelle a guide may be had to ascend Cader Idris, whose summit is about 6 miles distant.—2 miles north of Dolgelle, are the remains of y Vaner or Kemmer abbey ; and 4 miles beyond, on the left of the road leading to Tanybwlch, is Dolmelynllyn, the seat of W. A. Madocks, esq. and near it the cataract of the same name.—3 miles beyond Dolmelynllyn, are the cataracts, *Pistyll y Cain, Rhaiadr y Mawddach.* It will be necessary to take a guide in order to find the latter cataracts.

FROM DOLGELLE TO MACHYNLLETH, 15 MILES.

Five miles, Llyn Trigrainwyn, ' the pool of the three pebbles,' celebrated for a singular tradition respecting it.—7 miles, a small public house, the Blue Lion, from whence a guide may be had to the summit of Cader Idris, 4 miles distant.   The pool visible from the house is Llyn Mwyngil.—14 miles across the river Dovey.

At Machynnleth there is an old building, in which Owen Glyndwr is said to have assembled a parliament. The Eagles* is the best inn.

FROM MACHYNNLLETH TO LLANYDLOES, 19 MILES.

About half way betwixt these towns, and near one mile and a half on the right, there is a cataract called *Frwd y Pennant.*—Plinlimmon is visible at a distance

on the right.—19 miles, cross the Severn and enter
Llanydloes.

The new inn* here is a very good house.

FROM LLANYDLOES TO NEWTOWN, 13 MILES.

6¾ miles Llandinam.—13, Newtown.

The Bear* is the principal inn. Dolforwyn castle is
about 4 miles north-east of Newtown.—1½ mile from
Newtown, near the road leading to Builth, is a cataract,
but not worth visiting.

FROM NEWTOWN TO MONTGOMERY, 9 MILES.

At Montgomery the tourist will probably visit the
castle and the church.—The Dragon* is a good inn.

FROM MONTGOMERY TO WELSH POOL, 9 MILES.

7½ miles pass on the left Powys Castle.

The Oak* is the principal inn at Welsh Pool.

FROM WELSH POOL TO OSWESTRY, 15 MILES.

6 miles, pass the Breiddin hills, on the right,—9 miles,
cross the river Virnwy in a boat.—9½ enter the village
of Llanymynech. The Cross Keys, a small inn in this
village, is kept by Mr. Robert Baugh, a very in-
genious man, the engraver of both the copies of Mr.
Evans's map of North Wales.—13¼ miles, a house of
Industry.

At Oswestry the tourist may visit the church, St. Oswald's Well, and the mount on which the castle stood. The principal inn is the Cross Keys.*

FROM OSWESTRY TO WREXHAM, 15½ MILES.

5¼ miles the village of Chirk. The tourist may visit the church containing some tolerably good monuments in memory of the Middleton family; the aqueduct over the vale of Ceirog; and 2 miles distant, Chirk castle. 8 miles, New Bridge, near which the scene is remarkably picturesque.—10 miles the village of Ruabon. Near this place is Wynnstay, the seat of sir Watkin Williams Wynne, bart.—(5½ miles east of Ruabon, is the village of Overton, and 9 miles Bangor Iscoed, where there was formerly the largest monastery in Britain) 13½ miles from Oswestry, on the right of the road to Wrexham, is Erddig, the seat of Philip Yorke, esq.

See the church at Wrexham; and in it a most beautiful monument, in memory of Mrs. Mary Middleton.— 5¼ miles N. E. of Wrexham is Holt, where are the poor remains of a castle.—There are two good inns at Wrexham, the Eagles* and the Red Lion,* the former however is usually thought the best house.

FROM WREXHAM TO MOLD, 12½ MILES.

4½ miles Cegidog bridge.—5¼ the village of Caergwrle, near which are the remains of a castle.—6, Hope.— 12, Mold.

The tourist may visit Bayley hill, on which the castle stood, and the church.—1½ mile, north west of Mold,

2 M

is Rhual, the seat of the Griffith family, near which is
Maes Garmon, where in 448, the famous ALLELUIA
victory was obtained by the Britons over the Picts and
Scots.—The inn at Mold is the Dragon, a bad and
extravagant house.

FROM MOLD TO RUTHIN, 8½ MILES.

At Ruthin are the remains of a castle. I forget the
sign of the inn.*

FROM RUTHIN TO LLANGOLLLEN, 13½ MILES.

About 10 miles enter the vale of Crucis.—11½ pass
the pillar of Eliseg, in a meadow on the left of the
road ; and ¼ of a mile beyond it, on the same side, the
remains of Valle Crucis abbey. Castell Dinas Brân is
visible on an eminence behind the abbey.

The principal objects worth visiting about Llangollen,
are Valle Crucis abbey, and the pillar of Eliseg;
Castell Dinas Brân ; and the vale of Llangollen. It is
a pleasant morning's ride of about 10 miles, round the
vale. Near Pont y Cyssylte, 4 miles from the town
(at the end of this ride,) the tourist will see an immense
aqueduct for the Ellesmere canal, over the vale, and the
river Dee. The principal inn at Llangollen is the
Hand.*

FROM LLANGOLLEN TO CORWEN, 10 MILES.

About the third mile stone, see, on the opposite bank
of the river Llandysilio hall.—7 miles, the site of Owen
Glyndwr's palace.

5½ miles west of Corwen, on the road leading to Llanrwst, is Pont y Glyn, with a fine cataract beneath it;—and 2½ miles south, near one of the roads to Bala, and behind the village of Cynwyd, is a cataract called *Rhaiadr Cynwyd.*—On the hill opposite to the town, there is a great circle of stones, called *Y Caer Wen.*— The New Inn,* the sign of Owen Glyndwr, is the only one in the place.

FROM CORWEN TO BALA, THE DISTANCE IS TWELVE MILES.

Near Bala, the principal curiosities are the lake, and two mounts on different sides of the town, on which there have been British forts. It is a pleasant excursion of about 13 miles, on foot or horseback, to go round the lake.—Cross the bridge at the north-east corner, and proceed along the eastern bank.—4 miles, the village of Llangower.—6½ miles, cross the river Twrch, and see the immense stones carried by the stream in a thunderstorm in June 1781.—7¼, the village of Llanwchllyn.—A mile beyond this place there was an ancient British fort called Castell Corndochon.—8 miles on the left see Caer Gai.—12, Llanycil, the parish church of Bala. The Bull* is by much the most comfortable, though not, perhaps, the head inn in this town.

FROM BALA TO THE VILLAGE OF LLANRHAIADR, IN MONTGOMERYSHIRE, 15 MILES.

1½ miles, cross Pont Cynwyd.—2 miles, Rhiwedog.— 7, a pass over the mountains, called Millter Gerrig ;—10½ miles, the village and vale of Llangynog.—15 miles, Llanrhaiadr.

The celebrated cataract called *Pistyll Rhaiadr* is about 4½ miles north-west of the village.—At Llanrhaiadr there is a small public house, the Coach and Horses, where one bed may be had, and perhaps no more.

FROM LLANRHAIADR TO SHREWSBURY, 20 MILES.

About 3½ miles from Llanrhaiadr are the village of Llangedwin and Llangedwin hall, the latter one of the seats of sir Watkin Williams Wynne, bart.;—8 miles, Llanyblodwel;—10, Llanymynech;—14 miles, Knochin; 18 miles, Nesscliffe;—22, cross Montford bridge.

At Shrewsbury the tourist will find amusement in visiting the castle ; the remains of the walls ; the gaol ; the abbey ; the churches, particularly St. Alkmund's, in which there is a beautiful painting on glass, the performance of Eginton of Birmingham ; the Quarry ; the house of industry; the remains of the three houses of Augustine, Franciscan, and Dominican friars ; the free school, and some other public buildings.

THE END.

B. Bryer, Printer, Bridge-street, Blackfriars, London.

List of Subscribers to the 1998 Edition

R.A.Aitken	Rhuddlan
Rona Aldrich	Llandyrnog
Mr.F.W.Anderson	Criccieth
Clwyd Powys Archaeological Trust	Welshpool
Gwilym Austin Jones	Cefn Meiriadog
Rev. J.Barden Davies	Ruthin
Miss V.Barry	Tywyn
John Beagan	Colwyn Bay
Glenda E.Beagan	Rhuddlan
Mr.Richard Bebb	Kidwelly
Mrs A.Bedwell	Flint
Mr.J.Bedwell	Flint
Mr.R.Benwell	Menai Bridge
Roger Berrington	Chirk
Mr.Randall Bingley	Corringham
Bala Bodyrepair	Bala
The Book Shop	Mold
Castle Book Shop	Holt
Books Unlimited	Prestatyn
P.Boyle	Thatto Heath
Mr.R.Brocklebank	Prestatyn
Frank L.Brown	Gellifor
Mrs Y.Brown	Ruyton XI Towns
A.F.Burquest	Liverpool
Mrs A.Carmichael	Rhyl
Mr.John J.Chappell	Cyffylliog
Rhoswen E.Charles	Bwlch-y-Ddar
Mrs G.Charles	Morfa Bychan
Brian & Mary Clark	Rhyl
John G.Clay	Denbigh
Hefin Closs-Parry	Caernarfon
Dr.Stephen Constantine	Lancaster University
Dr.David Constantine	Lancaster University
Mrs C.E.Cooper	Llaniestyn
Mr.G.R.Coppack	Rhuddlan
Hafina Clwyd Coppack	Rhuthun
Jean Cotton	Corwen
Flintshire County Council	Mold

Liam & Loic Coyle	Provence
Mrs June Cross	Lancaster University
Cyngor Bwrdeistref Conwy	
Cyngor Sir Ynys Mon	
Dr.Edward Davies	Cerrigydrudion
Miss Heather Davies	Eryrys
Rev. & Mrs Geoffrey Davies	Childwall
Dr.K.Davies	Prestatyn
Judith Davies	Cwm
Mrs Margaret Davies	Denbigh
Mr.I.Davies	Abergele
Mrs Deborah Davies	Prestatyn
Keith W.Davies	London
Miss Mair Davies Jones	Wrexham
Mrs B.Dawson	Oxford
Denbighshire Historical Society	Erddig
Mr.& Mrs W.V.Dickson	St.Asaph
Mrs A.Downs	Nannerch
P.J.Duff	Wallasey
Ian & Linda Duncalf	High Wycombe
Mr.J.A.Durcan	Rhyl
Mike & Lynn Dynes	Blacon
Dyserth & District Field Club Library	Prestatyn
Phillip Ebbrell	Denbighshire County Council
N.Edwards	Abergele
Manon & Roger Edwards	Rhuthun
Violet Ellis	Llangollen
Brian Evans	Llangollen
Cllr. Dr.Morton Evans	Denbigh
Dr.R.Paul Evans	Erddig
Dr.W.Gareth Evans	Llanbadarn
Mrs H.J.Evans	Rhyl
Ieuan Evans	Bryn Coch
Mrs D.A.Evans	St.Asaph
J.Stuart Evans	Connahs Quay
Paul Evans	Kinmel Bay
Mr.D.Ffrancon Williams	Trefriw
Thomas M.Forde	Kings Sutton
Miss H.A.Formby	Ysceifiog
Fiona Gale	Rhosesmor
Trevor Gallagher	Llannerch

G.B. & J.R.German	Marchwiel
Peter W.Giles	Eastwick, Ellesmere
R.I.Green	Tremeirchion
Marion Griffith Williams	Dolgellau
R.G.Griffiths	Rhuthun
Mr.Jack Griffiths	Rhyl
R.Geraint Gruffydd	Aberystwyth
Gwasanaeth Llyfrgell a Gwybodaeth Sir Ddinbych	
Mr. & Mrs W.Harrison	Connahs Quay
Mr.Jeff Harrison	Connahs Quay
Trevor Harrison	Moreton
Susan Hilton	Rhuddlan
Ewart L.Hughes	Bersham
R.G.Hughes	Ffordd Llanrhydd
Vernon Hughes	Abergele
Mr.J.O.Hughes	Amlwch
Vernon Hughes	Rhuthun
Bethan M.Hughes	Rhuthun
Lisa, Grethe & Gordon Jervis	Sydney
Mr. & Mrs Berwyn & Diana Jones	Rhyl
J.R.Jones	Gellifor
Cllr. Ann Jones	Rhyl
Christine Jones	Denbigh
Michael Jones	Denbigh
Nicholas A.Jones	Gwynfryn
Robat Arwyn Jones	Rhuthun
Mr.Trefor Jones	Denbigh
Mrs V.M.Jones	Llanrhaeadr
Mrs A.J.Jones	Rhuddlan
David R.Jones	Erddig
Helen & Iorwerth Jones	Peniel
Margaret Jones	Bontuchel
Meira Jones	Groes
Nora Wyn Jones	Llandyrnog
Keith Jones	Rhyl
Mrs Sally Jurizyszyn-Jay	Denbigh
Susan Kayser	Denbigh
Edward H.Kirk	Cilcain
Margaret Lakin-Smith	Llandderfel
Colonel, The Lord Langford O.B.E.	Rhuddlan
Vicky Lavers	St.Asaph

George Michael Lebeau	Ruthin
Mr.Edgar Lewis	Wrecsam
Steve Lewis	Liverpool
J.B.Lewis	Chester
St.Deiniol's Library	Hawarden
North East Wales Schools Library Service	Mold
A.Wyn Lloyd	Llanfair D.C.
Mr.J.G.Lloyd	St.Asaph
Mr.Anthony Lloyd	Llanfwrog
Cyng. Meirick Lloyd Davies	Cefn Meiriadog
Meinir Lloyd Davies	Rhuthun
Rita Lloyd-Evans	Cyffylliog
Owain Llwyd	Saron
Mrs M.Lynch	Denbigh
J.M.Macaskill	Connahs Quay
C.MacMenigall	Meliden
Peter & Sheila Manley	Rhyl
Miss P.A.Martin	Leebotwood, Church Stretton
I.McAlpine	Oxton
H.G.Mclean	Prestatyn
Don & Ann Milne	Rhos on Sea
L.R.Moore	Rhyl
Mr.Derek A.Morgan	Barmouth
Hywel Morgan	Rhyl
Gregory P.Morris	Hawarden
R.A.H.Morris	Lixwm
Mr.A.Morris	Parkgate
Mr.A.Morris	Heswall
Roger & Meg Mullock	Denbigh
The Library, National Museum of Wales	Cardiff
Keith Pace	Moreton
Mr. & Mrs John & Norma Parker	Rhyl
Mrs D.Parker	Crosby
Richard Parry	Picton
C.M.Parry-Jones	Henllan
Stephen Perkins	Bramshott
Victor & Philys Perry	Yr Wyddgrug
David R.Price	Bangor
David Price	Abergele
John Price	Llannefydd
Mr.R.G.Prichard	Caernarfon

Mrs D.Prosser	Llanrwst
C.D.Pyke	Shotton
Mrs S.Quinn	Rhyl
S.E.E.Rawlings	Garth
Dr.Neil H.Ray F.R.C.S.	Llandyrnog
Mr.D.Richards	Abergele
D.H.Heddwyn Richards	Caerdydd
Mr. & Mrs D.Rickards	Prestatyn
Geraint Roberts	Caerwys
Mrs Rhona Roberts	Rhosymedre
Elizabeth & David Roberts	Wrecsam
Philip Roberts	Harpenden
Carys Roberts	Rhewl
Mr.Gwynfor Roberts	Rhosmeirch
Miss Elizabeth B.Roberts	Llangollen
Anwen Roberts	Llangefni
Dewi & Pam Roberts	Llanrhaeadr
G.Roberts	Tremeirchion
Glyn Roberts	Harlech
B.H.Robinson	Eastham
Carol & Phil Rotherforth	Herringthorpe
Gwyn Price Rowlands	Ruthin
John Rowlands O.B.E.	Four Mile Bridge
Mr.Reg Salmon	Colwyn Bay
Mr.K.V.Scrimmins	Colbren
Priscilla Shaw	Ewloe Green
The Book Shop	Rhuthun
Siop y Morfa	Rhyl
Mr. & Mrs Stephen & Janet Smith	St.Asaph
Mr. & Mrs C.Smith	Kinmel Bay
Mr. & Mrs P.Stockinger	Llithfaen
E.J.G.Swayne	St.Asaph
Mrs Sheila Symonds	Dolgellau
Jean & Ken Taylor	Rhostyllen
Mr.Michael P.Taylor	Mynydd Isa
Mr.Peter A.Taylor	Mynydd Isa
Alison Taylor	Bangor
Mr.H.O.Thomas	Wrexham
Mr.M.Thomas	Tranmere
Graham & Irene Thompson	Brynteg
Mr.P.A.Turner	Aigburth

Miss E.M.Uttley	Abergele
Mrs S.Walls	Moel y Crio
Joseph Wareing	Upholland
Dr. & Mrs T.B. & S.M.Webb	Dinbych
G.R.R.Whitehead	Rhewl
Mr.Clive Whitfield-Jones	Denbigh
Miss E.M.Whitley	Glascoed
D.W.Williams	Ruthin
F.Ron Williams	Llandudno
Delyth Williams	Cilcain
Mrs Lucy Williams	Rhuthun
Anthony Williams	Wrexham
Henry Williams	Criccieth
John Glynne Williams	Caernarfon
John H.Williams	Newtown
E.G.Williams	Rhos-on-Sea
Mr. Wil Williams	Abergele
Miss A.E.Williams	Rhewl
Mrs S.Williams	Abergele
Mr.W.Gwyn Williams O.B.E.	Pentre-Helygain
D.Geraint Williams O.B.E.	Penyffordd
Kenneth Willis	Abergele
C.D.V.Wilson	West Kirby
N.Winterton	Nr.Holywell
Esther Wintringham	Corwen
Mrs P.H.Witkowska	Sutton
J.D.D.Wood	Denbigh
Emma Wood	Denbigh
Edward Wood	Denbigh
John Barry Wood	Padgate
Miss J.Worrall	Prestatyn
Mrs Bronwen Wotton	Derwen
Anna Yardley Jones	Glyndyfrdwy
Mrs R.G.Young	Criccieth
Tony Young	Pen y Ffordd